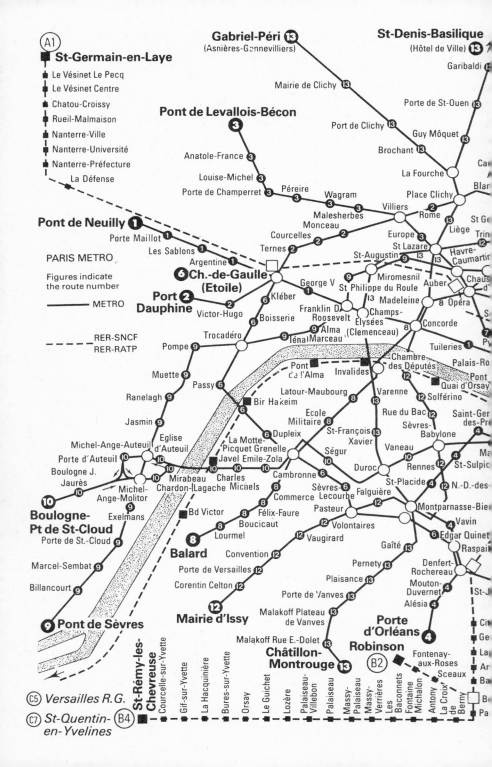

THE COMPANION GUIDE TO

PARIS

THE COMPANION GUIDES

GENERAL EDITOR: VINCENT CRONIN

*It is the aim of these guides to provide a Companion,
in the person of the author, who knows intimately
the places and people of whom he writes, and is able to
communicate this knowledge and affection to his readers.
It is hoped that the text and pictures will aid them
in their preparations and in their travels, and will
help them remember on their return.*

LONDON · OUTER LONDON · EAST ANGLIA
NORTHUMBRIA · THE WEST HIGHLANDS OF SCOTLAND
THE SOUTH OF FRANCE · THE ILE DE FRANCE · NORMANDY
THE LOIRE · FLORENCE · VENICE · ROME · NEW YORK
MAINLAND GREECE · THE GREEK ISLANDS · JUGOSLAVIA · TURKEY
MADRID AND CENTRAL SPAIN · IRELAND

In Preparation

OXFORD AND CAMBRIDGE
UNION OF SOVIET SOCIALIST REPUBLICS

THE COMPANION GUIDE TO

PARIS

ANTHONY GLYN

PRENTICE-HALL, Inc.   COLLINS
Englewood Cliffs, N.J. 07632   8 Grafton Street, London, W1
                1985

William Collins Sons & Co. Ltd
London · Glasgow · Sydney · Auckland
Toronto · Johannesburg

Prentice-Hall, Inc
New Jersey · London · Sydney · Toronto
New Delhi · Tokyo · Singapore
New Zealand · Rio de Janeiro

British Library Cataloguing in Publication Data

Glyn, Anthony
The Companion Guide to Paris.
1. Paris (France) – Description – Guide-books
I Title
914.4'3604838   DC708

Library of Congress Cataloguing in Publication Data

Glyn, Anthony
The Companion guide to Paris.

"A Spectrum Book."
Includes index.
1. Paris (France) – Description and travel – Guide-books.   I. Title.

ISBN 0-13-154410-1

First published in Great Britain and
in the United States of America 1985
© Anthony Glyn   1985

ISBN 0-13-154410-1 (p)
ISBN 0 00 217416 2 (Collins trade paperback)
ISBN 0 00 216368 3 (Collins hardback)

U.S. edition © 1985 by Prentice-Hall, Inc., Englewood Cliffs,
New Jersey 07632; William Collins Sons & Co., Ltd., and Anthony Glyn

A SPECTRUM BOOK

Printed in the United States of America

10 9 8 7 6 5 4 3 2 1

Prentice-Hall International (UK) Limited, *London*
Prentice-Hall of Australia Pty. Limited, *Sydney*
Prentice-Hall Canada Inc., *Toronto*
Prentice-Hall Hispanoamericanna, S.A., *Mexico*
Prentice-Hall of India Private Limited, *New Delhi*
Prentice-Hall of Japan, Inc., *Tokyo*
Prentice-Hall of Southeast Asia Pte. Ltd., *Singapore*
Whitehall Books Limited, *Wellington, New Zealand*
Editora Prentice-Hall do Brasil Ltda., *Rio de Janeiro*

Maps drawn by Leslie Robinson
Photoset in Linotron Times Roman by
Rowland Phototypesetting Ltd
Bury St Edmunds, Suffolk
Made and Printed in Great Britain by
William Collins Sons & Co. Ltd, Glasgow

CONTENTS

ILLUSTRATIONS

MAPS

All maps are orientated North/South

Introduction

One of the main objects of this book is to help you enjoy your visit to Paris. You may have come for the sightseeing or for business or on your way to somewhere else. But while in Paris, one of the most exciting cities in the world, you should contrive to enjoy yourself. There are many ways in doing this and Paris offers something for everybody. Whether your enjoyment lies in looking at masterpieces, street scenes, girls, or in eating, drinking or shopping, this book will suggest where to go and what to do.

I should also like to advise visitors, even those who already know Paris, to be adventurous, to strike out of their known quarter. Those whose business lies in the banking area of the Rue du Quatre Septembre might try exploring Saint-Germain-des-Prés. Those who have sentimental memories of a spring at the Sorbonne might consider a stroll along the Boulevard des Capucines or the Faubourg Saint-Honoré. Addicts of the Crazy Horse Saloon might think about a visit to the Comédie Française for a change.

Even those on a quest or a project should be aware of other sides of Paris. I had one young visitor who was only interested in Hemingway's Paris, perhaps for a thesis. Another, a stained-glass expert, would only look at twentieth-century glass; nothing would make her see the Sainte-Chapelle, even once. Another lady could not leave the Champs-Elysées, as her children did not fancy the idea of French food. All these were missing so much.

Anyhow, this book is intended to give at least a glimpse of the many things to be seen and enjoyed in Paris, of many different types and in many different *quartiers*, as they are called. This book has been divided into twenty chapters; eighteen cover different quarters of Paris, with their varying atmospheres and interests, and the other two are about Paris by night and shopping.

All chapters except Chapters 18 and 20 describe a walk or, indeed, are constructed round a walk. Walking is still the best way of exploring Paris. To drive round in a bus, listening to a taped commentary which may or may not be appropriate to the scene through the windows, is not the same. But the walks are guidelines only; they can be varied at will and, for those who prefer not to walk, I have also offered hints on driving in Paris and on how to get a taxi. These, as well as advice on how to use the Metro and other forms of public transport, can be found in Appendix A.

What I shall do is to take you past the most famous, the most interesting and, in their own ways, the most attractive parts of Paris. All walks begin and end at a Metro station so that we can identify them and reach them easily by any means. I shall also suggest a number of cafés and restaurants where we can sit down and refresh ourselves or lunch agreeably. The last may be quite modest – it is a mistake to combine a great artistic or historic experience with a gastronomic one; you should not eat at Le Grand Véfour as well as seeing the Louvre.

The walks vary a great deal in length. The one round the Opéra area (Chapter 6) is long, but it is mostly outdoor sightseeing. The Marais (Chapter 10) is fairly short, but it includes two museums. The shopping chapter (Chapter 13) describes, among other things, a walk round the boutiques of Saint-Germain-des-Prés. To make up for there being no recommended walk in the Seventh Arrondissement (which cannot be condensed into a walk), I have provided three in the Sixteenth (Chapter 12). One of these is an exploration of the 'Village' of Passy; the second is a short stroll down the hill from Trocadéro to the river, but it includes six major museums; and the third is simply a breath of fresh air in the Bois de Boulogne, where we can wander at will.

And so, on your way! Head for your chosen expedition and prepare to enjoy yourselves. The French have unfortunately no word for 'enjoy', but I can say *Amusez-vous bien! Régalez-vous!*

PART ONE

The Seine

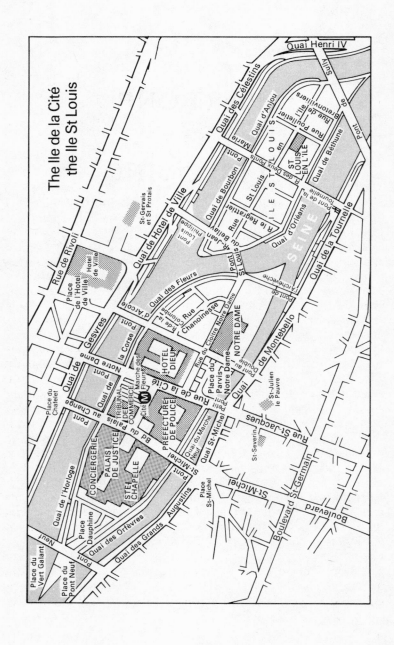

The Ile de la Cité
the Ile St Louis

CHAPTER 1
The Ile de la Cité

The French have a phrase for it – *le point de départ*. If you have your right departure point, you will have a good journey and arrive finally at the right place. If you have the wrong departure point, you will never arrive at the right destination, no matter how many changes (*modifications*) you may make on the way. The phrase applies not only to journeys, but to writing books, decorating rooms, going into battle or founding companies. And for an exploration of Paris, or for a book about Paris, the departure point is obviously very important. For us, it is Point Zero.

Point Zero is a compass star set in the pavement in front of the main façade of Notre-Dame Cathedral. It is the point from which all distances are measured in France, but it is clearly far older and more significant than that. It is the centre of the centre of the centre of the city, of France and, arguably, of Western civilization. Not the geographical centre, of course, but the spiritual, emotional and administrative heart of France. A few yards to the south stands a huge equestrian statue of Charlemagne and his vassals (erected in 1882), reminding us of the long-standing connection with Germany. Charlemagne, a Frank (AD 800), was the first Holy Roman Emperor and, in his way, the founder of a united Europe. Immediately to the east is Notre-Dame where Henry VI was crowned King of England and France, emphasizing the cross-Channel ties. A few feet below us are the remains of the Roman civilization, recalling the eternal link with Italy. The Ile de la Cité was the centre of it all.

But it is much older than that. Somewhere below Point Zero was one of the entrances to the Underworld. It was guarded by a god called Cernunnos, whose cult probably dates back to the reindeer-hunters of about 20,000 BC. He wore antlers on his head and sat cross-legged, yoga-style, an unusual position for a Western deity.

15

Over thirty altars to him have been found in various parts of France, guarding the Underworld entrances, but it seems that the Ile de la Cité was one of his most important sites and it has remained an important religious centre to this day.

This point is not only associated with the Underworld; other cults go back just as far. The star is slightly worn by the feet of people standing on it to wish. Many of them are young girls and, as they are standing between the statue of Mother and Child in the Cathedral and the maternity wards of the Hôtel-Dieu Hospital, it is easy to guess what they are wishing for.

The Ile de la Cité has changed its shape and its height many times since Cernunnos. In the pre-Roman era it was a sandbank and a primitive village, where the Seine boatmen and fishermen could find shelter and were protected on their river island from marauders. Later the local tribe, the Parisii, moved in and built a small town with massive bulwarks against the other Gaulish tribes (third century BC). Things changed with the Roman expansion. Vercingétorix, the hero of Gaul, rose in revolt, but he was defeated by Labienus, Cæsar's lieutenant, who burnt and then abandoned the Ile de la Cité, a smoking ruin.

The reconstruction began in the first century AD. The Gallo-Romans have left many traces of their civilization. They expanded on to the Left Bank, where they built, among other things, a large forum, three thermal baths, theatres, arenas and a fifteen-kilometre-long aqueduct, which brought clean water to the town, now renamed Lutetia Parisiorum. Temples sprouted on the island, the one on the site of Notre-Dame being dedicated to various Roman Gods, including Jupiter and the Emperor Tiberius.

All this lasted until the third century when Lutetia Parisiorum was destroyed by the German invaders. Later these invaders turned the Ile de la Cité into a small defensive fortress with ramparts, traces of which still remain. In 508 a major event occurred. Clovis, King of the Franks, established his capital and his seat in Paris, as it is now called. Paris was officially the capital of France, though France itself did not extend very far, scarcely more than the area now known as the Ile de France.

Christianity had some rather controversial appearances in Paris before that; the Bishop of Paris, St Denis, had been martyred, Julian the Apostate, the Prefect of Gaul, had been proclaimed

16

Roman Emperor by his legions, and Ste Geneviève had turned away the Hun invasion under Attila. But now Christianity became irresistible and Romanesque basilicas, rather small ones apparently, were built on the island in honour of the Virgin Mary, St Etienne (St Stephen, the first martyr), Ste Geneviève herself and St Christopher, who possibly replaced Hercules. The foundations of several of these can still be seen in the Archæological Crypt (see page 18).

Saint-Etienne was the earliest, a few feet north of Point Zero, but Notre-Dame, farther to the east, followed soon afterwards. There was naturally a certain conflict between the two, but gradually Notre-Dame expanded and enclosed Saint-Etienne. Long before the first stone of the present cathedral was laid, in 1163, the Virgin Mary reigned supreme in the area. She has done so ever since, except for a period during the Revolution when a Mademoiselle Maillard was enthroned on the high altar as Goddess of Reason, a surprising experience for a ballet dancer.

In the Middle Ages the Ile de la Cité was a crowded, congested little town and the streets were unbelievably narrow. One of them, the Rue de Venise, was only a metre wide. (Its former position is engraved on the paving, near the cathedral entrance.) The great stones from the Gallo-Roman period were re-used in the housing, with wooden upper storeys. Notre-Dame, either the earlier basilica or the later gothic cathedral, was scarcely visible. A narrow glimpse could be had along the Rue Neuve, which ran along the island, over Point Zero, to the great west door. A closer look, cricking the neck, could be had from the little square, called the Parvis (a corruption of Paradisus) immediately in front of Notre-Dame.

Many dramatic events have had their setting here and it does not require much imagination to see Hugo's Quasimodo, the deaf hunchback of Notre-Dame, on the gallery under the rose window, throwing back the scaling ladders and hurling down abuse at the crowd below. The Parvis was used for processions and mystery plays, and there the *amende honorable* took place. A small platform was erected and the criminal, heavily guarded and noosed, was led there. Kneeling, wearing a white penitential sheet, and holding a candle, he would mouth the formal words of penitence before being led away to a slow and horrible death across the river in the Place des Grèves (now the Place de l'Hôtel de Ville) on the right bank; the most notorious of these was Ravaillac, the hot-eyed fanatic who had

17

murdered the great and popular French king, Henri IV. Lesser criminals were left on the platform to be pelted and abused by the crowd, pillory-style.

Apart from churches, houses and taverns, the island had two hospitals: Hôtel-Dieu, on the south side, where the Charlemagne statue now stands, and a Foundlings Hospital on the north side, on the site of the present Hôtel-Dieu, which is the big building we see on our left. This last, in the eighteenth century, was an attractive neo-classical building by Boffrand (who was Mansart's partner in building the Place Vendôme, see Chapter 6). When the Hôtel-Dieu was burnt down in 1772, Boffrand planned to replace it with a twin building to his Foundlings Hospital, and widen the Rue Neuve, so that Notre-Dame could be seen better, without creating the huge empty square, the so-called 'paved prairie' which we now have. But Boffrand's excellent plans were never carried out, and indeed nothing remains above ground level of his Foundlings Hospital, except for some engravings.

Much of all this has only come to light in recent years. In the course of excavating a new underground car park in front of Notre-Dame, the foundations of Gallo-Roman and mediæval Paris were unearthed and preserved, thus greatly reducing the size of the proposed car park. The **Archæological Crypt** is well worth a visit. The entrance is at the western end of the present Parvis. It tells the story of Paris in visual terms with a (silent) commentary in English and French. Not a museum (the coins and pots have been moved elsewhere, some to Cluny), it is intelligently and rather spookily lit. Avoiding a rather unnecessary skeleton, we can study again the ground-plan of old Paris, examine the foundations of Saint-Etienne and Sainte-Geneviève, look at the heating arrangements for these old houses, and speculate on exactly where Cernunnos must have sat. We can also look with wonder at the old Rue de Venise and try to imagine why a distinguished man like Commissionaire Dela-mare, the colleague of Colbert, should have chosen to live there, within touching distance of a noisy tavern, when he could have been in a country château or at Versailles. Perhaps it was the island or the Seine which called him.

In the nineteenth century the Ile de la Cité was completely changed. Baron Haussmann, Napoleon III's Prefect of the Seine (the title

Mayor of Paris had been abolished by Napoleon I, and has only recently been restored – the man might have become too powerful), rebuilt Paris almost completely. We would hardly recognize the pre-Haussmann Paris and he has been much criticized. He disliked poky little streets and small corners where revolutionaries could plot together; better were wide avenues and big squares, which could be, if necessary, swept by bullets. However, in his defence, it can be claimed that he created the boulevards, a great benefit to modern traffic, pavements where people could saunter (*flâner*), and with them the pavement cafés, so much a part of the Paris scene nowadays. In any event his ideas were more glorious, more suitable to a great capital, than a huddle of mediæval houses, however picturesque.

On the Ile de la Cité he was quite ruthless. He removed twenty-five thousand people and about ninety streets, with their homes, shops and taverns, all in the cause of opening up the views of Notre-Dame. In their place he built the huge modern Parvis, and four enormous buildings of functional value, but of no architectural interest – the Hôtel-Dieu Hospital; the Préfecture de Police; the Tribunal of Commerce; and the Palais de Justice (the Law Courts). The first two of these can be seen from the Parvis. He was dismissed for extravagance before he could finish the work, and the part of the island which was not swept away by his cleansing operation is the area lying north of the Rue du Cloître-Notre-Dame, between the cathedral and the Seine. We shall return to look more closely at some of the houses here.

To reach Point Zero, the easiest way, short of emerging from the Underworld, is by the Underground railway, the Paris metro, at Station Cité. The metro runs deep here, under the Seine, and we ascend by an antiquated lift, followed by a staircase. The entrance to the metro station is worth more than a glance. This is the real Art Nouveau, with curly wrought-iron moulded into bushes and leaves, the lamps being amber tulips, or perhaps pears. No lines are straight, even on the lettering. Built by Guinard in 1900, this is the romantic line which took the hungry Modigliani from Montmartre to Montparnasse and back. It is still one of the quickest and most efficient underground systems in the world, but many of the original entrances have gone elsewhere; one, Metro Raspail, is in the sculpture section of the Museum of Modern Art in New York.

19

COMPANION GUIDE TO PARIS

In front of us lies the flower market, the **Marché des Fleurs**, a covered garden of cut flowers all the year round, a delight to the eye and very convenient for visitors to Hôtel-Dieu. On Sundays it changes to a caged-bird market, but gifts of these may be less acceptable to the hospital. Various plans to move the market to make more room for police cars have been successfully resisted so far.

Having walked round the market we return to Metro Cité and follow the sign 'Notre-Dame' into the Rue de la Cité and round the corner of the Préfecture de Police. There, suddenly making us catch our breath, is the Parvis and the great west façade of Notre-Dame, as Haussmann intended us to see it. Whether the original architects had any such grandiose notions is not known, but perhaps they did; it was built in an age of great faith on the part of everyone from expert stonemason to humble labourer. The original plans have hardly been altered despite many vicissitudes in the meantime (see Chapter 2).

Notre-Dame remains one of the glories of French Gothic art, its shape and proportions in perfect harmony. Some may regret that its height appears to be lower by being seen from a long distance. Others may regret that the towers were not, in the end, topped with steeples, as was at one time mooted. Some find it too perfect, too cold, too symmetrical and there are those who prefer the asymmetry of most French cathedrals, the feeling of random harmony which exists in Chartres, Rouen and elsewhere. But Notre-Dame remains one of the masterpieces of art and architecture, a worthy centre for the life, faith and culture of the French people, and Paris in particular.

We approach Notre-Dame across the **Parvis**. Far from being an 'asphalt skating-rink', as it has sometimes been called, it is a pleasant place to stroll or to sit on one of the stone benches. There we can enjoy not only the great façade but also the view across to the Left Bank, the old houses on the far quay, the distant dome of the Panthéon and, from some angles, the Eiffel Tower. And above everything the huge expanse of Paris sky, which could have been painted by Sisley, and which is always changing: blue, white, pink, grey.

For those who prefer wooden benches and the shade, these are on the south side, under the plane trees. The view from here is more limited, but much of Hôtel-Dieu is concealed by a double line of chestnuts; these are some of the first trees to come out in the springtime and they turn a beautiful colour in September. In summer the view may be obscured by a mass of scaffolding. A temporary theatre is often built on the Parvis for mystery plays, ballets and other spectacles, performed against the backcloth of the floodlit cathedral. This, of course, continues the mediæval tradition.

The Parvis has one more claim to our attention; it was the site of a battle. On 19 August 1944 the French police revolted. A thousand of them assembled in the courtyard of the Préfecture and sang the 'Marseillaise', a song not heard in France for four years. Then they sallied forth to fight. The Germans counter-attacked ferociously with tanks, field guns and armoured cars. The battle lasted for four days, with volunteers from Hôtel-Dieu crawling out under fire to drag in the wounded. But with the Allied armies encircling Paris, the Germans were forced to withdraw, and the Tricolor was hoisted over the Préfecture and many other places. The police, who lost 280 men in the fight, suddenly found themselves (temporarily) the heroes of France. The bullet holes can still be seen on the buildings, the scars of honour.

Before taking a closer look at Notre-Dame or going inside, we would do well to walk round the cathedral or, even better, the island itself and get the feel of the place. From Point Zero we cross the road and skirt Notre-Dame to the south, into a garden. This is a lovely place in the spring, the cherry trees in white blossom, the great rose window hanging above and, on the other side, the Seine with its barges. Moving on, we find that the garden widens into the Place Jean XXIII, where we can sit again, if we wish.

We are now at the east end of Notre-Dame and have one of its most beautiful (and most painted) views. It stands, or lies, as has been said, like a great ship becalmed in the flowing waters. The flying buttresses soar out of the chestnuts, which are white-flowering and, as they belong to the cathedral, have not been pollarded at the moment of writing. In summer the lime trees are in flower, and sitting there we can catch their sweet elusive scent. The children play on the swings, the tourists walk anxiously to and fro; it is a very Parisian place.

From the heights to the depths, from exaltation to degradation, is

21

a matter of seconds, of inches. We cross the road into another small gravelly garden, the 'stern' or east end of the island. And there we have the **Mémorial de la Déportation**.

Underground (like so many other things on the Ile de la Cité), suitably on the site of the one-time morgue, it is a worthy and much visited monument to the two hundred thousand Frenchmen who died in the Nazi camps. The Unknown Victim lies in state, but otherwise everything is understated. The surroundings are simply cells, prison bars and chains; the words on the walls are only the names of the camps (so many!) and the phrase '*Pardonne mais n'oublie pas.*' We, like others, emerge deeply moved.

Continuing to circle Notre-Dame, we are now on the Rue du Cloître-Notre-Dame. On the left is the cathedral, on the right a line of cafés and souvenir shops and the small Museum of Notre-Dame. This is the part of the island which Haussmann left untouched, and unfortunately much of it has been redeveloped piecemeal during the last century. In particular the fire station and the police motor-cycle garage could have been sited elsewhere. We turn off, therefore, into the **Rue Chanoinesse** and there we pause before the door of **No.10**. A plaque tells us that a comic singer lived there in the last century, but that is not why we are there. The site was the temporary home of Héloïse and Abelard – a plaque commemorating them is on the other (river) side of the house.

Peter Abelard (1079–1142) is a fashionable figure nowadays, the prototype of the with-it clergyman; not that he was ever a priest. In his private life he practised an extreme permissiveness; 'I feared no refusal from whatever woman I might deem worthy of my love,' he wrote. In public he preached against the Establishment, embodied in the person of St Bernard (no connection with the Alpine passes or the dogs).

In an age of faith and certainty Abelard was a questioner. Although not an atheist, doubt was his *point de départ*. In particular he had no use for abstractions, for certain types of thought and words, derived from Plato, which were then accepted.

For instance, Paris was (and still is) inhabited by thousands of dogs. But, if we take Abelard's view, they are all just separate animals; the idea of 'dogginess' as such is simply a name, without any reality of its own. As Abelard put it, it is a *nomen* and can be a *vox* (bow-wow!) but can never be a *res* or real thing. (For more about Abelard's thinking, see Chapter 15. Cluny and the Sorbonne.)

This down-to-earth type of thought, with its threads back to Aristotle, both undermined and renewed the scholastic Church. Abelard had a profound and long-lasting effect, both on philosophy and on Paris. He was one of the founders of the University of Paris which was at first orthodox enough, but later, permeated with his and parallel ideas, became the great Temple of Doubt, which it remains. When Abelard was finally forced to leave the precincts of Notre-Dame, he moved several times, finally ending up on the Left Bank. His followers went with him and the Left Bank was established as the intellectual centre of Paris and of France, which it still is.

But, standing before No.10 Rue Chanoinesse, we tend to think more about his private than his academic life. The house (1849) is of no interest in itself. It must have looked very different in 1118 when Canon Fulbert of Notre-Dame lived there with his niece, Héloïse (probably 'niece' was a euphemism for 'daughter'). He was, it is said, pleased when the famous teacher of theology came to tutor his niece and he encouraged Abelard, who was then thirty-nine. Héloïse was a pretty seventeen-year-old and it is uncertain how interested she was in the problem of the *nomen* and the *res*. Abelard wrote later: 'The lesson-times were spent in hidden places chosen by our love. We dealt more in kisses than words.'

The story of Héloïse and Abelard never seems to die, the ill-fated love that was doomed from the start. Héloïse became pregnant and was sent away by Abelard to Brittany, where she bore him a son, whom she named, curiously, Astrolabe (Sextant, perhaps, or Altimeter). This suggests that there were unperceived depths in Héloïse or, possibly, that Abelard's teaching was indeed unorthodox. She abandoned her baby and returned to Paris. At her uncle's instigation, she married Abelard in a ceremony which she insisted must be kept secret, to protect her husband's future career in the Church. This, however, was not enough for Abelard or, in the opposite sense, for the Canon. Abelard sent her away to a convent, the first of many, where she dutifully took her vows, and he then went on a long carouse through the taverns of the City in search of women and wine. This was too much for the Canon, who organized the famous revenge. Two thugs came to Abelard's bedroom at night and 'their knives separated me from those members of my body which were guilty of the error they resented'.

Abelard survived the attack, but vengeance was swift. The two thugs were caught, castrated and blinded; the Canon was deprived of his home, his position and his possessions. But Abelard was very sorry for himself. Since he was mutilated, he could no longer consider entering the Church. St Bernard taunted him cruelly with no longer being a man 'and Peter is a man's name'. He died aged sixty-three, soon after hearing that his latest book, a treatise on logic, was to be burnt by order of the Lateran Council. Héloïse, twenty-two years younger, outlived him by many years, becoming an abbess, dying in 1164. Their bodies, after many removals, now lie together in Père Lachaise cemetery.

Other personalities, perhaps less colourful, have been associated with the street and the area, among them the American writer Ludwig Bemelmans and the Aga Khan. The street has been too much rebuilt in the last century to be attractive but we catch occasional glimpses of Notre-Dame through the side streets and the sound of bells can be heard everywhere; the deep one, the only one to survive the Revolution, is called Emmanuel. The most pleasant building is No.24, in fact several houses with an old coaching entrance, now the Restaurant La Lieutenance. It was an old *hôtel* of the canons, sixteenth-century, but much altered since then. However, it carefully preserves a certain atmosphere (fairly expensive).

Turning right, we are in the Rue de la Colombe, a much prettier street than the Rue Chanoinesse. Many old houses, or parts of them, still survive. In particular we should look at No.5, a private house. With permission we can enter and see the cellar, the old chapel of St Aignan. Mass was celebrated there secretly during the Revolution, but it was obviously a place of hidden worship long before that. Little remains except rounded arches, columns with acanthus leaves on their capitals, a graceful plaque of the Madonna, a dignified head of the saint. It still has an atmosphere of secret religion and long-forgotten mysteries. Holy wells are usually very much a part of such places, and the well here is in La Lieutenance, a few yards away.

. At the end of the street are flights of steps, leading to the quay and the river, a reminder of the changing height of the island. We walk along the Seine past Hôtel-Dieu. The hospital was founded in

AD 651 by St Landry, Bishop of Paris, who sheltered the sick in part of his palace. The name might be translated as 'God's hostel'.

We turn back into the flower market, to Metro Cité. This is the moment to take a brief glimpse inside the **Préfecture de Police**. The immediate reaction is, how few police! Perhaps there are more of them on the far, river, side or perhaps they keep a careful low profile. What you see are thousands of ladies in mauve overalls, carrying files. No matter which entrance you choose, there they are, harassed but usually polite. There are also several thousand foreigners, mainly Algerian, waiting for work or residence permits, usually polite too. But the experience is Kafka-esque. Anyone, for instance a foreigner resident in France, who has business there, must have calm, patience, a good book and an ability to read standing up; a sharp eye for queue-jumpers is also a good idea. A major reorganization to diminish queueing is under way, but so far this has proved unsuccessful.

Emerging, after only a brief but adequate visit, we pause on the pavement in front of Metro Cité, and turn left. There, before us, are the gilded gates and the great staircase of the **Palais de Justice**. This is the ancient seat of authority in Paris and France. It was the palace of the Roman prefects, of King Clovis and his Frankish followers, of Hugues Capet and the Capetian kings, of St Louis and Philip the Fair. From Roman to Valois times it was the government centre of Paris, until King Charles V in 1358, following the bloody uprising of Etienne Marcel, moved the court to the Marais and then to the Louvre. Justice, however, remained.

The gilded gates are open, and justice is free for all-comers. We enter and climb the stairs where St Louis administered palm-tree justice (not the same staircase, of course; little of his palace survived Haussmann). At the top we are in a world of vast marble corridors. Advocates in robes and bands (but not wigs) walk to and fro talking to each other or to their clients, sometimes perching on the pedestal or toe of a statue. Many of the lawyers are women, wearing earrings. We are free to enter any of the court-rooms and listen to the proceedings. The civil courts can be rather dull, a long mumbling of wills or leases. The criminal courts (*chambres correctionnelles*) are usually more dramatic, but even here, it seems, much of the traditional rhetoric has gone out of French legal pleading in recent years.

The most beautiful and one of the best-known pictures of St Louis's palace is in the fifteenth-century Book of Hours (*Les Très Riches Heures du Duc de Berry*). The originals are in the museum at Chantilly, but it has been reproduced many times in art books and calendars. The picture illustrates 'June', and the palace is seen from the Left Bank, from the Hôtel de Nesle, the Duc de Berry's town house, now the site of the Bibliothèque Mazarine. In the foreground are peasants haymaking. Beyond the Seine the towers and walls of the palace are clearly seen against the blue sky, and can be easily identified. The whole complex of buildings is dominated by that soaring masterpiece, the Sainte-Chapelle. Alas, it no longer dominates the present Palais de Justice.

Nowadays the towers of St Louis are best seen from the north bank of the island or from across the river. The easternmost tower, square-built, is the Tour de l'Horloge, which dates from the fourteenth century and has a clock (sixteenth-century), which is claimed to be the oldest public clock in the world. Much restored and redecorated, it still keeps remarkably good time; it has a rather cryptic Latin quotation about time and justice. The next two towers, steepled, form the entrance to the Conciergerie, but the last one, the Tour Bonbec, is not open to the public. Thought to be a torture chamber, the name means 'babbling', which anyone might do under duress.

We have, however, come to the Palais de Justice to see its most famous monument, the **Sainte-Chapelle**. We pass through the main gates (survivors of the eighteenth century) but we do not climb the stairs. We follow the signs through a tunnel, round the chapel to the west end and enter the vaulted lower chapel, gaudily painted in pseudo-mediæval colours. This was where the servants worshipped. We climb a narrow winding stair, and at the top the great glory awaits us.

It is dazzling and must look today much as it did on the day it was finished in 1248. A church built entirely of stained glass! Henry III of England was overwhelmed by it. Even on a cloudy day it is like being inside a huge jewel. The very idea of such a building was new – churches had often been used as fortresses, but how to defend a glass shrine? How to keep the roof up without any supporting walls? The achievement of the architect, Pierre de Montereau, was immense and, seven hundred difficult years later, the slender buttres-

26

ses show no cracks, the chapel no sign of collapsing. Immense too was the cost, eight hundred thousand livres d'or, and we cannot think that St Louis grudged a penny of it.

There are fifteen hundred square yards of stained glass in the chapel, all of it (except for the later rose window) predominantly in red and blue. But there are so many shades of red and blue, carefully and harmoniously blended, that there is no monotony. The windows are a series of Bible scenes, a vast illustrated Bible, like the illuminated manuscripts. We can, if we wish, follow it round, up and down, scene to scene, window to window. We may notice the emphasis on kings and law-givers, for instance St Louis himself receiving the Holy Relics, on the immediate right as we enter, or Solomon on his throne, second window from right. This suits the chapel's theme of the Crown – it is possible to see the building itself as shaped like a mediæval crown. Most of the subjects are from the Old Testament, but the life of the Virgin, Christ's Passion and John the Baptist can be seen at the far end.

If we wish to study the scenes in full detail, we may get books and charts at the desk, or join a guided tour. These are arranged by the Hôtel de Sully. But to concentrate only on detail is to miss the great design.

All art students learning stained-glass design in Paris are taught, of course, to find first their *point de départ*. This, which is usually dictated partly by the architect or stonemason, is made by the black interstices, the shape like black lace, the *dentelle*. Only after this has been designed can the glass be planned. Standing in front of one of these windows, our eyes and minds closed to the Bible scenes, we can see the *dentelle*, the shape and construction of the window. Every one is different, but all are carefully harmonized. And then we step back and let the whole mediæval, mystical glory overcome us as it overcame the kings of France and England.

The west rose window was added over a hundred years later. Like many windows facing the sunset, it shows the Apocalypse. But it is very different in mood from the other windows. The lines of the *dentelle* are curly, not straight; the main colours are not red and blue, but green and yellow. It does not fit very comfortably with the rest of the chapel. Yet it is a masterpiece in its own right and it shows very clearly in the scene from the Book of Hours as the dominant feature of the chapel.

St Louis built the Sainte-Chapelle to be a worthy shrine for the Crown of Thorns, which he had acquired on his first crusade. In fact, he bought the Crown, for an enormous sum, from the Venetians, to whom Baldwin of Constantinople had pledged it as security for a loan. Later Baldwin sold St Louis directly a fragment of the True Cross and some more questionable relics, such as a feather from the wing of the Archangel Gabriel. These he adored in Notre-Dame, but the Crown of Thorns was apart and required special veneration.

The twelve statues of the apostles against the pillars have great quality. Six of them are the originals and one is thought to be a portrait of St Louis. Others, unfortunately, have been removed to the Cluny Museum, (6 Place Painlevé, Paris 5ᵉ. Metro Odéon or Saint-Michel).

St Louis (King Louis IX, 1214–70) has indeed left his mark on the Ile de la Cité, on France and on continents of which he was unaware. His austere life was dominated by two principles: one was Christian piety, which he doubtless learned from his mother, Blanche of Castile; the other was the ideal of kingship (what would Abelard have said!). St Louis has been called the embodiment of this mediæval ideal. To him, it meant not only to wear a crown, to reign, to rule, but to make peace everywhere and to dispense justice fairly. His principle in justice was a determination that every man should have his due. Coupled with this was an idea that, until the truth could be ascertained, the poorer man should be preferred – an arguable point, and startling indeed in feudal times.

In international affairs his principle was to make peace, imposing it, if necessary, by force. He succeeded in this in France, in Flanders and in Catalonia. In England he arbitrated between King Henry III and Simon de Montfort and his Parliament, giving judgment, naturally, for the King. As a king, he was a man of peace. What is paradoxical is that his other principle, piety, required him to bring war to the Middle East. Most of his time, his treasure, and finally his life were devoted to his two crusades.

But we must return to the Sainte-Chapelle, where the original services were splendid affairs, conducted by twelve canons and many chaplains. The King himself mounted a special stair to show the Crown to the faithful. Gradually things changed. A later king, Louis XI, a more secretive monarch but, all the same, the man who put France together, had a side oratory built where he could observe Mass without being seen. In the seventeenth century the Couperins played the organ. Even before the Revolution it had become a storehouse for flour. It was planned to demolish it, but it was found to be a convenient storehouse for legal files. Much of the glass was damaged.

Restoration began in the nineteenth century under Haussmann and his architect Viollet-le-Duc. The glass was painstakingly repaired by Steinheil (a friend of Balzac and Baudelaire – see Chapter 3) so that now it is impossible for us to tell the recent from the original. But secularization continued. In the present century the chapel was cleared, the relics being taken to Notre-Dame (the Crown of Thorns can be seen there on Good Friday), the altar, the organ and the furniture being removed. The chapel is now used for choral concerts, usually by choirs from Eastern Europe singing Rumanian carols or Croatian drinking songs. The windows are floodlit from the outside and the sense of being inside a luminous jewel is intense. St Louis would have been amazed.

Only one Mass a year is now said, in May, for the feast-day of St Ivo (or Yves), a bishop of Chartres and an expert on canon law, the patron saint of lawyers. Admission is by invitation only. The concierge is entitled to go, but, as she explained, she was not going to 'work' outside her normal paid hours.

Forty years later another king made his mark on the palace. Philip the Fair was far from being another St Louis. Indeed, he spent seven years of his reign quarrelling with the Pope (the same Pope, Boniface VIII, who canonized St Louis). The difficulty was over authority. The Pope claimed complete authority, temporal as well as spiritual, over all creatures on earth. The King retaliated by blocking the transport of all gold and valuables to Rome and attempting to bring the Pope to trial. The Pope replied by preparing a papal bull excommunicating the King, but was forestalled by the King sending a commando under the Chevalier de Nogaret to arrest and imprison the Pope. The Pope was released by Italian troops after a few days, but the shock was too much for him and he died a month later. His successor, Clement V, was more cooperative and King Philip was free to continue his own ambitions.

These were to create the most sumptuous royal apartments yet seen in France (his Sainte-Chapelle!) and to destroy the Templars.

He did not care for St Louis's bleak apartments, and it must have been agreeable to look out of his windows at the Templars being burnt at the stake, and reflect that it was their wealth which was financing his palace. However, the Grand Master, Jacques de Molay, called out from the stake, foretelling the deaths within the year of the King, the Pope and the Chevalier de Nogaret. These duly happened on time (1314), a possible example of the black magic of which the Templars were accused.

The sumptuous apartments are no longer sumptuous; they are part of the Palais de Justice. The Great Hall is the so-called Salle des Pas-perdus. But below it is the **Conciergerie** and, in particular, the Salle des Gens d'Armes, where the guards and servants of the royal household lived. It is a vast and splendid gothic room, about 20,000 square feet, supported by three lines of Gothic pillars. Adjoining it are the kitchens, with four great corner ovens which could serve up to three thousand people in the Salle and upstairs (a winding stair) in the Great Hall. At the west end of the Salle, separated by a grille, is a passage called the Rue de Paris, so-called because the public executioner, known anonymously as Monsieur de Paris, had his rooms adjoining.

The Conciergerie was originally the dungeon of the Palace. Many well-known prisoners spent a brief time there, and gradually they took the place over. Even by the standards of mediæval prisons the vileness and filth were notorious. Twice it was swept by plague and had to be cleared and cleansed. But its most famous time was during the Revolution, when it was filled to overflowing. The main activity, however, was in the Rue de Paris, and beyond it in the Salle des Prisonniers. This was always full, not only with aristocrats, but with soldiers, gaolers and lawyers.

On the left, leading off it, is the small room where the condemned had their final preparation – neck-cloths removed, hair cut and hands tied behind the back. From here they went through the dreary little courtyard, the Cour des Femmes, out through the main gates of the palace, twelve at a time, into the street, where the jeering public and the *tricoteuses* awaited them and the tumbrils took them to the guillotine. Nearby is a small cell where Queen Marie Antoinette was held for a time after the execution of her husband, Louis XVI. But after a rash escapade to rescue her through a door from the palace, she was moved to another cell, equally small but more secure, at the other end of the Salle des Prisonniers. In these barbarous conditions she existed from August to October 1793 (she was executed on 16 October – 'the Capet woman' or widow, as she was contemptuously called).

Next door is another tiny cell, occupied in turn, it is said, by Danton and Robespierre. Beyond is a chapel, which was turned into a prison for the twenty-two Girondins, who were moderate reformists and were guillotined in 1793. The prison has now been turned into a kind of shrine for Marie Antoinette – an altar, her crucifix, a letter trying to make provision for her children, and – grim reminders – a cell door and a guillotine blade (rather blunt!). The solemn relics seem pathetically unsuited to the Austrian queen's real character, frivolous, bewildered and sad.

The Public Prosecutor, Fouquier-Tinville, had his offices in the twin towers above the entrance to the Conciergerie; this was indeed convenient for the Tribunal next door. In due course he was led down to the Conciergerie, protesting volubly, and onwards to the tumbrils. He was followed by the members of his Tribunal, judges, juries and lawyers. It was 1794 and the Terror was over.

The Conciergerie can be hired for private parties and so may be closed to the public without notice. Some of these parties are held by wine-growers for their retailers and café-proprietors to taste (*déguster*) the new wine of the year, in particular the Beaujolais Nouveau. If we can arrange an invitation, we should certainly go. The great hall is full of barrels of the new wine, from which we help ourselves liberally; there are trestle tables piled with plates of cheese (including a rarity, blue Camembert), pâtés, sausages and bread. The throng, mostly male, talks about the new wine and café trade in particular. In our conversation we should hint that we are *courtiers-gourmets* (which means middlemen in the wine and food trade, and not what might be expected). Many candles light up the hall, the atmosphere is convivial, the wine is plentiful, though naturally it varies from year to year, but nothing can overcome the macabre feeling of the past horrors. Even after many glasses, the Terror still has us in its grip.

Emerging into the street, where no tumbrils await us, we walk along the quai and turn into the little funnel-shaped Place Dauphine. The east end is dominated by the Palais de Justice, but the rest includes a number of old houses, many of them restored.

There are several small restaurants, art galleries and one extremely modest hotel, the only one on the island. The square includes several trees, many parked cars and a well-known luxury restaurant, the Vert Galant which stretches from the Quai des Orfèvres to the Place Dauphine. This has a nice view and good wine, but the service is not what we expect at such prices. True to Henri IV's tradition, the restaurant's special dish is the *poule-au-pot* (boiled chicken) which he wanted every French family to have on Sundays. Modern Frenchmen may prefer something tastier. We emerge through the narrow end of the funnel between two beautiful houses (seventeenth-century, but well restored) of brick and stone. These are the houses which André Maurois thought about every night during his wartime exile in England; to him they embodied Paris and France. On the ground floor of one of these is the Taverne Henri IV, a pleasant wine-bar with a wide variety of good wines by the glass, especially the better Beaujolais (Morgon, Fleury, etc.) very reasonably priced. It is recommended by the Académie Rabelais which aims to improve counter-wines. We are offered cold plates of regional cheeses, pâtés, etc., which go well with the wine. Closed at weekends.

Beyond is the Pont Neuf, and there facing us in the middle of his bridge rides Henricus Magnus, Henry of Navarre, the Vert Galant, Henri IV of France. But he requires more space than is available in this first chapter. And so does his beautiful bridge, the oldest in Paris despite its name (see Chapters 4 and 9).

Beyond the Pont Neuf we reach the tip of the island, the bows, so to speak, of the Paris ship. We descend stairs to a little park, the Square du Vert Galant. (Vert Galant means 'gay old dog' or Merry Monarch, a reference to the many mistresses and illegitimate children of this popular king; the 'square' is in fact a triangle.) It is the only part of the island at river level, a quiet place full of worn cobblestones and chestnuts and dappled light from the river which is all round us. It is a favourite area for young loving couples and the Vert Galant himself would have approved strongly.

Unable to go any farther, we return along one or other of the quais, in search, probably, of refreshment. There are two groups of cafés on the island: one lot, in the Boulevard du Palais, between the Palais de Justice and the Préfecture de Police, is where the clerks and secretaries take their midday meals or snacks. The best is Les

Deux Palais, old-fashioned and unpretentious, which also provides meals.

The other group is, naturally, near Notre-Dame, either in the Rue du Cloître-Notre-Dame or in the Rue d'Arcole which meets it at right-angles. Cameras rather than briefcases are the impedimenta here and the cafés provide souvenirs, drinks and snacks such as hot-dogs or the ubiquitous *croque-monsieur* (a toasted ham and cheese sandwich), whose fragrance sometimes seems to permeate every café. The best of them is the Esmeralda, at the eastern end of the Rue du Cloître-Notre-Dame, almost at the Mémorial de la Déportation. This café offers not only simple meals of the steak and chips variety, but also the only pavement tables on the island. It is pleasant to sit here in the sun, drink a glass of beer and look at the fine view which extends from the old houses of the Ile Saint-Louis to Notre-Dame. The view may, however, be partly blocked by the parked coaches of many European countries, including Britain, which abound here. Nor are we likely to overhear much French at the neighbouring tables.

A word of warning is required about all these cafés. The Ile de la Cité is almost uninhabited. The tourists and the clerks depart, and at night it is virtually a desert island. All the cafés without exception close at about eight o'clock, which can be dispiriting for those who come to see Notre-Dame floodlit. The restaurants, however, remain open for dinner, unless they are closed on Monday or for the summer holidays.

To the restaurants already named we should add one more, my favourite in the Ile de la Cité, Le Vieux Bistro. It is in the Rue du Cloître-Notre-Dame, just across from the north tower and almost within touching distance of the cathedral. It is an unpretentious place, though larger than it looks, and the welcome is warm. It is also open every day in the year, except 1 January, and this is perhaps where we should go now. The roast quails, flamed, and served with a gin and cream sauce, are memorable and reasonably priced.

And now it is time to take a closer look at Notre-Dame itself. We must hope that it is a fine day, with the afternoon sun blazing on the rose windows.

CHAPTER 2

Notre-Dame

The foundation stone of the Cathedral of **Notre-Dame-de Paris** was laid in 1163 by the Pope (Alexander III) and it was finished about 1345. The site architects were Pierre de Montereau (who built the Sainte-Chapelle) and Jean de Chelles and doubtless many others; much of the labour was done by enthusiastic volunteers. But, in the end, it looked very like the original sketches of Bishop Maurice de Sully in 1159; and as it looks today.

There were, however, certain conspicuous though temporary differences. The statues on the west and north portals were painted in brilliant mediæval colours: blue, scarlet, green and yellow, all against a background of gold. The cathedral glowed with colour. Inside, instead of the present reverent hush, was a combination of a bazaar and a hostel for the homeless. Here was the whole cavalcade of mediæval life: merchants calling from their stalls to the passers-by, travellers from overseas showing or selling their souvenirs, crusaders taking their vows and fugitives in search of sanctuary. At one period there was also St Louis, who did not at all object to the hubbub of the people, adoring his relics.

But the French tired of Gothic in the Renaissance. First Mansart and then Soufflot were put in to modernize the building. The tombs, statues, some of the stained glass, choir stalls, rood screen and even the high altar were removed and replaced by some mock-classical statues of the Virtues. The colour was removed, the portals and the inside were whitewashed and the idea was to make the building look as much like a classical temple as possible. Then came the Revolution and its period as the Temple of Reason, after which it fell into decay.

Robespierre in 1793, finding that Revolution and Reason were not enough, pronounced his doctrine of the Supreme Being. As he

34

was guillotined soon afterwards, he had no time to explain exactly what he meant; whether the Supreme Being was an Immortal, a great leader, or even possibly himself. But the great leader was already there, waiting in the wings for his cue. When General Bonaparte became the Emperor Napoleon, it was natural for him to wish to be crowned in Notre-Dame.

After Napoleon's fall, the cathedral again fell fast into decay. The whole once-great building was sold to a demolition contractor. That it was ever saved and restored was largely due to one man – Victor Hugo, a professed atheist, though pantheist would seem to describe his faith more exactly. His long novel *Notre-Dame-de-Paris* (*The Hunchback of Notre-Dame*) aroused popular feeling about the derelict masterpiece in their midst. Napoleon III and Haussmann felt justified in the large effort and expenditure involved in restoring it. Viollet-le-Duc, an expert restorer (see later note in this chapter), was given the job, and in general it is felt that he overdid it. In every century, and particularly the nineteenth, there are those who prefer a building to be in ruins. In fact Viollet-le-Duc made Notre-Dame look very much as it does in the mediæval engravings. Apart from much-needed repairs, he replaced the missing statues and glass and he added very little of his own.

We should look carefully at the **west front**. At the rose window level are statues of Adam and Eve and, between them, in front of the huge window, the redeeming Virgin and Child. On the next level, above the graceful columns, is a veritable carved zoo of monsters, gryphons and demons, but these can only be seen by the tower-climbers. They are, in fact, nineteenth-century, the idea of Viollet-le-Duc.

It is the **three main portals** which should claim our closest attention. Even without the intended colours they remain master-pieces of mediæval sculpture. The central portal shows the Last Judgment. The tympanum above the doors shows the Resurrection and the Weighing of Souls, with Christ in Majesty, the Virgin and St John, at the apex. The statues in the embrasures are mostly recent, the originals (like the kings of Israel and Judah higher up) having been destroyed in 1871 by the Communards, who took them mistakenly for the kings of France. The left portal is dedicated to the Virgin. The tympanum, virtually unchanged for centuries, is a glory of mediæval art, full of flowers, fruit, angels, prophets and, by way of a change, the signs of the zodiac. The right portal is dedicated to St Anne, the mother of the Virgin. There in the congregation of Heaven, we can see St Marcel killing the dragon, Bishop de Sully (standing) and King Louis VII (kneeling) consecrating the cathedral.

In the Rue du Cloître-Notre-Dame we have another way of entering the cathedral, **the cloister portal**. This was built about 1250 by Jean de Chelles and is another major example of thirteenth-century sculpture. Later in date than the west portals, it is more elaborate and decorated with more detail, designed to harmonize with the rose window above. The tympanum illustrates the life of the Virgin together with scenes from a mystery play. In the centre is a fine thirteenth-century Virgin, a gentle Lady – though it is sad that her Child was lost during the Revolution.

The equivalent portal on the south side is equally elaborate in design, and illustrates the life and death of St Stephen. We can, however, only see it from a distance, because of the sacristy railings.

On the north side, also, is the **Red Door**, now closed, but once the private entrance of the canons. The tympanum shows the coronation of the Virgin by her Son, assisted by St Louis and Marguerite de Provence.

We must now enter Notre-Dame through one of the portal doors and immediately we are struck by the beauty and the size of the soaring **nave**. It is in fact not the longest mediæval cathedral or abbey (Winchester is) nor the tallest (Beauvais is), but it is nevertheless very large and can hold a congregation or a concert audience of about nine thousand. What impress us, however, are its beautiful proportions, its grace and lightness.

We can be grateful again that it was spared in some later ordeals. In May 1871 the Communards, fashionable revolutionaries of the moment, vowed to destroy all Paris in two hours. They piled the chairs in the centre aisle, poured on petrol and set fire. Fortunately for us, one of them had second thoughts and returned to put out the fire. Notre-Dame also survived the Liberation and Hitler's order to burn it down, together with much else. On 26 August 1944 the famous Liberation *Te Deum* was held there, with the bullets whizzing about the nave and the tall figure of General de Gaulle refusing, typically, to duck. Much may be still to come, but at the moment what we find there is peace and beauty.

We walk up one of the side aisles to the transepts, where we can see the **rose windows**. The south one, of course, gets the sunlight. It has had to be much restored (though very well) and it portrays Christ surrounded by saints and angels. These details are not discernible from floor level and we are left to admire the shape, the size and the colours of the much photographed window. The colours are mainly blue and red, as in the Sainte-Chapelle, and they blend into a many-toned purple. Another good time to see the window is at dusk, *l'heure bleue*, when the reds fade and we are left with a huge round-cut sapphire glowing in the twilight.

The north rose window, which never catches the sun, has been almost undamaged and unrestored since the thirteenth century. Said to be the personal gift of St Louis to the cathedral, it shows the Virgin surrounded by personalities from the Old Testament (though, once again, we have to take this on trust). To me it is even more beautiful than the south window, a study in blues of many different shades, the whole being more cobalt than ultramarine.

The windows of the nave at ground level are better left unseen, but we should look carefully at the windows in the triforia and clerestories (one and two storeys up) in the nave and transepts. These are modern, the work of Le Chevallier, the senior contemporary French designer. One can appreciate his problems, his difficult *point de départ*. Both the shapes of his windows and the general colour scale were unalterable. His designs are purely abstract, but he used mediæval colours and techniques, and the result is admirable. We should note particularly the blue window in the triforium of the north transept, a good example of modern glass. All these windows are visible from ground level.

Beside the central altar, at the chancel steps, are two statues, one of St Denis, the other (spotlit) a lovely Virgin and Child, Notre-Dame-de-Paris. This dates from the thirteenth century and was for many centuries in the nearby chapel of St Aignan, which is why it has survived. It shows a young, happy Madonna. There are three other Virgins in Notre-Dame, one on the high altar, and the other two either side of the entrance, surrounded by the lighted candles of the faithful. But – a curious thing for a Christian church – there is no conspicuous Crucifix or Cross. We are reminded again to venerate the Lady to whom the cathedral is consecrated.

Napoleon's coronation took place in front of the high altar on

2 December 1804. The occasion was unusual in many ways. French kings had normally been crowned in Rheims Cathedral. Coronations in Notre-Dame had been few, only Henry VI of England in 1430, and Mary Queen of Scots as Queen Consort to François II. Napoleon found the cathedral almost in ruins, but it was magnificently decked out with tapestries for the great occasion. The Pope was summoned from Rome to perform the crowning, but at the last moment the Emperor decided that the Pope was unworthy of the honour, and he seized the crown and crowned himself, and then his Empress Josephine, leaving the Pope with nothing to do. The whole scene has been vigorously portrayed by David in his big painting which we can see when we go to the Louvre.

On the pillar immediately to the west of Notre-Dame-de-Paris is a plaque, in English and French, commemorating the million British and Commonwealth dead from the First World War, who are mostly buried in France – a fact sadly unknown to many French people. On 11 November every year the Royal British Legion holds a service in their memory, complete with the Last Post. Recently, the veteran trumpeter sounding this call dropped dead in the middle – a newsworthy item for the French and, doubtless, how he would have wished to die.

The ambulatory, behind the high altar, has memorials to various bishops of Paris. On the south side is the entry to the Treasure (entrance fee required). Apart from an illuminated manuscript, some pieces from the eighteenth century (later gifts) and a grandfather clock, the treasure is mainly nineteenth-century, chalices and platters. Gold, however, always attracts a sizeable crowd.

From the central altar we can look backwards, along the nave, to the west rose window. Unfortunately the lower half is blocked from view by the **organ**. This is, in itself, and like most organs, a beautiful piece of sculpture, the masterpiece of France's best organ-builder, Aristide Cavaillé-Col (d. 1899), who built many of France's organs. But one could wish that he could have found a different position for his great work. It is, however, a marvellous organ, France's biggest, with over six thousand pipes, and it makes a great and very varied sound. Organ recitals are held every Sunday evening at 5.45 p.m. often given by visiting organists from Europe (including Britain) and America. Entrance is free, but we should go early.

France has produced and attracted many great organists, and

Paris is full at the moment of organ students from everywhere, studying at the Conservatoire, playing publicly whenever they can and hoping to follow in the footsteps of the Couperins, César Franck, Widor, Schweitzer, Marchal, Dupré, Messiaen, and Cochereau. Improvising at the organ is very old, going back to Bach and beyond, but it was Charles-Marie Widor (d. 1937, composer of the well-known Toccata) who transformed it into the complex art-form which it now is, rather a French speciality. Improvisation is very much a part of the French character and way of life. Anyone who has heard the late Pierre Cochereau in Notre-Dame improvising *aux grandes orgues*, creating an elaborate suite containing, probably, a fugue and a resounding climax, will not soon forget it. It was an experience made all the more poignant for the large hushed audience because the music was temporary, lost for ever in the air even as it was being played.

But even more memorable is one of the great services in Notre-Dame, for instance the Easter Eve vigil. The windows are dark, but the cathedral is lit mainly by the thousands of lighted candles carried by the congregation. The choir peal out their alleluias, the organ sounds in triumph, and we are reminded that Notre-Dame is not only an art museum and a concert hall, but a place of worship, as it has been for thousands of years.

Those who are more interested in the architecture than the Easter vigil will, of course, visit Notre-Dame in daylight, although many busloads come at night for the floodlighting alone. Parisians will sometimes tell us, with local pride, that Gothic architecture sprang into being for the first time at Notre-Dame. But in fact the style developed gradually, in several places at once. In England, Gothic was evolved locally from the Norman tradition, but there were some major exceptions such as Westminster Abbey; when French bishops were appointed, they brought French ideas with them. Italy too produced an indigenous Gothic, retaining the wooden roofs of the old basilicas, except in parts of the North, where French influence can be seen, for example in Milan, imitating Bourges.

The much higher buildings, which were characteristic of Gothic in the 'Anglo-Norman area' where it took hold, and which became almost an obsession in France, were made possible by the development of the ribbed vault. The previous barrel or groin vaults could not hold up such high naves and choirs. The ribbed vault was based on joining arches, which provided a framework, to be filled in later. It has been likened to an umbrella frame, but it is possible to see it as a palm-tree shape. At all events, the use of pointed arches, which was introduced with it, is thought to have been brought back from Syria or Palestine by returning Crusaders. The ribbed vault first appeared in Lombardy, Normandy and Durham, all at about the same time; the earliest which still survives is in Durham (1093).

In France transition from Romanesque to Gothic was gradual. The first cathedral which is classed as truly Gothic (although still transitional) was Abbot Suger's at Saint-Denis (1135–40). Chartres came next, but that building was burnt down in 1194 and replaced. Several others followed, all together, but Notre-Dame-de-Paris was the first to develop fully the ideas which were to dominate Gothic architecture in France, and spread to Belgium and Germany. In particular Notre-Dame perfected flying buttresses, here seen at their best, and its other glories are the rose windows and the *chevet* – the forest of stone at the east end. In these, Parisian pride is justified and Notre-Dame was a pioneer of the great period of church-building in France. This only lasted until the fourteenth century, when the Hundred Years' War brought it to an end. When building resumed in the fifteenth century, it was in the 'Flamboyant' style, which many think exaggerated and less successful.

Superimposed on the original Gothic, Notre-Dame has, of course, the work of restoration by Eugène-Emmanuel **Viollet-le-Duc** (1814–79), architect and writer. He also restored many other cathedrals, abbey-churches and churches throughout France, notably Amiens, Vézelay and Saint-Denis, and the walls of the old town at Carcassonne. He wrote many books about architecture, including the ten-volume *Dictionnaire de l'Architecture française du XIe au XVIe Siècle*. In 1863 he was made Professor of Artistic and Aesthetic History at the Ecole des Beaux-Arts.

Viollet-le-Duc was a specialist in Gothic architecture and one of the figures in the 'Gothic Revival'. He claimed that the integration of form and structure was the chief virtue of the style. He also propounded the dubious theory that an analytical study of the past, combined with the application of constructive principles to modern building materials, can create a new contemporary style. It was this theory which inspired Auguste Perret to build his pseudo-classical façades in reinforced concrete. Viollet-le-Duc is also credited with having influenced many later architects, including Gaudi and Frank Lloyd Wright – temporarily, one must think. His work and ideas have not been admired for some time now, but enthusiasts for Victorian Gothic are beginning to see new virtues in him.

Viollet-le-Duc at Notre-Dame also introduced the popular gargoyles, of which replicas and photographs can be found in all the souvenir shops. Less forgivably, he added the sixteen green copper statues which surround the base of the central spire – apostles and evangelists, among whom he included himself. The spire rises to nearly three hundred feet and tapers more gracefully than it does in the mediæval engravings, where it seems more of a sharpened pencil stood on end. Sometimes at night intrepid revolutionaries climb the spire – an airy experience, indeed! – to hoist the flag of their particular cause at the masthead, above the crow's nest. They are followed the next morning by equally intrepid policemen or alpinists, removing the offending emblem. On one occasion in recent years a fireman was lowered from a helicopter to remove the flag of North Vietnam, to the entertainment of thousands of spectators.

For those who wish to see the view legally, the way is up the towers (entrance outside the north tower in the Rue du Cloître-Notre-Dame). It is a long climb. We traverse the front of the cathedral and finally emerge on to the roof of the south tower, surrounded by a wonderful roofscape of towers, belfries, gargoyles and the spire. We also have a great view of the Seine and most of Paris.

CHAPTER 3

The Ile Saint-Louis

The Ile Saint-Louis is the second of the two Paris islands, the
smaller; the dinghy, it is sometimes said, towed behind the ship of
the line. If we are on the Ile de la Cité, we simply walk across the
Pont Saint-Louis, beside the Café Esmeralda. Or else we can go to
Metro Pont Marie and walk across the beautiful bridge of the same
name. The two islands are in great contrast: one an almost uninhabited ancient centre of religion and administration; the other a
secluded and compact island village, dating back only to the seventeenth century. And although about six thousand people live there,
it is still a village in spirit, where everyone knows everyone and
neighbours greet each other daily in the shops and cafés.

An island in the heart of Paris! The thought is still scarcely
believable, and so romantic. It is not possible to leave it without
crossing water by a bridge, and it is this which has kept the Ile
Saint-Louis a little different from the rest of Paris during its three
centuries of existence. Until recently there were plenty of Louisiens
who prided themselves on never having been to the 'mainland'.
They were usually very small, with mediæval names like Basseporte
or Crèvecœur, and they seemed to spend much of their time on
games of skill. Even thirty years ago there were at least four cafés
with billiard tables for the customers, and one with chess facilities.

Things have changed a little since then, since the island was
'rediscovered'. The Louisiens have grown taller and have acquired a
taste for travel, going to the mainland to work or to shop – the prices
in the markets of the Place Maubert or the Rue Saint-Antoine are
noticeably lower. Strangers (like myself) have moved in, the billiard
tables and chess sets have given way to candlelit restaurant tables;
Crèvecœur and Basseporte have gone. But the atmosphere of the
secluded island still remains, with its narrow streets and old houses,

and even relative newcomers have a feeling of 'belonging', of being members of a special community, rare nowadays in a great city.

One of the glories of the island is, and still remains, its **river quays**. At a time when so many of the famous quays of the Seine have been given over to motorways, including the whole of the Right Bank, the Ile Saint-Louis still retains its charm and it is possible to walk almost round the island at river level. We descend from the upper level by one of the many flights of stairs and immediately we are on cobbles, away from the traffic, a few inches from the Seine (which in spring sometimes floods the lower quays). Here we find the loving couples kissing, the fishermen, the sunbathers, the students reading Bergson or Lévi-Strauss, the *clochards* (the old-established and beloved tramps of Paris) sleeping under the bridges, families picnicking, and hundreds of poplars, including some of the biggest and oldest trees in Paris. From time to time we may also find a fishing competition or film-makers shooting a film on location or models posing for the fashion magazines, their clothes always six months ahead of the weather. And beside us always is the Seine with its unceasing procession of barges and *bâteaux-mouches*; around us is the dappled light from the trees and the river.

The Ile Saint-Louis is delightful at any time of day or year. But one can single out one or two highlights: a hot June afternoon, ourselves eating ice-cream, and the whole island in a cloud of cottonseed from the poplars, a pleasure to those who identify it with summer, asparagus, raspberries and the approaching holidays, a misery to those afflicted with carpet-brushing or sneezing; or a misty autumn morning with the river scarcely visible, and the sun coming through in a pearly light, gradually revealing the Seine and, beyond, the towers, spires and domes; a wet night, with the cafés and restaurants glowing with light and life; or indeed night at any time, with the lights from the mainland shimmering across the water – in their path the Seine always seems to be fizzing like champagne. An island in the centre of Paris! Balzac said that the place made him feel uneasy. But he came often, just the same.

The island was originally two (a third was incorporated into the Right Bank to form the Quai Henri IV); the Ile Notre-Dame with the Ile des Vaches upstream, the divide coming at what is now the Rue Poulletier. They were uninhabited and frequently flooded, but people came to them for occasional fairs or duels. St Louis visited

them on occasion and a temporary oratory was erected for his
frequent devotions. The islands belonged to the canons of Notre-
Dame, but early in the seventeenth century they sold the land, to
their later regret, to three architects, Marie, Le Regrattier and
Poulletier. The king, Louis XIII, approved and himself laid the first
stone of the Pont Marie in 1614. The islands were joined together
and embanked, and building began. The oldest buildings (1616) are
at the corner of the Rue Saint-Louis-en-l'Ile and the Rue Le
Regrattier.

The island is laid out on a simple grid plan. The houses on the
quays naturally face the Seine; down the centre runs a straight
narrow street, the **Rue Saint-Louis-en-l'Ile**, the commercial street,
dominated by the almost transparent spire and hanging clock of the
church, Saint-Louis-en-l'Ile. There are fine great houses on both
quays and in the central street. Crossing the island at right angles are
narrow side streets, with more modest but equally attractive houses.
Behind these houses, particularly the big ones, are large courtyards,
originally for coaches and horses, and these courtyards give a
further depth of secrecy to an already secret island.

The architecture of the big houses (*hôtels*) deserves our attention.
The seventeenth century was a particularly good period of French
building and many of these splendid *hôtels* (including one for
himself) were built by Louis Le Vau, certainly one of the greatest of
French architects. The island was not a place for the aristocracy,
who already had their *hôtels* and châteaux elsewhere. They were the
homes of ambitious bourgeois who had made their fortunes in the
Royal Chamber or the Royal Accounts, and became the ancestors
of a new generation of aristocrats.

The north quay (Quai de Bourbon, Quai d'Anjou) was the
fashionable side, being protected from the sun. In the seventeenth
century its inhabitants included the Corrector of Accounts in the
Royal Chamber, one of the twelve hautbois players in the Royal
Chamber, the Grand Master of Waters and Forests, the Queen
Mother's private portrait-painter and valet (a versatile man, it
seems), the Captain of the Queen's Regiment, an iron merchant,
the Governor of the Bastille, the President of the Chamber of
Accounts, a gentleman with the baffling title of Lieutenant de la
Robe Longue à la Connétablie de France, the Professor of Arabic at
the Collège de France and Le Vau himself. Many talents, much

ambition, a certain lack of incorruptibility – but we may wonder what they talked about on social evenings.

In the eighteenth and nineteenth centuries the island became less fashionable, though still the home of some interesting people. Except at the western, downstream, end in the nineteenth century, there was little rebuilding. The island was 'rediscovered' in the present century, after World War Two. But now it was the south-facing quays (Quai d'Orléans, Quai de Béthune) which became fashionable in a sun-loving time. Among the personalities who have lived there recently we find Georges Pompidou, Helena Rubinstein, the writers Francis Carco and James Jones, the actor Claude Dauphin, and the distinguished couple Mr and Madame William Aspenwall Bradley, literary agents, whose work and friendships covered over half a century. Their Saturday-night receptions were a welcome rendezvous for writers from France, Britain and America.

The **Pont Saint-Louis** is a modern prefabricated affair, linking the two islands. As it is chained off from traffic at both ends, it provides a pleasant viewpoint for walkers and a paradise for roller-skaters. It is hoped that it may be the precursor of a pedestrian area on the Ile Saint-Louis, despite the ill-founded opposition of many restaurateurs and shopkeepers, who fear that this may damage their trade.

The Pont Saint-Louis is the ninth bridge on the site, a series of disasters having destroyed the previous ones. There is, perhaps, a reason for this. In 1472 a group of swarthy people encamped round Notre-Dame. They were, it is said, a duke, a count and ten knights from Lower Egypt, Christian refugees from the Saracens. They had confessed their sins to the Pope, who ordered them as a penance to wander the world for seven years without sleeping in a bed. With their wives, families and hangers-on, they numbered, remarkably, twelve hundred people. They had black hair, wore ear-rings and masses of jewellery and told fortunes, and it seems clear that they were gypsies. The canons of Notre-Dame, weary of their presence, which both fascinated and annoyed the faithful, drove them away (17 April 1472), and, as they crossed to the Ile Saint-Louis in boats, they cursed the strip of water beneath them.

The curse seems to have been effective. The first permanent bridge between the islands, built by Marie in 1634, collapsed on its opening day, drowning twenty and injuring forty more. A later bridge, the Pont Rouge (painted red to protect it from the weather) was destroyed by floods. Others were severely damaged by barges or blocks of ice, or became inexplicably shaky. So perhaps there is a grain of truth in the old legend.

Crossing the bridge, we find ourselves in a little square, the junction of the quays and the Rue Jean-du-Bellay, the only street wide enough in the island to have pavement cafés (it is named after the sixteenth-century Cardinal, bishop and writer, the uncle of Joachim, the poet). We are surrounded by parked cars, cafés, restaurants and brasseries. The Brasserie de l'Ile Saint-Louis is on the site of the old Taverne du Pont Rouge – but more about this at the end of the chapter.

We, however, turn sharply left either on the street level or down a flight of steps to the river level, in order to reach the western tip of the island, downstream, with its trees, cobblestones and old lamps. From here we get a fine view of the splendid seventeenth-century house by François Le Vau, younger brother of Louis, which dominates the Seine here (45 Quai de Bourbon), the home for a long time of the Princess Bibesco, the uncrowned 'Queen' of the island; and now used by her descendants, mostly British.

From here to the other end of the island we have a choice of three routes, on the north or south bank or down the middle. But it would be a mistake to confine ourselves to one or the other; better to feel free to wander, to find the buildings, the shops and the views which appeal most. We can suggest a few.

The Ile Saint-Louis was not planned as a symmetrical whole like the Place Vendôme or the Place des Vosges. But there is a feeling of harmony and of place which is appealing. The *hôtels* which face the Quai de Bourbon (facing north) are remarkable for their stateliness and their pediments. They are now all converted into flats, with wide stone staircases and tall rooms with painted ceilings between the old oak beams. At night we can get many glimpses inside, as the French do not often draw their curtains. The inhabitants usually seem to be sitting at tables or desks, writing. These hotels are in contrast to the Polish Library on the Quai d'Orléans (south side), a severe neo-classical façade, which is much admired. The Ile Saint-Louis has been for centuries the centre of Polish culture in Paris.

Walking along the centre street, the Rue Saint-Louis-en-l'Ile, we find butchers, bakers, hairdressers, boutiques and many antique shops, where devotees can browse. But above the horse-butcher (No.51) we must note the florid pediment of the **Hôtel Chénizot**, supported by two elaborate gryphons and a sea-god. The *hôtel* was at one time the residence of the archbishops of Paris; one of them was fatally wounded at the barricades of the Faubourg Saint-Antoine during the 1848 revolution, and was brought home to die. But its most famous inhabitant was undoubtedly Theresia Cabarrus, the sex symbol of the 1789 Revolution, nicknamed Notre-Dame de Thermidor.

She lived there with her first husband, the Chevalier de Fontenay, and they were an ill-matched and unhappy couple. The marriage had been arranged by their parents to unite two family fortunes. She was only fourteen, partly Spanish, luscious; the curves of her bosom and hips, which were later to become so famous, were already conspicuous. He was small, red-faced and ugly, and she was ashamed to be seen about with him. His main interest was in raising himself in the aristocracy (the title Chevalier was self-awarded), but in the month of August 1789, when some of the nobility were thinking of packing and leaving, he finally succeeded in buying a genuine marquisate. His young marquise was not interested in this sort of thing, and her drawing-room was full of young cocktail-party revolutionaries, at least theoretically so; they included the La Rochefoucauld brothers and Lafayette, the more progressive nobility. Theresia even joined the reformist Club des Feuillants and, it is said, played with the Revolution like a child with a toy.

It could not last, of course. The moderates were swept away by the Terror. The couple parted and left, the marquis to America, she to Spain and her relations. However, she never got there. She was captured and put in a dungeon in Bordeaux. She did not remain there long, her intelligence and her attractions were too great. She soon became the mistress of Citizen Tallien, the bloodthirsty dictator of Bordeaux, and from there she returned to Paris, to her famous rôles in the Revolution. She was usually dressed as Liberty or Calypso, or just vaguely in gold and ostrich feathers, appearing at galas or riding in carriages. She was, however, usually pregnant and she had eleven children altogether. Napoleon said that she had the bastards of the whole world, though it is unlikely that he was one of the fathers. She made a last return to the Ile Saint-Louis, to the bedside of her eldest son, Antoine de Fontenay, who was dying of wounds received in 1815.

The **Rue Le Regrattier** was named after one of the original developers of the island. It is a narrow cross-street where Coffinhall, the friend and colleague of Robespierre lived until their execution on the same day in 1793. The northern half of the street was for some time known as the Rue de la Femme Sans Tête, a more pronounceable name than the original and present one. Her statue stands in a niche on the corner overlooking the Seine. 'Headless' seems a mild way of describing a lady who was decapitated, apparently, at her knees. She was probably a Virgin or Séquana, the goddess of the Seine, fished out of the river, and nothing to do with the guillotine.

Half way down the island we find the **Rue des Deux Ponts**, which connects the Pont Marie and the Pont de la Tournelle and funnels a great stream of traffic across the island, dividing it in two. Among the shops and restaurants we should certainly stop at the Boulangerie Haupois (No.35) which sells those crusty loaves, so appreciated by Louisiens and visitors from further afield. The loaves (parisiens, baguettes or bâtards) will be still warm from the wood-fired oven where they are baked.

Crossing the street, but still in the Rue Saint-Louis-en-l'Ile, we find another gastronomic attraction of the island, Berthillon's ice-cream shop (No.31). It sells ice-cream or *sorbets* (water-ices tasting of real fruit juice) in twenty-eight different flavours, the best of which is passion-fruit, to take away or eat on the premises, and it attracts a long queue in hot weather, many coming from distant parts. It is closed on Mondays and Tuesdays, holidays, and at other less predictable times. When it is closed the same ices can be bought, for consumption on the premises, at the Café Louis IX, a few yards away on the other side of the cross-roads.

The spire of **Saint-Louis-en-l'Ile** dominates the narrow street. It is one of the few spires in Paris which defies the Renaissance's obsession with Greek columns and Roman domes. The spire is pierced with a pattern of ovals which, seen from the side, gives a strange asymmetrical, almost kinetic effect, as we walk by. It was built in 1765 to replace Le Vau's original campanile, destroyed by lightning. The clock, which chimes the half hours loudly (at night too), is worthy of attention. To an Englishman the whole building

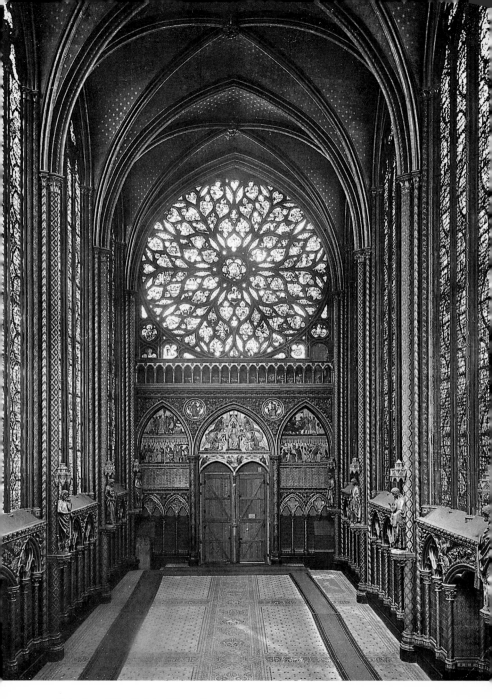

Interior of the Sainte-Chapelle.

The Horloge Tower and the Conciergerie.
Right 'June' from *Les Très Riches Heures du Duc de Berry.* A view of the
Ile de la Cité from the Left Bank, it shows clearly the Conciergerie Towers
and the Sainte-Chapelle.

A King of Judah, originally
on the façade of Notre-Dame,
now in the Cluny Museum.
Below Notre-Dame and the Parvis;
on the left, the Hôtel-Dieu Hospital.

says 'Wren' and it would not look out of place in the City of London. Similarly, the carved wooden doors remind us of Grinling Gibbons, and, indeed, both the church and its doors are contemporary with the English masters.

Saint-Louis-en-l'Ile was begun in 1664 to the designs of Le Vau, but it was not finished until 1726, which perhaps explains the more elaborate baroque interior, with its decoration, gilded scrollwork and marble. It is a fashionable church for weddings, not only for islanders but for those living farther afield. It is also used for concerts, attractive candlelit occasions.

Crossing the Rue Poulletier (another of the developers of the island), we find the **Arch of Bretonvilliers**, which spans the short street of the same name. It was originally part of the huge Hôtel de Bretonvilliers (another developer), which has been demolished to make the Boulevard Henri IV. But much remains to show the splendid style of the seventeenth century. The building and the arch are now pierced with windows, out of which schoolgirls looked, giggling, until 1984, when the school closed.

Madame de Bretonvilliers, the wife of the *nouveau riche* contractor, was also the mistress of the Archbishop of Paris. For some reason her husband objected to this and, when the Archbishop tried to slip away discreetly, he was escorted to his residence by many servants in full livery carrying torches, as was fitting to a personage of his rank. The Archbishop, it is said, did not return.

Strolling down the short street to the Quai de Béthune, we find two houses on the corner. The left-hand one is reputed to be haunted by a ghost – whose and why is not known. The right-hand one carries a plaque, recording that the Princesse de Poix, '*très haute et très puissante*', bequeathed the house in 1728 to the Maréchal de Richelieu. The military achievements of the Marshal and Duke (a great-nephew of the cardinal) were mainly against the British in Minorca. But his more famous victories were in the bedroom. His sexual appetite was almost inexhaustible, and there were no lengths he would not go to, even tunnelling through walls, to get the girl. Duchesses, actresses, servants, he pursued them all tirelessly, though he was often plagued by jealous husbands, duels and, occasionally, marriages. With such vitality it is hardly surprising that he lived to the age of ninety-two, and his final score, it is

said, was three wives, forty-four 'official' mistresses and an uncountable number of more informal seductions.

Returning to the Rue Saint-Louis-en-l'Ile, we find the **Galerie
Lambert**, a Polish enterprise. Many of the art galleries in the Ile
Saint-Louis cater for the tourist and have a general show of 'souvenir art'. The Galerie Lambert is more serious, if often more
macabre. But on one occasion it showed an exhibition of artists who
live on the island (there are seventy-five, including at that time
Chagall). The result was a varied and surprising revelation of the
artistic depths of the islanders. It is to be hoped that one day one of
the bookshops will do the same for the writers.

On the Quai d'Anjou (north side), we find the **Hôtel de Lauzun**,
No.17, the only old *hôtel* on the island open to the public (see
start of chapter). Apart from the gutters, the outside is rather
severe, and is incomplete, as the contractor was arrested for selling
non-existent fuel to the army. It is built with the principal rooms on
the first and second floors, to avoid flooding. This allowed secret
exits on to the Seine for clandestine visitors. It also allowed, during
the Terror, the young son of the house to escape while his father, the
Marquis de Pimodan, was arrested upstairs by the patrols of the
Committee of Public Safety.

The house was known at the time as the Hôtel de Pimodan. The
name of Lauzun was only given to it in 1850 by the then owner, who
put up the present plaque which has both Lauzun's name and date
wrong. Lauzun in fact only lived there for three years (1682–5),
escaping from his enormous, dominating wife, La Grande Mademoiselle, the King's niece (for more about this extraordinary
couple, see Chapter 16). The first floor is fairly plain seventeenth-
century, the second a riot of French baroque, covered with clouds,
rivers, swathes of flowers, trumpets, goddesses, masks and false
perspectives.

The Hôtel de Lauzun looked like that when its most distinguished
tenant, **Baudelaire**, lived there in 1843, in a small room under the
roof. His friends were amazed when he abandoned his usual haunts
on the Left Bank and went to live in outer darkness. It was the river
which drew Baudelaire. Water without limit symbolized genius
without form. The fixed quays symbolized (symbols were very
important to him) the form and the discipline necessary to his poetry
and his life, which he found so hard to find. He would stare at the

Seine for hours from his window, and one day he saw, bathing in the river, the beautiful mulatto girl, Jeanne Duval. (The Seine was relatively unpolluted and bathing was permitted.)

Jeanne's origins are mysterious. She is supposed to have come from the West Indies, and there are conflicting accounts of her appearance: tall, crinkly-haired, graceful, farouche, full-breasted, though others have described her as of medium height, ungainly, queen-like and flat-chested. Baudelaire fell passionately in love and installed her nearby in the Rue Le Regrattier; she became for him the symbol of carnal and profane love.

Baudelaire's two years in the Hôtel de Lauzun were the happiest years of his life, and the longest he ever spent in one lodging. He wrote nostalgically in '*L'Invitation au Voyage*'

> *Là, tout n'est qu'ordre et beauté,*
> *Luxe, calme et volupté.*

Perhaps he was thinking not only of Jeanne's dark skin, but also of the Hôtel de Lauzun and the Seine.

But troubles were crowding in – lack of recognition, debt, the sea of madness like the Seine without banks. He stabbed himself in her presence. It was ineffective and he recovered in a few days, but the romance was over. So was his life on the Ile Saint-Louis.

However, Baudelaire did return many times to the Ile Saint-Louis, to the Hôtel de Lauzun. He came to meetings of the Club des Haschichiens. The Hashish Club met in the small east room of the Hôtel de Lauzun, where one could get a good smoky fug very quickly. The chairwoman (La Présidente, as she was known) was 'Madame' Sabatier, a demi-mondaine and courtesan and, like others (La Dame aux Camélias, for example), an important influence in French literary and artistic life. Aglaë-Apollonie Sabatier was a jolly, pretty girl of twenty-four, but she became for Baudelaire his symbolic angel of purity, his chaste guardian, his embodiment of sacred love, to be contrasted with Jeanne – not that there was anything very chaste about Madame Sabatier.

The Hashish Club, however, was neither a brothel nor merely a den for druggers. Among its distinguished members were many who came for the company and not for the hashish. Théophile Gautier (who wrote the preface to Baudelaire's *Fleurs du Mal*) presumably smoked, judging from his own hallucinatory writings. So did Boissard, who introduced the cult and was the real president. Balzac, on the other hand, inspected the spoonful of yellow-green paste, which gave out a strong smell of rancid butter, and declined. He had, he explained, consumed so much alcohol and coffee that he was immune to such stuff. We do not know about the habits of the others – Delacroix, the Goncourt brothers, Daumier (who drew caricatures of the smokers and lived almost next door), Meissonier, Steinheil (who restored the glass of the Sainte-Chapelle) and, of course, Baudelaire himself. Visitors from abroad included Sickert, Rilke and Wagner. The East Room has long since been redecorated, but a small, very black patch has been preserved, a reminder of what hashish-smoking does to the wallpaper and, presumably, to the human lung.

The Hôtel de Lauzun was bought by the City of Paris in 1928 and has since been used for official receptions. One of the most famous was the one given in 1957 for Queen Elizabeth II and the Duke of Edinburgh on a state visit. Powdered footmen waited on the glittering guests and, above, musicians in eighteenth-century clothes played suitable music.

Moving along the quay, we pass Daumier's modest house and Le Vau's own *hôtel* with its convex front, shaped to the river line. And there we meet Le Vau's masterpiece, the **Hôtel Lambert**, with its bow windows overlooking the *hôtel* garden and the river. It was built for Lambert *le riche*, who had studied the art of embezzlement under Louis XIII's superintendent of finance, named (suitably) Claude de Bullion. After Lambert, it was owned by a Monsieur Dupin, whose wife's lover was Jean-Jacques Rousseau, and then by the Marquis du Châtelet, whose wife's lover was Voltaire, briefly. In the nineteenth century it was owned by Prince Czartoryski and it became the centre of Polish life; among its distinguished guests was Chopin, who often played there. During the Second World War it became the secret hide-out of Allied airmen shot down over France. When the Germans searched the house, the concierge would give a special ring on the bell, and the airmen would lose themselves in the complicated cellars until the danger was over. When they needed a breath of fresh air, other than the gravelly and rather bare garden, they would be allowed to wander about Paris, on strict condition that they did not speak a word. Later they would start on the long secret journey to Spain.

More recently the *hôtel* has been famous for the parties given by the Comte de Rédy. The guests, who never arrived before midnight, would be greeted in the courtyard by enormous floodlit papier-mâché elephants. Now it is the town-house of the Baron de Rothschild and closed to the public. But we can admire the main entrance (at 2 Rue Saint-Louis-en-l'Ile), with its big, plain but beautifully proportioned portico. If the doors are open, we can look in at the courtyard. On the far side is the double staircase, and, behind it, Le Sueur's fresco of the Seine (seen as a very old man) being rejuvenated by the Ile Saint-Louis (rather a fierce young woman); this is a curious concept, the Seine being normally shown as a chaste young goddess, Séquana, and St Louis as his royal self. Le Sueur also did the frescoes and ceiling, which show the labours of Hercules, of the upper bow window overlooking the Seine. These can be glimpsed from a distance.

Crossing the last boulevard, we find another gravelly garden, typically French, and we take the steps down to the river level, the upstream point of the island, a pleasant place for a sunbath. But our reveries may be disturbed by the local fishing school and the casting of beginners' lines.

We cross to the mainland, the Right Bank, by the unattractive **Pont Sully**. But, half way across, we should pause and look downstream at one of the finest views in Paris: the curving Seine, the old houses, the poplars, the distant towers and the Pont Marie, the most graceful bridge in Paris. On the mainland, at the entrance of Metro Sully-Morland, we shall probably pause for a drink on the terrace of the Café Sully (excellent omelettes too). From here we have a pleasant view of the Hôtel Lambert with its harmonious lines; perhaps the lights are coming on in the Hercules Salon and we can see, romantically, the glittering chandeliers and the painted ceiling. Across the Boulevard Henri IV we have a closer sight of the ruins of the Bastille prison, moved from the original site. But that is for another chapter.

Or perhaps we shall prefer to remain on the Ile Saint-Louis and eat there. At the moment of writing, there are thirty-six restaurants on the island – this includes brasseries, cafés which serve meals and tea-shops offering light lunches. They are much frequented by visitors from all parts of Paris and the suburbs. Some are closed on Mondays, some on Wednesdays, some close in the evening, others only open then and stay open late. But, with such a choice, we shall not go hungry, whether we want *haute cuisine*, simpler grills, provincial dishes (Alsace, Auvergne, Burgundy), exotic food from other countries or just a pancake (*crêpe*). The price range is wide too, but we can study the menus posted outside, before we commit ourselves.

The smart place is the Orangerie, opposite the church. It is a place for the rich and famous, a mini-Maxim's. The food is fairly simple, well-served in a neo-Empire decor. But it is a place where we will expect high prices; there is no menu card in the window. At the main crossroads is L'Ilot Vache; despite the name and the golden calf's head on the corner, it is an excellent fish restaurant. Not cheap, but we could be tempted by the *Gratin de barbue a l'oseille*.

At the corner of the Quai de Bourbon and the Rue Jean-du-Bellay we find a café-restaurant, Le Lutétia. The food is Burgundian in flavour and we could consider *Lapin à la moutarde dijonnaise*. The prices are reasonable and we may be able to eat out of doors, looking across the Seine at Saint-Gervais.

Or there is the Brasserie on the corner beside the Pont Saint-Louis, where we started this exploration. It is on the site of the old Taverne du Pont Rouge and often nicknamed the 'Oasis'. It is inexpensive, informal, crowded and fun. It is also well-known for its beer, Alsace white wine and *choucroute garnie*. Its warm (in both senses) hospitality has made it a rendezvous for the British, especially at weekends – and for other nations too. It is difficult to leave the old wooden bar without having found an old friend or made a new one.

CHAPTER 4
The Seine

The Seine is the heart of Paris – or rather, the great artery that feeds everything else. It is hardly possible to move about the centre of Paris without travelling along or across the river at some point. All streets, even if they do not actually lead to the river, are numbered from their river end. Paris, despite its size and growth, is still 'on the Seine'.

The seven miles of the Seine in Paris are without doubt the most famous river-front in the world, celebrated in paint, romanticized in song. Just as the Seine originally created Paris, so the Parisians have cherished the Seine, turning it into a long park or garden, full of trees and water. There are no factories or cranes or dockyards beside the Paris Seine (unlike the Rouen Seine). In Paris the river has been designed for pleasure, for strolling, cruising, fishing, loving, sunbathing, sprawling, picnicking, drinking, living and, for some, sleeping *sous les ponts de Paris*.

Keen Seine-watchers will notice its colour – that special blend of green and grey which can only be called Seine-coloured and which was captured so successfully by Sisley and Monet. It is, of course, heavily polluted, but its colour and appearance have hardly changed since the time of the Impressionists. Another curiosity should be noted; the Seine often seems to be flowing upstream. This is not romantic fantasy. The Seine is a very slow-moving river. The total drop between the source near Dijon and the sea is only 470 metres, and most of this takes place in the Côte d'Or when the river is still only a trickle. There are no snow mountains to give it spate and the tributaries are all equally gentle. The Seine is not like the rushing Rhône, full of snow-water. At its widest at Rouen it only reaches an average of 500 cubic feet a second (compare the Danube's 9000 at Vienna). It meanders gently across the plain of the Ile de France, making enormous bends, most of which are downstream from Paris. It is, as nearly as such a thing exists, a stationary river and the slightest breeze is enough to move the surface of the water downwind, upstream. And with a winding river like the Seine, every breeze blows upstream somewhere.

There are, of course, many locks and weirs, mostly very shallow, and the Seine is a very useful waterway. Paris is the fourth largest port of France (after Marseilles, Le Havre and Dunkirk). The barge traffic increases every year, but most of these unload at Gennevilliers, downstream, or at Charenton, upstream, and more ports are being constructed upstream from Charenton. It is rare nowadays to see a barge moored in central Paris. Instead we have a picturesque and almost continuous procession of boats, many of them carrying petrol or sand for the new suburban constructions. Some of them have Belgian, Dutch or German flags, for the Seine is connected to the canal systems of the Low Countries and the canals of France. But they all fly, gaily like flags in a regatta, an almost unbelievable amount of washing, particularly children's knickers.

The life of a French bargee is rather separated from that of his brothers on land. For one thing, he takes pride in setting foot as little as possible on the soil of France. So do all his friends, relations and future sons-in-law; they wave as they pass, meet briefly in the locks (where there is usually a shop), and for longer periods in the two great centres of Saint-Mammés (upstream) and Conflans-Sainte-Honorine (downstream). In the latter the church is on an old barge, so that the bargee and his large family can attend mass without setting foot on shore.

But the life is changing, naturally. The Impressionists showed us strings of barges, each separately steered and towed by a small tug. With the rising cost of labour (and the social security contributions for employees) the single barges arrived, self-propelled and probably owned by the skipper, and these still form the greater part of the Seine river-traffic. More recently the *pousseurs* (pushers) have arrived. These powerful boats, owned by the big oil, chemical and construction companies, can push up to six barges, two abreast, before them. With a fine disregard of the old nautical principle of sharp-end-first, they consume a great deal of fuel and save a great deal of manpower. Whether this will prove finally to be economic is uncertain.

Barges are not allowed to carry passengers, but bargees are hospitable people and if we find one moored, they will certainly invite us on board and show us over their immaculate and highly-polished boat. There will be up to fourteen people living on board in extremely cramped conditions; it is thought lucky for a baby to be born on the barge. If they are about to leave, they will perhaps give us a ride to the next stop or lock. Their life, however, is changing. The demands of education and midwifery are forcing them to have more contact with the mainland. Most now have television and many carry their owners' cars, made fast on the hatches. But they still remain an essential part of the Paris scene.

It is easier and less chancy to take one of the river cruise boats which ply up and down from Easter till the autumn, and we should certainly take one of these trips, preferably on a fine day when we can sit on deck. We shall have a beautiful view of the Seine and its incomparable architecture, though we may be irritated on some trips by the loudspeaker commentary, which seems obsessed by the weight of the bridges and the names of the visible ministries. The biggest boats (*bateaux-mouches*) look like huge insects made of glass. These also run at night, offering a longer cruise, a leisurely candlelit dinner (rather expensive) and a view of the buildings, floodlit by the boat itself. The view may be partly obscured by condensation, in which case we can console ourselves with *sole meunière* and a bottle of Chablis.

But the best way of exploring the Seine, like the rest of Paris, is on foot. The quays of the Seine are tree-lined double-decker affairs, plane trees above, poplars below on the verges of the Seine. The walk along the right bank at river level has been obliterated by the barbarous new motorway (named the Voie Georges Pompidou, after the politician who authorized it) which channels another hundred thousand vehicles a day beside the Seine, through the centre of Paris. The project to build a similar motorway along the Left Bank was vetoed by President Giscard d'Estaing and so we can still enjoy a walk of several miles along the bank of the Seine, shaded and in parts still cobbled. It extends from near the Gare d'Austerlitz to the Gare des Invalides (both metro stations), at which point an older motorway takes over. On our way we can admire not only the river scene, but many of the most beautiful buildings of Paris.

Or we can take the upper level along either bank. The traffic is daunting but there are many compensations: the chance to see the buildings more closely, the glimpses down narrow streets into the Marais (Right Bank) or the Latin Quarter (Left Bank), and, especially, the bookstalls. These are mainly in the Notre-Dame area and for a long time were frequented by those who wished to buy porn novels forbidden in other countries. Things have changed recently and now the bookstalls sell old books, prints, maps, posters and the inescapable, international pictures of doll-like children with huge eyes. Even if we do not wish to buy (and the prices are not as cheap as one would hope), we can enjoy browsing. The stall-owners, though keen to make a sale, are tolerant.

The buildings along the Right Bank will be described in later chapters (9 and 10) but here we are walking along the upper level of the Left Bank, starting at the Quai Saint-Bernard. The first thing we notice is the smell of animals; we are passing the **Zoo** and the **Botanical Gardens**. These contain Paris's celebrated Cedar of Lebanon which the botanist Jussieu is said to have brought back from the Middle East, watering it with his own drinking water. In fact it was a gift from Kew Gardens. The Zoo was originally stocked with animals 'borrowed' from travelling circuses. The arrival of the first giraffe, a present from the Pasha of Egypt in 1827, caused a sensation. The animals were all slaughtered for food during the Siege of Paris in 1870, but it has since been amply restocked. The animals are kept in more or less natural surroundings and we can see the antelopes through the railings as we walk by.

On our left was until recently the Halle aux Vins, the wine market of Paris. This has now been replaced by the Science Faculty of the University (Jussieu), a modern glassy building with a dominating tower, another of Pompidou's gifts to the city – he was one of its few admirers.

Crossing the end of the Boulevard Saint-Germain (which continues across the Pont Sully to the tip of the Ile Saint-Louis and the Right Bank, the Boulevard Henri IV and the Bastille), we find ourselves on the **Quai de la Tournelle**. The Tournelle was originally a fort guarding the entrance to Paris, part of the walls of Paris which King Philippe-Auguste built in 1190. There was another tournelle on the Right Bank and a chain was hung between them. The forts were also used as transit posts for galley-slaves on their way to

Marseilles, but happily nothing of this remains except the name of the quay.

A few yards further on, on the corner of the Rue du Cardinal Lemoine, is a building which is still very much in business. On the top floor is the celebrated restaurant La Tour d'Argent, thought by some to be the best in Paris. It is luxurious and expensive, with a fine view over the Seine, the Ile Saint-Louis and Notre-Dame. During dinner the lights are lowered for a few minutes to let us see the floodlit view, which, however, may be blurred by condensation on the windows. The menu cards are printed in pink and blue; the pink ones have no prices marked so that the ladies may order in ignorance of what they are costing their menfolk.

The principal food here is game, served in dishes decorated with feathers to look like the bird in question. The speciality is duckling (*caneton*) cooked in several ways, including the well-known *canard à la presse*. This is roast duck or duckling, flamed in brandy; over it is poured a sauce made of the crushed carcase and giblets, blood, mousse of foie gras and other undisclosed ingredients. In the repertory of *haute cuisine* it is probably the richest dish of all, popular also in Normandy (*caneton rouennais*) and in New Orleans. But modern Frenchmen, worried about their livers and figures, are beginning to shy away from that sort of cooking.

The reaction has produced *la nouvelle cuisine*, popularized by the figure-conscious President Giscard d'Estaing. This means simpler food, the best and freshest ingredients which taste of themselves and, often, dishes from the regions. It has been described, unkindly, as a grilled chop served with absolutely fresh, almost calorie-free watercress; or as 'more shopping, less cooking'. But for those foreigners less obsessed with their livers, who would like for a change a taste of *haute cuisine*, the Tour d'Argent can be recommended. Reservations are essential, credit cards desirable. After dinner we shall be encouraged to visit the cellars. These are dramatically lit, with information about the bizarre circumstances in which some of the bottles were acquired. It is a wine museum. The oldest wine, although priceless, is not for drinking.

We are now beside the **Pont de la Tournelle**, one of the most graceful in Paris. It is a modern bridge, replacing the old wooden footbridge mentioned by Hemingway in his first novel, *Fiesta*. In a single span it reaches the Ile Saint-Louis, allowing plenty of room for modern barges and also, shaped like a flying buttress, repeats the flying buttresses of Notre-Dame. The simple statue of Ste Geneviève, facing east at the invading Huns she defied, is placed off-centre so as not to interfere with the view of the cathedral.

The other bridge, the **Pont Marie**, connecting the Ile Saint-Louis with the Right Bank, is also beautiful but much older. Designed by Marie, the original developer of the island, its first stone was laid by Louis XIII in 1614. On either side of the road were rows of four-storey houses and shops and these can be seen in old prints. Two of the arches and twenty-two of the houses were destroyed in 1658 by floods, many inhabitants being drowned. The arches were rebuilt without the houses and, following more floods, the remaining houses were removed in 1740. The spans of the Pont Marie are too narrow for modern barges so the bridge is left to the cruise boats. From them we can enjoy the proportions of the bridge and its mellow stone, which is floodlit at night.

The other bridges of the two islands are, excepting the Pont Neuf, useful pieces of nineteenth-century engineering and need not excite our curiosity. We should concentrate, rather, on the riverside buildings as we walk along the Seine on the edge of the Latin Quarter. We pass many restaurants, cafés and shops, one of which sells empty tins, 'The Air of Paris'. We reach the Place Saint-Michel, a large square on the river, surrounded by student bookshops, cafés, restaurants and traffic.

Crossing the Place, still beside the river, we are on the Quai des Grands Augustins (there was a monastery here in the sixteenth century) with a line of fine eighteenth-century houses; fashionable apartments, though nowadays the roar of the traffic has made them less desirable. Here we also find another well-known restaurant, Lapérouse. It is a restaurant in small rooms and on more than one floor in an old building. Its reputation grew in the present century because of its chef, Topolinsky, who invented among other things a cheese sauce, a blend of gruyère and parmesan, to be put on roast duckling, a dish almost as rich as those to be found further up the quay. Outside, only a few paces away, is one of the great monuments of Paris, the Pont Neuf.

Despite its name, the **Pont Neuf** is the oldest bridge across the Seine; the most famous, the grandest, the solidest and a triumph of bridge design. It crosses the river at its widest point in Paris, with five arches to the tip of the Ile de la Cité and seven more to the Right Bank. The piers supporting the bridge are surmounted by round bays with stone seats – the bridge was always intended for leisure as well as traffic. Below the rim a theatrical frieze of grimacing masks runs right round the bridge.

The Pont Neuf is always associated with Henri IV, whose statue stands in the middle (a nineteenth-century replica, the original was melted down during the Revolution). But the idea had been mooted for a long time without anything happening. The first stone was laid in 1578 by Henri III. It was a sad occasion: the King was in deep mourning and tears; three of his favourite *mignons* (boyfriends) had recently been killed in a duel with the Guises (see Chapter 10) and he was almost speechless with grief. Nothing more happened for twenty years until Henri IV, his cousin, and brother-in-law for a time, ordered the bridge to be finished. He made two changes in its design: there were to be no houses built on it and there were to be pavements for those on foot. He himself opened the bridge in 1607, riding across it on his charger.

Immediately it became the promenade of Paris. The city was not a pleasant place for walking. The streets were narrow, deep in filth, crowded with horses, wagons and the carriages of the great. The unfortunate pedestrian would be jostled by lackeys and footmen, possibly set on by thieves. But now at last Paris had a pedestrian precinct. It was, in a sense, Paris's first boulevard and it was thronged, day and night, by a crowd endlessly moving up and down, the first *flâneurs*.

It was also a permanent fair. The bays were occupied by booths, stalls and merchants crying their wares, including plenty of prostitutes. A carillon played every quarter of an hour, jugglers, acrobats and strolling players entertained the passers-by. Under one of the arches was a large pump and statue, 'La Samaritaine', which provided water for the Louvre. It was the social centre of Paris and it continued for nearly two hundred years until the Revolution, which swept the fair away. The jugglers, singers, actors, prostitutes and bookstalls can still be found plentifully in Paris, but no longer on the Pont Neuf.

One of the traders who cried his wares on the bridge was a Monsieur Cognac-Jay, who prospered, founded museums, and, in particular, transferred his business to the end of the bridge on the

Right Bank, where he renamed it **La Samaritaine**, after the fountain. It is now one of Paris's largest department stores and it is there that we should now go. Crossing the quay, we enter the big building, Magasin Deux; we ignore the attractions round us, the heat and the crowds (we shall think about Paris shopping in another chapter, 13), and head for the lift to the ninth floor, the roof terrace. Here, over a drink, we can see possibly the finest view of Paris: not as remote as the Eiffel Tower or the Montmartre terrace, not as exhausting as the Notre-Dame towers or the Arc de Triomphe, we can see them all from here and much else. Below us lies the Seine and its bridges and beyond it the façades of the Left Bank. On every side are the domes, the towers and the spires of Paris, and we can identify them all from a helpful circular map on the turret above, reached by a small winding stair. Is the Panthéon dome more beautiful than those of the Invalides or the Institut below us? Is the Monnaie more beautiful than the Louvre? Is the Montparnasse Tower an eyesore or a masterpiece? Is the Pompidou Centre at Beaubourg the most startling building we have ever seen? We can decide it all over a cool drink under an awning. (The terrace is open during the store's shopping hours, but the café is closed from the end of October till April.)

We descend reluctantly and re-cross the Pont Neuf. It is the moment to consider the personality of **King Henri IV**, Henry of Navarre (1553–1610). In a long line of mediocre kings, he stands out like a star. Soldier, statesman, man of ideas, he became France's most popular king since St Louis – though the two men had little in common except a concern for the welfare of ordinary people. The leader of the much-persecuted Protestant Huguenots, he believed in freedom of worship, which he achieved in the Edict of Nantes (13 April 1598).

His economic idea was summarized in his hope that there would be no Frenchman too poor to have a chicken in his pot every Sunday. This *poule au pot* philosophy (an early example, perhaps, of *la nouvelle cuisine*) was to be achieved by ending the Wars of Religion and giving the peasants time to breed chickens and grow vegetables. He was helped in this by his able minister and closest friend, the Duc de Sully. Sully said, 'Grazing and ploughing are the two breasts from which France is fed, the true mines and treasures of Peru.' This was a crack against rich Spain, whose wealth came, temporarily, from the looted altars of South America. Sully also forbade the gentry to ride over growing crops and vines, and introduced a close season for hunting. He reorganized taxation; many rich people had bought themselves out of the system. He reconstructed roads, built bridges and started the Canal de Briare, joining the Seine and the Loire. The royal treasury overflowed.

But ending the Wars of Religion was a hard task. The Huguenots were outnumbered by the Catholic League, led by the powerful Guise family and able commanders such as Mayenne and Farnese. Henri IV was often outnumbered two to one; on one occasion his cavalry were outnumbered five to one. Several times he took refuge on the coast, where he received help from England; indeed, he even considered marrying Queen Elizabeth I. In the end he won, and the treaty of Vervins was signed (1598). It was a generous peace; Henry was a man to forgive and forget.

But the problem of Paris, firmly Catholic, remained. 'What can I do?' the King in tears asked Sully. 'If I do not forswear Protestant-ism, there will be no more France.' The question is often misquoted as the cynical 'Paris is worth a Mass.' In 1594 he became, in Chartres, a Catholic for the second time. A month later Paris opened her gates to him and he was given a rousing welcome. It was not, however, completely unanimous. Some, like the mad Ravail-lac, thought it was all part of a cunning plan to murder the Pope; others were suspicious of his conversions and thought that he was still at heart a Protestant. There was some reason for this. In his last year he was preparing an army to prevent Austria from imposing Catholic princes on the Protestant Rhineland.

Despite the Massacre of St Bartholomew, the long years of civil war and two unhappy marriages, Henry was a man who enjoyed life. He liked riding his horses down the corridors of the Louvre. Especially he enjoyed the feel of female flesh, which he preferred unwashed. His favourite mistress, Gabrielle d'Estrées, bore him two children, but this did not prevent him having children by her sister and by many other young women. At one moment he parked fourteen of his children with their various mothers at Saint-Germain-en-Laye, which brought a moment's quietness to the Louvre. He also liked riding through the narrow streets in his carriage, greeting the ordinary people, a habit which made him an easy target for assassination.

But beyond all this was his vision of peace. He dreamed of a federal Europe, a *république chrétienne*, with a Senate which would settle all international disputes of frontiers and religion. He was foreseeing and trying to prevent the horrors of the Thirty Years' War, which lay just ahead. As an idea it was three hundred years in advance of its time, and it was not to be fulfilled. When Ravaillac stabbed him in his carriage in the Rue de la Ferronnerie on 14 May 1610, everything changed. All France was in tears. He was remembered, and still is, as Henri le Grand, who brought peace, prosperity and reconciliation to the country.

Regaining the Left Bank, we find ourselves on the Quai Conti, in front of the **Monnaie**, the Mint. Originally the Hôtel de Nesle, the town house of the Duc de Berry, there has been much rebuilding on the site. In 1670 it was the Paris residence of the Princesse de Conti. In the eighteenth century Louis XV moved the Mint there and an unknown architect, Antoine, was commissioned to make the necessary alterations. The façade which we now see is plain and almost severe, but pleasing in its formality. In the age of baroque it was a surprising addition to Paris. But it pleased the Parisians, who were beginning to tire of ornamentation; it also pleased the architect who, disconcertingly, decided to live there.

It is open to the public. We find ourselves in a fine entrance hall with a coffered ceiling. Turning right, we climb a beautiful double staircase to the gallery, a succession of panelled rooms displays the medals, medallions and coins of the Monnaie, from many dates up to the present. There are also temporary exhibitions. Beyond is the shop (it can also be reached from the entrance hall) where bronze medallions can be bought. These vary from replicas of old coins to new work, specially commissioned by the Monnaie as its contribution to modern art. They are reasonably priced and make attractive souvenirs and presents. The coinage of France is now minted elsewhere, mainly in the Gironde.

The next building is the **Institut de France**, a landmark for its fine gold-ribbed dome, and the Mazarin Chapel, containing the Cardinal's tomb but otherwise secularized. Originally part of Philippe-Auguste's fortifications, and later the Hôtel de Nesle, it was completely rebuilt in the late seventeenth century by the orders of Mazarin on his death-bed (1661). He had ruled France during the boyhood of Louis XIV and amassed a huge fortune; he left two million *livres* for the building of his memorial chapel and a college and library for students from four 'acquired' provinces. The two curved wings end in square pavilions on the Seine and were designed by Le Vau, although not actually built by him; the Corinthian columns are not typical of his style.

The east wing contains the **Bibliothèque Mazarine**, originally the Cardinal's own library, but with many later bequests. This lovely room, with its leather-bound books and its view over the river, is open to the public, readers and sightseers alike, and is much used. Many of the books are in manuscript and the students, often rather elderly, find a magnifying-glass a help.

The rest of the building is given over to the **Académie Française**. It is closed to the public, but there are lecture tours every Saturday and Sunday starting at 3.0 p.m. The French Academy was founded by Richelieu in 1635 in the Louvre and moved to its present site, on Napoleon's orders, in 1806. Its members include distinguished people from all the professions, but it has a strong literary flavour and it is responsible for the official French Dictionary. Its meetings are spectacular and widely publicized, the members wearing knee-breeches, swords and green robes. It was exclusively male, but a woman was recently admitted (the novelist Marguerite Yourcenar); it was reported that she did not wear a sword. The members think highly of themselves and write '*de l'Académie Française*' after their names, even, it is wickedly said, on cheques. They are called the Immortals, though the majority were and are rather obscure. The list of those, from Descartes to Proust, who have been refused admission, is starry indeed. The Parisians regard the Academy with a mingled awe and amusement, which is typically French.

Crossing the Seine in front of the Institut is the **Pont des Arts**, a footbridge opened in 1803. The first iron bridge in Paris, it attracted a huge crowd, about sixty thousand, and the pattern of the curved arches is very pleasing. Unfortunately the task of navigating it and the Pont Neuf in rapid succession was too much for many bargees and it was increasingly damaged by collisions. The bridge has recently been rebuilt on the old design, but with fewer (seven) and wider arches. There are no longer seats and flowers, but we have pavement artists and, in particular, the wonderful view. We are poised in air above the Seine between the Mazarin Dome of the Institut and the classical Cour Carrée of the Louvre. Upstream are the Pont Neuf and the Ile de la Cité; downstream is the river and its bridges. Elsewhere there are pleasant houses with well-proportioned façades. Add trees, water and sky and we have what Lord Clark, speaking of this view, called a humane and reasonable solution of what town architecture should be.

After the Quai Conti we are on the Quai Malaquais. Queen Marguerite de Valois, known popularly as Fat Margot, the estranged first wife of Henri IV, built herself a sumptuous palace here, deliberately facing the Louvre and her former husband. She lived a debauched life, but much may be forgiven her (except perhaps strangling her lovers with her garters); she was the daughter of Catherine de Medici and had had a sad life, including the St Bartholomew massacre on her wedding-day and a long period of house arrest in the provinces. Nothing now remains of her mansion except the name Malaquais – ill-acquired (the means by which she got her estate from the University of Paris, which owned the land, were very suspect).

Now we have, here and on the Quai Voltaire, a pleasant line of eighteenth-century houses, and the enjoyment of looking at them is much increased by recalling what a distinguished collection of writers, painters and composers lived here beside the Seine, sometimes briefly, sometimes for long periods: Anatole France (at No.19 Quai Malaquais), Ingres (No.11 Quai Voltaire), Delacroix and Corot (at No.13 in the same studio, but not of course at the same time). At No.19 Quai Voltaire, in the same hotel, were, at various times, Baudelaire, still gazing at the Seine, Wagner finishing *Die Meistersinger*, and Oscar Wilde in exile. Voltaire himself was at No.27 in 1724, aged thirty. Fifty-four years later, after years of exile in Geneva, he returned in triumph to the same house and died a few weeks later.

The Pont de Carrousel, joining the Left Bank and the Louvre, carries much traffic, but our admiration should be reserved for the next one, the **Pont Royal**, Louis XIV's gift to the river. Its simple grace and curve are an example to bridge-builders, which was later sadly forgotten. It is in strong contrast to the Pavillon de Flore on the Right Bank, the downstream end of the Louvre, built in the nineteenth-century under the Second Empire, dignity without beauty.

On our left is the dark hulk of the **Gare d'Orsay**. Recently scheduled for demolition, it has been rescued and preserved as a monument of the railway age. No trains leave there now, though it is connected by the suburban RER line to Orly airport in the east and Versailles in the west. The building will house the Musée d'Orsay with an important collection of nineteenth-century art (including Lautrec and Seurat, formerly in the Jeu de Paume), also furniture and decoration. The opening is planned for 1986. (See Chapter 12.) Across the river are the formal Tuileries Gardens.

We also pass (or, if it is a hot day, perhaps visit, for a swim) the Piscine Deligny, a floating swimming pool moored in the Seine. The idea of a floating swimming pool is intriguing and, unlike the river, the water is filtered and even said to be drinkable. The pool has been there since 1842.

The Pont de la Concorde is a plain austere bridge, which does not take the eye from its surroundings. It merely joins the Chambre des Députés with the Place de la Concorde (see Chapter 5) and carries a huge amount of traffic. The Chambre, or **Palais Bourbon** as it is often called, is the French Parliament, but architecturally it is a Roman temple built by order of Napoleon, who saw Paris as another Rome. The façade of columns is false, the real entrance of the eighteenth-century building is on the far side of the building. Since a presidential system of government was adopted by the French under de Gaulle, the Chambre des Députés has lost much of its newsworthiness. Governments no longer fall weekly at three o'clock in the morning and the deputies no longer slam the lids on their desks. Or, if they do, nobody reports it. But we can attend a debate, if we wish, by prior application to the Quaestor (No.126 Rue de l'Université).

But, as Seine-watchers, we should reserve our attention for the next bridge, the **Pont Alexandre III**. It was built for the 1900 World Exhibition and named after a Tsar. It is the most sumptuous and the most flamboyant of all the Seine's bridges. Every spare centimetre is encrusted with decoration: cupids, scrolls, garlands of flowers, wreaths, shells, birds, shields, trumpets, lions – they are all there, some in stone, some in bronze, some gilded. It is the supreme example of the architecture of the Third Republic and the Belle Epoque. At the Exhibition and ever since it has been a popular promenade, and, if we tire of the decoration, we can enjoy a superb view of the dome of the Invalides, Hardouin-Mansart's great golden bubble floating over the Esplanade (see Chapter 18), and meditate on the changes in architectural fashion in little over a hundred years.

We can no longer stroll along the water's edge; a motorway took over at the Gare d'Orsay, but on the quays we can still enjoy fine and famous views. On the right we have the huge glass mound of the Grand Palais; on the left we are increasingly aware of the Eiffel Tower. We pass the Quai d'Orsay, the French Foreign Office, and the Pont des Invalides, again built at the turn of the century, but since rebuilt. We should, however, notice the **Pont d'Alma**. Originally nineteenth-century, it is remarkable for the huge statue of a *zouave*, a French-Algerian soldier. This is popular as a marker for the height of the Seine. Has it reached his waist? His neck?

The **Pont d'Iéna** is also encrusted with eagles and horses, and was built at the start of the nineteenth century, though it has been much altered since. On the Right Bank is the Palais de Chaillot and its gardens; the bridge is a fine place to see the fireworks which are let off on 14 July and other national occasions. On the Left Bank we can see the Champ-de-Mars and, distantly, the Ecole Militaire. Overtopping everything is the Eiffel Tower, at whose foot we now stand.

The cruise boats do not go further than this, but on foot we can persevere a little longer. On the left is Grenelle, a working-class area full of factories, builders' yards and the Citroën works. Efforts have been made to raise the *'standing'* of the area by building seven high-rise apartment blocks, two of which are reserved for low-rent tenants ('Where our servants will live,' it was explained to me). On the right is the Seizième Arrondissement, full of fashionable homes and small gardens. The circular white building beside the Pont de Grenelle is the Maison de la Radio, the Broadcasting House of Paris. The Seizième spreads down the hill from the Arc de Triomphe to the Bois de Boulogne and Auteuil. At Auteuil we are at the city limits and the Seine leaves Paris.

We need not walk as far as this, but we could continue as far as the Pont Mirabeau before we descend into Metro Javel. There we should recite, if we can, the opening lines of Apollinaire's celebrated poem:

Sous le pont Mirabeau coule la Seine
    Et nos amours
Faut-il qu'il m'en souvienne
La joie venait toujours après la peine . . .

PART TWO

The Right Bank

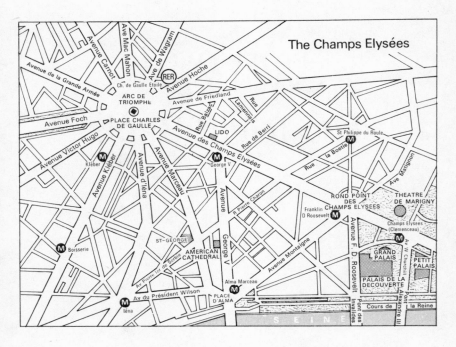

The Champs Elysées

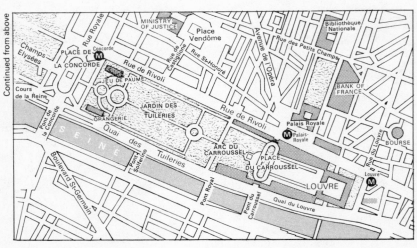

Continued from above

CHAPTER 5

The Champs-Elysées

We take our *point de départ*, once again, from a star, but this time from a much bigger star, the **Etoile**. The circle round it has now been renamed Place Charles de Gaulle, but everyone, Gaullist or anti-Gaullist, still refers to it as the Etoile – the star. In the centre of it stands the **Arc de Triomphe**, one of the best-known monuments in the world. From here, or better still from the top, we can see the twelve avenues radiating out in all directions. Nine of them are not very interesting, unless we have business there. Two of them, Victor Hugo and Foch, are fashionable residential streets leading to the Bois de Boulogne, and we shall come to them later. The one we are concerned with at the moment is the main one leading down the hill to the Place de la Concorde and the Louvre, the Avenue des Champs-Elysées. The whole area and idea is generally thought, in France and abroad, to be the high point of French town-planning.

However, it was not planned like that. Beyond the city limits, it was simply fields and marshes in the time of Henri IV. His wife, Marie de Medici, in 1616 created the Cours-la-Reine, a fashionable carriage-drive. But it led, not through the fields, but along the Seine to what is now the Place d'Alma. In 1667 the great landscape-gardener, Le Nôtre, who loved distant prospects and formal perspectives, planted chestnut trees in rows and named the area the Elysian Fields. It did not, however, lead anywhere, scarcely to the Rond-Point. In 1724 the Director of the Royal Gardens, the Duke of Antin, prolonged the avenue to the top of the Butte de Chaillot, now the Etoile. His successor extended it to the Seine at Neuilly. To improve the perspective and make the avenue easier for horses, Soufflot, in 1774, reduced the height of the Butte by sixteen feet (five metres), the spare earth being dumped in the nearby Rue Balzac, where it remains. The top of the hill became a grass lawn and it was Napoleon, in 1806, who had the idea of placing a huge triumphal arch on the summit.

His choice of architect was Chalgrin and his ideas were monumental indeed. The arch was to be fifty metres high and forty-five metres wide, encrusted with large flamboyant sculptures, friezes, shields and hundreds of names. Less elegant than the Arc de Carrousel at the other end of the Champs-Elysées, it dominates the Etoile and the avenues, as it was intended to, particularly at night when it is flood-lit.

We reach the arch by the underground passage (from the north side of the Champs-Elysées); no one dares to cross the Place Charles de Gaulle on foot. Beneath the arch lies the Unknown Soldier with his flame, and several other plaques record historical events. In the very centre, worn by many feet, is a bronze Napoleonic eagle.

Outside we should note the four sculptured reliefs. Facing the Champs-Elysées, the one immediately on our left is generally considered the finest of the four; by Rude, it shows the departure of the volunteers in 1792 and is usually called '*La Marseillaise*'. It is full of life and revolutionary vigour, but it may seem rather too flamboyant for some tastes. The other three sculptures have less life and are less admired. On our right is the Treaty of 1810 ('*La Triomphe*') by Cortot. On the other side of the arch, facing the Avenue de la Grande Armée, we have 'Peace' on the right, 'Resistance' on the left, both by Etex. On a higher level are six panels showing battles and funerals. The battle of Austerlitz faces the Avenue Wagram, the battle of Jemmappes the Avenue Kléber.

We re-enter the arch and there, standing between the imperial eagle and the flame of the Unknown Soldier, we realize that we are, in a sense, in a cathedral. The Arc de Triomphe is Napoleon's Notre-Dame, his Sainte-Chapelle, great in size and dedicated to the glory of the Grande Armée. On the walls round us are the names of battles, marshals and generals, founders of the Napoleonic Empire.

Some well-known names are, of course, missing and many of the battles may be unknown to us. Which of us could write an impromptu essay on the battle of Dietikon? (Near Zürich in September 1799, French troops and Swiss levies under Masséna checked the advancing Russians under Suvarov. Switzerland, *la république helvétienne*, had been quietly absorbed into the French Empire, a shocking thought for those who fondly imagine that the little neutral country has been independent and free of foreign invasions for five hundred years.)

But, standing in the middle of the arch, we can certainly find it an awe-inspiring building. We can forgive its ungainliness, its megalomania. It dominates the avenues and the landscape, much as Napoleon dominated continental Europe for fifteen years.

However, the arch got off to a shaky start. The Empress Josephine had not produced an heir, though she had children by her first marriage. In 1810 he divorced her, to the disapproval of the Pope, Pius VII, who was taken into captivity, in Valence and elsewhere. As his second wife, Napoleon took a prize of war, the young Princess Marie-Louise of Austria. On her way from Vienna to Paris she was unexpectedly waylaid by Napoleon himself, who virtually raped her – in her carriage, some say. He then returned to Paris. The nineteen-year-old princess made her way to the Arch, through which she was to make her triumphal entry, and so down the Champs-Elysées to the Tuileries. Unfortunately the arch was only a few feet high, Chalgrin having had problems with the foundations. A false arch of canvas was hastily erected and the future Empress passed through this in her procession down to her bridal bed. Despite this unpromising start, she produced an heir the following year, Napoleon François, King of Rome. His short, sad life has been eloquently described in Rostand's weepy play *L'Aiglon* (The Eaglet).

The arch was finally finished in 1836, after years of neglect. Four years later Napoleon's body, brought home from St Helena by permission of the British (Palmerston), passed through the arch on its way to the Invalides. Since then there have been many moving events there: the Victory procession through the arch in 1919; the crowd of enthusiasts, led by de Gaulle, in 1944; the annual large ceremony held there every 11 November, in memory of the Unknown Soldier. On major festivals and state occasions, a huge Tricolor flag hangs and billows inside the arch, reminding us that it is an arch of celebration as well as a cenotaph.

The summit platform is open to the public during daylight hours. It is an ascent of two hundred and eighty-four steps; there is also a lift and a queue. But it is an ascent which we must certainly make, one way or the other. We find a great panorama. Around us lies Paris, or at least the Right Bank, which most visitors consider to be Paris. The Champs-Elysées, beneath us, leads to the Place de la Concorde, the Tuileries Gardens and the Louvre. We are in the centre of the Etoile, the star with its twelve radiating avenues. It is a memorable experience.

The Etoile was completed in 1854 under Haussmann (who else?). He added the seven further avenues to complete the twelve-pointed star and commissioned Hittorff to design the uniform façades which ring the Place between the avenues. It is the type of majestic town-planning which the French admire, though some visitors prefer the narrow streets and picturesque corners elsewhere, which time has forgotten to develop.

We return through the tunnel to the 'mainland'. Two addresses nearby may be useful to the British visitor. One is St George's Anglican (high) Church at 7 Rue Auguste Vacquerie. It is not easy to find, although it is only a short walk from the Etoile (up the Avenue Iéna). It has a tradition of good music and an excellent choir, but the great organ which Susan Landale used to play has gone, along with the nineteenth-century building. The site has now been redeveloped into a block of flats, with the church squeezed into part of the underground garage. It is always full and many people stay for wine and cheese, or lunch, on Sundays, after the 10.30 a.m. service. Social activities include the Cardew Club for young people and lunchtime organ recitals on Mondays.

A few yards away, at 5 Rue de Presbourg, we find the Sir Winston Churchill Pub. This is an interesting hybrid of a Victorian pub, with engraved glass and brass rails, and a French restaurant, with plush banquettes on a higher level, for those who wish to eat and be served by waiters. It is a popular rendezvous for the British, both visitors and locals, especially on Saturday nights. In addition to food and a large variety of beers, the pub also offers Glenmorangie and other malt whiskies, toasted tea-cakes in the afternoon, and opening times which are very far from British licensing hours.

Remontons les Champs-Elysées! – though in fact we shall be going downhill. The phrase was much used at the turn of the century, when the carriages of the well-to-do, several abreast, passed up and down the avenue, greeting each other and the strollers on the pavements. The ladies wore large hats, the gentlemen top-hats, unless they were alongside on horseback. Above them were the chestnuts, nostalgically always in candle. The world of Gigi and her admirers. It is not quite like that now. The chestnuts have been replaced by planes, supposedly more resistant to traffic fumes. The carriages and horsemen are now cars, going much too fast to greet anybody, but often honking their horns. But the magic remains. It is partly due to the wide pavements and the vast crowds which wander up and down, all day and most of the night, French as well as visitors. It is still the great Promenade of Paris. *Remontons les Champs-Elysées!*

In addition to the ever-moving cavalcade, the Champs-Elysées is also a street of more formally organized events; for instance, the big parade on 14 July, the moving procession on the 11 November, the state visits of foreign potentates, when the avenue is hung with flags; and lighter events such as the summer day when the avenue is closed for the Tour de France bicycle race and the sweating riders go up and down for more than two hours. There is talk of a grand prix rally there, similar to the one through the streets of Monte Carlo. A simpler spectacle, though not without its dangers, is to cross the Avenue on a wet winter night and pause at a traffic island; from here we can watch the twinkling red tail-lights of the cars, and their reflections, as they mount to the Etoile or descend to the Place de la Concorde, also floodlit. And at Christmas there are lights in the trees along the whole avenue.

But there is more to it than that. The Champs-Elysées has become an idea, an emotional rallying-point for Parisians. We can mention such spontaneous and unorganized events as the huge demo on 30 May 1968, when the long avenue was crowded from end to end with thousands of Frenchmen, waving Tricolors and singing the 'Marseillaise'. It was a counterblast by the silent majority to the much-publicized riots in the Boulevard Saint-Michel, which preached anarchy and revolution. The *événements* on the Left Bank, as they are tactfully called, petered out soon after this. Two years later there was a big silent march, equally unorganized, in memory of de Gaulle. When we stroll down the Champs-Elysées on a summer afternoon, we are not only making the scene; we are also, in a small way, part of history.

Architecturally it is not much, apart from the two perspectives up and down, and an occasional glimpse through a side avenue at the

77

Invalides dome. It is a commercial street of banks, airline offices, car showrooms, cafés, cinemas, hamburger bars and even a drugstore, which bears as little relation to its American origin as a French 'pub' does to its British counterpart. It is another Piccadilly. But recently it has become a good shopping area, especially for women. Less expensive than the Faubourg Saint-Honoré, less way-out than Saint-Germain-des-Prés, it is popular with those wanting fashionable clothes and shoes. Many of the boutiques are in shopping arcades, leading off the main avenue and often on several levels.

Two of these may be mentioned. The Arcade de Lido was rebuilt on the site of the well-known cabaret, which has now moved a few yards further along the street (see Chapter 20). In the centre is the Café de Paris, where we can have a cheap meal, standing or seated – the *tarte aux poireaux* is recommended. While we eat, we can windowshop, and afterwards visit those boutiques which attract us. The other is the Elysée-Rond-Point, further down. We can refresh ourselves beside a big waterwheel with dolphins (not alive) and a quotation from Leonardo about perpetual-motion machines, while the ladies buy dresses and shoes in the surrounding boutiques.

Many avenues and streets lead off the Champs-Elysées and we cannot explore them all. But we can note the main ones and their points of interest. Descending from the Etoile, we find on the right, leading down to the river, the **Avenue George V**, named after the English king. Lined by chestnuts (which seem to survive the traffic without difficulty), its most prominent feature is the spire of the **American Episcopalian Cathedral**. This is a nineteenth-century Gothic building, dignified inside as well as out. Its services, always crowded and not only by Americans, are noted for their music; each one is almost a concert and the choir is very well-rehearsed.

Otherwise the Avenue is very typical of this part of Paris, the Eighth Arrondissement. It contains three fashion houses (Givenchy, Balenciaga, Nina Ricci), two embassies (China, Mexico), two luxury hotels (George V and Prince de Galles), a popular night-spot (the Crazy Horse Saloon, see Chapter 20), any number of banks and business offices, cafés, restaurants, boutiques and the Paris office of a big firm of British chartered accountants. Such a mixture is very Parisian and we shall meet it again in the Opéra area, but it is scarcely conceivable in London or New York. The avenue ends at the Seine, at the Place d'Alma, a semi-circular area of cafés and restaurants, where four avenues meet the quay and the Right Bank expressway. It is also the embarking point for the *bateaux-mouches*, the big boats which provide evening dinner cruises (see Chapter 4).

Back on the Champs-Elysées, we find ourselves at Fouquet, the famous old café and restaurant. It is not exactly fashionable, but its good food, splendid wine-list and attentive service have kept it very much in the swim. It is mainly used by business people, including a sprinkling of show-business types and those staying at the nearby hotels. The décor is mainly veneer wood. We should start at the bar, perched on stools in front of the celebrated notice that unaccompanied women are not admitted to the bar; a notice which has given much annoyance to Women's Lib and female journalists. The champagne cocktails are excellent. For lunch we should choose the terrace facing the Avenue George V, glassed in in cold weather, open in summer, so that we can enjoy the chestnuts. We should choose a meat dish for our main course, perhaps *Agneau de lait* or *Médaillon de veau à l'estragon et pointes d'asperge*, so that we can drink a bottle of red Bordeaux. I recommend a red Graves, a Domaine de Chevalier, about fifteen years old. At night we should eat upstairs under the chandeliers, in a quieter, more luxurious setting and, if we can get a window table, we can enjoy the twinkling lights of the Champs-Elysées. Reservations are essential and prices are high, but Fouquet remains after many years and despite much competition, my favourite Paris restaurant.

On the other side of the Champs-Elysées, a little lower down, is a narrow business street, the **Rue de Berri**. It has a luxury hotel (the Lancaster), two good Italian restaurants and a seafood restaurant in an intriguing ski-resort décor (the Val d'Isère). The Alpine resort is, of course, far from the sea.

Passing the long Rue La Boétie we find a small café, La Colisée, now only a fraction of its former size. But I once saw a man there order a cheese soufflé and then give it to his dog. Almost opposite is the most graceful building on the Avenue, No.25, the Travellers Club (members only), a haunt of homesick British, and French bridge-players. The architecture reminds us of how the Champs-Elysées must have looked a hundred years ago.

Not that we are doing badly. We are now at the **Rond-Point**, the roundabout where six avenues meet, a point bright with fountains and flowers and trees, and splendid views in all directions. Two good façades remain here; on the south side the buildings of the magazine *Jours de France* (behind the big black and gold railings); on the other, the buildings occupied until recently by the newspaper *Le Figaro*. It was planned to demolish both and replace them by high-rise developments. This was prevented. The façades were retained and restored, while the buildings behind them were rebuilt – a typical French compromise, and one pleasing to the eye.

The first avenue on our right at the Rond-Point is the **Avenue Montaigne**. Formerly the Ruelle des Veuves, it was a bright spot with many 'dancings' and three thousand gas-lights. Many people went to the Winter Garden there to hear Monsieur Sax play his new instrument, the saxophone. The avenue is now very like the Avenue George V, and it also leads down to the Place d'Alma and the river. Apart from hundreds of big business addresses, it has high fashion (Dior, Laroche, Balmain, Revlon), the Canadian Embassy, a luxury hotel (the Plaza-Athenée) and two theatres, the Comédie des Champs-Elysées and the **Théâtre des Champs-Elysées**, almost on the Place d'Alma.

We should note the Théâtre, one of the first reinforced concrete buildings to be built in Paris, completed in 1912. It was designed by Auguste Perret and he tried to soften the bleakness of the material with pilasters and reliefs (by Bourdelle). His reputation soared and, many years later, he was commissioned to re-plan and re-build the city of Le Havre, totally destroyed in 1944 by the Germans, who wanted to deny the Allies a Channel port. Le Havre is the only modern city in Europe planned and designed by one man and, whatever we may think of it now, we have a foretaste and sample of his architecture here in the Avenue Montaigne. Grandiose, we may think, and uninspired.

The Théâtre des Champs-Elysées is now almost wholly given over to concerts; it is the main concert hall of central Paris. It is also used by visiting ballet companies, and it was here that the Diaghilev Ballet gave the notorious first performance, on 29 May 1913, of *Le Sacre du Printemps*. The conductor, Pierre Monteux, had prophesied that the work would cause a scandal, but even he did not foresee the riot that actually occurred. Stravinsky, it was said, was trying to destroy music, though little of his score could be heard

Unforgettable Paris – Seine bookstalls and Notre-Dame.
Below An informal 'Parlement'; in the background, the Ile de la Cité.

The gold-ribbed dome of the Mazarin Institute; in the foreground, the delicate Pont des Arts. *Below* The seventeenth-century Pont Royal, a graceful contrast to the nineteenth-century Louvre behind it.

The Pont Alexandre III, completed in 1900, the most flamboyant
of the Seine bridges; in the background, the Grand Palais.
Below The Pont Marie and the Ile Saint-Louis.

The view from the roof of the Samaritaine department store.

through the booing and catcalling. After the performance Di-aghilev, Stravinsky, Nijinsky and Cocteau took a cab and drove round the Bois de Boulogne, to calm themselves. Diaghilev wept, nobody spoke.

By 1921 the work had achieved respectability and was placidly received at a London concert, conducted by Goossens. Fifty years after the first performance the music was performed with Monteux still conducting, and Stravinsky present, and this time it was the coronation of a masterpiece.

Also leading off the Rond-Point is the **Avenue Franklin D. Roosevelt**, reaching the Seine at the Pont des Invalides. This is another typical avenue of the area. Of note is the Restaurant Lasserre, of which more later; the stark West German Embassy; the France-Amérique club, a pleasant mansion, often used for public dinners; and the **Palais de la Découverte**. This is the Science Museum of Paris. It is a centre of scientific research and general instruction, with demonstrations and lectures. The planetarium is a popular feature. (We must not confuse the avenue with the Rue Franklin, called after Benjamin, which is in the sixteenth Arron-dissement. The French call them both Franklin, pronounced *à la française*.)

From the Rond-Point to the Place de la Concorde, the Champs-Elysées has quite a different character. The buildings are few and set well back from the Avenue. We are in a garden, or perhaps a wood, with avenues of mature chestnuts, azaleas and other shrubs and no fences. We (and dogs) are free to roam as we wish. On the left side, almost hidden among the trees, are the Théâtre de Marigny and the well-known **Espace Cardin**, once the Théâtre des Ambassadeurs. It is now in two parts. One is a television studio (visitors admitted after queueing) where we can watch our favourite programmes going out live. The other is a large hall, with plate-glass windows, used for exhibitions and sometimes for ballet. If we happen to go in May, to see, perhaps, the Salon de Mai, our eyes may be distracted from the works of art displayed for us by the Salon to the view through the windows, the chestnuts in candle, the azaleas in flower, the Champs-Elysées in the springtime. With an effort we bring ourselves back to contemporary art, which often seems all too keen to emphasize the ugly side of the modern world.

81

On the right side, at the statue of Clémenceau (by Cogné, 1932), we find another Avenue, the **Avenue Winston Churchill**.* This is quite different from the other avenues we have seen. For one thing it has no houses. Instead it has two palaces, the Grand Palais and the Petit Palais, one on either side. It also has a superb view, down to the Seine, across the Pont Alexandre III, over the Esplanade to the final dome of the Invalides. It is the kind of formal perspective which the French love and which they do so well.

The **Grand Palais**, built for the 1900 World Exhibition, is a huge building of stone, glass and steel. Normally it is divided into parts. The north end, nearest to the Champs-Elysées, is an art museum usually devoted to one-man shows of the great. The retrospective exhibitions of Picasso, Léger, Chagalle, Mirò and Cézanne attracted enormous crowds. The central part houses the Salon d'Automne, the Salon des Indépendants, the Triennale Européenne de Sculpture and others. At times the whole area is cleared, with immense work, dust and rubble, to provide space for the Motor Show, the Boat Show, the Ideal Home Exhibition, etc. It is the Earls Court or Olympia of Paris.

Opposite it is the **Petit Palais**, built mainly of stone, best known for its temporary exhibitions. I specially recall the Tutankhamen treasures which attracted long queues. Frescoes from Florence and Pompeii have also been shown with success. The Petit Palais also has the Museum of Fine Arts of the City of Paris. This covers the long period from antiquity to the Renaissance, also Flemish and Dutch paintings. Two other collections, Tack and Dutuit, consist mainly of objects – enamels, porcelain, books, drawings and furniture, also tapestries.

At the end of the Champs-Elysées, on the right, we find the Restaurant Ledoyen, a pavilion set on a lawn (closed Sundays). It was once a country inn where people went to drink milk still warm from the cows which grazed outside. It is not like that now, but it is still one of the best-sited restaurants in Paris. On the corner of the Champs-Elysées and the Place de la Concorde, we can, in warm

---

* Paris has honoured many well-known Englishmen by naming streets after them. Apart from George V and Churchill, Queen Victoria has an avenue, Edward VII a square and an equestrian statue. Streets are also named after Roger Bacon, Byron, Dickens, Newton and Stephenson. There are also a Rue des Anglais and a Rue de Londres.

weather, eat on the terrace beneath the chestnuts, surrounded by flowers and lawns, and enjoy the great sights around us.

Fouquet and Ledoyen are the only major restaurants on the Champs-Elysées itself. But if we explore the quarter a little further, we shall find three further restaurants; Le Berkeley, No.7 Avenue Matignon, notable for its oysters, profiterolles and fairly simple food, served in a draped setting at high prices. It is usually full and reservations are essential. At No.15 Rue Lamennais, near the Etoile, is Taillevent, thought by many discerning Frenchmen to be the best restaurant in Paris. It specializes in regional dishes, a different region each day, and it also offers *specialités de la maison* such as *gratin de langouste* and truffles in pastry. It is mainly used by businessmen for lunch; the well-dressed ladies come in the evening. The décor is Versailles-style and the prices are high.

And then there is Lasserre, No.17 Avenue Franklin D Roosevelt, arguably Paris's top restaurant, though it is not a haunt of the international jet-set. It is more a place for private luxury. The restaurant is best-known for its first-floor dining-room, where the painted ceiling (by Touchagues, who also did the murals) can be rolled back in warm weather, so that we can dine under the stars and look out on a roof garden. The décor has been compared to a transatlantic liner of the 1930s. However, we should not forget the food, which is very special – *poularde Grand Palais*, lobster *feuilleté*, hot foie gras and so on, plus a great wine list, all impeccably served. It is, of course, very full and expensive; reservations are essential (closed Sundays and in August, when the weather is usually at its warmest). But if all this is rather above our budget, it is only a short walk to the Matignon Drugstore or the Renault Pub (behind the car showroom). The Champs-Elysées caters for everybody.

As we enter the **Place de la Concorde** we should pause to admire the **Marly horses**. These superb statues flank and, in a sense, guard the entrance of the Champs-Elysées. They are eighteenth-century, the work of Guillaume Coustou, and originally in the Château de Marly, one of Louis XIV's houses destroyed in the Revolution. The horses were brought to the Champs-Elysées in 1795, dragged by sixteen live horses. The statues, magnificent wild animals, rearing, are shown being tamed by Africans. There is a delightful description of a small boy riding one in Nancy Mitford's novel *The Blessing*. How he got up there, and what the police thought, I do not know. The marble horses have recently been replaced by exact, pollution-proof replicas; the originals will be housed in the Louvre.

We are now in the huge square. It was intended to impress, and impress it does, by its size and by its position beside the Seine, between the Gardens of the Champs-Elysées, framed by the Marly horses, and the Tuileries Gardens, framed by two winged horses by Coysevox, erected in 1719. Replicas will replace these too. The one on the north side is called Mercure, the other La Renommée. Everywhere there are long vistas, great perspectives. André Maurois went so far as to write: 'There is not on this planet a more beautiful architectural ensemble than that which leads from the Arc de Triomphe to the Louvre and from the Madeleine to the Palais Bourbon' (the Chambre des Députés, across the river). There are certainly plenty of columns and arches to be seen: Rome in the heart of Paris.

The best place for seeing these vistas is at the centre, on the island by the obelisk. Getting there is hazardous, as thousands of cars cross the square every hour (or minute). While waiting for a chance to return to the 'mainland', we can pass the time by counting the lamps – I have got as far as two hundred. More romantically, we can look at the distant skyline of towers and domes, and the huge sky with its sailing clouds, which might have been painted by Monet. In spring and summer we shall enjoy the flood of fresh green from both gardens, turning to gold in the autumn. Even in winter the square has its charm, especially on a wet night when the buildings and fountains are floodlit.

The square also has eight large statue groups, dedicated to French cities, and two statue-fountains (copied from St Peter's Square, Rome), in honour of River Navigation and Maritime Navigation. It is difficult to tell these last apart, but River Navigation is, surprisingly, the one farther from the Seine. The French love to fill their squares with statues of large, semi-nude, full-breasted, gesticulating ladies representing Peace, Liberty, Eloquence, Consular Jurisdiction, the city of Bordeaux, Lyric Poesy and Maritime Navigation – to give only a few. Personally I find them lovable and am sad that this type of art has recently been discontinued.

The square was originally given by the bourgeois of Paris to King

Louis XV, *le bien-aimé*, with a statue of him by Bouchardon in the centre. A competition to design the square was won by Jean Gabriel, ahead of Souffiot, Servandoni and others. However, famous events intervened and the square was only finished in the reign of Louis-Philippe (1830–48) by Hittorf. Gabriel's two immense buildings remain on the north side of the square. Neo-classical in design, they deliberately remind us of the Louvre and of Italy and, with their arcades, their colonnades, and their pediments, they are justifiably admired as masterpieces of eighteenth-century architecture.

They are, however, simply façades, flanking the Rue Royale. To an eighteenth-century architect, a building meant a façade. The idea of 'the use of space' or the '*machine à habiter*' (Le Corbusier's phrase) is modern. Gabriel himself had no idea what was to be behind his great façades, nor what the buildings were to be used for. At the present time, the right-hand building houses the Navy and Environment Ministries, the left the French Automobile Club and the **Hôtel Crillon**. This building has long been associated with French-American relations. It was here that the Treaty of Friendship (1778), recognizing the independence of the thirteen states, was signed by Louis XVI and a number of American diplomats, including Benjamin Franklin. The Hôtel Crillon has kept its American connection; it is a convenient place for distinguished American guests, the Embassy being only a few yards away. The bar (good, very dry martinis) is also a rendezvous for international journalists.

But, back in the great square, our minds naturally turn to history, in particular those events which took place between 1792 and 1795. It was the Place Louis XV, but his statue was toppled and the Square renamed the Place de la Révolution. On Sunday, 21 January 1793, the first guillotine was erected there, on the west side near the present statue of Brest. The King, Louis XVI, walked calmly down the Rue Royale to his death. He tried to make his last words heard above the rolling drums; it was something about his blood assuring the future happiness of France. But the blood-lust was now high and, four months later, the guillotine was re-erected near the present statue of Strasbourg and the march of the tumbrils, the Terror, began. The guillotine was a portable machine and it moved, like a travelling circus, to the Place du Carrousel, the Place des

Grèves (Hôtel de Ville), the Bastille area and the Place de la Nation, where in fact most of the executions took place.

However, the guillotine was moved back to the Place de la Révolution for the execution of Robespierre. Robespierre, the austere tyrant, whom Danton had teased for never having been drunk, for never having laid a woman, whom Carlyle nicknamed 'the Sea-Green Incorruptible', was thrown unceremoniously on to the guillotine platform, as if he had been a mere marquis or fellow-politician. It was seven o'clock in the evening of the 28 July 1794. Over 1300 people had been beheaded in that square before him.

After the Revolution the Directoire tried to cleanse the blood-soaked square. The guillotine was removed and the square renamed Place de la Concorde. (It was temporarily renamed Place Louis XVI in 1823.) The square became a place for celebrations and festivities. The statues were erected on the unfinished plinths originally designed by Gabriel, and the **Egyptian obelisk** from Luxor raised in the centre. Louis-Philippe, a king who liked to keep a low profile, thought that an antique obelisk would be less controversial than a statue. The obelisk, over 3000 years old, was a gift to France from Mehemet Ali, the Viceroy of Egypt (he also gave Cleopatra's Needle to London). The obelisk, made of rose-red stone, is covered with hieroglyphs recording the achievements of Rameses II, too obscure to excite popular wrath. Twenty-three metres high and weighing 230 tonnes, its transport from Luxor to Paris was a great engineering achievement, the details of which are recorded in the Musée de la Marine in the Palais de Chaillot (see Chapter 12).

The Place de la Concorde is now a great sea of cars, except on certain festive occasions. On 14 July there is dancing there to live bands. The square also had one of the main entrances to the sewers of Paris. This has recently been closed and the main entrance for visitors is now on the left bank of the Pont d'Alma (see Appendix G).

We climb the steps to the **Tuileries Gardens** and pause for a moment on the terrace to admire the view. The Tuileries are sometimes called, and often thought of as, 'the noblest gardens in Paris'. They extend for a kilometre, from the Place de la Concorde to the Place du Carrousel and the Louvre, between the Seine and the Rue de Rivoli. But to the British it is hard to think of them as gardens; how can there be gardens without grass and flowers?

Instead we have gravel, clipped trees in straight lines and many statues.

We have to remember that this is a formal, symmetrical garden, intended for strolling and the contemplation of distant views, in the Italian manner. Indeed, the gardens were first planned by Queen Catherine de Medici on the site of an old tileworks (*tuileries*). However, the present gardens owe everything to Le Nôtre, who designed or re-designed so many gardens for Louis XIV. His passion for geometry, for straight avenues and formal ponds and patterns, for clipped trees and regular statues, found its expression here. And we should take it, as the French do, in the spirit in which it was planned, rather than wonder what an English gardener like Capability Brown would have done with the site. Anyway, we can admire many of the statues, especially those by Coustou, Coysevox and, more recently, Maillol.

The gardens were first opened to the public, reluctantly, by Colbert at the beginning of the eighteenth century and have been a popular promenade ever since, especially during summer lunch hours. The **Tuileries Palace** was at the far end, almost adjoining the Louvre and many historic personalities have gazed out on these gardens.

Louis XVI was brought there ignominiously from Versailles by the Parisians, who thought it was time that their king lived among them. Later, after his abortive flight abroad, which was stopped at Varennes, he was brought back to the Tuileries, again in ignominy. On 10 August 1792 he again escaped from the Palace, across the gardens to a temporary haven in the Palais Bourbon; most of his Swiss guards were massacred in the gardens by the mob. After the Revolution the Palace was Napoleon's home in Paris, where he held court with his marshals and other leading Bonapartists. The Bourbon kings lived there after the Restoration (except for the Hundred Days in 1815, when Louis XVIII fled to Ghent). The Tuileries was also the home of that unloved Emperor, Napoleon III, whose bones the French are happy to let lie in England. (But in his defence we can claim that he created the modern Paris that we love.) The Palace was destroyed by the Commune in 1871, and nothing now remains of it, except the gardens.

We can stroll along the south side beside the Seine and above the expressway, the Voie Georges Pompidou, which is hidden below us, the noise partly diminished. On the main avenue, we turn and admire once again the long view up to the Arc de Triomphe. From here, however, the vista is slightly marred by the off-centre high-rise buildings of the La Défense complex beyond Neuilly on the other side of the Seine. Pompidou said that this did not bother him, but it bothers many Frenchmen.

Before returning to the Place de la Concorde we should look out on the north side at the **Rue de Rivoli**, a very long street running from Concorde almost to the Bastille, getting shabbier and seedier as it goes on. The street was laid out in 1804 and named after Napoleon's first great victory, in Italy. The present buildings facing the Tuileries Gardens are grandiose enough for any emperor. Built in the early nineteenth century, they are suitably Italianate, with the long formal arcade and lighting. The arcade allows us to window shop, sheltered from the rain or the sun.

There are many boutiques here, catering for our need to buy presents. There are also several smart hotels, among them the Meurice, the Intercontinental (formerly the Continental) and the Saint-James-and-Albany. There are also two English-language bookshops, W. H. Smith's (paperbacks, stationery, a restaurant and a popular tea-shop, a rendezvous for the British) and Galignani's, which caters more for the American market. And plenty of places where we can buy a scarf, a watch or a not very avant-garde picture.

However, back in the Tuileries Gardens, we may have noticed on the edge of the Place de la Concorde two large pavilions. The one beside the Seine is the **Orangerie**, the greenhouse of the gardens; the other, beside the Rue de Rivoli, is the **Jeu de Paume**, the tennis court. Both are now art galleries. The Orangerie is now used only for temporary exhibitions; a recent exhibition of Henry Moore's works attracted a large crowd. The drawings were inside the Orangerie, the sculptures, of course, lying outside. The Jeu de Paume is the present home in Paris of the French Impressionists and many people come to Paris to see this, and this alone. The collection is due to be transferred in 1986 to the d'Orsay Museum. The museum is pure pleasure, whether we come as casual visitors or as art historians, and the Impressionists draw us, as few other artists have done since the Renaissance. The entrance is on the Concorde side. Since every picture is clearly marked with its name, that of the painter and his dates, there is no need to buy an expensive catalogue, unless we want one for later study. A certain rather limited attempt has been made to group the works of single artists in one room. But in general the collections of donors have been left intact, giving a somewhat random feeling; we can come upon a Monet or a Sisley anywhere.

We shall therefore stroll through the two floors of the museum, pausing every time we see something which gives us pleasure. (Room-numbers given here are those at date of going to press, but changes are frequent.) Myself, I can never see enough pictures of the Seine valley, of huge skies with moving clouds, of the reflections of light on water. Others may prefer to linger in front of race-horses, circuses, ballerinas and portraits of interesting people, both famous and unknown. The range of subjects for the Impressionists was wide.

But not wide enough for many contemporaries. The **Impressionists** deliberately rejected all the traditional subjects of art. We shall not find any Annunciations, any scenes from the Bible or classical mythology, any court portraits, battlefields or disembowelled horses. We are a long way from David and Delacroix; in size, too, these pictures are generally much smaller. What we have are pictures of everyday life: a bridge over the Seine, a cottage, a pretty girl in a smart dress (or nude, probably bathing), someone in a café, lunch, a boating party, a plate of fruit, a glass of wine. The artists were trying to avoid both the classical and the romantic, but we may well find their works romantic in our nostalgia a hundred years later.

The word Impressionism derives from an early picture by Monet, 'Impression, Dawn', which gave the name to the whole movement. But it is a mistake to imagine the artists as a coherent group, inspired only by the idea of painting light effects – this was confined to the 'hard-core' Impressionists, Monet, Sisley and Pissarro. They were a group of individualists, held together by their rejection of traditional art, of the rigid laws of design, content and colour laid down by the Ecole des Beaux-Arts and by the jury of the Paris Salon, which rejected their works again and again. This meant that they were deprived of public recognition and success; it was a permanent battle against loneliness, poverty and usually ill-health. When Monet took refuge in London from the 1870 war, it is thought that he was influenced by Turner; certainly there is something Turneresque about his paintings of Westminster, with the light filtering through the mists. We may compare Turner's 'Rain, Steam and Speed' in London with Monet's '**Gare Saint-Lazare**' (on the first floor, **Room X**). Nobody had ever thought of painting a train before. But there was a great difference in their lives. Turner was given commissions and honoured; Monet died of hunger. Yet the quality which emerges from so many Impressionist canvases, whatever their subjects and techniques, is joy and happiness.

In their despair they fell back on each other, encouraging each other, exchanging ideas and even teaching each other – they were nearly all self-taught. Some were country-lovers, some were town-birds, some were gregarious, some were solitary, but they were held together by their wish to paint their own pictures in their own way. For ten years after 1871 seven of them (Monet, Renoir, Sisley, Dégas, Manet, Caillebotte and Berthe Morisot) lived at Argenteuil, meeting, talking, and painting each other; the year 1872 was a high point of their collective achievement. However, it was an on-and-off business; they did not all share the countryside vision. The real meeting point was in Paris, at the Café Guerbois in the Avenue de Clichy, near Montmartre; or else they were entertained by Manet in his Paris home; he was better off than the others and became an unofficial president of the group, for that and for his spectacular rejections by the Salon. Others who helped the group were the photographer Nadar, who lent his studio in the Boulevard des Capucines for their first show on 15 May 1874; the dealer Durand-Ruel who bought many of their pictures, and thereby made himself a fortune; and their fellow-painter Caillebotte, who soon realized that he had more money than talent and contented himself with buying their work. A shy bachelor, he bequeathed his collection to the Louvre, with Renoir as executor. An acrimonious debate followed, with Clemenceau intervening on behalf of the Impressionists. The Louvre finally accepted only half of the pictures, to their great regret now – the Jeu de Paume is part of the Louvre.

Manet's rejection can be seen most spectacularly in his '*Dejeuner sur l'herbe*' (ground floor, **Room VII**). This large picture shows a picnic in a wood, the girl being naked. It was rejected by the Paris Salon and finally shown in the *Salon des Refusés* [sic] where it caused a scandal. It is not especially 'impressionist' and there had been plenty of nudes in French art before that girl. The trouble was that she was not labelled Venus or Justice, but was quite anonymous.

(Incidentally, the talkative young man on the right is Manet's son, who later married Berthe Morisot, not the girl in the picture). Two years later, in 1865, the Salon again rejected Manet's '*Olympia*,' a marvellous study in black and white, for the same reason – it now hangs next door in Room VI. After that he became, temporarily, a true Impressionist, as his pictures of the Monet family in a garden or boating at Argenteuil show. However, his heart was in Paris and in portraits; we should consider his portrait of Clemenceau in Room VIII. Other notable pictures in the museum are '*The Balcony*' – equally rejected (the girl is Berthe Morisot) and '*The Piper*', a strange picture, often thought to express solitude. Denied the popular and critical success for which he longed, Manet died prematurely, of locomotor ataxia. His last work was the well-known '*Bar aux Folies Bergère*', now in London.

Monet, however, was the real leader of the Impressionists and he really was obsessed by light: light on water (his 'Bridge at Argenteuil', his 'Regatta', his lily-pond at Giverny in Room XI) light in the sky, light on buildings. He was reacting from the sombre colours of the Barbizon school and from the dark-varnished masterpieces of earlier centuries. He preferred not to mix his colours on his palette, but to apply them plain in juxtaposition. The blending and the vividness comes in the viewer's eye and for this reason we should stand well back from them – a difficult thing to do in an always crowded gallery. His compositions are those of a child snapshotter; he did not often bother to include the end of the bridge, the top of the palazzo, the side of the cathedral. It was the light he was interested in, the rippled Seine, the sun coming through the mist, the ever-changing façade of Rouen Cathedral. He painted parts of this unchanging building twenty times going from one canvas to another as the light moved. Five of them hang together in Room X and we should remember that they are not pictures of the cathedral, but studies of changing light on the same stones. In the same room is one of his Westminster series, his '*Gare Saint-Lazare*', a murky triumph, and also his '*Haystacks*', arguably the finest picture in the whole museum. It really glows with light.

Sisley, of British parentage although he lived all his life in France, was also obsessed with light, in the sky and on snow. He was a solitary man, withdrawn and irritable, too poor to buy shoes – he wore clogs. There are rarely any people in his pictures, and then

91

only in the distance. But his works give great pleasure and we should enjoy his '*Floods at Port-Marly*', his '*Snow at Louveciennes*', and his many pictures of the Seine with its barges and regattas. Nor should we miss his picture of Argenteuil, that white little town, as it then was.

Pissarro, another true Impressionist, was less interested in water. Instead he preferred country lanes, orchards, gardens, trees and cottages (note his 'Village of Voisins' and his 'Red Roofs'). Finally he returned to Paris where he was fascinated by the streets, especially if they were wet. His well-known '*Boulevard des Italiens at night*' evokes the dark, lamplit city, but that is now in London.

Coming to the **Semi-Impressionists**, we reach Renoir, a painter whom we either love or hate. His flirtation with Impressionism was comparatively brief (note his 'Hillside Path'). A cheerful, gregarious man, he preferred painting people to landscapes; in particular he enjoyed painting female flesh and he returned to eighteenth-century colour, seeing himself as the successor to Boucher and Fragonard, whom he greatly admired. But whatever we feel about his too, too fleshy flesh (did those girls never use powder?), nobody can fail to enjoy his big picture in **Room XI** '*Le Moulin de la Galette*', with its happy, dancing, drinking crowd.

Cézanne, in **Room XIII** at the top of the stairs, was only an intermittent Impressionist. He lived, from 1872–4, in Auvers-sur-Oise, near to Argenteuil, where his close neighbour, Pissarro, influenced him strongly, particularly by the idea of working in the open air. He knew most of the others in the group and his 'House of the Hanged Man' was shown in the group exhibition at Nadar's studio. But his tendency was towards geometrical construction, very different from Monet, as were his preferred colours, which were not at all to the taste of juries. His shy, fierce temperament made it hard for him to make friends, and his rejections by the Salon hurt him. He was happier in his native Provence, to which he returned for a yearly visit. He was in the end officially accepted by the Salon, but it no longer meant much to him. He was trying to move beyond Impressionism to a kind of new classicism, and in this area he did his greatest work. The Salon d'Automne showed many of his works in 1907, but he only commented that he was making slow progress. The Jeu de Paume has few of his works, but we should notice two of his still lifes (bottles and apples, of course); his

Provençal landscapes, full of sunshine and warmth; and a wonderful but rather grim double-portrait, 'The Cardplayers'.

Rooms XIV and XV have Van Gogh and Gauguin. The Impressionists normally stayed on friendly terms, but these two quarrelled so bitterly (about what we do not know) that Van Gogh cut off his ear. His '*Restaurant de la Sirène*' reminds us that he was once an Impressionist, but most of the works shown are from his final period, after his return from Provence to Auvers-sur-Oise and momentary peace in the house of Dr Gachet, whose portrait hangs here. There is also a picture of the local church, very wavy. But the two pictures here which remain in the mind are both portraits. One is a 'Self-Portrait', a haunted, agonized man on the edge of suicide; the other is an earlier work from Provence, '*L'Arlésienne*', a formidable woman, seated against a yellow background.

Gauguin hangs on the opposite wall. Two works are from his Impressionist period, but the others are in his well-known Tahiti style, with its vivid colours, its total rejection of perspective and his flat-nosed women. Two of them command our notice: 'Tahitian Women' and 'Arearea', two girls and a dog beside a blue tree. Compelling, but a very long way from Monet, whom he had rejected.

There is no space here to consider the others – Bazille, Boudin, Jongkind and Fantin-Latour. But we shall leave the Museum through **Room II**, mostly devoted to Dégas. For Dégas an impression was a picture of movement, not of light. It was said of him that his idea of the countryside was a racecourse. Certainly he liked painting horses and also ballerinas, on stage or in their dressing-rooms. Or people at work, laundresses yawning, a moment in time, an impression captured. Yet the picture which will surely remain in our minds is '*Absinthe*', a sad picture of stillness, a man and a woman sitting motionless at a plain table, the glasses before them.

The Jeu de Paume is a big Salon des Refusés, the life's work of men of genuis, disappointed, ignored and often coming to sad ends. Yet, as we walk out into the Paris scene and see the skies of Monet and Sisley, the streets of Pissarro, our feeling is one of exhilaration, as if we had just had a glass of champagne. These men had something inside themselves, a *joie de vivre*, which could not be extinguished by any failure, any illness or any jury or critic.

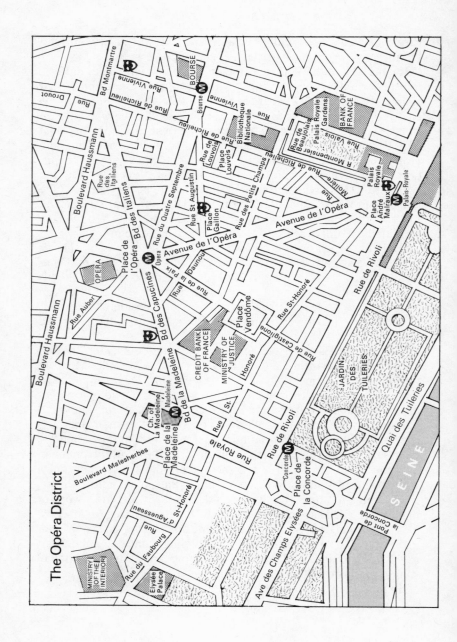

The Opéra District

CHAPTER 6
The Opéra District

The north-side of the Place de la Concorde is filled by Gabriel's two great façades, described in the last chapter. They form a kind of portal, framing yet another of Paris's perspectives, the Rue Royale leading to the Madeleine; and the Rue Royale is the start of our walk (Metro Concorde). Almost immediately, on our left, we find one of the landmarks, the most famous restaurant in Paris, and possibly in the world: Maxim's.

Originally an eating-house for cabmen waiting in the Place de la Concorde, it has moved a long way to its present eminence as the main rendezvous of the international jet-set. In other ways it has not moved at all, preserving its original turn-of-the-century décor, which we call Art Nouveau and the French call Belle Epoque or Style Rétro – the Beardsley-like world of mauve, Pernod-green and mustard, dim mirrors and drooping exotic flowers. As we enter, we step back ninety years.

Reservations are essential, unless we are very important indeed and well-known to the management. At lunchtime Maxim's is mainly used by rich businessmen, but it really comes into its own in the evening and after the theatre. Evening dress is compulsory on Friday nights (closed all day Sunday). As we sink on to our comfortable banquette, we can imagine ourselves to be millionaires or royalty or film stars or other sorts of celebrities. They will be all round us. Musicians will play 'Sous les Ponts de Paris' at our table and we can dance a waltz or tango in the small space available.

The service is superb; there must be more waiters to the square metre than anywhere else. The wines and the brandies, which carry the house label, are equally splendid. But – dare one say it? – the food is rather less so. Despite such celebrated dishes as chartreuse of partridge or Sole Albert, we may feel slightly disappointed (avoid

95

the Irish Stew). But then we do not really go to Maxim's to eat; we go to see and be seen in a luxurious, old-fashioned setting.

Changes, however, are afoot. Maxim's is now part of the Cardin empire and Pierre Cardin is not a man to mark time. There is talk of a monthly gala evening with a top pop singer, thus bringing us brusquely into the present day. Or there may be a literary prize, although Maxim's has no literary associations; few writers can afford its prices or want that sort of formal luxury. Maxim's products (spices, jams, teas, mustards, etc.) have long been on sale in a thousand shops throughout France, and it is planned to expand this side of the business. Further, there is to be a chain of Maxim's Restaurants round the world; the first one is to be, surprisingly, in China. But when I suggested Maxim's Calcutta, the wine waiter banged down the bottle of brandy on my table and left me to pour it myself. (He returned for his tip.)

Moving along the Rue Royale, we find ourselves at a crossroads. On the right is the Rue Saint-Honoré, a long narrow street of shops and business offices. The street becomes more interesting as we go farther east and approach the Beaubourg area. On the left is the **Rue du Faubourg Saint-Honoré**, which has more to interest us.

At No.33 is the **Cercle d'Union Interallié**, grandly placed in the old Rothschild Palace. It is an international Businessmen's club and we may well find ourselves invited there for lunch or a cocktail party. We should certainly accept.

Next door (35–39) is the **British Embassy** (note that the Consulate is much farther along the street at No.109). It is an eighteenth-century building, the former Hôtel de Charost. In 1800 it was bought by Napoleon's sister, Pauline, who, after a stormy life of loves and marriages, had become the Princess Borghese. Fourteen years later she sold the Palais Borghese to Wellington, who moved in immediately, though his stay was interrupted by Waterloo. Now, as the British Embassy, it is not open to the public, but we can peer in through the gates at the gatehouse (the comfortable residence of a diplomat) and the courtyard, a fine piece of architecture, described by Nancy Mitford in her last novel, *Don't Tell Alfred*.

If we get the chance to go inside, we shall see immediately busts of Napoleon and Wellington, side by side, with Winston Churchill at the foot of the marble staircase. There are imposing reception rooms covered with crimson brocade, used for lunches and parties;

and even Queen Victoria's throne-room, now used mainly for films, concerts and when the annual garden-party is rained out. Upstairs are more reception rooms and, finally, the bedrooms and Pauline Bonaparte's bed. This is a splendid affair, with gilded curtains hanging from the claws of a Napoleonic eagle. Some Ambassadresses enjoy sleeping in it, others find it intimidating and prefer one of the guest rooms. Outside is the garden, leading down to the Avenue Gabriel. This is a true English garden with lawns, borders and unclipped trees. The French regard it as more of a field. Where are the statues? Where is the gravel? Why not clip the trees?

Almost opposite the Embassy, at 5 Rue d'Aguesseau, is the **Embassy Church, St Michael's**. Like St George's Anglican Church, it has recently been rebuilt as a modern block, with the 'church' in the basement. It looks rather like a small boardroom and the altar can be screened off to allow meetings. The 'low' services are crowded and emphasis is on youth, informal dress and Christian names. Gone are the days when the Ambassador sat in the front and read the lesson. Coffee and lunch are served on the church premises, after the 10.30 a.m. Sunday service. There is a Thursday lunchtime service at 12.45 p.m. Meetings and outings are organized.

Farther along the Rue du Faubourg Saint-Honoré we find the portico of the **Elysée Palace**, the official home of French Presidents. Another eighteenth-century building, it was at one time the home of another of Napoleon's sisters, Caroline, and then of his first wife, the Empress Josephine. Napoleon's nephew, Louis-Napoleon, lived there, planning the 1851 *coup d'état*, after which he became the Emperor Napoleon III and moved to the Tuileries. The Elysée has only been the Presidential palace since 1873 and for much of this time the President was only a figurehead, choosing prime ministers, often in the middle of the night. It is only since the introduction of Presidential government by de Gaulle in 1958 that the Elysée has become the centre of power. But, even now, some Presidents, including Mitterrand, prefer to live at home and visit the Elysée daily for work and entertaining. The fear of being 'A Prisoner of the Elysée', out of touch with Paris and France, is one that haunts French rulers.

The principal attraction of the street for us, however, is less the three fine buildings described than the large number of fashionable boutiques, which cluster between the Rue Royale and the Avenue

Matignon. These expensive shops deal mainly in clothes for men and women, scent, beauty and hairdressing. They include, among others, Heim, Lanvin, Hermès, Lapidus, Laroche, Saint-Laurent, Cardin, Courrèges; Lancôme, Roger & Gallet; Helena Rubinstein, Harriet Hubbard Ayer; Alexandre. (See also Chapter 13.) There are also a number of art galleries here and in the Avenue Matignon, which show and sell what is called 'Right Bank' art: recently painted works in fairly traditional style, landscapes and still lifes, all in big gilt frames. For more avant-garde art we shall have to go to the Beaubourg area or the Left Bank.

Back in the Rue Royale, we approach the **Madeleine**, the huge Roman temple which has been dominating us ever since we left Concorde. There had been at least two attempts to build a church there before (one was to be another Panthéon dome), but neither got very far. In 1806 Napoleon decreed that it was to be a temple to glorify the Grande Armée and the chosen architect was Vignon. But it was not finished till 1842 and by then the original idea had evaporated; the Grande Armée, it was felt, was already sufficiently glorified in the Arc de Triomphe and the Invalides. One can imagine the problem of the French in finding a use for the huge brand-new Roman temple in their midst. As a church it would be (and is) a discouraging place, pagan and windowless. As a railway station, another suggestion, it would be too small, despite its size. There had also been thoughts of using the place for the Banque de France, the Bourse or the National Library. However, it was finally consecrated to St Mary Magdalen, whose picture is above the high altar.

Vignon had produced an enormously inflated version of the charming Maison Carrée at Nîmes and, even if nobody could call the Madeleine charming, we can be struck by its dimensions and dominating site, by the twenty-eight steps which lead to the entrance, by the fifty-two Corinthian columns, each over sixty feet high, which support the frieze. We can even bring ourselves to admire the vast bronze door, inspired by the Ten Commandments, and the huge pediment above it, by Lemaire. It shows the Last Judgment and has one of the fattest Christs in Europe.

The Madeleine is set in a large square and the flower-market brings happy memories to many British people of weekends or honeymoons in Paris. The Place de la Madeleine is a place of memories and ghosts and we should have the eyes and the imagination to see them. On the corner of the Rue Royale, where the shirt shop now is, we can see the portly figure of King Edward VII, a great lover of Paris and French food, emerging, after a large lunch, from Larue's, his favourite restaurant. On the other corner we can see men in top hats entering Thomas Cook's to book their *wagon-lit* on the Blue Train or the Orient Express. Cook's happily remains in business, although it now shares its premises with a British bank. A few yards away, No.4, a jeweller's shop, was until very recently Durand's, the well-known music publishers, a victim of the cassette age. It was here that Chopin first met Liszt in 1831, but the story that they played the A-Flat Polonaise as a duet, shaking hands in the middle, is probably mythical. Chopin's funeral was held in the Madeleine; the Conservatoire performed Mozart's *Requiem* before a congregation of four thousand.

At No.26 Place de la Madeleine, the far end, is a shop which is definitely not for ghosts – Fauchon, the most sophisticated food shop in Paris (see Chapter 13.) The smell from the kitchen ventilators of baking tarts and cooking chocolates is worth a visit for itself alone, even if we are not planning to buy anything. There is a cafeteria on the ground floor where we can eat a good light lunch (standing up), in company with many luxury-minded ladies. The desserts are much recommended, especially the mango ice. Fauchon is closed on Mondays, but the cafeteria and pâtisserie are open.

We stroll along the **Boulevard de la Madeleine**, the start of the long boulevard which, though often changing its name and its style, would eventually lead us to the Place de la Bastille, should we wish to walk so far. This part is a street of banks, boutiques, shoe shops and airline offices and we may prefer to observe our fellow boulevardiers – and the ghosts. Passing Aux Trois Quartiers, Paris's most expensive department store (see Chapter 13) we can glance at No.11. Here lived and died a fashionable courtesan, Mlle Plessis, who was the original of the younger Dumas's *La Dame aux Camélias* and Verdi's *La Traviata*.

The street becomes the Boulevard des Capucines and on our left we have the **Olympia music-hall** (see Chapter 20), a mecca for successful pop singers, French and international. It was here that the Beatles made their first appearance when they started on their world travels. But the ghost here is surely Edith Piaf, probably singing '*Milord*', the never-forgotten *chanteuse*, who held all France in her spell.

At No.35 was Nadar's photographic studio, where the Impressionists, tired of being rejected, held their first group show on 15 May 1874. The building is now a shoe shop and, above it is a popular self-service restaurant, Le Rallye, much used by coach tours from abroad.

The **Cognac-Jay Museum** at No.25 has fine examples of work by Fragonard, Greuze, La Tour, Canaletto and Gainsborough. Set in panelled rooms with furniture and cabinets of the same period, it is a lost corner of eighteenth-century grace in a bustling nineteenth-century street.

On the corner of the Place de l'Opéra is the Café de la Paix, a well-known rendezvous for people from many lands. It has recently been completely restored, but the Beaux-Arts insisted that the original style be followed faithfully. Inside, it still has the Ionic columns in green and gold and the painted-sky ceilings; and it looks very much as it must have looked when Oscar Wilde tried unsuccessfully to borrow money from Lord Alfred Douglas there. The two restaurants are international in intent (complete with taped music), but the terrace still keeps its old style. It has been said that if you sit there long enough, you will see someone you know walk by. The experience has only happened to me twice and on the second occasion the man did not recognize me. I recalled later that he was the man who sometimes made announcements from the stage at Covent Garden, and my face must have been quite unknown to him.

We are now at the **Place de l'Opéra**, dominated by the enormous **opera house**, the brainchild of the Emperor Napoleon III and Haussmann. It has sometimes been called a gigantic wedding-cake; and, though it does resemble a cake, we can appreciate the pale stone, the pink and green colours, the gold frills, now that it has been cleaned. The architect was Charles Garnier, a fairly unknown young man, who won the qualifying competition; a golden bust of him stands on the Rue Auber side of the theatre. The Empress Eugénie complained that the still unfinished opera house had no style, it was neither Greek nor Roman. Garnier answered that it was the style Napoleon III. Indeed, Garnier hoped to found a new school of architecture, but his work, a mishmash of many styles and lands, could have no followers. Nevertheless the Opéra remains as the most grandiose monument of the Second Empire, even though it was only finished in 1875, after the fall of Napoleon III.

From the start the Opéra was intended as much for balls as for opera and ballet. The annual Polytechnic Ball and occasional Presidential galas are still held there. It is also a place of many statues; hundreds inside, some outside. From the entrance hall we can glimpse the great staircase, the steps made of marble, the banisters of onyx; framing the entrance to the auditorium are two huge caryatids. But, to see the house properly, we should really attend a performance. Then we can climb the staircase to the Grand Foyer, fifty-four metres long, with mirrors and allegorical paintings; we can step out on to the big balcony to look at the Place de l'Opéra at night, and then head for the ridiculously small bar for a sandwich and a bottle of beer. (There are also guided tours.)

Or we can descend to the basement where we find a vast cavern of mirrors, reflecting us from all sides, fountains and pools. It was the idea of this underground grotto which gave Leroux the idea of **The Phantom of the Opera**.

The bells ring, we leave the caverns and return to our pleasure-dome. The auditorium is as sumptuous as everything else. Five tiers of boxes rise round us. In front of us is the famous painted curtain, behind which is one of the biggest stages in the world, capable of holding the most extravagant productions. Above us is a chandelier, weighing six tonnes, and above that a false ceiling painted by Chagall in 1964. This shows sketches of scenes from well-known operas and ballets mingled with the tourist monuments of Paris. Some find it childish, others typically Chagall.

Musical standards have tended to be low, for various reasons. But recently they have been much improved by importing singers, dancers, conductors and producers from other countries, including Britain. This has pleased a discerning public and given some annoyance to the resident company. It has also cost a lot of money and in a time of budget cuts it is uncertain if the new standard can be maintained. One of the problems is that the Opéra, though it is the biggest theatre in the world, only seats 2,200 people and many of these have no view of the stage. Garnier was designing for an élite, and not a very musical one at that. The Duke of Brunswick played chess with Paul Morphy during a performance of *The Marriage of Figaro*; the game is one of Morphy's masterpieces.

The big Place de l'Opéra was planned by Haussmann to be an imposing junction; the buildings round it are of uniform style, nineteenth-century classical, complete with pilasters, and only tasteful white neon signs are permitted. The Place seethes with traffic and pedestrians; six main thoroughfares meet there. The metro station underneath is also a main junction where several lines meet.

But the Place de l'Opéra is more than a traffic junction. It is a meeting place of three different Parisian worlds, who mingle, even if they do not actually meet, in the many restaurants and cafés of the neighbourhood. The ladies at the next table may be buying leather goods at Lancel's or watches at Clerc's, or having their pearls restrung at Cartier's; or they may have been shopping in one or more of the big department stores in the Boulevard Haussmann, immediately behind the opera house. The area is an attractive shopping quarter for the rich and the thrifty alike – and especially for windowshoppers. At the table on the other side the men in their dark suits are probably businessmen. The Opéra is the business area of Paris. There are big banks everywhere, the head offices of the main French banks, the Paris branches of foreign banks. The Bourse (the Stock Exchange) is nearby. The buildings are filled with business offices, commercial law firms, accountants, brokers and agencies. The area is also Paris's theatreland. There are many theatres here besides the Opéra and at night our restaurant will be filled with theatre-goers.

Three different worlds, shopping, business and theatres, all in the same place! This gives the area an extraordinary variety and vitality; it also means that the Place de l'Opéra is as lively at midnight as it is at midday – something which cannot be said of Threadneedle Street or Wall Street.

More will be written about shopping and theatres in Chapters 13 and 20. But in the meantime we should windowshop our way down the smart **Rue de la Paix**. It was originally called the Rue Napoléon; he had ordered its construction in 1806. (There is, incidentally, no Rue Napoléon now in Paris.) However, as we stroll down the 'Street of Peace', our minds will be less on battles than on luxury, and we shall pass such familiar names as Dunhill, Cartier and Mappin & Webb. At the end we find ourselves in that masterpiece of French seventeenth-century architecture, the **Place Vendôme**.

The square was originally conceived as a backdrop for a huge equestrian statue of Louis XIV by Girardon. The Duke of Vendôme's town house and the Capuchin convent were bought in 1685 and demolished, and Jules Hardouin-Mansart was commissioned to build the new square. The nephew by marriage of the distinguished architect François Mansart, Hardouin had added his surname to his own and, confusingly, is often referred to as 'Mansart'. The square was finished in 1699 and named the Place des Conquêtes.

It is built of pink-grey limestone and is completely formal and symmetrical. Above an arcade, Corinthian pilasters rise for two storeys between the windows. The roof is steeply pitched and broken by curved dormer windows. These are replaced by classical pediments in the middle of the two long sides and on the four buildings which cut off the corners. Such a rigid formality could easily be monotonous, but instead it is pleasing and graceful. The style of the architecture, the size and shape of the square, and the proportions of the façades add up to an artistic achievement, typical of its century. A sense of proportion was one of Hardouin-Mansart's greatest gifts as an architect; we have another example of it in the Invalides dome.

He was, however, only building a façade. The buildings behind it were added later and could be entered only from the back. Nothing must be done to spoil the uniformity of the square. But, on a prime site, such a state of affairs could not last indefinitely and now every building opens on to the square; many of them have shop windows showing diamonds glittering on black velvet. The Place Vendôme has long been known as a centre of jewellery and fashion and there are still a number of jewellers, including Boucheron, Van Cleef & Arpels and another branch of Cartier's. But fashion and beauty are being squeezed out by yet more banks and by such enterprises as IBM and the British Tourist Authority (surely 'Authority' is an odd word to use in connection with tourism). Charvet's, however, still remains, the shop where Edward VII bought cravats and where we can still buy beautiful silk shirts and ties. The west side of the square is mainly occupied by the Ministry of Justice and the Ritz Hotel, a contrasting pair to find behind the same façade. In a different key, Chopin died in 1849 at No.12; a plaque reminds us of the composer and of the time when people actually lived in the square.

The central statue of Louis XIV was destroyed in the Revolution.

A Rome-style column was erected by Napoleon as yet another monument to the Grande Armée. It is covered with a spiral of bronze plaques made from guns captured at the battle of Austerlitz (1805) which are said to show scenes from the campaigns. The column was toppled by the Commune in 1871 and many of the plaques had to be recast when the column was re-erected by the Third Republic. Several statues have stood on its top – Napoleon in military uniform, Henri IV, a giant fleur-de-lys. The present incumbent is Napoleon dressed as Julius Cæsar, in accordance with his original order.

On the south side of the square the Rue de Castiglione leads across the Rue Saint-Honoré to the Rue de Rivoli. This too is a windowshopper's paradise, but the jewellery here is more likely to be costume jewellery than diamonds.

We should, however, retrace our steps up the Rue de la Paix and turn right into the **Rue Daunou**. At No.5 we find a popular landmark for businessmen and visiting Anglo-Saxons, Harry's Bar, known to the owner, Andy MacElhone, and many Americans as 'Sank Roo Doe Noo'. It is decorated with British and American college shields and pennants, to remind us of our youth, and it is the only bar in France to serve Californian wine. With this we can eat a club sandwich or a pork pie, while we survey our fellow bar-flies, many of whom will be French, fascinated by the atmosphere of the place. The bar was started early in the century by a successful American jockey, who went broke and sold it to his bartender, Harry MacElhone. It became a fashionable supper club downstairs, its clients including Gloria Swanson (then a marquise), the Duke of Windsor (in his young Princely days), Noel Coward and Charles Chaplin. Upstairs, writers and sportsmen mingled near the bar, among them Jack Dempsey, Big Bill Tilden, Hemingway, James Joyce (usually at a secluded table), Marcel Achard, O'Flaherty, Thornton Wilder, James Jones and Jean-Paul Sartre during his pro-American phase, sipping Bourbon and eating hot dogs. The bar is open until dawn, so see also Chapter 20.

Refreshed, we continue our walk along the Rue Daunou to the Avenue de l'Opéra, a long dull street, one of Haussmann's lesser achievements, and now filled with banks and airline offices. Its best feature is its view of the Opéra and to this we should now return, turning right at Clerc's into the Boulevard des Capucines.

There are many boulevards in Paris, but the phrase **Grands Boulevards** is usually only applied to the string of boulevards which, under different names, lead from the Opéra to the Place de la République and the Bastille. The names are: Capucines, Italiens, Montmartre, Poissonnière, Bonne Nouvelle, Saint-Denis, Saint-Martin, Temple, Filles de Calvaire and Beaumarchais (see also Chapter 9). The total distance is about three miles. The smart end is near the Opéra; it gets seedier as we go east – not that we shall go so far today.

The Grands Boulevards, originally 'The Boulevard', were constructed in the reign of Louis XIV on the site of the old ramparts and moats which had fallen into decay. The Boulevard was wide and lined with trees; triumphal arches replaced the old gates of Paris, the Porte Saint-Denis and the Porte Saint-Martin. It became a fashionable place to drive in carriages or ride, though it was not till 1828 that the first bus travelled the length of the Grands Boulevards. Capucines and Italiens became fashionable places to live in the eighteenth and nineteenth centuries and many theatres were built. The eastern end seemed to be a non-stop fairground and circus.

Much changed with the arrival of Haussmann, the motor-car, the cinema and neon lighting. The Boulevard des Italiens may not still look as it did in Pissarro's picture of the boulevard at night. But, though much has gone, including fashionability, much still remains, the vitality, the people. To sit on a café terrace on a warm summer evening and watch the crowds walking up and down on pleasure or business is an enjoyable and interesting experience. These are the real Parisians, the descendants of the Gauls and Franks.

At No.8 Boulevard des Capucines, almost beside the Opéra, Offenbach composed *The Tales of Hoffmann*, but he died there before the work, on which he rightly set great store, could be performed. Le Grand Café, at No.4, was another of Wilde's haunts during his prosperous years, before his fall. It is now a good, though rather expensive fish restaurant, which serves oysters right through the summer. Almost next door, and much cheaper is the Bistro de la Gare, which serves good beef in a style Rétro décor. But then there are many good cheap restaurants on these boulevards.

We are now on the Boulevard des Italiens and trying not to see the ugly Berlitz Building. Why Italiens? In 1782 the Duc de Choiseul built a theatre in the grounds of his house to attract people to the area, where he was a big landowner, and to house the Italian Comic Opera Company. This became eventually the Opéra-Comique, performing operettas, particularly the works of Offenbach and Johann Strauss.

On the north side of the Boulevard, we find the dog-legged Rue des Italiens and the premises of **Le Monde**, France's most respected and influential daily newspaper. In theory an evening paper, its first edition is on the bookstalls at eight o'clock in the morning. It used to sell half a million copies a day and was one of France's few papers to make a profit. But it is now losing readers and money and may have to close. Important Frenchmen read it from cover to cover every day, all forty pages. It is a journalists' cooperative, electing its own editors but remaining faithful to the principles of its founder, Hubert Beuve-Méry, forty years ago. There are few concessions to popular attraction such as headlines, photographs, gossip columns, strip cartoons or crossword puzzles. Every article is an essay, but we can be sure that the reviewer has actually read the book or seen the show he is writing about, something which cannot be said of all newspapers. Officially it is independent of all party politics, but behind its sober exterior and the solid pages of print, we can detect a strong left-wing slant, sometimes even sympathizing with terrorism; many of its readers never notice this, regarding it as objective and impartial, which it often is. But *Le Monde* is one of the few Western newspapers which can be bought in Moscow.

At the end of the Boulevard des Italiens, we are joined by the Boulevard Haussmann. On the left is the Rue Drouot; No.9 is the **Hôtel Drouot**, one of Paris's main auction rooms, where you may, if you are lucky and in ample funds, pick up a Louis XV chair or a Fragonard painting being sold by an impoverished marquis. In stark contrast is the **Musée Grévin** in the Boulevard Montmartre; full of waxworks, distorting mirrors and conjurors, it attracts many children and reminds us of the old Grands Boulevards, as does the Wrestling Theatre ('Catch') a little further on.

We should, however, turn right into the Rue Vivienne, leaving the Grands Boulevards. On the left, the Théâtre des Variétés was for a long time the stage home of Sacha Guitry; the theatre is still associated with light comedy. A little farther on we find the **Bourse**, the Stock Exchange, another Roman temple. There are galleries inside, which we can visit, if we like, to watch the market; there are also guided tours in the mornings for those who are interested. Round the Bourse there are plenty of cafés and restaurants, full of stockbrokers; there are also sometimes demos by anti-capitalist factions.

We will leave the Bourse by the Rue Saint-Augustin, avoiding the Rue du Quatre Septembre, a business street which leads back to the Opéra. The Théâtre de la Michodière, nearby, was for many years associated with Yvonne Printemps and Pierre Fresnay. But our goal is the charming **Place Gaillon** (a triangle more than a square), which was reconstructed by Visconti in 1827, and we should note the fountain with a boy on a dolphin which was erected in 1707. However, the dominating feature of the little square is the Restaurant Drouant, one of the best in Paris and specializing in fish. Much recommended is the grilled salmon with either Sauce Choron (Béarnaise and tomato) or Sauce Marine (dill and fennel), followed by a Grand Marnier soufflé, which must be ordered at the start. The service is particularly attentive and expert.

Drouant's is best known for the November morning each year when the Goncourt Academy meets there to choose the Prix Goncourt, France's most prestigious literary prize. A crowd gathers in the rain to watch the great men arrive, something which one can scarcely imagine in another city. On one occasion one of the Academicians paused to address the damp crowd. 'Have no fear!' he said. 'We shall be at lunch within an hour.' This was not to reassure them about his possible starvation, but to tell them that the short list was short indeed that year. The choice made, the jury is served with a large lunch, ending traditionally with Reblochon cheese from the Savoy mountains. Meanwhile, telephones ring, reporters interview the happy winner and booksellers rearrange their windows.

The prize is still only fifty francs and most winners prefer to frame the cheque rather than cash it. The real reward comes with the vast sales and fame which follow; the French respect the judgments of their seniors and dutifully buy their choices. But recently some controversial choices, involving resignations, have damaged the prestige of the prize and with it its value. Revelations have been made about how the winner is chosen; the book almost always comes from one of the same three publishers. Nobody can win the Goncourt twice, yet Romain Gary is said to have done this, with the

107

help of a pseudonym. Advice has been published to aspirants telling them where to be seen lunching (Lipp's) and how to dress (prosperously). Favourites boast openly of their friends on the jury; it is desirable to have parents or ancestors who lived in a distant country and endured great hardships, though the author himself now lives comfortably on the Left Bank.

All this is saddening, though perhaps inevitable where so much money is involved. Yet a good deal of glamour still remains in the Place Gaillon on that damp morning in November. The ordinary Frenchman who rarely buys a book still regards the Goncourt with awe. Edmond de Goncourt wrote: *'Il n'y a de bon que les choses exquises.* A better period may have begun for the prize with the selection in 1984 of Marguerite Duras. This suggests a new trend.

Leaving the Place Gaillon, we make our way to the pleasant Square Louvois and to the **Bibliothèque Nationale**, facing us across the Rue de Richelieu. The façade is eighteenth-century, by Robert de Cotte, but the building is of many dates. The old Hôtel Tubeuf was rebuilt in the seventeenth century by François Mansart, who made many additions including the Mansart and Mazarin Galleries. The Reading Room and the rest of the Library are mainly Second Empire.

We enter the courtyard and, turning right, we go, with many others, into the main vestibule. The two offices there, Information and Readers Service, are staffed by some of the most helpful people in Paris, full of knowledge about the Library and all the other Libraries in Paris, and indeed in France, and about temporary exhibitions, present and future. Across the vestibule is the Reading Room and through a window we can see the rows of desks, the green glass lamps, the studious faces, the leather booklined walls. But you need a reading card to enter; this can be obtained in the vestibule on production of your passport, publishers' contract, commissioning letter or similar document. Casual browsing is not encouraged. The half-price card, allowing twenty-four visits to the Reading Room, is a good bargain, especially as the card is not always stamped each time.

The Library originated as the royal library in the Louvre, Blois and Fontainebleau. In 1537 François I, a great book collector, brought in a law that the royal library must possess a copy of every book printed. When the library reached two hundred thousand

books, Colbert decided to move it to his own house in the Rue
Vivienne; fifty years later it was moved across the street to the Hôtel
Tubeuf, its present home, which held Cardinal Mazarin's personal
collection of pictures and works of art. At the present time the
Library has about seven million printed books, including two
Gutenberg Bibles and first editions from Villon onwards; manuscripts dating back to AD 800; prints and engravings; newspapers
and periodicals; maps, photographs, music, records. Many of these
are far too valuable for daily display and are only shown in temporary exhibitions. But the **Médailles collection** is open to the public
every afternoon from 1 to 5 (entry fee payable at the bookstall) and
is well worth a visit.

This is not purely a collection of coins or military medals. The
medallion, as an art form distinct from coinage, was developed in
the fifteenth century in Italy and France, where it still flourishes,
principally at the Monnaie (see Chapter 4). One of the earliest
medallions shows a knight on a galloping horse and commemorates
the expulsion of the English from France in 1455. Other good
examples are shown here, notably portrait medallions of Erasmus
(1519), Catherine de Medici, Henri IV (1602), Monet by E. Rousseau and Stravinsky by Berthe Camus (1972).

The collection also contains fine small works of art from many
dates, from prehistoric fragments (spirals) to the present day. As we
go in, there are urns, heads, small figures, vases, and wrought-silver
ewers. One of the finest bigger pieces is an amphora of 470 BC,
found in Agrigento, Sicily, and representing Poseidon and Theseus.
A head of Nero as a baby is improbably cherubic and innocent-
looking, but a great silver platter is very fine: fourth century BC, it
shows the death of Patroclues at Troy, and was discovered in 1656
between Arles and Avignon. Upstairs are more recent works. In the
case marked 'nineteenth century', the chief feature is remarkable
rather than beautiful, a 'great cameo' crowded with heavy flying
bodies in togas, in true Napoleonic vein (1806) and intended for, of
all places, the Sainte-Chapelle.

Sadly the Mansart and Mazarin Galleries are closed to the public
for security reasons, except for temporary exhibitions, which occur
fairly frequently. Should one be on during our visit, we should
certainly go, if only to see these splendid rooms. But before leaving
the Bibliothèque we should look at the **State Room** on the ground

floor, which is open to the public. The eighteenth-century wooden panelling is remarkable. So is Houdon's famous seated statue of Voltaire (1787). Here we have the original plaster statue – the bronze cast from it is in the foyer of the Comédie Française. In both we can glimpse the wry, cynical philosopher, the essayist, novelist and satirist; not the serious writer of solemn (and now forgotten) tragedies – Voltaire's own image of himself. His heart is buried in the pedestal, the strangest object in the whole Bibliothèque. One would have expected his brain to be of more interest.

Leaving the Library, we turn left into the Rue des Petits Champs. Here we can see the Hôtel Tubeuf as François Mansart left it, a pleasant brick and stone courtyard with a steeply-pitched roof. Turning left again into the Rue Vivienne, we can see through the railings the Library Gardens and the façade of Mansart's library, which contain the two galleries – a fine example of seventeenth-century architecture.

Returning to the Rue des Petits Champs we cross into the Rue de Beaujolais, one of three streets built in 1780 by Philippe-Egalité when he enclosed and 'developed' the gardens of the Palais-Royal. (The other two streets are called Montpensier and Valois, all good Bourbon and Orléans names.) Almost facing us is the house where Colette lived for much of her life. The house faces the **Palais-Royal gardens**, and Colette used to love looking out at them, when she was too crippled to walk any more. We turn right and, circling round the famous restaurant Le Grand Véfour (of which more at the end of the Chapter), we enter the gardens.

The façades here are far more pretentious than the simple buildings in the three surrounding streets. Here we have royal grandeur, stonework, pilasters, arcades; an out of proportion imitation of the Place Vendôme a hundred years earlier. The gardens themselves – trees and a fountain – are a huge courtyard of peace and silence in one of the busiest parts of Paris. A few, very few, strollers, readers and pram-pushers – that is all. The shops in the arcades are mostly empty; those still in business seem to deal mainly in philately, a quiet trade. At night the arcades are silent to the point of eeriness, despite two theatres, a busy restaurant and a café. It is as if the customers were overawed by their surroundings; time, we may feel, has passed the Palais-Royal by.

It was not always thus. Philippe-Egalité (Prince Louis-Philippe of

110

Orléans) was a man who liked to have it both ways. On inheriting the palace and the gardens, he found himself one of the richest men in France and he saw a good commercial outlet for his money in his gardens and the streets he built round them. But the façades had to look royal, even if the arcades below them were full of gambling houses and brothels. He lived in the palace but he renamed it the Palais-Egalité. A good revolutionary, he called himself Citoyen Egalité. He was one of those who signed the death warrant of Louis XVI, his cousin. None of this saved him from the guillotine himself in 1793.

The gardens were at first a fashionable promenade and meeting place for Parisians, but standards deteriorated quickly. Revolutionaries gathered there to hear the inflammatory speeches of Camille Desmoulins. The palace became, like the arcades, a big gambling den and brothel, and the gardens held not only revolutionaries and prostitutes but also circuses, dance-halls and all the attractions of a funfair. It is said that Napoleon had his first sexual experience there; it was certainly he who later had the gardens and the palace cleaned up. But the gambling houses in the arcades continued until 1838, when they were closed by Louis-Philippe and, with them gone, the popularity of the arcade shops began to fade away and the gardens to assume their present respectability.

The palace itself is at the south end of the gardens. It is now occupied by the Council of State (a mysterious body) and closed to the public. It was originally built in 1624 by Jacques Le Mercier (born in 1585) for Cardinal Richelieu and called the Palais-Cardinal. Le Mercier was also the architect of the Sorbonne Chapel. After Richelieu's death and that of the King, Louis XIII, the Queen Mother, Anne of Austria, lived there with her young sons Louis XIV and Philippe, Duke of Orléans; the palace was renamed the Palais-Royal. Louis XIV, grown up, had, however, grander ideas and moved back to the Louvre for a while. In the Palais-Royal lived Henrietta-Maria, widow of Charles I of England, and her daughter Henrietta, who later married Philippe of Orléans. The palace remained in the Orléans family for many generations. Altered by Philippe-Egalité and the Bourbon Restoration after Napoleon, burnt by the Commune in 1871, restored by the Third Republic, nothing now remains of Richelieu's palace except a gallery on the Rue de Valois side.

Richelieu, as well as running the country, took a great interest in the theatre and indeed had ambitions, but not the talents, to be a playwright himself. It is said that he asked Corneille to write a play for him, but insisted on dictating its contents. Corneille naturally declined; he never regained official favour. The east wing of the Palais-Cardinal contained a theatre which at last gave a permanent home to Molière and his troupe of comedians, after many years of wandering on the Left Bank and in the provinces (see Chapter 4). Molière's major works were first performed in the Théâtre Richelieu, from 1661 to 1673, when he collapsed on stage and died a few hours later. He was only fifty-one and the part he was acting was *Le Malade Imaginaire* – an ironic end indeed for the ironist.

The statue of Molière nearby, at the corner of the Rue de Richelieu and the Rue Molière is nineteenth-century, by Visconti. The figure of the playwright, seated, pen in hand, by Seurre, is compelling; we can note his bluff face and his big moustache. The surrounding muses and cherub are unnecessary and distracting.

Seven years after Molière's death, Louis XIV founded the **Comédie-Française** from the remains of Molière's troupe and the company at the Hôtel de Bourgogne. The new company and the irreverence of the works they performed brought it much anger, both from the conservative-minded and the universities. However, it continued to enjoy the support of the all-powerful king. Napoleon also supported them, perhaps because of his *tendresse* for the leading lady, Mademoiselle Mars. At any rate he gave the company state patronage, a subsidy and a measure of state control, all of which it still has.

The name Comédie-Française is now applied less to the company, some of whose leading members are frequently lured away by film and television contracts, than to the theatre itself. This is at the south-west corner of the Palais-Royal, built for Philippe-Egalité by Victor Louis and restored in the nineteenth century. It faces on to the Place André Malraux (formerly the Place du Théâtre Français) at the southern end of the Avenue de l'Opéra. It is dignified without being overwhelming; indeed it is rather small for France's most prestigious theatre, though it manages some lavish productions. It also has an enormous collection of wigs and costumes; in the foyer are the chair in which Molière collapsed on stage and Houdon's

The Opera, Second Empire – the biggest theatre in the world.

La Renommée by Coysevox, in the Tuileries Gardens. *Below* One of the horses of Marly, which frame the Champs-Elysées.

Mercury by Coysevox, overlooking the Place de la Concorde.

A medallion of Catherine
de Medici, now in the
Bibliothèque Nationale.
Below The Palais-Royal
and garden.

bronze statue of Voltaire, referred to earlier. But Voltaire's plays are no longer performed.

The Comédie-Française has always been the home of French 'classical acting'. In this a couple stand on the stage, scarcely moving, never touching each other, while they confess, in rhythmical alexandrines, their uncontrollable, and probably incestuous, love. This type of acting is normally only used for the works of Corneille and Racine and it must not be thought that French acting is always so static. The great Sarah Bernhardt, as Cleopatra, on hearing the news of the defeat of Actium, stabbed the messenger, smashed much of the scenery, raved and howled, and finally collapsed in a shuddering heap in the centre of the stage. (In the silence after the applause an English lady was heard to remark, 'How very different from the home life of our own dear Queen!')

The 'Divine Sarah' also played Hamlet, the Prince himself, and indeed is partly responsible for the appreciation of Shakespeare in France. In a modern translation, the French public is well able to understand the plots, characters and humour, though the poetry is, of course, lost. But things are gradually changing; Shakespeare in English is becoming increasingly a set book for exams, but modern French youth finds Elizabethan English rather opaque. Visits by visiting English companies are now considered more as exam aids than as dramatic experiences. Nevertheless we may well find *Le Roi Lear* or one of the comedies being performed during our visit.

The Comédie-Française has for centuries specialized in the classics (though Molière's plays were contemporary enough – he would have been surprised to find himself a classic). Apart from those playwrights already mentioned, the theatre stages Marivaux, de Musset, Beaumarchais, Hugo and Rostand – not that the last two are exactly classics. Modern plays produced here include works by Montherlant, Pirandello, Giraudoux and Ionesco. Claudel's *Le Soulier de Satin* was first produced here during the war, with the approval of the German military governor. A poetic drama about sin, set in sixteenth-century Spain and lasting eight hours, should, it was thought, be quite harmless and nothing to do with the Resistance. (Gide commented that we must be grateful that he did not also write about the other slipper too.) But eventually the Governor realized that the play was not as innocuous as was at first thought and it was dropped from the repertory. It was, however, revived, in a shortened version and the production was seen in London as well as Paris.

It was performed at the Odéon, not at the Comédie-Française, which seemed then to be devoted to the farces of Feydeau, as de Gaulle pointed out to his Minister of Culture, Malraux. It was time to revive the classics. But Corneille and Racine were no longer the draw they had once been; they were for exams only. This is the dilemma of a National Theatre. At the moment of writing, the Comédie-Française is showing plays by Molière, Marivaux, Hugo and the little-known Henri Becque. The great standby is Rostand's *Cyrano de Bergerac*, popular with both French and foreigners.

The **Place André Malraux** is the end of our walk and we are back in the nineteenth century. It is, in fact, an attractive square, as Pissarro knew, with its fountains, globe-lights, the perspective to the floodlit Opéra and the ponderous bulk of the Louvre. But before we descend into Metro Palais-Royal, we could stop for a drink at the Ruc-Univers, once a well-known literary café. And we can consider where to eat.

The whole area is full of restaurants and several have been mentioned already. But three more must be added, very different from each other. Lescure, in the Rue Mondovi, is a small, inexpensive restaurant where, if we are lucky, we can eat Limousin and Auvergne dishes out of doors.

In the Square Louvois there is a tiny family bistro, **Au Fleur de Lys**, where we can enjoy *rable de lapereau Dijon* for very little. It is almost at the entrance of the Bibliothèque Nationale, and much used by researchers. And, finally, **Le Grand Véfour**.

For many people this is Paris's best restaurant and certainly the *cuisine* is *haute* indeed, specializing in the dishes of Bordeaux, such as lampreys, ortolans and various meat dishes with bordelaise sauces. If we order foie gras, we shall get the biggest portions imaginable, possibly served with grapes. The wine list is celebrated and we should certainly consult the learned *sommelier* before ordering. But it is hardly a place for the impecunious or those on a diet.

The décor has hardly changed since it was the rendezvous of the fashionable world in the Palais-Royal Gardens. A glass plate tells us that it was once the Café de Chartres; another advertises 'Sherry

Goblets'. Inside, copper plates remind us of the celebrities, including Napoleon, who have been there. When we enter we step back nearly two hundred years, but this has not prevented the chef-owner, Monsieur Oliver, from becoming a television personality, greatly to the profit of his restaurant. The address is No.17 Rue de Beaujolais, but we can also enter from the Palais-Royal gardens or arcades. Closed on Sundays and in August, and reservations are quite essential.

CHAPTER 7

The Louvre

THE PALACE

The Louvre is the largest palace in Europe, some say upon earth and
the statistics are enormous. It took six hundred and sixty-six years to
build and it spans the history of France from mediæval fortress to
Second Empire folly. Seventeen sovereigns and uncountable numbers of architects were involved in its construction. The size too is
breathtaking – on and on it goes beside the Seine and the Rue de
Rivoli. One is scarcely surprised that so many of France's rulers
decided to live elsewhere.

Originally it was part of the walls of Paris. Like the Tournelle,
which protected Paris from upstream invasion, the Louvre guarded
the downstream end, which was vulnerable to attacks by pirates and
other invaders. The original tower was enlarged and in 1200 King
Philippe-Auguste completed the military fortress, of which no
traces now remain above ground. Although several kings lived
there, it seems to have been an uncomfortable place, occupying less
than a quarter of the present Cour Carrée. The word 'Louvre' is of
obscure origin, but the theory most generally held is that it comes
from an old Flemish word meaning Fortress.

It was François I, the contemporary of the English Henry VIII,
who decided to reside in the Louvre, as part of an agreement, it is
said, with the Parisians, who had paid his ransom when he was
captured in Italy. The King ordered much demolition and rebuilding, in particular the Renaissance façade of the Cour Carrée, and
this continued with interruptions for a long time. Catherine de
Medici built a new Palace, the Tuileries, at the far end of the present
Louvre and the two palaces were joined together by Henri IV.
Artists were allowed to live and work there – an example of state
patronage of the arts unsurpassed even in our times – and it is

entirely appropriate that this should be the site of the Grande Salle and other galleries, where most of the great works of the Louvre are now hung.

Louis XIV decided to reconstruct the Cour Carrée and various architects submitted plans, including Le Vau, Bernini, and Claude Perrault, and it is the latter's work, mainly, that we can see and admire there now. Napoleon made further alterations to the palace, including the addition of the Arc du Carrousel, at the western end. In the Second Empire, Napoleon III and Haussmann decided finally to complete the building with the north wing and the two pavilions, Flore and Marsan, which ended the palace and joined it to the Tuileries. Much reconstruction was unfortunately carried out elsewhere. In 1871 the Commune burned down the Tuileries, damaging the two pavilions, but these were rebuilt under the Third Republic. Soon afterwards the Ministry of Finance installed itself 'temporarily' in the north wing.

Architecturally, the Louvre has only two parts which we can enjoy. Facing the Place du Louvre at the extreme eastern end of the building, **Perrault's colonnade** (1673) is a good example of neoclassical style. Behind it is the finest part of the Louvre, the **Cour Carrée**; the façade on the left has changed little since Pierre Lescot designed it in the sixteenth century, a fine piece of Renaissance architecture, with its grace and harmony. The sculptures are by Goujon.

At the other end of the palace stands the **Arc du Carrousel**, erected in 1806 to celebrate Austerlitz and other victories. The columns, however, are older, from the Château de Meudon. At one time it was even decorated with the famous horses of St Mark, looted from Venice by Napoleon. But, even without these, it is a delightful work of art, relatively small and well-proportioned, and many people prefer it to the Arc de Triomphe. The famous vista of the Concorde obelisk, the Champs-Elysées and the Arc de Triomphe can be seen at its greatest length through the Carrousel arch.

Otherwise the palace of the Louvre is monstrous and mediocre and our reason for visiting it, of course, is to see the art treasures inside.

117

The Museum

The original art collection was plundered by the English after Agincourt but in the following century a new collection was started by François I, partly by looting in Italy and partly by encouraging artists to live and work in France. One of those who profited by this invitation was Leonardo da Vinci, who brought the 'Mona Lisa' with him, among other works. Art, like music, was then thought to be a specifically Italian product, and the Italian collection in the Louvre is among the finest in the world. Later kings, usually discerning art collectors, added further acquisitions, but the idea of letting the public see them, first mooted by the Encyclopédistes, was stalled by Louis XVI's ministers. However, the palace was opened in 1793 and the museum consisted of the royal collections from various palaces, the collections of émigré aristocrats, and works taken from the suppressed Church. After the Restoration many more works were acquired by purchase or bequest, and the museum now has about 400,000 works of art, including antiquities and furniture.

The Louvre rapidly became not only a museum for the people, but a shrine of the Revolution and Napoleonic periods. Earlier art, in particular French art, was frowned on as either religious or decadent, and the pre-Revolutionary painters had been, it was thought, far too interested in aristocratic life and in the female body. Female nudes, as in Boucher's paintings, were 'out', but male nudes, as in Delacroix's works, were 'in' because they were classical. This helps to explain the enormous amount of space given to the vast canvases of David and Delacroix and their contemporaries; moreover, these are hung in the first gallery we reach, through which we have to pass if we wish to see anything else. So we arrive at Leonardo or Van Eyck, our eyes already dazed by dozens of battlefield or Revolution corpses, rearing cavalry horses seen from the back, gesticulating generals and goddesses.

Some distinguished modern art historians, among them René Huyghe and Pierre Quoniam, both Louvre curators, have reminded us that French art flourished before the Revolution. Huyghe points out 'the almost unique quality of self-renewal' in French art. There is a growing feeling that insufficient emphasis and pride of place have been given to the art of earlier centuries and this, together with

118

the French obsession for the hanging and re-hanging of all art exhibitions, have promoted ambitious plans for a super-Louvre, to be opened, it is hoped, in 1988.

The plans for Le Grand Louvre are ambitious indeed. The Ministry of Finance will move, at the end of 1986, from the North Wing to new premises not yet built at Bercy. This will free a great number of new galleries and the space will be used, not only for re-hanging the present exhibition, but for putting on show works now lingering in cellars or country depots. The works will be shown in a more logical order and all the French pictures will be hung together. Indeed much re-arranging is going on at the moment. Many pictures have been moved and some well-known ones are not at present on view. The Egyptian antiquities, including the Sphinx, have been put into a crypt and the Greek and Roman sculptures have been re-arranged. It was thought at one time that the display of French nineteenth-century art might be reduced, but this now seems improbable. David is unlikely to be de-throned just before the bicentenary of the Revolution; and, as for Delacroix, his head of 'Liberty' taken from the huge picture (see later) has recently been chosen by President Mitterrand for the new postage stamps.

In the main courtyard, the Cour Napoléon, behind the Arc de Carrousel, will be the main entrance. This will be underground and will be connected by escalators with all the surrounding galleries. There will also be ticket offices, bookstalls, information desks, modern lavatories, rest-rooms, conference and lecture rooms, restaurant and buffet. There will also be coloured maps and signs suggesting tours of the Louvre for those who have limited time to spare. These improvements will, it is thought, bring half again the number of visitors to the Louvre, a further four and a half million a year – a surprising thought for those who had fondly imagined that people came to the Louvre to see the Mona Lisa rather than to drink orangeade.

In the course of the preparatory excavations for all this, a great deal of archaeological material has been discovered. The most interesting is the base of the keep of Philippe-Auguste's original fortress, which was destroyed by Francois I in 1527. There are also other *donjons*, moats and cellars which will be preserved and opened to the public. The area will also be used as an archaeological museum, similar to the one at Notre-Dame, with maps, engravings and models showing the history of the Louvre.

The stables, latrines and wells used in the later centuries have also been discovered. These are full of bric-a-brac, coins, ornaments, pottery, glasses and household utensils, mainly dating from the eighteenth century. The Louvre was at the time occupied by a strange mixture of homeless aristocrats, artists and riff-raff, and their personal belongings are of historic rather than aesthetic interest. However, they are at the moment attracting large crowds and will be in due course catalogued and put on show in the archaeological museum. But it will take time and may delay the opening of the Grand Louvre.

All this will be underground. The main visible feature will be above-ground and is already very controversial. It is to be a giant transparent pyramid, containing only fountains and lights. This is to be the design of a Chinese-American architect, I. M. Pei, and many are asking 'Why not a Frenchman, if we must have it?' The plan has its supporters, those who find it modern and photogenic and those who feel that anything must improve the present Louvre architecture. But most people are against it. A leading critic has called it 'perfectly useless, expensive, inaesthetic, out of place and degrading to the surrounding architecture.' Officially it is to be in memory of a President – which one is not yet known. A fairly amiable comment is that it is a visible example of Mitterrand's Pharaoh-complex, and perhaps he will be buried there eventually.

In the meantime we have to take the Louvre as we find it and perhaps this is the moment, before considering any of the works separately, for some practical advice. One guidebook recommends comfortable shoes and a light breakfast – as if a Paris breakfast were ever anything else. More to the point is to allow as much time as possible; opening hours are rather short and there is much ground to cover.

The first thing is to find the main entrance, the **Porte Denon**, and not go into the Ministry of Finance by mistake. Passers-by and policemen will not be able to help you, as they have not been to the Louvre since they were schoolchildren. The Porte Denon is in fact inside the main courtyard on the north side of the south wing, about halfway between the Arc de Carrousel and the Cour Carrée. As most of the ticket-offices are always closed, we shall have to queue for half an hour in summer, longer probably in the high tourist season. Inside is a large hall which once held Græco-Roman sculpture and now has bookstalls and information desks manned by helpful, well-informed and polyglot ladies. From here we can easily reach all the most popular galleries.

After that light breakfast, if we feel the need for refreshment, we should not leave the building. There are no restaurants nearby and we will have to queue and pay again to re-enter. Better is the cafeteria on the first floor. But here too we will have to queue for a good half-hour, and the rather expensive food can charitably be described as 'airline style'. However, we can at least carry our trays out on to the terrace overlooking the Arc de Carrousel and, if we cannot face eating our sliced sausage, the pigeons, who share our table, will enjoy it.

After lunch we may have further needs and here we will not find any signs or advice. The secret is, on leaving the cafeteria, to go straight on, across the courtyard, to the Aile Mollien and look for a large picture of an elaborate picnic in the woods by Van Loo (!). One must hope that this helpful work at least will not be re-hung elsewhere. Beyond it is a small room full of Watteaus, and just behind this are some lavatories. They do not seem to have been modernized lately, and Henri IV might have approved of the lack of hot water, soap or towels, so it is as well for the prestige of modern France that so few people succeed in finding them. But at least you will not have to queue.

Guided tours, with English-speaking guides, start from the main information hall every twenty minutes or so. Ladies in particular are advised to join one of these groups, in order to avoid being pestered, a growing nuisance.

And now, finally, to the works of art. Unless we are with a guided tour, we shall naturally wish to spend most of our time with those artists or types of art which appeal to us most. But there are three works – the three Mediterranean ladies – which are obligatory. If we have not seen them, we have not been to the Louvre: the Winged Victory of Samothrace, the Venus de Milo and the Mona Lisa.

The **Winged Victory** is still splendidly placed on the landing of the eastern staircase, on the left as we enter. This superb work dates from the third or early second century BC. Found in many pieces, it has been carefully put together into its present (and original)

121

soaring lines; the hand and finger alongside it were discovered in 1950. Like a ship's figurehead, it stands on a prow, though, being made of marble, it was never on any ship. It stood on a cliff overlooking the sea at Samothrace, erected to commemorate a naval victory. While admiring its lines as they are now, we should also try to imagine how it looked originally, with its head and arms, startling eyes and bright paintwork, like all Greek statues.

The **Venus de Milo** has now been relegated to the farthest end of the Græco-Roman sculpture. This is a controversial work. It was discovered by a French archæologist on the island of Milos in the last century. He proclaimed it to be the masterpiece of classical Athens, even of Praxiteles himself, and on this basis he sold it to the Louvre. There was consternation when it was found that, far from being classical, it was of late date (second century BC) and was not from Athens. It was then thought that the statue was the ideal of feminine beauty; but larger-than-life pear-shaped bodies, long noses and big feet are not at the moment thought to be signs of great beauty. What we can genuinely admire is the contrast of spirals between the smooth body and the folds of the draperies which are slipping down. We can also appreciate the feeling of balance and serenity, and also of softness; the goddess seems to be made of some material much less hard than marble. But, this said, it can be added that a large number of distinguished people would gladly see it sent back to Greece.

The 'Mona Lisa' is on the first floor, in a smaller gallery linking the two long galleries. However, we will have no trouble in finding 'La Gioconde', as she is known in France. We simply follow the signs, the crowds and the hubbub. Once there, we have to stand well back behind a rope and look through a glass protective screen, placed to avoid vandalism. This screen reflects our faces and the goggling bewildered eyes and cameras of the crowd around us. We see the picture dimly through a ghostly mirror or our own selves, which adds greatly to the sense of mystery and religious awe which surrounds the experience. But if we wish to examine the picture closely, we would do better to buy a good reproduction.

Its origins, like everything else about it, are mysterious. Leonardo finished it about 1505 after four years' work (some say seven). He brought it with him when he came to live at the Louvre, and the portrait was one of the first pictures in François I's collection. The lady is thought to have been the wife of a rich Florentine merchant, Francesco di Zanobi del Giocondo. The name 'Mona Lisa' is a contraction of Madonna Elisabetta, and 'La Gioconda' has a double meaning. She was, so to speak, Lady Elizabeth Smiley, and the portrait is a visual pun, one which perhaps Messer Giocondo and his wife had grown rather tired of.

As we gaze at the picture, a number of questions must jump into our minds. Who is this lady really? What is the picture about? Why did Leonardo take so long to paint it? Why did it remain in the painter's possession, rather than in the Giocondo family's? Why is she sitting in a wild, uninhabited landscape, unlike that of Tuscany, rather than in her own home or garden? And, finally, why should this small, drably-coloured portrait of a not very beautiful woman have become the most famous picture in the world?

'Hers is the head upon which all the ends of the world are come,' wrote Walter Pater in his *Renaissance Studies* (1873). An ambiguous sentence, but suggesting finality and universality. Pater continued, in his purple style:

> She is older than the rocks among which she sits; like the vampire, she has been dead many times, and learned the secrets of the grave; and has been a diver in deep seas, and keeps their fallen day about her; and trafficked for strange webs with Eastern merchants; and, as Leda, was the mother of Helen of Troy, and, as Saint Anne, the mother of Mary; and all this has been to her but as the sound of lyres and flutes, and lives only in the delicacy with which it has moulded the changing lineaments, and tinged the eyelids and the hands.

A master of a very different prose style, P. G. Wodehouse, often used her nickname to describe a sorrowful girl: 'You're looking like the Mona Lisa today.' In 1934 Cole Porter wrote the lines:

> *You're the Nile, you're the Tower of Pisa,*
> *You're the smile on the Mona Lisa . . .*

The picture has also been used as an advertisement for a laxative, perhaps because of the lady's greenish complexion. It is an enigmatic smile indeed!

Smiling portraits are rare and usually famous (Murillo; Franz

Hals, whose '*La Bohémienne*' hangs in the Louvre). But there is something special about the Gioconda smile. It is not the toothy grin of a modern politician or television personality. She is clearly not saying 'Cheese'. It is not the mocking smile of Voltaire, nor is it brave or false. La Gioconda is smiling at some inner thought, which we shall never know.

The background is also mysterious. Men have obviously been there, making roads and bridges, but nobody is there any more. If we ignore for a moment the central figure, we can see that it is in fact two landscapes, which can never meet. What does this mean? Past and Future? Left Hand and Right Hand? Possibility and Achievement? Leonardo, of course, does not tell us. Mystery was an integral part of his own many-sided, volatile genius, as is shown by his passion for mirror-writing.

Leonardo has several other works in the Louvre, nearby, unguarded and relatively ignored. 'The Virgin of the Rocks' is a beautiful, imaginative work, showing a young, fair girl, seated in a fantastic Dolomite setting, holding out her hands to an angel and two cherubs. It is almost exactly the same as the picture in the National Gallery, London, and it was the custom of Renaissance painters to paint the same picture several times, obsessed with the idea. 'The Virgin and Child with St Anne' is the same as the cartoon in London; perhaps one was based on the other, or possibly there were originally two paintings and two cartoons. It is rather a spooky work, and some have identified the figure of St Anne with the apparition of Death.

All these works give good examples of Leonardo's *sfumato* style. This is a painter's skill, making use of light to make the figures seem alive and even in motion. But this is a technical point. We shall be more interested in the subjects and the cryptic meaning of the pictures.

The **Italian school** is the heart of the Louvre and the chief reason why it has become so famous as a museum. Occupying much of the Grande Galerie, its collection spans the centuries from Cimabue and Giotto in the thirteenth and fourteenth centuries, through the Renaissance to Titian who died in 1576, aged ninety-nine, and, in the eighteenth century, Guardi. There is no space here to write an essay on the development of Renaissance art, nor is this the book for that. All I can do here is to show you some works which I find particularly attractive and some artists which I find of special interest. But you may well have other views.

The primitives are now more admired than they once were and we may well pause before Giotto's 'St Francis receiving the Stigmata'. Painted mainly in white and gold, it is basically a Byzantine icon (painted about 1320). A hundred years later Fra Angelico's 'Coronation of the Virgin' glows with colour, in particular cobalt blue. The simple theme is complicated by the large crowd, and the artist did not know about perspective. This technique was developed by Paolo Uccello (d. 1475), who never seemed to tire of painting the battle of San Romano (there are other pictures of it in London and Florence), and the profusion of lances, horses and bodies gave ample opportunities for his skill. Perspective, creating a third dimension in a two-dimensional art, with its vanishing points and in-going lines, was an essential part of painting from then on – one cannot imagine Vermeer or Velazquez without it – until our own times, when it was eliminated by Matisse and some of his contemporaries.

Botticelli is represented here by a 'Madonna and Child' and his 'Lady with Four Allegorical Figures'. Although they are beautifully drawn, and full of grace and charm, I personally find them rather wan, and much prefer Mantegna's works. His 'St Sebastian' is much reproduced and in his 'Calvary' (painted about 1456) we should note the fine rock-formations, a Renaissance speciality. Ghirlandaio's 'Old Man and his Grandson' remains one of my favourite pictures; apart from the old man's comic nose, it is a touching portrayal of mutual affection.

Raphael is represented by several religious works. The Madonna and Child, popularly known as '*La Belle Jardinière*', is very typical both of Raphael and of the high Renaissance (1507). There is the fine draughtsmanship, the formal construction (triangular in this case), the colour, especially Madonna blue, the distant hilly landscape. But there are those who find it sugary, and personally I much prefer his fine portrait of Balthazar Castiglione.

Venice was a long way, artistically, from Florence. Titian's splendid 'Entombment' (1525) is full of energy and movement, very far from Raphael's calm. Giorgione's 'Pastoral concert' brings in secular sensuality, in particular the female nude, even if the two couples are doing nothing sexier than playing music. We should note the sky, a speciality of this artist. And so to Tintoretto ('Susanna Bathing') and Veronese, whose 'Marriage at Cana' occupies so much space and manages to include such unlikely wedding-guests as the Emperor Charles V, nobles from Venetian society and the artist himself playing the cello (late sixteenth century). Italian art had moved far away from the times of Giotto and Fra Angelico.

Flemish art has been almost as important and influential in France as Italian, and the Louvre has a good though not very large collection, representing most of the great masters. Van Eyck's 'The Virgin and Chancellor Rolin' (1433) is rightly famous, though we must regard it as more of a conversation piece or an interior scene than a religious picture. The Chancellor, who commissioned the work, is clearly reading the Madonna a stern lecture, while she meekly sits with her eyes closed (note her red hair and red robe, a daring innovation). But our eyes will be mainly caught by the details – the tiled floor, the clothes, the capitals on the columns. All the lines lead us to the arches, the garden and the landscape beyond, with its river, little town and distant mountains. The two main figures do not hold the centre of the stage.

The same cannot be said of 'The Annunciation', probably by Rogier Van der Weyden. The Virgin and the Archangel dominate the picture. But, although it is of the same date as 'Chancellor Rolin', it is a simpler, more Gothic work. The domestic details, however, are painted with the same fidelity; we shall enjoy the Angel's gold cope, worthy of an archbishop. Memling, a little later, is represented by 'The Mystic Marriage of St Catherine'. It is in fact a Madonna and Child, she in traditional blue, against a landscape of distant trees and mountains. The usual Flemish domestic details are missing and, apart from the Virgin's oval Flemish face, we might be looking at an Italian picture.

With Gerard David's 'Marriage at Cana' (1505) we are back among the pots and pans, or at least among the platters and goblets. We are at a pleasant family party in Bruges, some of which is visible outside. There is no sense of wonder at the miracle. Hieronymus Bosch's 'Ship of Fools' and the two Breughels are also shown here. Van Dyck has a superb portrait of Charles I of England, painted in 1635. This is possibly the finest of Van Dyck's royal portraits, capturing so many facets of the King's character, his dignity, his stubbornness and his elegance. How it came to France is not known, but it was, ironically, much admired by Louis XVI.

The Medici Gallery, which adjoins, contains the twenty-one pictures which Marie de Medici commissioned from Rubens for the Luxembourg Palace (see Chapter 16). This series was intended to show the life of the Queen in historical terms; an unpromising commission, but one which turned out to be a masterpiece. It is thought that much of the detailed work was done by his apprentices, among them Van Dyck. Apart from Marie de Medici, we can also see his 'Adoration of the Magi' and a late, great work 'The Country Fair', in which he contrasts a peaceful evening countryside with the crowd of drunken peasants.

Dutch seventeenth-century painting is admired in France as elsewhere. The collection may not be large, but it contains several masterpieces; tiresomely, it is hung in the Salle des Sept Mètres, at the far end of the Grande Galerie from the Flemish and German pictures. No one will want to miss the four Rembrandt self-portraits, but we should also notice his 'Bathsheba' (painted in 1654). This is in fact a portrait of his servant-mistress Hendrickje Stoffels, nude in her bath. As Bathsheba she is reading a letter telling her of the death planned for her husband, Uriah the Hittite. It is difficult to imagine that King David should have so much desired her heavy, unshapely body, but her face is moving, so full of love and sadness.

At the other end of the emotional scale is Franz Hals's '*La Bohémienne*' (about 1625). Daringly painted in red and white, the girl's smile is far from enigmatic and her sidelong glance has a come-hither look. A merry peasant, she is a contrast to Van Eyck's Madonna. More serious is the girl in Vermeer's 'The Lacemaker', a quiet picture of someone ruining her eyesight. Hobbema's 'Watermill' is a typical Dutch landscape, full of sky, trees, water and perspective.

And now for the **French school**. Two-thirds of the paintings in the Louvre are French. (One may note the contrast with London, where the National Gallery at one moment was apparently not showing any English art, about which I complained in *The Times*). However, French art is not uniformly represented over the centuries. Much of mediæval art, a time when France was supreme artistically, has been lost, some of it in the Hundred Years' War, some of it by the periodic French wish to destroy their heritage. However, some has survived and can be seen in the Salon Carré, at the eastern end of the Grande Galerie. The two Pietàs, by Malouel (about 1400) and from Villeneuve-les-Avignon (about 1460), are both fine examples of mediæval art.

French art, especially portrait-painting, has benefited from France's central geographical position, touching both north and south, Flemish and Italian. The north provided, it is said, the verisimilitude, the south the intellectual content. France has also benefited much from its traditional hospitality to foreign artists, begun by François I, which still continues. So it is right that one of the finest French portraits should be of that king, by Jean Clouet (1524); this shows the King's sumptuous tastes, his intelligence and education and also his cunning.

Philippe de Champaigne's magnificent portrait of Cardinal Richelieu has unfortunately been sent upstairs to the second floor. However, identically the same portrait may be seen in London. On a lower social level are the characters in the works of Le Nain and, especially, Georges de La Tour. The latter's candlelit groups, the faces alive in the light of the flame, are rightly admired. No one knows for certain how he did them; it is said that he used wooden boxes with slits for his dramatic effects, but others think that he worked from sketches made in the low taverns which he liked to haunt. Card-sharpers, pickpockets, sneak-thieves – these were his models. The picaresque, I feel, inspired him more than religion, and his Bethlehem scenes in the Louvre I find less exciting, though 'The Adoration of the Shepherds', being down to earth, is a fine picture.

The seventeenth century, *le grand siècle*, did not only produce portraits and groups. It also produced a great nostalgia for the classical world, an alternative to the too-established Church. Poussin, a Norman, spent most of his life in Rome, painting imaginary classical scenes. Some discerning art critics find these very great, but I fear I am not among them; to me they look like bad productions of a Shakespeare 'Roman' play, sombre fantasies. Equally 'classical' – that is to say, full of buildings with columns – are the pictures of Claude Le Lorrain. Here the architectural landscapes are bathed in an agreeable sunset haze and populated by figures in seventeenth-century clothes.

The passion for ancient Rome had gone to extremes. Poussin produced 'laws' of Nature and Art which were rigidly applied by Louis XIV's expert, Le Brun. René Huyghe, not a man to devalue his fellow-countrymen, writes that the reign of Le Brun at Versailles produced, artistically, 'almost nothing of value'. But the fine portraitists escaped his influence; the Louvre shows many good examples. The eighteenth century reacted, going from the grandeur of Rome to what Huyghe calls 'frivolity' – nudes and shepherdesses. Madame de Pompadour's painter, Boucher, may well be so criticized, but it is a little unfair on Fragonard, whose landscapes often have a pastoral fairytale quality. In a different class is Watteau, the first of the Romantics, a movement which was to find its climax in Delacroix. His 'Embarkation for Cythera' (1717) is full of romantic yearnings and nostalgia, and so well painted that the Beaux-Arts accepted the unknown young man immediately. Portrait-painting did not flourish in the new reign. Quentin de La Tour's portrait of Louis XV is a good picture and probably a good likeness, but it is hardly a Van Dyck. French creative genius, during the eighteenth century, was more interested in architecture, furniture and interior decoration.

Everything changed with the Revolution and the Empire. The nineteenth century is still the pride of the Louvre's French collection and its largest feature, in numbers and size. It takes up much of the first floor, including the whole of the Salle Mollien, the Aile Mollien, the Salle Denon and the Salle Daru. And at once we are faced by the works of Jacques-Louis David.

David (1748–1825) was the foremost French painter of his time and ruled French art 'with an iron hand', laying down further laws of art, derived theoretically from Rome. He was a talented portrait-painter, as we can see from his famous picture of Madame Récamier on her sofa, Pope Pius VII and a self-portrait. But his political theories inspired him to attempt huge canvases on classical or military themes. A close friend of Robespierre, they were together in prison and David was lucky to escape the guillotine in 1793. He was visited in prison by his estranged wife, a royalist, and he was so touched by this that he was later inspired to paint his 'Sabine Women'. In this the women are shown stopping the fight between the Romans and the Sabines. This is not the popular angle on the legend and indeed is surprising from an artist devoted to martial

129

glory. But it is a powerful work, full of sincerity, especially the pleading women.

David became a Bonapartist and official painter to Napoleon. We see his coronation here, but he also painted Napoleon in battle, and riding across the Alps, showing a remarkable skill in horsemanship. After 1815 David went into exile and painted no more.

The men in the 'Sabine Women' are all naked, as indeed are all his soldiers, except Napoleon. This was partly due to his early training by Boucher and partly due to his studies of classical statues. But it introduces a certain credibility gap. Do all soldiers always go into battle naked? And, if so, would they have been quite so pale-skinned? David would have us think so. The Louvre has thirty-nine of his works, and, for one visitor at least, that is quite enough.

David had many pupils, but his mantle fell upon Delacroix, who was not one of them. Once again we have the huge violent canvases, full of corpses, massacres and heroism, some of it mythical or classical, some of it more contemporary. We shall certainly admire the energy, the feeling of line and construction, though this some-times seems to be a little repetitive. But 'Liberty leading the people' (1830) is a powerful and striking picture. Here the bare-breasted goddess of Liberty (the one whose face is on the postage stamps), barefoot, waving a Tricolor, strides across the corpses, followed by a street urchin (like 'Le petit Gavroche') waving pistols, a bourgeois in a top hat brandishing a shotgun, and other revolutionaries. In the distance, through the smoke of the barricades, we can see the towers of Notre-Dame. The contrast in styles, in realism and, especially in clothes, is startling, as Delacroix doubtless intended it to be. The obvious comparison is with Victor Hugo, who held similar views and wrote about the same revolution and barricades. But Delacroix much disliked being compared with his literary counterpart; he also resented being called a Romantic, when he insisted that he was a 'pure classicist'.

As a change from all this vast violence we can contemplate the classical nudes of Ingres. A follower of Raphael, a pupil of David, he spent most of his life in Rome where he became Director of the French Academy. Draughtsmanship was all-important to him, colour of far less importance. Line and shape were supreme and his figures based on classical statues sometimes seem rather lifeless –

not that there is anything asexual about his '*Odalisque*', a seductive girl indeed. His portrait of M. Bertin, too, is very living.

For landscapes we shall certainly admire Courbet, whose realism makes a change after the eighteenth century; we can almost smell the leaves and the grass, feel the cool water. With Corot we are back with the eye of the artist, muddy colours, blurred shapes and diffused woodland. But in a long career his early works and his last works show a clarity and an interest in light which he lost for a while. His 'Bridge at Mantes' (1870), one of his last works, shows this very clearly. It might almost be by an early Impressionist, and indeed some have seen Corot this way. The Louvre, incidentally, has over a hundred Corots, not all, of course, on view. And with Corot the Louvre collection of French art ends. For the Impressionists we shall have to go to the Jeu de Paume and the Marmottan and for later artists to the Palais de Tokyo, until the d'Orsay Museum opens.

Although these Louvre nineteenth-century artists were contemporary, are now hung together and may seem to us to have a good deal in common, it must not be thought that they were a mutual admiration society like the Impressionists. David's pupils attacked Delacroix for breaking the Laws of Art, a very French offence. Ingres attacked him savagely for being a Romantic and not a Classicist. Ingres himself, despite his draughtsmanship, was criticized for deforming the human body. Courbet was attacked for being self-taught and for making trees look like trees instead of feather-dusters. And it is this conflict of strongly held, if rather esoteric views, which has provided the mainspring for so much of French art.

Compared with Italian, Flemish and French painting, other schools – Spanish, German and English – have always been dismissed as 'peripheral'. However, belated efforts have been made to put this right. Velazquez's own copy of his portrait of Queen Marie-Anne of Austria has been acquired from the Prado. The English school has been enlarged by some Constables and a fine portrait of Lady Alston by Gainsborough, presented by Baron Robert de Rothschild.

The **Spanish paintings** are at the western end of the first floor – the Pavillon de Flore. The controversial Picasso Donation collection (not his own work) is also here at present. Here we shall find a

131

typical El Greco 'Crucifixion' and a good portrait of the old architect Covarrubias, a study in black, grey and elongation (1600). Zurbarán's 'Burial of St Bonaventure' (1629) is a dramatic construction; the diagonally placed corpse robed in white, with a green decomposing face and a scarlet hat, is surrounded by mourners, some sorrowing, some like the Pope and Emperor, uncaring. Ribera's 'Clubfoot' (1652) is an attractive picture, the boy so merry despite his deformity. There are two good Goyas, the 'Woman in Grey' and the portrait of the Marquesa of Solana, thought by some to be his finest portrait.

German painting is in the Pavillon des Etats, near the Flemish. Here we shall find a Dürer self-portrait, an excellent picture of himself as a young man. Holbein's 'Anne of Cleves' and 'Erasmus' catch the eye but the elder Cranach's 'Venus' seems rather mannered.

English (and Scottish) art is on the second floor, in the west wing of the Cour Carrée, and few people succeed in finding it. This is a pity, because, apart from the excellent Gainsborough, the collection includes portraits by Reynolds ('Master Hare'), Lawrence and Raeburn; and landscapes by Bonington, Constable and Turner. Whistler's famous portrait of his mother is also here.

Besides Paintings, there is a drawings and pastels section, most of which is not on public view. The Louvre also has important sections on **Sculpture** (Mediæval, Renaissance and French, including Michelangelo's famous 'Captives'), Oriental Antiquities, and Objet's d'Art, mainly furniture such as Boulle cabinets. All these contain great treasures, but they are not always open. They are closed on a rotating basis, announced on a board near the entrance. If we wish to make sure of seeing any of them, we should go on a Monday or Wednesday, avoiding the lunch-hour.

We can, however, look at the Greek and Roman statues every day. Few people do, except for the obligatory visit to the Venus de Milo. This is partly because so many of the Greek statues are replicas, and partly a change in public taste. David would be astonished. Should we decide to explore, we should notice the 'Lady of Auxerre', one of the oldest known Greek statues, a stern work; also the section of the Parthenon frieze. Among the Romans, the most popular, in a gruesome way, is the head of Caligula.

We end our visit in the **Crypt of Osiris**, a new creation, which holds the Egyptian Antiquities and is much visited. The 'Squatting Scribe' is famous. The small figure is Old Kingdom (between 2750 and 2625 BC) and represents the governor of a province. We should note the eyes; opaque white, with quartz cornea, rock crystal iris and ebony pupils; they stare over our right shoulders in a most disconcerting way.

A recent acquisition is the compelling head of Amenhotep IV (Akhnaton, the first monotheist). It dates from about 1360 BC and was presented by the Egyptian government. The Sphinx is a popular attraction; sixteen feet long, made of pink granite, it dates from the Middle Empire (2100–1780 BC). A lion with a human head, the Horus with two horizons, it symbolizes the sun or pharaoh invigorating the earth. But others see it as something puzzling, questioning and, like the Gioconda lady upstairs, mysterious.

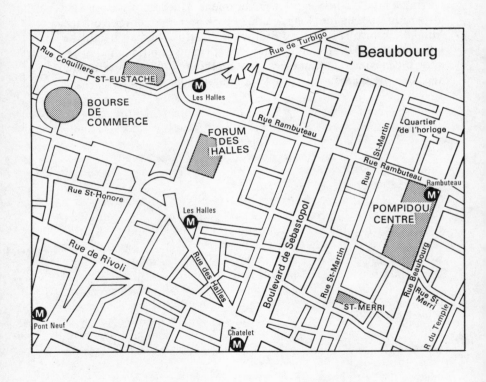

CHAPTER 8
Beaubourg

Beaubourg, fifty years ago, was an old, slummy village with narrow picturesque streets, squeezed between the church of Saint-Merri and Les Halles. Saint-Merri was once the centre of the haberdashery and clothing trades, while Les Halles was the great food market, the stomach of Paris, as Zola put it. Round the edge of Les Halles were a number of restaurants which catered for the local tastes at those hours of the night when food wholesalers normally work. These restaurants were discovered by a better-heeled class who had spent the night at a ball or a nightclub and wanted a bowl of onion soup before going to bed. The two classes mixed together very prettily.

Much of this has gone. Haberdashery and clothing have moved to the department stores, the *couture* houses and the boutiques. Beaubourg has been redeveloped into precincts and pedestrian areas; the new apartment blocks have been well designed to fit in with the old streets that remain and the original inhabitants have been rehoused in them alongside new and better-off tenants – not, it is said, without some conflict of lifestyles. And Les Halles have gone to an area near Orly airport; their glass arcades have been demolished, despite protests that the arcades were themselves of artistic merit. In their place is a large shopping and leisure centre, not yet completed. Only the church of Saint-Eustache and the onion-soup restaurants survive – and thrive, despite the disappearance of the pork butchers and the oyster-sellers.

But the most spectacular innovation in the area is in Beaubourg: the **Georges Pompidou Centre**, opened in 1977 and already one of the main attractions of Paris. The idea of a multi-cultural centre had been around for some time, particularly in the head of André Malraux, but it was President Pompidou, a great lover of change

and modernity, who brought it into existence, with the encourage-
ment of Mme Pompidou, an active supporter of contemporary art.
Completed after his death, it was rightly named after him and an
op-art portrait of him by Vasarély hangs on the ground floor.

But the building itself – what are we to think? The winners of the
international competition to design it were then little known –
Richard Rogers (British) and Renzo Piano (Italian). Their building
is in shape a simple parallelepiped five storeys high, made of steel
and glass; there are no towers or skyline features, other than the
tops of ventilator shafts. But it is far from being a plain geometric
block. The outside is encrusted with steel rods like scaffolding,
pipes, ventilator shafts, painted bright red, blue, green and yellow.
A pleasing feature is the outside escalator which leads to all floors;
encased in transparent material on a red base, it resembles a giant
caterpillar climbing up the west face.

Naturally such a building must arouse great controversy. Some
regard it as daringly original, others as an eyesore. There are many
jokes; When are they going to take the scaffolding down? How are
they going to repaint it? Why did they have to put an oil refinery in
the middle of Paris? So this is where the *Titanic* sank?! But this at
least can be said: the building has personality. It is not just another
glass egg-box.

The idea of the centre has also been under attack, for putting too
much power and patronage in the hands of the state, for absorbing,
like the opera, too much of the limited cultural budget. Such funds,
it is argued, would be better spent more widely and diversely; art in
France has always thrived on the small galleries and purchasers, the
many salons with their different committees and attitudes. A single
monolithic authority, the Versailles of our time, may not encourage
the best art. Or, again, it may – the point is highly debatable. But
what cannot be denied is that the Pompidou Centre is making a
great effort to bring contemporary art – in all senses of the word –
into the everyday life of ordinary people and not keep it as something eclectic for Sunday afternoon. Beaubourg has become a must
for every visitor to Paris, like the Eiffel Tower and the Louvre, no
matter what the height of his brow.

Entrance is free or half-price for certain categories such as
children, art students, pensioners, employees past and present of
the Ministry of Culture, and so on. Details are available in the

leaflet of weekly activities obtained at the information desk on the ground floor. The main entrance is in the Rue Beaubourg; after 2.30 p.m. we can enter the escalator direct from the Rue Rambuteau. There is also an exit into the main piazza on the west side.

The main attraction of the centre is the **Museum of Modern Art** on the third and fourth floors. The biggest collection of contemporary art in the world, it covers over a century of painting and sculpture, beginning with Douanier Rousseau's 'Snake Charmer' and ending with the museum's latest acquisitions. Everything is splendidly lit and hung, and clearly labelled, so that we can identify and date any work without trouble; we should allow an hour and a half to see the main works, more if we are interested in any particular artist or style.

The works are arranged approximately in chronological order, but this can be misleading as many different types of art were going on at the same time; for example, Utrillo and Léger were exact contemporaries, but their pictures have nothing in common. Conversely, Picasso went through many periods during his long working life and his pictures are shown in many different places in the collection. We must not regard modern art as a chain of men, each 'doing his thing' and then passing on the torch to his successor. Certainly many of them knew one another and were influenced, favourably or otherwise, by one anothers' work. But several hundred geniuses are not put into a historical line as easily as some art historians would like. And one thing more must be said before we begin. The Beaubourg collection is international, deriving from many lands and origins. But we will be aware, as we go round, how many of the artists, from Kandinsky and Modigliani to Poliakoff and Calder, chose to live in France, for its opportunities and its quality of life. Through this, many of them knew one another and were aware of one another's work, even if they chose to go their own ways. Whether this will continue is uncertain, but one of the objects of the Pompidou Centre is to make its continuation possible.

We start at the point where Impressionism made way for new ideas. One of the first canvases we see is by Bonnard (d. 1947); he seems to belong to the previous century, except that his happy pictures, so full of colour and light, are already looking forward to Matisse and Delaunay. Then we are among the Fauves – Dérain,

137

Dufy, Vlaminck, early Matisse, Van Dongen – who used Impressionist subjects, but applied the paint more boldly and dramatically,
with more violent colours. Contrasting with this are the Cubists –
Braque, Juan Gris, Léger, Picasso (emerging from his rose and blue
periods) – who were more interested in line and construction than in
colour, which they suppressed completely, preferring uniform
browns and greys. Léger's work now seems the most interesting,
partly because he painted other things besides mandolins and old
newspapers; in his work we find parts of the body, geometric shapes
and the cogwheels of the machine age. He ended with pure abstract
work.

Colour, however, returned with the Delaunays; both Robert and
his wife Sonia are shown to advantage, particularly Sonia, with
whom clear primary colour was the main subject of her pictures, the
simple geometric patterns being of secondary interest. She was
among the first to find her way to abstraction. Matisse, another
colourist, continued to paint the world round him, but vividly and
with a great loosening of shape, including the elimination of perspective. With Kandinsky the loosening went much further, with
lines wandering everywhere, belts and stars of colour floating in
space, as he moved away from the figurative.

Two other artists here attract our attention. Utrillo could make a
street, a house, a flight of steps, a wall come to life so that it speaks
to us as it once spoke to him. The human body, however, meant
nothing to him. Marc Chagall's early work, '*Double portrait au verre
de vin*', already shows his unique blend of realism and fantasy.

We take the escalator to the fourth floor and are immediately
confronted by Matisse's four sculptures of a woman's back, each
more simplified than the last and showing that this artist had other
interests than colour. On the other side of the escalator is a typical
Picasso, 'The Minotaur' (1928), one of his works fixated on men and
bulls, here combining both.

Continuing round in the main 'corridor' we find ourselves in the
world of pure abstraction; Mondrian's coloured rectangles, '*Composition 2 avec bleu et rouge*' and Moholy-Nagy's '*Composition
AXX*' – titles have been simplified as well as shapes. There is
nothing simple, however, in Kandinsky's '*Jaune rouge bleu*'; the
primary colours were his *point de départ*, themselves dictating the
wild and seemingly random shapes. By contrast we have Pevsner's

sculptures, geometric shapes beautifully balanced and looking as if they could spin and float.

On our right we find examples of the works of Montparnasse painters of the 1920s. There is only one Modigliani painting on view, but it is enough to give us a glimpse of his unusual vision; elongated heads and bodies, eyes without pupils, but the personality of the artist and the model always comes through. There are also some Modigliani busts, which may make us feel that the artist was always more a painter than a sculptor. His friend Soutine, who allowed him to work in his studio, tended to see everything and everyone as still life: deformed, still bleeding, but dead. Even his nudes are dead. Lipschitz, the close friend of Modigliani, has several sculptures in the collection; smooth, pleasant shapes, they yet remind us of Lipschitz's own head, blobby, lopsided, familiar to us from Modigliani's portraits of him. Lipschitz, incidentally, tried to reform Modi's bohemian lifestyle, but the aspect of this which most distressed him was Modi's habit of putting salt on his food before tasting it. 'When I began to urge him to put some kind of order into his life, he became as angry as I had ever seen him.'

The next gallery brings us to Surrealism, the world of dreams and psychology. Max Ernst, the most profound and sinister of them, is shown at the end of the gallery. Magritte, the careful painter of the impossible object, shows us bisected heads. And Dali who, among other things, rediscovered perspective, gives us a picture of six little portraits of Lenin dancing on piano keys. Dada-ism, founded in Zürich during the First World War and thought to be a consequence of or a protest against it, is usually associated with Surrealism, and so here we find a fantasy by Arp and a weird infantilism by Mirò.

It comes as something of a shock to find Picasso again in the next section, at the height of his powers. There are also a late work by Matisse and, at the end of this part of the gallery, a smooth pleasantly-shaped sculpture of Brancusi, '*Le Phoque*'. It is, however, rather dominated by the Henry Moore which lies beyond.

The 'corridor' narrows and we squeeze between Moore's big reclining figure and a triptych by Francis Bacon, Britain's contribution to the collection and both typical of their styles. We are now in the part of the museum devoted to the latest in art: abstract, tachiste, action, new figurative, op, pop, neo-realist, geometric – names are merely names, it is the works themselves which either have or have not something to say to us. But I may perhaps mention those artists here who say something to me.

Poliakoff – a gold and dark abstract, reminding us of an icon. Hartung – his sharp black lines which yet seem to glow with light. Soulages's big belts of black have a similar quality on a larger scale. Mathieu's big red tachiste painting '*Les Capétiens partout*' (the title is typically irrelevant) dominates one wall with its vitality; unfortunately his fellow action-painter Jackson Pollock is represented only by two small monochrome works, which do not do justice to his vision. There is, however, nothing small-scale about Barnett Newman's picture, vertical stripes on a neutral background. Nicolas de Stael's '*Les Toits*' hovers on the edge of landscape and abstraction, like Klee before him.

Neither the Warhol nor the Lichtenstein can strictly be called pop art – no soup tins, no strip cartoons; yet both are unmistakable in style. The big scale was important to Lichtenstein, as it was to Newman and to Calder, whose large stabile dominates the sculpture here; more of his works, both mobiles and stabiles, are outside on the terrace. By way of a sculptural contrast we can admire the spindly figures of the Swiss Giacometti, who was able to reduce the human shape almost to one vertical dimension. We are supposed to take off our shoes if we go into Jean Dubuffet's 'sculpted room' '*Jardin d'Hiver*'. (Not because it is holy, but because the floor is part of the sculpture, which we shall be standing *inside*.) He makes his effect by the use of black and white.

Modern art is something which can never come to an end, and the Museum is continually acquiring new works. This means a frequent rearrangement of this part of the fourth floor, with some works going temporarily to the reserve collections. These are open to the public; for details we should consult one of the hostesses or the information desk.

But perhaps we have seen enough modern art for one day and we should end our visit by looking at Ben's Store. From 1958 to 1973 Ben Vautier had an art and record shop, which was also a gallery, in Nice, where it became an avant-garde centre. Covered now with objects and slogans by Ben, it has been re-erected here as a piece of pop art sculpture or, as Ben prefers to call it, a *chose exposée*. One supposes, perhaps wrongly, that the original must have been more spacious and less cluttered. But anyway it makes a delightful end to our visit and to what has been, I hope, an exhilarating experience.

Besides the Museum of Modern Art, the Pompidou Centre also has galleries of graphic art, photography, a library and a small cinema. The ground and fifth floors are used for temporary exhibitions, while the ground floor also has a children's studio, full of gimmicks and gadgets; a reconstruction of Brancusi's studio; and the Centre de Création Industrielle (CCI), which considers various aspects of modern life, such as the problem of noise, with the help of the latest audio-visual techniques and displays. These are popular with children as well as with sociologists.

At No.31 Rue Saint-Merri is the part of the centre devoted to modern music (**IRCAM**) a laboratory where a team of electronic engineers and musicians, directed by Pierre Boulez, discover strange and sometimes beautiful new sounds. Admission is only permitted to specialists after application, but concerts and lectures are given two or three times a week – details from the information desk or telephone 277–1233. Some of the compositions are also broadcast on France-Musique (MHz 98.6) at 11.0 p.m., Continental time. However, one of the problems of listening to radiophonic music is the uncertainty whether we are tuned in correctly, whether the heterodyne whistle is intended or not. Easier are the 'songs' where, against a humming, gonging background, a sonorous voice declaims:

> . . . *mère d'amour,*
> *Mer de glace, Maire de Paris,* . . .

At least we know we are on the right station.

To the west of the Pompidou Centre is a large **piazza** extended as far as the Rue Saint-Martin, itself closed to traffic, at least in theory. This open space naturally attracts the crowds and with them the fire-eaters, acrobats, jugglers and other street entertainers. It makes a lively spectacle and it was intended that the area should become a cultural and social centre. Indeed, there are a couple of private art galleries, several boutiques and snack-bars, pizzerias and so on. But the problem is that the Centre, its visitors and its life also attract a considerable number of *voyous* – pickpockets, bag-snatchers and rowdies. Efforts are being made to deal with this, which is not a new problem in this area, but it has delayed the elegant and artistic development. However, we shall probably have no difficulties in daytime.

If we are waiting for the Pompidou Centre to open, we could well explore the **Quartier de l'Horloge**, a new area which lies just to the north. We pass through a shopping arcade, *le passage de l'horloge*, into the Rue Bernard de Clairvaux. There, on the right under an archway, is the **horloge** itself, Paris's newest clock, 'The Defender of Time'. It is a remarkable piece of sculpture and engineering by Jacques Monestier, commissioned in 1975 and unveiled by the Mayor of Paris, Jacques Chirac, in 1979.

Four metres high and weighing one tonne, it hangs from the wall, a rocky seashore made of oxidized brass. In the centre stands a lifesize man, wearing armour of polished brass (or is he naked?). Beside him is a brass clock on a pillar; round him are a dragon, a sharp-beaked bird and a crab, all also made of polished brass. The dragon breathes in and out regularly. Shortly before the hour, lights come on, drums roll and the Defender limbers up for action. A gong sounds the exact hour (quartz timing) and the man is attacked by one of the beasts, selected at random by the computer. This is accompanied by the noise of an earthquake, hurricane or rough sea, for whichever beast is attacking the man. He defends himself with his sword and shield, counter-attacks, and the beast retires. This happens every hour from 9.0 a.m. till 10.0 p.m. But at midday, 6.0 p.m. and 10.0 p.m. he is attacked by all three at once. It is an energetic fight, but he emerges victorious and the crowd of watching children cheer. Time is safe from nature for another hour. I personally deplore the basic idea of nature being always hostile to man, though I know that many people do hold it. And on another level French dinner tables would be poorer without birds of shellfish. But there is, all the same, something intriguing about the mixture here of primitive terrors and modern technology. There is also something rather Wagnerian about the central figure himself; it is said that the clock was inspired by the Rathaus clock in Munich.

We return to the piazza and turn west along the Rue Rambuteau. In due course we reach the vast area occupied until recently by the food market of Les Halles. Much of this is now taken up by a big shopping and leisure centre, the **Forum des Halles** (*le Forum* for short, or *le trou*, the hole). It is indeed a big hole in the ground, the

142

idea being not to obscure the view of the church of Saint-Eustache or the other buildings in the district.

The architects, Vasconi and Pencreac'h, have produced a pleasing symmetrical design in glass and steel, the entrances suggesting fountains, the sides waterfalls. The Forum extends down four levels and at the bottom is a piazza where we can rest our feet and drink a cup of coffee in the company of a statue called 'Pygmalion', of a four-breasted woman and several strange beasts including a pig (Pygmalion, see? The sculptor, Julio Silva, presumably speaks some English, as the pun does not work in French). At Christmas we shall also have a live Father Christmas on roller-skates to cheer our Christmas shopping.

Of course, shopping is what we are here for, especially on Saturdays, when there will be many others. Behind the glass walls are three tiers of boutiques, 180 altogether. The emphasis is on clothes, the most expensive and the smartest being on the top level (*quatrième niveau*). Leather is much featured, including coats, bags, shoes from Charles Jourdan and accessories. Many established boutiques from elsewhere have branches here. We can also buy scent, jewellery and watches. Men are also catered for with clothes, wine, cheese and, for both sexes, chocolates. Many of the boutiques are cafés or snack-bars, so that a man can enjoy a glass of Beaujolais Nouveau, while his girlfriend looks at the scarves. There is also a small theatre, a branch of the Musée Grévin on the Grands Boulevards, which gives us a brief glimpse of the Belle Epoque and the cancan; and FNAC. This branch of FNAC is possibly the most popular part of the whole Forum. Originally selling records and cassettes, it has moved on to electronic goods, sports, ticket reservations and a whole range of further possibilities. It looks rather like a bank, but it has become a rendezvous, almost a way of life, for men and this naturally attracts the girls too.

The Forum has direct access to the metro, the RER, and the Gare du Nord and Charles de Gaulle airport, also the underground car parks. On street level we can reach the surrounding streets. The main entrance at the moment is in the Rue Rambuteau, but there will presumably be access to the gardens, which will cover the rest of Les Halles district, a quiet place covering twelve acres in the middle of a crowded area. There was some argument about the design of the garden. The architects wanted an 'English' garden, but this was overruled by President Giscard in favour of a traditional French garden, Tuileries style, complete with gravel, pools and statues – we may hope that they will not all be of pigs. The gardens will be on several levels and we shall enjoy a good view of the great church of **Saint-Eustache**.

It is an imposing building, immensely tall, with flying buttresses and steeply pitched roofs. Originally it was a small chapel dedicated first to St Agnes and then to St Eustace, a Roman general converted to Christianity by seeing, like St Hubert, a cross between the antlers of a stag. He was martyred, it is said, by being enclosed, with his wife and children, in a large bronze bull which was then heated – a very expensive form of martyrdom, we must think.

However, it is not of General Eustace that we think now when we look at the church, but of rich pork butchers and their families. The parishioners wanted a church worthy of their wealth, a building to rival Notre-Dame a short distance away. Indeed Notre-Dame was the model for the ground plan. But the church took so long to build that tastes changed; new benefactors gave lavishly, but there were often conditions. The original gothic shape was retained, including the flying buttresses, lancet and rose windows. But the façade of the transept became much decorated in Renaissance style, covered with mouldings and grotesques, including a stag's head with the cross. The west front was remodelled into classical style, with Doric, Ionic and Corinthian columns. For some there are too many styles mixed together, too much decoration, but the parishioners were very proud of it, and we would not expect them to have had simple or severe tastes. During the Revolution it was renamed, not unsuitably, the Temple of Agriculture. It was badly damaged by fire and restored by Baltard, who also designed the glass and iron food halls of the great market, now gone for ever. The church belfry too was partly demolished to suit a semaphore station. However Saint-Eustache remains an imposing building, better seen from a distance. It is well-known for its music, a continuing tradition.

Entering the church through the west door, we are immediately struck by both the height and the light. There are several low dark churches in Paris, lit mainly by stained glass, but here is one with the full upspring of gothic architecture; it is of cathedral stature and one thinks of Amiens or indeed of Notre-Dame – so to speak, its sister church. The nave is in fact 112 feet tall and the aisles are the same,

The Sphinx in the Crypt
of Osiris, the Louvre.
Below The foundations of
Philippe-Auguste's keep,
the original Louvre.

An early fifteenth-century
Pietà, in the Louvre.

François I by Le Titien,
a fine character portrait.

Richelieu by Philippe de
Champaigne.
Below Napoleon by David.

The Winged Victory of Samothrace, in the Louvre.

without galleries. The length of the church is also impressive. We should stand at the west door and look through the chancel towards the Lady Chapel, and see space behind space; or from the east end, look back at the rose window and organ. The church is 100 metres long, 330 feet.

But once again we have the feeling – did they not overdo it? Is there not too much decoration and ornament? The vaulting is a good example of flamboyant gothic with its hanging keystones. But is it not too florid and encrusted? Are soaring gothic pillars made more beautiful by the addition of one or more Corinthian capitals?

The churchwarden's pew is eighteenth-century, a gift from Philippe of Orléans. On the left of the Lady Chapel is Colbert's tomb; note the statue of Abundance by Coysevox. Inside the chapel is a statue of the Virgin by Pigalle. There are also an early Rubens, a sixteenth-century statue of St John in the south transept and a bust of the composer Rameau. As one might expect, such a big and important church, the parish church of the Palais-Royal, was the scene of many ceremonial events. Among them were the baptisms of Cardinal Richelieu, Molière and Madame de Pompadour, the fishmonger's daughter; the funerals of La Fontaine, Molière, Rameau and Mirabeau; and, rather unexpectedly, the First Communion of Louis XIV, who was living with his mother in the Palais-Royal.

Back to the market, to the pigs and fish. Outside the church was the market pillory, used for the punishment of dishonest stallholders. Somewhere here too was the 'Astrological Tower' built by Catherine de Medici for her doctor and adviser, Nostradamus. Nothing remains of it and we do not know what it looked like.

By now we will be thinking of our stomachs; indeed, it is hard to think of anything else here, what with the old market and the hundreds of restaurants, mainly medium-priced or cheap, which remain. We can, of course, eat simply in the Pompidou centre or in one of the nearby snack-bars. Opposite the Defender of Time clock is a friendly brasserie, Les Automates, where we can eat or drink while waiting for the hour to sound. The Forum is full of places to eat, mostly small. But we shall probably choose one of the 'onion soup' restaurants for which Les Halles is famous; either Le Père Tranquille in the Rue Lescot beside the Forum, which is open till 1.0 a.m., or the well-known Au pied de Cochon, 6 Rue Coquillère beside Saint-Eustache, which is open all day and night, every day.

Onion soup is known as a *gratinée*, as it is full of grated and melted cheese. It goes down very well on a cold day and is quite indispensable after a long night on the town. Once, after a ball, I was enjoying a *gratinée* at 5.0 a.m. when I noticed a wedding reception in full swing and I asked why they had chosen that hour for the great occasion. '*C'est normal*,' the waiter commented. And time, whatever its Defender may feel, is of little consequence *aux Halles*.

Of course, it does not have to be onion soup. The Pied de Cochon has received a diploma for its shellfish, and a dozen oysters eaten standing at the bar makes an agreeable Sunday brunch. But those who prefer to eat at normal times sitting down will certainly choose pork. Other meat is available, but pork is the thing here: pigs trotters, snout and tail (called *Tentation de St Antoine*), the real andouillette, *tripe à la mode des Halles*. The roast sucking-pig has too much garlic for my taste, but the piglet stew (*civet de porcelet à la moutarde*) is excellent. We should finish our rather heavy lunch with *La Vie en Rose*, a concoction of fresh strawberries, water ice, syrup, whipped cream and – it hardly needs saying – a pink sugar pig.

CHAPTER 9

Eastern Paris

The **Place du Louvre** (Metro Louvre) is an old and attractive square. It was here that the Roman general Labienus had his headquarters when he defeated the Parisii in 52 BC. The Norsemen in AD 885 were checked here when they sailed up the Seine. But the square does not look the same now. On the west side is the neo-classical façade of the Louvre; on the east side the old church of Saint-Germain-l'Auxerrois; and to the south, the Seine flowing by.

It must have looked very pleasant too on the night of 23 August 1572, a hot Paris summer night, the eve of St Bartholomew's Day. Paris was *en fête*; there was to be a royal wedding the following day. Princess Marguerite (Margot) of Valois was to marry her cousin Henry of Navarre in Notre-Dame. Royal weddings are normally joyful occasions, but this one was especially important. Margot was a Catholic, Henry a Huguenot, and the marriage would end the civil wars of religion which were plaguing France. It was, however, to be rather an odd wedding. The bride would be at the high altar, while the bridegroom, being a Protestant, would have to wait outside the main door. The rings presumably would be taken to and fro by messengers. But nobody was troubled by this and thousands of Huguenots were in Paris to support their leader at the great event.

During the night the Queen Mother, Catherine de Medici, looked out of her window in the Louvre and gave a signal to watchers in Saint-Germain-l'Auxerrois opposite. The bell in the church tower began to peal and other belfries across Paris took up the signal. The massacre had begun. It had been carefully plotted by Catherine de Medici, her sons King Charles IX and Prince Henri (later King Henri III) and the Cardinal Duke of Guise, the head of the powerful Catholic family. For three days the French were overtaken by a frenzy of killing, which spread rapidly to other

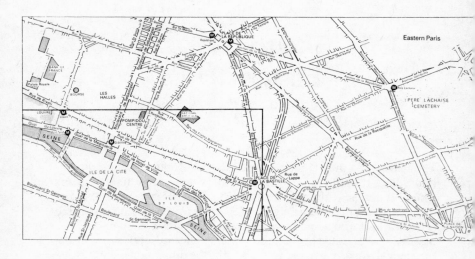

Eastern Paris

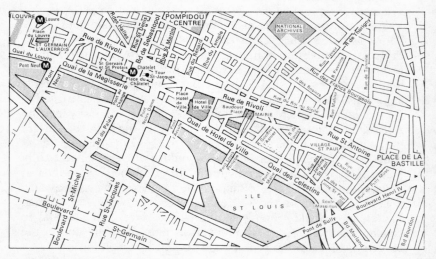

towns. In that time about eight thousand Huguenots were killed, the ghastliest wedding present ever given by a mother to her daughter. Henry of Navarre saved himself by kneeling before the King and swearing to abandon Protestantism. In due course the marriage took place but it is hardly surprising that it was brief, unhappy and childless.

The signal was given from the church tower which we can see from the side street; and not, as is often thought, from the big belfry which stands conspicuously in the square beside the church. This is a nineteenth-century mock-Gothic erection whose great interest is its carillon of thirty-eight bells, which weigh in total ten thousand kilos. The thirteen small bells are all of the same diameter, the different notes being caused by varying thicknesses of metal. There are carillon recitals every Wednesday from 5 to 5.30 p.m., the secular music being mainly improvisations on popular tunes. The belfry is controlled, not by the church, but by the Mairie on the other side (housed in a mixed style, nineteenth-century building by Hittorf).

The church of **Saint-Germain-l'Auxerrois** is very old, built on the site of a sanctuary destroyed by the Norsemen. St Germain, Bishop of Auxerre, (AD 378–448), was himself a remarkable man. He was originally trained as a Roman advocate and he died in Ravenna while pleading the cause of the rebellious Armoricae. St Patrick of Ireland, St Illtyd of Wales and Ste Geneviève of Paris are claimed as his pupils. He came to Britain twice; in 447 he led British troops to victory over the invading Saxons and Picts, shouting his war-cry 'Alleluia!'

Apart from the older Romanesque bell-tower, his church is mainly Gothic, spread over several centuries. The centre doorway is thirteenth-century, but the rest of the porch was built between 1435 and 1439. Lovers of Gothic architecture will enjoy the porch vaulting, Flamboyant in the central bays, simpler at the ends. The church was much damaged in the Revolution and the statues are modern replicas.

Inside we shall be struck by the unusual proportions. Gothic churches are normally tall, but this one is wide and comparatively low, with double aisles running right round the church. In the transepts the vaulting is late Gothic; the stained glass, including two rose windows, is late fifteenth-century. Two painted statues, one on wood, one on stone, flanking the chancel grille are of the same date and represent St Germanus and St Vincent. The chancel columns were given their classical aspect in the eighteenth century – regrettably, one may think. The big wooden churchwardens' pew dates from 1684 and was probably used by members of the royal family living in the Louvre. Behind it we should note a good Flemish altarpiece from the fifteenth century. In the Chapel of the Holy Sacrament, to the right of the entrance, we can see a coloured stone statue of the Virgin from the fourteenth century and an older statue of St Germanus, together with other statues and a modern 'Last Supper' by Van Elsen.

The church is the centre of a 'Community of Fine Arts' which aims to encourage a continuing Christian tradition both in music and the visual arts. Organ recitals are held every Sunday at 5.0 p.m.; the organ was originally in the Sainte-Chapelle. We must notice the striking modern altar and lectern and a series of bold carved figures by Albert Dubos, particularly a fine 'Resurrection' in the north transept. But the contemporary glass seems to be less successful. A special service for artists is held on Ash Wednesday, according to the will of the painter and caricaturist, Adolphe Willette (d. 1926). Those present receive ashes and pray for the souls of those artists who will die in the coming year. This gloomy event is, it seems, well attended.

Outside, we get a good view of the east end and the bell-tower from the side street near the Samaritaine department store. Many will enjoy the gargoyles and the elaborate carvings. And then we are back beside the Seine at the Pont Neuf. Leaving, for the time being, the three big stores here (see Chapters 4 and 14), we continue along the **Quai de la Mégisserie**, one of the most delightful strolls in Paris. On the right is the river and the Ile de la Cité. On the left is a line of pet shops; the pavement is lined with parrakeets, cocks, guinea-fowls, white rabbits and tropical fish. A friend of mine bought a swan here, a present to the Seine and to a solitary errant swan which had become attached to the Ile Saint-Louis. Recently a cuddly black bear with very sharp claws escaped from a cage here and made its way through the pedestrians and traffic to the nearby Avenue Victoria, where it climbed a plane-tree, to be brought down some hours later by an intrepid fireman. *Oui, on peut s'amuser sur le Quai de la Mégisserie.*

The **Place du Châtelet** is on the site of a mediæval prison, said to be even viler and more horrible than the Conciergerie. Nothing now remains of this. Instead we have a square overlooking the Seine and the Pont au Change (once a haunt of money-changers). In the centre is a monument to, once again, the Grande Armée. On either side are two symmetrical theatres, built by Davioud in 1862. The Théâtre du Châtelet (now officially renamed the Théâtre Musical de Paris) has the largest auditorium in Paris, seating half as many again as the Opéra. Both theatres are state-owned but there is little love lost between them. The Châtelet is now given over to concerts, operettas and ballet, but any performer or musician from the Opéra who appears at the Châtelet will not be re-engaged by the Opéra. Opposite, the Théâtre de la Ville, originally the Théâtre Sarah Bernhardt, caters for pop culture.

Below the square is the world's biggest underground station. The junction of several metro lines, including the RER, it is really four stations joined together. It is possible to cross a great deal of Paris here without seeing daylight and it can be said that if you have not changed at Châtelet, you have not really experienced Paris. There is something about the endless corridors, the sudden corners, the little flights of steps leading up and down, the moving platforms which do not always work, the same advertising poster repeated over and over again along the corridors, the feeling that you may be lost or going the wrong way – all this makes Metro Châtelet hypnotic as well as fatiguing.

The Parisians have a fascination with their underground world, something which goes back to the Roman catacombs or even beyond. Catacombs, sewers, two metro systems, underground car parks, nightclubs, modern churches – the ground beneath Paris is honeycombed with tunnels and mines. There is a certain anxiety in case the city collapses into its subterranean world.

However, we should continue our walk in daylight. Behind the Hôtel de Ville we find the Avenue Victoria, named after the British Queen. Here also is the **Tour Saint-Jacques**, one of the landmarks of the Seine. The Gothic belfry is all that remains of the sixteenth-century church of Saint-Jacques, one of the starting points of the pilgrimage, by way of the Rue Saint-Jacques on the Left Bank, to Santiago in Spain.

At the end of the Avenue Victoria we emerge into The **Place de**

l'Hôtel de Ville. Architecturally it is not very interesting, but it has seen much of Paris's tumultous history. Indeed, for many centuries it was the only big square in the city. Until 1830 it was called the Place de Grève; *grève* means foreshore and it was here that unemployed longshoremen and others would gather. The phrase *faire la grève* meant first to be unemployed; it now means to be on strike. *Grève*, a familiar word in the newspapers, now means a strike.

It was in the Place de Grève that public floggings and executions took place, among them the execution of Ravaillac, the murderer of Henri IV. The flesh of the condemned man would be slit at several points and boiling lead poured in, to give a foretaste of things to come. Finally the body, still alive, would be pulled in pieces by four strong horses. It was no worse than the English method of 'hanged, drawn and quartered', but the merciful invention of Dr Guillotin did not come a moment too soon.

The Place de l'Hôtel de Ville has been the centre of municipal authority for a long time. Etienne Marcel in 1357 established the assembly in the Pillared House in the square; he raised the whole of France against the monarchy, sacked the Palace on the Ile de la Cité, encouraged the English and Navarrese invaders, and was killed by the Parisians the following year. However, the Mayor of Paris and the municipal assembly did not have much authority under the Valouis or Bourbons, nor indeed until the Revolution, when the Committee of Public Safety met here.

Robespierre was arrested here in 1793 by the patrols which he himself had instigated to safeguard the Revolution and which were in many people's minds the start of the Terror. In 1837 Carlyle put it in his own inimitable style: 'O Sea-Green Incorruptible, canst thou not see where this Patrollotism leadeth? O Patrollotism! O Patrollotism!'

In 1830 Louis-Philippe was proclaimed king from the steps of the Hôtel de Ville, then a seventeenth-century building. When he fled eighteen years later, the Second Republic was proclaimed from the same place. Baron Haussmann, Prefect of the Seine, had his offices here when he was redesigning Paris into the city we know today. The Commune had their headquarters here in 1871 and, on departing, burnt the building to the ground.

The present **town hall** was finished in 1882, an example of Third Republic architecture, a blend of Renaissance and Belle Epoque.

The outside is encrusted with 136 statues. Guided tours of the inside are available on Mondays at 10.30 a.m. We shall find a great staircase, chandeliers, coffered ceilings, statues and caryatids by the dozen; we can console ourselves with a Rodin bust ('La République') and some caricatures by Willette. At the river end of the building are the offices of the elected Mayor of Paris, at present Jacques Chirac.

Behind the Hôtel de Ville we find a remarkable church, **Saint-Gervais et Saint-Protais**, both Roman soldiers martyred by Nero. What we see is a vast classical façade which might be a lecturer's slide of the three orders of classical architecture, Doric columns at the bottom, Ionic on the first storey and Corinthian on the second. It is the earliest classical façade in Paris, finished in 1621, and behind it is a beautiful Gothic church which was not finished till 1657. The two styles of architecture do not mix at all well, to my mind, but obviously others must disagree, since both were being built at the same time.

The inside is well worth a visit for its Gothic vaulting and its organ, built in 1601 and the oldest in Paris. Eight members of the Couperin family have held the post of organist here and made the church famous for its music. Just off the north transept is a fine Flemish painting of the Passion from the sixteenth century. In the Lady Chapel, behind the altar, is a hanging keystone, eight feet in diameter, like a floating crown. The church is now used by the Monastic Brotherhood of Jerusalem, who sing their offices in the Lady Chapel. The chanting of the brothers has replaced the playing of the Couperins. Saint-Gervais is built on a rise, with steps at either end. Its sixteenth-century belfry, floodlit at night, is another Seine landmark, visible from a considerable distance.

We return to the Seine at the nineteenth-century Pont Louis-Philippe, and continue along the Quai. On our left is a long modern building (1965), the **Cité des Arts**. This provides accommodation and facilities for artists and composers, foreign as well as French. Nobody is allowed to stay there more than a year; by this time the artist is expected to have found a niche elsewhere. The Cité des Arts helps to combat the loneliness of the creative artist and provides opportunities for his work to be shown or heard by other artists and by anyone whom he can cajole into coming along. The underground art gallery is sometimes used by outside groups. The concrete façade, however, pleases nobody; fortunately in summer it is mainly concealed by trees.

Immediately beyond, there is a large gravel area called, for some reason, the Square Albert Schweitzer. Behind it we can see the Hôtel d'Aumont, with Mansart's austere façade. On our right is the mediæval Hôtel de Sens. We are now skirting the area of old Paris called the Marais, full of big *hôtels* and narrow streets; but this requires a separate chapter. In the meantime we should continue along the Quai des Célestins. At No.32, now a modern office block, was once the Barbeau Tower, guarding the eastern entrance to Paris like the Tournelle on the left bank.

Continuing along the Quai, we note the house on the corner of the Rue des Jardins-Saint-Paul. Rabelais died here in 1553, as a plaque records. At the end of the Quai is the little Square Henri Galli with a children's playground and the remaining stones from the Bastille prison, moved here from the original site. Their size gives some idea of that formidable fortress. To reach the Place de la Bastille, where it stood, we must walk (or take a bus) along the Boulevard Henri IV.

The Bastille is a legendary name in French and indeed world history. Frenchmen often say, 'I must do this or I shall be sent to the Bastille', hardly knowing what they are saying. The details of exactly what happened on 14 July 1789 have been overlaid by revolutionary propaganda, popular myth, romantic novels and historical films. Yet the words 'Quatorze Juillet' can still fire the French imagination and the Fête Nationale is celebrated in France in a way which is hardly comprehensible across the Channel. Processions, bands, fireworks, dancing in the streets – we can all take part in the rejoicing of a great city. The Place also has a lasting association with defiance and protest, and many demos and marches (*manifs*) begin or end at the Bastille. And all this because 633 men captured an almost disused and undefended detention centre.

The **Bastille Saint-Antoine** was built in 1370 as a fortress to guard Paris and provide a safe residence for the king, Charles V. Like the Tower of London, it served several purposes. It had eight towers and high walls, and its vast bulk dominated the whole area. Yet it was besieged several times and only once did it manage to hold out – it was not as large or formidable as it looked. In the seventeenth

154

century Richelieu converted it into a prison, for which it was not very suitable as it held only fifty prisoners.

However, they were special prisoners, guilty of irritating somebody important, or of suspected insanity. Untried, they were sent to the Bastille by a *lettre de cachet*, a blank order signed by the king, the names to be filled in by anybody who might get hold of one. Voltaire's father filled one in to imprison his son and prevent his marrying a Protestant; however, he changed his mind and tore it up. But Voltaire was twice in the Bastille for impertinence and writing malicious verse. He whiled away the first time by writing a tragedy, *Œdipe*. The Marquis de Sade spent time there, before being transferred to the Charenton asylum. Nobody knows to this day the name on the *lettre de cachet* of the mysterious Man in the Iron Mask, though there have been many guesses.

The system of *lettres de cachet* was obviously a great abuse of personal liberty, a threat hanging over the head of every independent-minded citizen. It was much attacked and finally abolished in 1784, five years before the fall of the Bastille. But the *lettres* were revived in the Empire and Napoleon's Police Chief, Fouché, made use of them as never before – but not for the Bastille, which was no more.

The Bastille was not the Conciergerie. There was no shame attached to being there and no fearful death awaited its prisoners. They lived for the most part in considerable comfort. They had their own servants and entertained guests. One, the Cardinal de Rohan, gave a dinner party for twenty at the state's expense. Indeed, expense was one of the factors which made Louis XVI decide in 1784 to close the prison. In its place there was to be a big square to honour him, as the Place Vendôme honoured Louis XIV. The Bastille was to be demolished, except for one symbolic tower. Beside it was to be a huge statue of the King, holding out his hand in mercy. The plans were never carried out; they can be seen in the Hôtel Carnavalet (see Chapter 10). But the Bastille legend had started.

Early on 14 July the mob, of which only 200 were Parisians, inflamed by Desmoulins' speeches, by the King's dismissal of the popular minister Necker, and by looted wine, marched to the Invalides where they captured a number of muskets, but little ammunition. A rumour went round that there were more than a hundred barrels of gunpowder in the Bastille. Shouting '*À la Bastille*' they marched off, thinking more of powder and shot than of liberating prisoners.

On arrival they burned the outlying buildings and fired at the walls. The Governor, the Marquis de Launay, was in a dilemma. Though the walls were thick enough, he commanded only thirty-two Swiss guards and a larger number of French pensioners. Talks were held, followed by more shooting, more talks and an assault on the main gate. In the late afternoon the Governor decided to surrender. The Swiss stacked their arms in the courtyard and the Governor handed over the keys, which immediately became symbols of the people's victory; the key of the main gate was given by Lafayette to George Washington. Without their help the mob smashed its way in but, to its dismay, found no arms or powder. Somebody remembered the prisoners, but there were only seven there, forgers or lunatics. These were paraded round in carts to their great bewilderment. The Governor and some of the Swiss guards were lynched.

Such were the events of the great day. The King wrote in his diary: '*Rien!*' – it had been a blank day's hunting. Charles James Fox wrote in a letter dated 30 July: 'How much the greatest event it is that ever happened in the world! and how much the best!' Both comments may seem to us somewhat exaggerated.

Forty-one years later, almost to the day, it was all to do again. In the Bastille area, the Faubourg Saint-Antoine, there were three days of street fighting at the barricades in July 1830, at the end of which Charles X, the reactionary Bourbon king who had 'learned nothing and forgotten nothing' was dethroned and the bourgeois king Louis-Philippe put in his place, the so-called July monarchy. The fierce fighting, costing over six hundred lives, has been described by Victor Hugo in the 'Petit Gavroche' episode of his novel *Les Misérables*; and by Delacroix in his picture in the Louvre.

Eighteen years later the Saint-Antoine barricades were up again, and this time the Archbishop of Paris was among the casualties. Louis-Philippe was replaced by the Second Republic, which soon gave way to the Second Empire. There had been three revolutions here in sixty years and they had all led to autocratic dictatorships – as do all revolutions everywhere.

In the centre of the huge Place stands the July Column, a solitary spike 170 feet high and surmounted by a winged and male Mercury (and not by 'La Liberté', as is sometimes said). It is closed to the public. There are a number of Frenchmen who regret the disappearance of the old Bastille; it would have made a fine historical monument, open to the public, probably with *son et lumière*. Paris has gained her National Day and a legend, but she has lost her 'Tower of London'.

Efforts are being made to provide other attractions in the area. The projected Opéra de la Bastille is due to be opened in July 1989, on the site of the old station. The winning design, chosen by an international jury, is by Carlos Ott, a Canadian-Uruguayan architect, almost unknown in France. It carefully combines simplicity and a modest appearance with the most sophisticated modern equipment. But doubts are expressed whether Paris needs yet another opera house – especially as the present Opéra is to remain open for concerts and ballet – and whether the Bastille is the right site for such an ambitious project. Nine hundred and sixty thousand seats a year will be available, but who is to sit there? Another prestige project is a Yacht Club on the adjoining Arsénal Canal, but details are not yet disclosed. Doubts have been expressed about this, too: whether it is the right amenity for a workaday area, many of whose inhabitants work in the cheap furniture trade of the Faubourg Saint-Antoine.

A typical street of the area is the **Rue de la Roquette**, leading off the main Place; narrow, winding, full of small businesses, the façades of the buildings being gradually cleaned and restored. We should take the first turning right into the **Rue de Lappe**. This is old and picturesque and we should note the wrought-iron balconies, some curved, some straight. There are several *bal musette* dancehalls, probably with accordion bands; also small restaurants and shops specializing in Auvergne food (sausages, tripe, cheese and Cahors wine). The clog (*sabot* or *galoche*) is the symbol of Auvergne and we shall see many in the street for decoration or sale. One small shop sells both clogs and Auvergne sausages.

However, if we do not wish to eat *tripoux*, we should go elsewhere. For many the chief attraction of the area is the Brasserie Bofinger in the Rue de la Bastille. As we circle the Place on our way there, we should note the names of the Boulevards which now meet at Bastille: Henri IV, rather off course, though the Hôtel de Sully (see Chapter 10) in the Rue Saint-Antoine may account for it; Richard Lenoir, an unknown workman (why, it was asked, should boulevards always be called after famous people?) and Beaumarchais, the playwright, whose statue stands in the Rue Saint-Antoine at the corner of the Rue de la Bastille.

Beaumarchais would certainly have wished to be remembered in this area, but not for the obvious reason. His plays satirize the aristocracy and their way of life. In *The Marriage of Figaro*, the barber-turned-valet savages his master Count Almaviva with the words *'Vous vous êtes donné la peine de naître, et rien de plus'* – hardly a respectful greeting from a servant to his lord. But then the dialogue of Beaumarchais was intended to attack the whole principle of aristocracy. Yet his revolutionary spirit was distinctly at odds with his personal life. A watchmaker named Caron, he changed his name to Monsieur de Beaumarchais. A middleman in the slave trade, an arms dealer in the American War of Independence, he had made himself one of the richest men in France. Shortly before the Revolution he built himself a sumptuous *hôtel* opposite the Bastille – the other Bastille, it has been called. Here he proposed to entertain the fashionable world in style, much like Theresia Cabarrus on the Ile Saint-Louis. But luxury homes, no matter to whom they belonged, did not find favour with the mob on 14 July, and many of them had the idea of sacking the place. However, Boulle tables and snuff-boxes, enticing though they were, did not have the same attraction as gunpowder, and the Hôtel Beaumarchais was spared and later forgotten. No trace of it now remains.

A few yards away is the Brasserie Bofinger. It calls itself the oldest brasserie in Paris and it began as a small draught-beer house in 1864. In 1919 it was much enlarged and redecorated in Style Rétro of twenty years before, which it still retains, complete with coloured glass, leather banquettes and Art Nouveau storks. There are plans by its new owner, Monsieur Alexandre, to expand it further to provide takeaway services and outside catering, especially for oysters, for which the restaurant is celebrated. Although it is large and spacious (with excellent service), it is usually full with hungry customers who come from all over Paris, especially so in the evenings with theatre-goers, although there are no theatres in the vicinity. Credit cards are much used.

Should we not wish to eat oysters or other seafood, we may try a *magret de canard au poivre vert, pommes sautées à cru*, and those with a sweet tooth may enjoy a *tarte tatin*, a hot apple and caramel tart.

Helpings at Bofinger's are large and afterwards we may not feel like a long walk, especially as the Boulevard Beaumarchais is not a very interesting avenue, even though it is the end of the Grands Boulevards. But we might get as far as No.21, where, through the railings, we can glimpse the fine classical façade of the Hôtel Mansart, built by Hardouin-Mansart in the late seventeenth-century for his own use. Otherwise we should take the metro direct to République.

We are now in the Temple area, once the stronghold of the Templars, the order suppressed and looted by Philip the Fair in 1314. Some of the land was given to the Knights of Malta, who were in turn suppressed in the Revolution. All that remained was the turreted Temple Tower, where Louis XVI and his family were imprisoned in August 1792. The following year the King was guillotined and his queen, Marie Antoinette, and his sister, Elisabeth, transferred to the Conciergerie (see Chapter 1). The young son, theoretically King Louis XVII, remained behind; in June 1795 a boy died mysteriously in the Temple, but it has never been established whether it was the young king (who was never seen again) or someone else. To prevent further investigations and possible pilgrimages, the tower was pulled down in 1808. Haussmann completed the work and all that remain now of the Temple are the street names.

The huge **Place de la République** is one of Haussmann's less happy inventions. It was part of his plan to open up Paris and discourage revolution and plotting, but it is now much used, like the Bastille and Nation squares, for demos and political marches. In 1958 de Gaulle proclaimed the constitution of the present Republic here, rather than in one of the more obvious places. The enormous statue of *La République* in the centre is by Morice (1883) and the plaques round the base show events from the previous hundred years.

However, we are still on the Grands Boulevards. A little way down the Boulevard du Temple is the **Cirque d'Hiver**, the last of the many circuses which once abounded in the area. It is a permanent building (hence the name) and still active, but it is on the small side and the more spectacular circuses have to go to the Palais des

Sports, at the extremity of Paris. At the corner of the Place de la République and the Boulevard Saint-Martin is the **Caveau de la République**, one of the last two *chansonniers* left in Paris (see Chapter 20). For refreshment we have the new Holiday Inn, whose restaurant has the nerve to call itself 'La Belle Epoque'! However, it provides a good lunchtime buffet.

Back in the metro, we take the train direct to **Père Lachaise**, Paris's famous cemetery, visited by thousands of tourists every year, as well as by those who have business there. Père Lachaise was the confessor of Louis XIV and gave generously to the Jesuit house of retreat, which became nicknamed after him. Under Napoleon it became a municipal cemetery and for nearly two hundred years it has been the fashionable place to be buried. Marshals, politicians, writers, painters, composers, philosophers, singers, together with thousands of ordinary French people. There are nearly a million graves and the cemetery extends for more than a hundred acres; on undulating ground, it is landscaped with 12,000 trees. It was here that the survivors of the Commune made their last stand in May 1871, shooting among the graves. The 147 survivors were shot against the Federalists Wall, at the north-east corner, at dawn the following morning and buried in a common grave, now an object of political veneration.

However, as we wander along the cobbled paths of the cemetery, lined by thousands of tombs, like stone bathing-huts, our minds are less likely to be on revolutionary violence than on autumnal peace and melancholy. The best time to go is in October, when the chestnuts have turned and a grey light filters through the yellow leaves. Every year at Toussaint (1 November) French people flock to the cemeteries to lay chrysanthemums on their family graves. We should do well to go a week or two before this, if we want the quiet solitude necessary to appreciate the atmosphere. But we shall not find it completely, as there will be other visitors, including mothers pushing prams.

The most romantic spot, undoubtedly, is Chopin's grave, with the falling ground and the trees meeting overhead; the tomb is beautiful too, with its mourning nymph. There will be many flowers and probably a group being eloquently lectured about the 'Raindrop' prelude. Chopin chose the site himself, near the grave of his friend Bellini, and a little of the earth here is soil from Poland, brought by

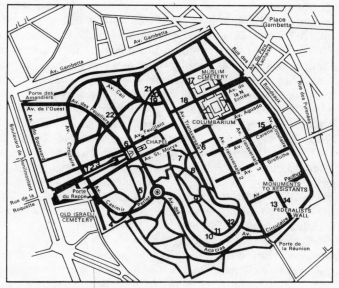

Père Lachaise Cemetery

1) Colette
2) Rossini (cenotaph)
3) Baron Haussmann
4) Abelard and Heloïse
5) Chopin
6) David
7) Corot
8) Molière and La Fontaine

9) Hugo family
10) Marshal Ney
11) Beaumarchais
12) Murat and C. Bonaparte
13) Modigliani
14) Edith Piaf
15) Oscar Wilde
16) Sarah Bernhardt

17) Marcel Proust
18) Guillaume Apollinaire
19) Delacroix
20) Gérard de Nerval
21) Balzac
22) Bizet

the composer himself in a silver box when he left Poland aged twenty-one. He was always 'half in love with easeful death', half in love with his native land.

The biggest names do not always have the biggest tombs. Delacroix and Colette have simple slabs, Apollinaire a rough-hewn dolmen. The most lavish sepulchres have probably the least known names, but much of the sculpture is striking in itself: sad, naked ladies, holding flowers or books, sitting on the edge of graves or beds – in one case actually in bed. The withered flowers, the dog-eared books, the rumpled bedclothes are faithfully carved in stone or marble. At the Rond-Point there is an eerie piece, a veiled ghost beside a barred window; whether the spirit is trying to get in or out is unclear.

One of the most dramatic tombs is Epstein's monument to Oscar

161

Wilde, donated by an anonymous lady admirer. The big sculpture shows a winged pharaoh, flying from one world to the other. Impressive indeed, though its connection with Wilde is not easy to see. On the reverse side is an inscription giving the bare facts of his birth, education and death and – in case we might have forgotten that he was a writer – four lines from 'The Ballad of Reading Gaol'. Wilde's grave naturally attracts some rather special visitors, and the tomb has been marked by graffiti, and the pharaoh castrated.

Under the gravestones lie many romances, some known only to their families, some to all the world. Abelard and Héloïse are here, together at last, though their grave is hard to find. (A map is essential, since the cemetery is not signposted, except for a few unhelpful 'street names' like Avenue des Peupliers.) But everyone will direct us to Edith Piaf's grave, surrounded by flowers. She lies there with her young husband Théo, for whose career she sacrificed her health and, indeed, her life.

Across the way lies Modigliani with his girlfriend, Jeanne Hébuterne, the mother of his daughter; we know her Gothic face and fair plaits well from his portraits. Modi died in 1920, aged thirty-six, killed by his bohemian life, by drink, drugs, tuberculosis and poverty. But recognition had come to him before the end and all Montparnasse was here at his funeral. But not Jeanne. Hearing of his death in hospital, she rushed to the morgue and covered his dead face with kisses, even though it was a mass of open sores. She was dragged away and went to her parents' home, from which she had been expelled some years before. After a bitter altercation she threw herself off the roof, even though she was almost nine months pregnant with a second child. Her parents refused to let her be buried with Modi; nevertheless they are together now. The slab has a touching inscription in Italian.

Chopin, Wilde, Piaf – but the greatest number of pilgrims are at the grave of Allan Kardec (near Delacroix's grave). They stand round the thousands of flowers, praying. One by one they go round to touch the left shoulder of his bust, their eyes closed. Kardec was the father of modern spiritualism. After this experience we may find it a relief to see the down-to-earth features of Balzac a little way away.

CHAPTER 10

The Marais

The Marais is the 'lost' quarter of Paris. It is hard to find and hard to find one's way around; even taxis get lost here. Public transport is remote and walking is the best way of getting about. Yet it is very rewarding. The Marais contains Paris's oldest square, which to many people, including myself, is the most beautiful. There are many fine seventeenth-century houses, with elaborate façades and courtyards, some of which we can visit. There are narrow, winding old streets and a population which has been there for centuries, probably the descendants of coachmen and housemaids and still looking like the *jacquerie*. And, permeating everything, there is the sense of history, the feeling that we may well meet a Guise or a Valois on the next corner, who will certainly challenge us to a duel.

The word *marais* means a marsh and that was what it was, a swamp on the right bank of the Seine, unhealthy and often flooded. Attempts had been made to drain it since the sixth century AD, with little success. In the twelfth century, King Philippe-Auguste enclosed it inside his great wall of Paris, of which a long section can still be seen here. In the following century, the marsh was finally drained and permanent building started.

Charles V (1364–80) was the first king to live here. He built more walls and two *hôtels*, the Tournelles and Saint-Paul, now both lost. He, and many of his successors, thought that the Marais, protected by the city walls and the Bastille, was a safer place to live than the Ile de la Cité or the Louvre. But it was in the seventeenth century that the great building boom began. Henri IV decreed a new square for the area on the site of the ruined Tournelles. When completed, in the reign of his son, Louis XIII, the square, the Place des Vosges, became the fashionable part of Paris. The nobility and the *nouveaux riches* built themselves imposing houses; indeed, the idea of an

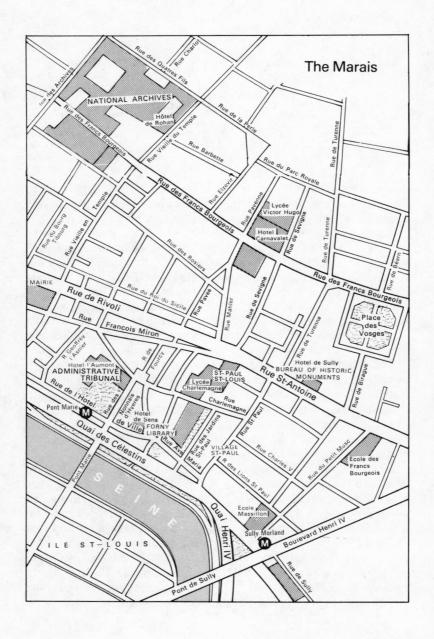

The Marais

elegant town house, not a palace, not a château, but simply a house to live in, was a novelty in itself. The architects of the time, Le Vau, François Mansart, Jules Hardouin-Mansart and others, excelled themselves in building beautifully proportioned houses which looked to the Classical rather than the Gothic tradition. The age of French Baroque had begun.

Something else had begun too, the idea of a civilized, urban society which was distinct from the court or country estates. The seventeenth and eighteenth centuries were the great time of the *salons*. The party conversation in these *hôtels* would be sophisticated, thoughtful, witty and often advanced in its thinking, much concerned with politics, philosophy and the arts; a long way indeed from Versailles' wars and hunting. Richelieu invited many of the more prominent members to join the French Academy, and among the names of those who haunted the *salons* over the years we may note Madame de Maintenon (Madame Scarron, as she was then), Madame de Sévigné, Ninon de Lenclos, Molière, Racine and Voltaire. For about a hundred and fifty years the Marais was the glittering intellectual centre of France.

All this came to an end, here at least, with the Revolution. The Marais was too close to the Bastille for comfort and it began to get a bad name as a rough district. The fashionable world moved further west and the Marais fell into a state of shocking dilapidation from which it seemed it would never re-emerge. However, Malraux's efforts to clean Paris have had a noticeable effect in the Marais, as elsewhere. The façades of the ordinary houses as well as the *hôtels* are being cleaned and restored. Flats are being modernized to attract a better class of owner or tenant. Cultural events are being organized. To walk along the Rue François-Miron or the Rue des Francs-Bourgeois is now a pleasure, even though some of the inhabitants may have preferred it the way it was ten or twenty years ago.

The *hôtels* are more of a problem. Twenty-nine have disappeared over the centuries, but a hundred still remain. They are nearly all of historic or architectural interest, protected from redevelopment. Some house museums, libraries, the National Archives, cultural centres and schools. Others are derelict. The Hôtel Salé, 5 Rue Thorigny, after a period of occupation by *clochards* and squatters, is being turned into a Picasso museum, though we may wonder if a seventeenth-century *hôtel* is the right setting for this particular artist. The opening is planned for 1985. Meanwhile the Picassos remain in store or on tour.

Many of the *hôtels* have been cleaned, restored and put to good use and we shall see several of them during our visit. I suggest that our walk should begin at Metro Pont Marie, beside the Seine. Standing with our backs to the river, we see, across a playground and a formal French garden, the façade of the **Hôtel d'Aumont**. This correct, though rather severe, *hôtel* was originally built in 1645 by Le Vau for Monsieur Scarron, one of the earlier enthusiasts of the Marais. It was altered and redecorated inside by François Mansart on the orders of Marshal d'Aumont, Scarron's son-in-law. The house is now occupied by the Administrative Tribunal and not open to the public, except for the main courtyard which we reach by the Rue des Nonnais d'Hyères, the street on our right.

The steep roofs with dormer windows are typical of Mansart and have been called after him. The courtyard itself, which is open to the public, is less severe than the façade, decorated with garlands and masks, as is the rounded entrance arch.

Returning towards the river we find on our left the **Hôtel de Sens**. This is in startling contrast to the Hôtel d'Aumont, being still Gothic in style. It is in fact much earlier in date, built between 1475 and 1507, and is one of the only two remaining Gothic secular houses left in Paris – the Hôtel de Cluny on the Left Bank is the other. Even at the time it must have seemed something of an anachronism, with its turrets, gables and battlements. Perhaps the explanation lies in the fact that it was built as the Paris residence of the Archbishop of Sens.

Outdated though it may have been, we can enjoy a glimpse of mediæval Paris, especially the side overlooking the very formal French garden. Every afternoon (except Sundays and Mondays) we can enter the courtyard through the flamboyant Gothic porch to see the square tower with its *bretesse*, a kind of battlemented balcony. We can also go inside, since the *hôtel* houses the **Forney Library**, which is mainly concerned with the technology of art and architecture, including a good collection of technical magazines.

While thumbing through these, we can recall that it was in one of these quiet reading rooms that Cardinal Pellève, in 1594, died of rage while a *Te Deum* was being sung in Notre-Dame to celebrate

166

Henri IV's entry into Paris. Eleven years later the King allowed his first wife, Margot de Valois, the daughter of Queen Catherine de Medici, to return to Paris after long years of exile in the Auvergne. Aged fifty-three, very fat and sexy, she resided here with her lovers. In 1606 the Count of Vermont, the current lover, jealously killed her young page, Dal de Saint-Julien, who was replacing him. The murder occurred in the royal carriage and two days later Vermont was beheaded in front of the *hôtel* on the Queen's orders.

Later Margot built herself her own palace on the Left Bank, facing the Louvre (see Chapter 4), where she continued her scandalous and violent life. The Hôtel de Sens at one time became the Paris terminal of the Lyons stage-coach, a journey famous for its danger. And from this glimpse of history we return to the present day and our technical magazine.

We walk along the Rue Ave Maria, past the Rue des Jardins Saint-Paul and turn left into the **Village Saint-Paul**, which is well-signed. This is an example of the 'New Marais'; a cobbled pedestrian area of interlinking old courtyards with trees and shrubs. Below are antique shops and cafés, upstairs are flats. It must be a quiet and pleasant place to live in and one hopes that the antique shops will be successful, though they are rather off the beaten track. We emerge through one of the archways into the Rue des Jardins-Saint-Paul. Facing us, across a school playground, is a long section of Philippe-Auguste's wall, a formidable piece of masonry. At the end of the street is a fine view of the dome of Saint-Paul.

At the end we turn right into the delightful Rue Charlemagne and then left into the Rue Saint-Paul. On either side there are pleasant glimpses of little streets, the *impasses* of old Paris. At the end is the **Rue Saint-Antoine**, the main street of the Marais and for many centuries the widest street in Paris. It is in fact the eastern end of the Rue de Rivoli, which we first met at the Place de la Concorde, but it looks very different here, a busy workaday market street where much of the business is conducted on pavement stalls.

However, it has a good deal of historical interest, going back to Roman Paris, when it was raised above the marsh, the only solid street in the town. We shall note the church of **Saint-Paul-Saint-Louis**, built in the seventeenth century by the Jesuits on land given to them by Louis XIII. Architecturally the fine dome is of interest, one of the first church domes since classical times. The façade, with columns, is also neo-Classical. The twin water-stoups inside the entrance were given, surprisingly, by Victor Hugo. Who would have thought that a famous anti-clericalist would wish at any time to make gifts to Catholic ritual! But Hugo was a man who moved on several different levels of thought and emotion.

At No.62 Rue Saint-Antoine we find the **Hôtel de Sully**, one of the finest of the Marais *hôtels*, which has recently been well restored. The imposing street façade consists of a large gateway, with two large pavilions and a gallery. Inside we find a courtyard, a splendid example of Marais architecture. Beautifully proportioned, the courtyard has carved pediments, dormer windows, statues of the four seasons, the four elements, (female nudes, of course) and two sphinxes. Less severe than some *hotels*, it manages to avoid a feeling of clutter and the name of its architect, Jean Androuet du Cerceau, should be better known.

The inside is open to the public on Wednesday, Saturday and Sunday afternoons (guided tours). Of note are the panelling and painted ceilings in Sully's study and bedroom, which look out on to the garden; the decoration is not strictly contemporary but is thought to date from soon after his death in 1641. The floral tapestries are, however, thought to be contemporary with him and have recently been recovered from his château on the Loire.

The *hôtel* was built in 1624 for a notorious gambler called Petit Thouars, who lost his whole fortune in one night. Ten years later it was bought by Sully, the former minister of Henri IV. He was then seventy-five and no longer able to satisfy his young wife Rachel, who had nine children by various lovers. Sully tolerated all this with good grace, doling out money for his wife, the housekeeping and the lovers, provided that these last were kept away from the main staircase. He himself preferred more intellectual company. On a later occasion Voltaire, dining at the Hôtel de Sully, was called to the main door by a visitor – only to find himself well thrashed by lackeys of the Chevalier de Rohan, whom he had insulted in his verses.

The Hôtel de Sully often has temporary exhibitions, usually dealing with scenes from French city life. It also has the information office of the **Bureau of Historic Monuments**. This helpful office will provide information and booklets about the Marais *hôtels* and much else.

Androuet de Cerceau was also responsible for the **Hôtel de Mayenne**, further along the street at No.21. This was built for Charles de Lorraine, the son of the Duc de Guise, who was the great enemy of Henri IV and Sully. But, architecturally, the two *hôtels* have much in common, in plan and in decoration. The Hôtel de Mayenne is now a school and a chemist, with neon signs. The fine façade is badly in need of restoration.

In the sixteenth century this part of the Rue Saint-Antoine was often used for tournaments and jousting, in particular by King Henri II. The road was wide and strong enough for galloping chargers. But in 1559 the King, jousting with Count Montgomery, the captain of his guard, got Montgomery's lance through his eye. He was carried to his room in the nearby Hôtel de Tournelles, where he died. His queen, Catherine de Medici, in her fury, ordered the Tournelles to be destroyed. Montgomery, however, managed to escape to England. But, fifteen years later, he rashly returned to France, leading a Protestant force to support the Huguenots. He was captured, imprisoned and beheaded. The Medici queen had waited a long time for her revenge, but she had it in the end.

From jousting to duelling is only a short step and the Marais became the favourite place for duels. And it was beside the ruins of the Tournelles that the most famous and terrible duel in French history took place.

Henri III was the favourite son of Catherine de Medici, the youngest of three decadent and childless brothers. It is said that he was brave in battle and interested in the arts; but he is best remembered for his sexual perversion. He often appeared in woman's clothes and he filled the Louvre with his *mignons* (darlings or boyfriends). These young men behaved outrageously, with extravagant manners, screaming insults or compliments at each other, playing cup and ball, gaudily dressed as parrots – indeed, the palace resembled a parrot-house. Sometimes the *mignons* would flagellate each other for the King's pleasure. Many people could not stand them, especially the Guise family, but the King loved them all dearly, especially little Quélus, his favourite.

One day in April 1578 three Guises challenged three *mignons* including Quélus, a challenge which could not be refused. They met at dawn the following morning at the Tournelles. The Guises were in sober black, the *mignons* wearing their full finery, jewels, silks, velvet cloaks, the lot. They bowed elaborately to everyone and then the fight began. It was a sword and dagger affair and the Guises soon found that they had underestimated their opponents. The darlings fought with the greatest ferocity. Of the six duellists, four died *sur le champ*, Quélus, with nineteen wounds lived on for a month and the only survivor, a Guise, was crippled for life. The King was in tears and mourning until his own assassination.

Duelling was forbidden by Richelieu, but many felt that honour or self-defence were more important than the decrees of a not very popular Cardinal. On 22 June 1627 François de Montmorency-Bouteville, seconded by the Comte de Chapelle, fought two other noblemen, Beuvron and Bussy d'Amboise in the Place des Vosges. Richelieu was living at the time at No.21 and the duel took place under his windows; it was indeed an act of provocation. Beuvron was killed and Montmorency-Bouteville and de Chapelle were arrested. Despite appeals by other members of the nobility, they were executed and their headless bodies taken to Montmorency-Bouteville's home, the Hôtel Lamoignan in the Rue Pavée.

Despite this, duelling continued and in the century which followed became something of an epidemic. A gentleman had to be a good swordsman to survive either the formal duels with seconds or the casual street brawls; nobody wished to be set on by the lackeys of another house. The vendettas gradually ceased with time, but the duels for honour continued, although swords gave way to pistols and the preferred site moved to the greater seclusion of the Bois de Boulogne. The most recent duel, and probably the last, took place twenty years ago, when two politicians fired formally at each other in the Bois, much to the annoyance of President de Gaulle, who thought such behaviour unseemly in responsible men. Such is the changing code of manners.

We turn left off the Rue Saint-Antoine into the Rue de Birague and, passing through an archway under the King's Pavilion, we arrive in the splendid **Place des Vosges**. It was the idea of Henri IV who wished to replace the ruined Tournelles and transform the Marais into a royal area. He would himself live in the big house on the south side (under which we have just passed) and his estranged wife, Marie de Medici, in a similar building on the other side. Building began in 1605, by the architect Clément Metezeau, and it was finished in 1612, two years after the King's assassination, in the reign of his son, Louis XIII. It was named the Place Royale, though in fact no king ever lived there, Henri IV's sons preferring the Louvre and his grandson Versailles and elsewhere. During the Revolution it was renamed the Place of Indivisibility, and under Napoleon the Place des Vosges, in honour of the first *département* to pay its taxes. Under the Bourbon restoration and the Second Empire it became the Place Royale again, and then after 1870 reverted to the Place des Vosges.

Metezeau's plan is totally symmetrical. The thirty-six houses or *pavillons*, nine on each side, are of brick and stone, with steep slate roofs and dormer windows. On ground level is a stone arcade running right round the square and here there are some antique shops and art galleries and restaurants. In the centre is a garden, a French garden of gravel, lawns, trees and a statue – though some commentators have thought it not French enough; that the trees, particularly the four big central chestnuts, are too big, spoil the view and hide the statue. This statue is of Louis XIII, in Roman clothes on horseback, but the original was destroyed in the Revolution and the present statue, by Dupaty and Cortot, dates from the last century.

The garden is a very pleasant place, especially in spring and autumn when the maligned chestnuts are coming out or turning. Children hang upside down on the parallel bars of the playground, mothers knit, and young people read. Under the arches, or, in colder weather, inside, we can eat or drink. On the east side, the restaurant La Chope des Vosges is medium-priced and has a pleasing three-level seventeenth-century decor. The *tarte tatin* is particularly good. On the west side the café-brasserie Ma Bourgogne is more modest. Inhabitants of the square like to breakfast here on Sunday mornings, especially in summer under the arcade; this is an agreeable and sociable occasion.

The square was officially opened in 1612 with a big tournament in honour of Louis XIII's marriage to Anne of Austria, and of his sister to a Spanish prince. The tournament went on for three days and was called the *Chevaliers de la Gloire*. According to contemporary prints, it was a lavish affair. Because of or perhaps despite the tournaments and duels, the Place Royale became the fashionable place to live. The great king might be dead, his sad, near-impotent son elsewhere, but Richelieu lived there from 1615 to 1627. French society moved in to the magnificent new houses; *Tout-Paris* (as it is now called) had arrived.

The central garden became a parade of elegance and big receptions, the first *salons* were held in the large first-floor rooms. The sword was giving way to the pen, or at least to the tongue. Many receptions were held in No.9, the home of the Duc de Chaulnes and, later, of the actress Rachel. It is now the Academy of Architecture. Madame de Sévigné was born at No.1 *bis* in 1626. More than two centuries later the house became the Paris home of the rich and eccentric Singer family – eccentric because the Marais was no longer a fashionable place. I recall dining there; the huge, dark, candlelit room with a minstrels' gallery running right round; the feeling that everyone ought to have been wearing clothes like the Three Musketeers and carrying swords. But in fact both the conversation and the food would have given more pleasure to Madame de Sévigné than to the Duc de Guise.

The Place Royale was also the centre of a group who called themselves *Les Précieuses*. They practised an affected, mannered style of speaking and writing and laid down lists of words which might or might not be used. The French are fond of laying down detailed laws for literature, art, cooking, fashion and so on. When somebody breaks these laws, there is usually a scandal and the miscreant, whether deliberate or not, is abused. However, a new impetus has been given and possibly a new movement or fashion started. One of the reasons why Victor Hugo's tragedy *Hernani* came to grief in 1830 was that he used the forbidden word *mouchoir* (we may wonder how the Précieuses would have staged *Othello*, not that the occasion ever arose.)

Hugo himself lived in No.6 from 1833 to 1848, before his exile in Guernsey. The first floor is a **Hugo museum**; the second floor, where he actually lived, is now closed to the public. Nevertheless the museum is of great interest to admirers of Hugo, especially his drawings and self-designed furniture. Théophile Gautier, who lived next door at No.8, has described how Hugo would take an ordinary household object, even an ink-blot, and make a drawing out of it. These 'doodles' are fascinating psychologically and they show us the black, Gothic side of his nature. They are nightmare fantasies of weird, twisted castles and towers, huge gnarled trees, everything seen in chiaroscuro against moonlight or storm. There is also an alarmingly prophetic giant mushroom. This is the dark night of Hugo's soul, the hunchback-and-sewers aspect of his character. It is a long way from his feeling for the sky, for the beauty of nature, for the great trees of Villequier and for freedom.

His furniture is equally weird. We do not know why he wanted to take cabinets and dressers and put them together, turning them into mock-Gothic court-cupboards of mixed style. The result is interesting rather than enjoyable. To see beautiful furniture we shall have to walk the few yards to the **Hôtel Carnavalet** at No.23 Rue de Sévigné.

Even without being a museum, the Hôtel Carnavalet would be worth seeing as an example of Marais architecture. It was originally built for President de Ligneris in 1548. The keystone of the entrance and the porch pediment are the work of Jean Goujon, whose pupils sculpted the Allegories of the Seasons between the windows of the main building. The next owner was a Breton nobleman, Monsieur de Kernevenoy, a well-known horseman written about by Montaigne and Ronsard; but the Parisians, who like to re-spell everything their own way, changed his name to its present form. The carnival mask, a visual pun, over the main entrance, was added later.

François Mansart in 1655 altered the building a good deal, adding another floor both to the street and side buildings. More reconstruction was done in the nineteenth century; the Nazarene arch, which previously spanned the Rue des Francs-Bourgeois, is now part of the *hôtel*, looking on to the street. Other façades, notably the Pavillon de Choiseul, were reconstructed. None of this much changed the appearance of the building, but important additions were made to the interior. Whole rooms were moved in from other *hôtels* in the Marais, preserving what might so easily have been lost. In particular we shall note the Gold Cabinet on the ground floor, the work of Le Vau and Van Obstal, which was originally in 14 Place des Vosges. From the same house comes the drawing-room with a ceiling showing Mercury introducing Psyche to the gods. The furniture has been collected from many *hôtels*, including the Temple, the apartments where the royal family were imprisoned (see Chapter 9). The statue of Louis XIV by Coysevox in the main courtyard comes from the Hôtel de Ville. The municipal council saved it from being destroyed at the Revolution by claiming it as their own property. The statue of Victory in front of the Pavillon de Choiseul was originally on top of the Châtelet fountain.

The museum is the municipal museum of Paris and devoted to the city. It is, incidentally, a good museum for children; the models of the sixteenth-century Ile de la Cité, the Bastille and the guillotine are striking, as are the old inn-signs which fill a whole room. But in general the ground floor is concerned with the Revolution and Empire, the first floor with the eighteenth century.

In Room 72 we cannot fail to be horrified by the portraits of three revolutionary leaders, which are hung together. Marat seems crazy, Robespierre mean and hard, and even the idealistic Danton gross and brutal. Beside these portraits, and contrasting strongly, is a Louis XVI inlaid chest-of-drawers, a masterpiece of elegance and an example of the civilization which the revolution was trying to destroy. In Room 80 we shall note the portrait of Madame Réca-mier by François Gérard (1805). Her sofa seems surprisingly small, almost a chair, unlike the famous one in her portrait in the Louvre.

On the first floor we shall enjoy the decoration and the furniture from the reigns of Louis XIV, Louis XV and Louis XVI, though the building is of course older. These suites of rooms look much as they must have done at the time. The furniture includes some *chinoiserie*, as popular in France as it was in England. Madame de Sévigné's apartments are on the south-east corner. Some of her own belongings have been preserved, and the rooms remind us strongly of the witty and warm-hearted woman, whose letters have helped us to appreciate her age and Marais life. She lived here from 1677 to 1696, with various members of her family (her husband had been killed in a duel), enjoying the Carnavalet and the *salons* of the Marais.

She has been called, rightly, the *grande dame* of the Marais. Born in the Place des Vosges, christened in Saint-Paul, married in Saint-Gervais, she felt most at home in the Carnavalet. However, when she was seventy and very rheumatic, she went to live with her disagreeable daughter, Madame de Grignan, in Provence, where she died and was buried. During the Revolution her body was dug up, beheaded and the skull brought back to Paris, where it disappeared. The reasons for this atrocity are not known; perhaps some sort of witchcraft, perhaps political hatred, a feeling that she should not be allowed to escape decapitation merely by being dead.

But the Carnavalet is where she would wish to be remembered. And it is here that we end our walk. We turn right at the main entrance, down the Rue de Sévigné, one of the prettiest streets in the Marais with the dome of Saint-Paul dominating it, to the Rue Saint-Antoine and the few steps to Metro Saint-Paul.

Our walk will have taken us through the most attractive parts of the Marais and shown us some of the best and best-known places. But there is much, much more to be seen in the Marais, some of it mainly for keen Marais-explorers. Within the limits of time and space available, we must be selective and brief. But here are some more *hôtels* of interest.

The **Hôtel de Rohan**. No.87 Rue Vieille du Temple. This is sometimes called the Hôtel de Strasbourg, because the three Cardinals de Rohan who lived here successively were also bishops of Strasbourg. The building dates from 1704 and has scarcely been altered since. The architect was Delamair and the Cardinal an intelligent young man, a friend of the king. The *hôtel* is a little later in date than some we have seen and the great façade on to the garden shows this. With its tall windows, columned porticoes, pediment and rather flat roof, it is very different from the Place des Vosges. The courtyard is more modest and leads to the stables. There, between the drinking troughs, we find Robert Le Lorrain's superb relief-sculpture, 'The Horses of the Sun'. Against a background of the sun's rays, four horses rear or drink from shells held by men who may be heroes or even gods.

Inside we can visit the Cardinal's apartments. The *grand salon* is the eighteenth century at its most splendid, and it contrasts with the little *Cabinet des Singes*, the Monkeys' Room, an entertaining example of popular chinoiserie, by Huet. The Aubusson tapestries in the suite, which also have Chinese motifs based on designs by Boucher, were not originally in the building. Of the smaller rooms the 'Fable Room', with its medallions, dates from 1738 and was originally in the nearby Hôtel de Soubise. The other small rooms are decorated and furnished in the same style – rococo. Some people love this, the climax of baroque; others find it overdone, frivolous, decadent and likely to provoke revolutions. But probably we should avoid judgment and simply accept it for what it is – decoration de luxe. Those wanting something more severe can enjoy the towers of the next *hôtel*.

175

The **Hôtel de Soubise** (No.60 Rue des Francs Bourgeois) also belonged to the Rohan family and is twinned with it – the same entrance ticket does for both. The Hôtel (or Palace) de Soubise has a long history and many architects and artists. On the corner are the fortified turrets of the original Clisson Manor (1380) which recall the Hôtel de Sens. The manor later became the property of the Guise family, who enlarged it and renamed it the Hôtel de Guise. In 1700 it was bought by François de Rohan, Prince de Soubise, for the enormous sum of 326,000 livres; and he commissioned Delamair to redesign it.

Delamair had ambitious ideas. He retained the old Clisson turrets, but he created the great courtyard on the site of the old riding-school and he added a majestic neo-classical façade to the Guise *hôtel*. This much-photographed façade is indeed imposing, with its double porticoes, its fifty-six double columns, the four statues of the seasons (only copies now) and the reclining statues on the pediment, suitably named 'Glory' and 'Magnificence'. The distinguished sculptor was Robert Le Lorrain.

The Prince was succeeded by his son, who lived in the Guise apartments behind the façade. But at the age of sixty he married a nineteen-year-old widow, Marie-Sophie de Courcillon. As a wedding present he gave her a new house, built on the site of the old Clisson keep. Boffrand, a pupil of François Mansart, was the architect and the best-known sculptors and artists, including Boucher, were employed. The result is a riot of rococo, especially in the Princess's apartments on the first floor; the Prince's on the ground floor are slightly more severe, as befitting his age (did they not live together?). We shall certainly enjoy the lushness of it all, the panelling, the ceilings, the chandeliers and, especially, the shape of the Oval rooms, Boffrand's original idea.

The **National Archives**, housed in both *hôtels*, contain about six thousand million documents kept on nearly two hundred miles of shelves. Some of the more interesting can be seen in the Historical Museum in the Hôtel de Soubise, which is open to the public every afternoon except Tuesdays. Here we can see, among other things, St Louis's Acts founding the Sainte-Chapelle and the University; the Edict of Nantes 1598, and its Revocation by Louis XIV, and Napoleon's will.

The **Hôtel des Ambassadeurs de Hollande** (No.42 Rue Vieille du

Temple) has a misleading name. It never had any connection with the Dutch Embassy, though one of their chaplains may have been a tenant. Its most famous occupant was Beaumarchais, who wrote *The Marriage of Figaro* there, in intervals of organizing his arms traffic and slave trade business (see Chapter 9).

The main portal is richly decorated by Regnaudin and covered with gorgons and allegorical figures representing War, Peace, Strength, Truth, Flora, Ceres and so on. Inside are two courtyards. In the first we should note the four painted sundials. The passage between the two courtyards is decorated with Mock-Tuscan pilasters and a *trompe l'oeil* painting hiding a blank wall. The *hôtel*, privately owned, is not open to the public and this is probably all the concierge will let us see.

The **Hôtel de Beauvais** (No.68 Rue François-Miron) has a colourful history. It was built in 1657 by Lepautre for Pierre de Beauvais and his wife, Catherine Bellier. She was the daughter of a porter in Les Halles and chambermaid to Queen Anne of Austria, the Queen Mother of Louis XIV. Catherine Bellier had the duty, among others, of giving the Queen her enema and, during this intimate activity, she became confidential enough to say with certainty that the young king, fifteen years old, was strongly sexed; she spoke from personal experience. The Queen, recalling her sad years with her inadequate husband, was delighted by the news. Honours ('de' Beauvais and the lordship of Chantilly) and wealth enough to buy two adjoining houses were showered on Madame de Beauvais, who continued to enjoy a full sex life into old age. The Queen had the pleasure of watching her son's wedding procession in 1660 from the windows and of knowing that all would be well.

A hundred years later the *hôtel* was the home of Count Eych, the Bavarian Ambassador, and it was in the drawing-room here that the seven-year-old Mozart gave his first Paris recital.

Lepautre's problem, as architect, was to design a building to fill the seventeen-sided site, and he showed remarkable skill. A wide corridor leads to a circular vestibule with Doric columns and a cupola; this, in turn leads to a triangular court ending in a loggia. Unfortunately the building was split up in the nineteenth century, so that the complete effect can no longer be seen. Much of the decoration, too, was lost, but we can still enjoy the main façade, the doorway and the richly decorated staircase. We should also note the pervading *motif* of rams' heads (*bélier*, a corruption of Catherine's maiden name, is the French for ram).

The **Arsénal** (No.1 Rue de Sully, Metro Sully-Morland) is one of the oldest *hôtels*. The arsenal of François I blew up in 1564 – the sound could be heard as far away as Melun – and Sully built a house for himself. Sully's successor, Marshal de la Meilleraye, took over the house and redecorated it for his marriage to Marie de Cosse. These rooms are some of the finest surviving examples of seventeenth-century style on view. In particular we should note the Cabinet des Femmes Fortes. The panels show military scenes and pictures of famous tough ladies, whom the bride was to emulate; all rather intimidating for the girl to have in her bedroom.

The contrast in centuries can be clearly seen when we move to the Duchesse de Maine's music room. A hundred years later the proportions are equally pleasing, but the decoration is infinitely more elaborate, especially the wood-carving. But, by using white, gold and pale colours, the rooms seem much lighter, if more artificial. The music room in the nineteenth century was the setting of the literary salon held by the librarian, Charles Nodier. Among the regular guests were Hugo, Vigny, Musset, Lamartine and Dumas.

The Arsénal was first used as a library during the Revolution and grew in size and importance until it is now the second biggest in France. Apart from a million books, it has a large collection of manuscripts, many of them illustrated, engravings and a unique collection of theatrical books, plays and annotated scripts. The library is open every weekday from 10.0 a.m. to 5.0 p.m.

CHAPTER 11

Montmartre

The skyline of Montmartre has been familiar to us ever since we arrived in Paris – or even before, since it is clearly visible from the train entering the Gare du Nord. The domes and the campanile stand on the highest point of Paris – 424 feet high, Montmartre, the Mount of Martyrs and known generally as *la Butte*, the hill. It is a steep hill with winding, stepped streets, squares and terraces with tremendous views and a funicular to ease our ascent and descent. We walk to it from Metro Abbesses, asking for '*La Butte*'. Montmartre was a country village, a windy one, to judge from the windmills, and it still preserves a good deal of that atmosphere, despite the tens of thousands of tourists. We can either go in the middle of the day, see the church and the view, explore the streets and then have lunch, or we can go up in the evening, dine and make a night of it. Most people do the latter, and we shall find the Place du Tertre very crowded at night.

Originally a sun-worship centre, it was later dedicated to Mercury, the favourite god of Gaul, and then to the martyrs who were beheaded there. The best known is St Denis (a corruption of Dionysius), the first Bishop of Paris and later its patron saint. About AD 250 he was tortured and decapitated there, after which he picked up his severed head and carried it a long way to the part of northern Paris where his basilica now is.

The basilica now standing on the summit of Montmartre is, however, not named after him, but after the Sacred Heart, the **Sacré-Cœur**. This huge church, better seen from a distance floating above the river mists on an autumn morning, was begun in 1876 and only finished in 1910. It was not consecrated until 1919. Many architects were involved, the original being Abadie, a specialist in Roman and Byzantine architecture. The interior is full of

179

Montmartre

mosaics, but the crypt is sometimes used for temporary exhibitions of modern religious art, of very different style. But the best thing about the basilica is the view from the main steps and the terrace. Luminous or hazy by day, twinkling by night, it is seen most romantically at dawn. And if, as is possible, we have spent the night in a Montmartre nightclub, we may well be there to see it.

Beside the Sacré-Cœur is **Saint-Pierre**, whose simple belfry is in great contrast to its neighbour's ponderous campanile. Saint-Pierre is all that remains of the big abbey of Montmartre and contains some old arches and stones which are said to have been originally in a Roman temple on the site. It also contains the tomb of Queen Adelaide, who had founded the abbey in 1133.

Many pilgrims still visit the area, especially on Good Friday, when the Archbishop of Paris does the Stations of the Cross which are scattered around the Butte, himself carrying a cross. But the thousands of tourists who visit the Butte every year do not usually go for religious reasons any more. They go for the views, the picturesque streets, the night-life and the reputation of Montmartre as a centre of art, which it no longer is.

The artists arrived on the Butte towards the end of the nineteenth century, though many of them were already in the Place Pigalle; painters, caricaturists, poets, singers, models, dancers, attracted by the bohemian life. From there it was only a short move up the hill to the Butte itself, which offered an easy-going village life, literary and artistic conversation in the Lapin Agile (which still continues as a nightclub) and the studios in the Bateau-Lavoir (No.13 Place Emile-Goudeau), recently burnt down. It was here that Picasso, Braque and Gris created Cubism, encouraged by poets like Apollinaire and Max Jacob. Other artists who live here (mainly in No.12 Rue Cortot) were Renoir, Van Gogh, Dufy, Suzanne Valadon and her illegitimate son, Maurice Utrillo.

Utrillo is the painter we chiefly think of when we visit Montmartre today. The little streets, the old houses which he painted so vividly, are still there. The Rue Norvins and the Rue Lepic still look much the same, apart from the crowds, as they do in his pictures. His walls glow with life, even if the occasional humans seem to be stuffed dummies. The famous *boulangerie* in the Rue Norvins still sells bread. To look at, Montmartre has changed little since his day. But something has gone – the genuine artistic spirit. It moved in the 1920s to Montparnasse.

Nevertheless a great deal of artistic life still goes on and the main centre is the **Place du Tertre**. This pretty little square, surrounded by old buildings and restaurants, still looks like a stage setting, the second act of *La Bohème*. In summer the paved centre of the square is full of restaurant tables, waiters and entertainers. Round the edge is a ring of colourful artists at their easels, and the occasional argument between an artist and a waiter adds to the operatic quality of the scene.

However, let no aspiring artist think that he can simply set up his easel and paint; the sites are as carefully guarded as booths in a fairground. Each artist is allowed to show two pictures, one which he has completed and one to which he is putting the final touches. These touches may take many months to complete and the artist working on it after lunch may not be the same as the one before lunch. Should we pause to consider a work which is simply standing on an easel, an artist, who has been eyeing us from the window of Le Clairon des Chasseurs, will be instantly at our side, suggesting a price. The works are mainly landscapes (not necessarily of Mont-martre), children and animals, and the fact that they are always complete, or almost, has prompted the ribald thought that they are imported from a wholesaler elsewhere. Better value are the carica-tures, which are very much part of the Montmartre tradition. Often amusing and pointed, a good likeness of ourselves, they have the advantage of being done by the artist while we sit meek and still.

As for the restaurants, there is little to choose between them. We can either sit outside in the square or, in cold or wet weather, inside – the restaurants are far larger than they seem. They are usually filled by coach tours and we shall overhear little French during our meal. But the food is acceptable and not overpriced, the service efficient and the entertainment appropriate. **Eugène's** is the cheapest and least touristy, but I have also spent some enjoyable lunches and evenings at **La Mère Catherine**.

This restaurant is said to have been founded by the Cossacks in March 1814. The villagers of Montmartre, who have an indepen-dent nature, had put up a strong resistance to the Cossacks in the Place Clichy and at the Moulin de la Galette. But the Cossacks won and the Montmartre leader was crucified on the sails of the Moulin –

one more martyr on the mount. In 1870 the villagers once again held out, this time against the Prussians. They formed an independent *commune* which became the Paris Commune, a brief and bloody episode which left its scars on the city, though not on the Butte. In 1940 Montmartre was again occupied; a vivid description of this can be found in Peter de Polnay's book *Death and Tomorrow*.

Those wishing to find something of the old cultural traditions of Montmartre should go to the **Museum of Montmartre**, No.12 Rue Cortot, the house where Utrillo and others lived, referred to earlier. The museum here, devoted to writers and painters who found their inspiration on the Butte, is open every afternoon, Sundays included. On Wednesday evenings the group Art et Humour Montmartrois meets for art exhibitions, poetry readings and discussions. On Saturday evenings the Societé du Vieux Montmartre organizes evenings of poetry, music, sketches and lectures on some aspect of Montmartre culture, particularly its poets, who seem at the moment to be more prestigious than its artists. These evenings are wholly French, both in spirit and in language, and we shall enjoy meeting Jean-Louis Vallas or Lo Celso; it is all very different from the Place du Tertre. A small entrance fee is payable and telephone reservations should be made in advance.

For those in search of night-life the choice is wide indeed. Practically every restaurant and café offers some form of entertainment, either professional or spontaneous, and we may well wish to wander from one to another, as the mood takes us. Among night-clubs the best-known is the Lapin Agile on the north side of the hill (closed Mondays). The Moulin de la Galette, on the south-west side of the hill, is not open at present. Both of these have long histories and both were painted by Utrillo – the outsides, of course, and in daylight. Utrillo's idea of a nightclub was very different from Toulouse-Lautrec's.

Descending the south side of the Butte, we can either take the funicular or, if it is a fine day, make our way on foot. Below the Moulin de la Galette, in the Rue Caulaincourt, we find the **Montmartre Cemetery** where a number of famous writers, painters and composers are buried (Zola, Gautier, Dumas the younger, the Goncourt brothers, Stendhal, de Vigny; Heine, Guitry; Fragonard, Greuze, Dégas; Berlioz, Delibes, Offenbach).

We continue down the street until we meet the busy Boulevard de

Clichy, a street full of cinemas, theatres, nightclubs, cafés and restaurants specializing in seafood. Going eastwards we find at No.100 the Théâtre des Deux Anes, one of the two remaining *chansonniers* (see Chapter 20) in Paris. But the main landmark of the Boulevard is at the Place Blanche, where we find the much photographed sails of the Moulin Rouge. This famous cabaret was opened in 1889 and is still going strong. Everywhere we find memories of La Goulue, Jane Avril, Yvette Guilbert and, of course, Toulouse-Lautrec who painted them. There are three performances a night, during one of which we can have a rather rushed dinner, and, during the others, drink fairly expensively and possibly rather far from the stage. The show is all that we could wish, featuring the cancan, the female body and, sometimes, the Eiffel Tower, which was opened the same year as the Moulin Rouge.

The Moulin Rouge is often associated in the minds of visitors with another famous music hall, the **Folies Bergère**. This is not, strictly speaking, in the Pigalle area, but the two *spectacles* have a good deal in common. The Folies is a theatre, not a cabaret (see Chapter 20).

A little further along we find the **Place Pigalle**. Jean-Baptiste Pigalle was a nineteenth-century painter and sculptor, who was known for his pictures and statues of the Virgin, some of which hang in Lady Chapels, for example in Saint-Sulpice. We may find it ironic that the name of this pious, Virgin-minded artist should now have become almost synonymous with sex. And sex is what the Place Pigalle nowadays is about; the area and in particular the side streets leading off the boulevard are full of sex shops, porn films and books, erotic pictures, houses of pleasure, and girls of all ages and types. Once they were part-time, working in the daytime as artists' models or seamstresses, but now they are full-time professionals.

I regret that I cannot guide you here – it is every man for himself. But I would remind you that commercialized sex often attracts some undesirable hangers-on. If you venture away from the well-lit boulevard at night – and many thousands of visitors do – you should leave behind your valuables, your credit cards and your wife.

To end this chapter we must mention two more restaurants, both with a special and quite different quality. The first is Chartier's (No.7 Rue du Faubourg Montmartre). This restaurant has style; the waiters wear white aprons, the décor suggests good living and the food is both acceptable and reasonably priced. The result is that it has become popular and well-known; it has now overflowed into two further restaurants nearby. The problem is to get a table, since reservations are scarcely possible. The unscrupulous will note a suitable table, where the diners are finishing their main course, and then crowd them, breathing down their necks and occasionally kicking the legs of their chairs. After a while the diners may decide to skip their coffee and possibly even their dessert. The moment they rise, others sit down in their seats. We may find this trick being used to move us on in due course, but in the meantime we shall have had a good and jolly evening. Chartier's is not Maxim's, but, in its own way, it is as much fun and far cheaper.

The other restaurant is less well known; Androuet's (No.41 Rue d'Amsterdam), behind the Gare Saint-Lazare. This is a place for lunch. If we should think of dining there, we should telephone beforehand (874 2690). The restaurant, which claims to have an old history, is on the first floor, over the cheese shop of the same name (see Chapter 13). And the speciality is, naturally, cheese.

There are seven *plateaux de fromage*, covered with different sorts of cheese, over a hundred different types in all. If we like, we can make our entire meal out of cheese, choosing which and what we want, as the whim takes us. This is called *une dégustation*, a tasting, and it should be accompanied by a red Bordeaux, perhaps a Pomerol. However, it is not exactly cheap; a *dégustation* is not a snack. If we should prefer a hot dish, the restaurant specializes in meat dishes with cheese sauces; we might consider a veal chop with a Roquefort sauce. And afterwards we shall, of course, have some cheese. It will be a memorable, though rather rich, meal.

CHAPTER 12

The Seizième Arrondissement

The Seizième (the sixteenth Arrondissement) is '*le beau quartier*', the beautiful part of Paris, more even than the Septième, another '*beau quartier*'. Not that there is anything very beautiful about it as an area; it is simply where the beautiful people live, and would be ashamed to live anywhere else. It is an area of good addresses, of streets people are proud to put on their visiting cards. And, incidentally, it is a quarter where a large number of interesting people do choose to live.

It is a very large quarter, stretching from the top of the hill at the Etoile down to the Bois de Boulogne and the Seine. But it should not be called beautiful; architecturally it has little to offer. There are a few old houses which survive, and some modern blocks set in lawns with statues and possibly fountains. But, otherwise, it consists of long streets and avenues of buildings from the last century, all six storeys high, all a hundred years old, all similar; you have to look at the street signs to know where you are. Behind the elaborate but uninteresting façades are thousands of flats, all identical, all furnished with similar antiques or reproductions, all with portraits in large gold frames. They are inhabited by similar people, rich, class-conscious, traditional, hospitable and, to be fair, intelligent.

The Seizième is not an area for shopping or restaurants or hotels or theatres, although there are some important museums, about which more in a moment. But the principal reason for visiting the quarter is to visit friends or go to a party, one of those small, select 'cocktails' which the French like to give. Only a carefully chosen few are invited and they usually know each other already. There will be a little champagne, or whisky, which is more fashionable, and plate after plate of 'eats'. The other guests will be expensively and quietly dressed. The main attraction is the conversation, which may be amusing or deadeningly polite – the one thing in this quarter which is variable.

Perhaps we shall be going to a reception given in the Duchesse Edmée de La Rochefoucauld's large drawing-room overlooking the Place des Etats-Unis. These are much larger parties, centering on her own literary-feminist personality. Most of the guests are writers, though there will be a sprinkling of politicians, diplomats and artists. 'The last *salon*', one of the other guests remarked once to me, and indeed it may be. The Duchesse herself would far rather be remembered for her books, in particular for her books on Paul Valéry, on whom she is an expert, than for her parties and her *salon*.

A new type of *salon* is growing up, many of which take place in the Seizième. These are more formal gatherings, with lectures, readings and debates. These may be rehearsed and are probably recorded, with the hope of selling the tape to the France-Culture radio programme. We shall not have much chance to exchange news and views with friends. If we are not called on to speak, we may find ourselves sitting on a hard chair, or even on the floor, for two hours, silent, stiff and thirsty.

Or we may be going to dinner in the **Avenue Foch**. This wide tree-lined street, leading from the Etoile to the Porte Dauphine and the Bois de Boulogne, is still the most fashionable residential street in Paris and everyone here is very rich, or wishes to be thought so. A dinner party here will consist of many courses, served by waiters wearing white gloves. A fine series of wines will be offered to us, preceded by whisky and ending with champagne. And we may sit next to the daughter of the family, known to her fellow-Parisians as Mademoiselle Avenue Foch.

She is well brought up and well-off, though she never seems to have much pocket-money. She does not have a job, but she is studying fashion design or Science-Po. She rides in the Bois, and is often to be seen at Longchamp, Maxim's or the newest disco. She eats little and drinks less, being figure-conscious and afraid of a complaint called *cellulité*. She buys her clothes in the Faubourg Saint-Honoré or even at one of the *haute couture* houses; she favours navy blue and a fawn raincoat. She lives at home and spends her weekends and holidays with her parents at their château in Burgundy. She has been a member since infancy of a '*rallye*', a group of similar people of the same age, one of whom she is

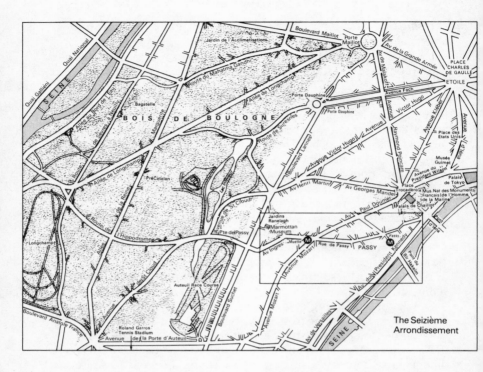

The Seizième
Arrondissement

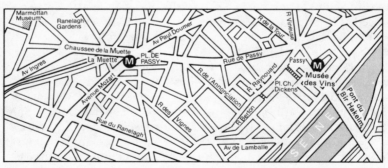

intended to marry. She has been schooled since childhood never to be *remarquée*, never to do or say anything interesting in public, especially if there are men present. We may feel that her total vocabulary consists of two words, '*Ah bon*,' which can be inflected in various ways.

This traditional image, the *jeune fille rangée*, has undergone some modifications in these trendy years, though they may not be noticeable at first glance. She is now more likely to be interested in the possibility of a television film part than in Science-Po. She goes further afield on her holidays and may even speak English. If questioned, she will readily admit that her baby is not by either of her husbands. But she still likes to wear navy blue and she still lives in the Avenue Foch.

Apart from the Duchesse and Mademoiselle, what are the attractions of the Seizième? Well, the village of **Passy** for one. The old village on the side of the hill overlooking the Seine still keeps an atmosphere of its own. Haussmann overlooked Passy, and, though many old houses and walled gardens have gone, some remain, together with narrow streets and sudden unexpected views. Passy provides us with a pleasant and interesting walk.

We should start one of our walks at Metro Passy and walk a little way across the bridge (Pont du Bir-Hakeim) to look at the view: the Eiffel Tower, the new towers of Grenelle, the modern Maison de la Radio (which is the biggest single building in France, built in 1963), Passy on its steep hillside, the river full of petrol barges – this is not the typical Parisian view of the city. But it became more familiar about ten years ago, with the film *Last Tango in Paris*, which was shot mainly in Passy. We can amuse ourselves by wondering in which flat all that sex-on-the-floor took place.

We return to Metro Passy (by the escalator) and make our way to the Square Charles Dickens; the connection with the novelist is only nominal. At No.5, at the corner of the Rue des Eaux, we find the **Musée du Vin**, recently constructed in the cellars of the old Abbey of Passy. The monks were known as Minims, because of their poverty, or *bonshommes*, because of their age. They were, however, energetic and commercially-minded and, in warmer centuries, grew vines on the sunny Passy hillside. Their wine was sold in all the Paris taverns and some local street names, Rue des Vignes and Rue Vineuse, remind us of Passy's wine-producing past. In the seventeenth century mineral water was found there (hence the Rue des Eaux); it contained iron and was supposed to be good for feminine sterility. A new and more fashionable crowd was attracted to Passy, which was beginning to lose its country feel. The Abbey was closed during the Revolution, although it was not completely demolished until 1906.

The Musée du Vin, also called the Caves de la Tour Eiffel, is rather a theatrical experience, with its audio-visual gimmicks and its waxworks. But it gives us a good idea of wine-making in a suitably dramatic setting, and we can taste some of the wines and buy bottles if we wish.

We walk to the Place de Costa-Rica and turn left into the **Rue Raynouard**, which winds pleasantly along the hillside. Architecturally it is not of interest; it must have looked very different when Lauzun and Rousseau lived here. But **Balzac's house** at No.47 still looks much as it did in his day, a comfortable country house with shutters. Balzac lived here from 1840 to 1847 and the house is open to the public. The walls are covered with caricatures of the novelist, so that we feel his personality strongly. Of interest is his study with his chair and table; we can imagine him sitting there, working in non-stop bouts all day and night, pressed on by debt and black coffee; and then going to relax on the Ile Saint-Louis.

The garden is charming, full of flowering trees and shrubs. On one wall is a bronze relief showing characters out of *La Comédie Humaine*. On the other side we peer over into the Rue Berton below us, an unexpected street with blank walls, ivy and old lamps; it is hard to believe that we are in Paris. Beyond, we have a good view of the Château Lamballe, a fine eighteenth-century building, the home of the Princesse de Lamballe, Marie Antoinette's best friend. Later it was a clinic for the insane; Dr Blanche tried to treat Maupassant's terminal syphilis here. It is now the Turkish Embassy.

At the end of Balzac's garden, No.51–5, is a grim block built by Auguste Perret, the architect and town-planner. Here he lived and died (1954), much admired. But looking now at his concrete pilasters we may regret that his enthusiasm for his new material, reinforced concrete, was not matched by an equal talent in design – a continuing controversy in art and architecture.

Almost opposite, at No.66, was the home of Benjamin Franklin from 1777 to 1785. During this time he was trying to forge an alliance between his new country, the United States of America, and Louis XVI's France. In between diplomacy and politics, he followed another of his interests, physics. On his house he installed the first lightning-conductor seen in France. It was not, presumably, his famous 'kite and key' but something more durable. The present building, not a hundred years old, has several television aerials, and it is difficult to see if it has a lightning-conductor as well.

We retrace our steps and at the Rue de l'Annonciation we turn left. We are in a quiet Passy street with little traffic and an old but much renovated chapel. At the end we arrive in the **Place de Passy**, the old village square and hardly altered over the last centuries. We can sit under the trees of the open-air café Paris-Passy or eat at the modest but good restaurant. Beside the square – a triangle, really – we find the Rue de Passy, the old village street and one of the few shopping areas in the Seizième. One of its surprises, as it winds down the hill, is the way we keep seeing the Eiffel Tower almost in the street, although it is, of course, on the other side of the river. The shops are becoming more fashionable, as befits a rich neighbourhood, and we shall find smart boutiques with familiar names – Daniel Hechter, La Bagagerie, Burton's, the Scotch House, the last well-placed for Turks wanting tartans.

We can end our walk at Metro La Muette, but perhaps we would like to go further, across Ranelagh Gardens to see the Marmottan museum. The Ranelagh Gardens were originally created in the eighteenth century in imitation of the celebrated pleasure-gardens in London, owned by Lord Ranelagh. The present gardens (in Paris) were laid out in 1860, but they still have a very English feeling with their lawns and huge, unpollarded chestnuts. For children there are donkey-rides, peepshows and sweet-stalls.

The **Marmottan museum** originally housed the collection, mainly paintings of the Napoleonic period, of Paul Marmottan, a civil servant and art collector, whose house it was. It is now known for its wonderful collection of Monets, most of them bequeathed to the museum by the artist's son in 1971. Here we can see the picture which gave its name to the movement: 'Impression of Sunrise at Le Havre'; The Gare Saint-Lazare in grey steam; the façade of Rouen Cathedral, one of the celebrated series, in bright sunlight; and Westminster on a murky evening. But most of the pictures are of his garden at Giverny on the Seine, a world of ponds, water-lilies, roses and trees.

The collection covers fifty years of Monet's life, from the 'Impression of Sunrise' in 1872 to the final weeping-willow tree-trunks, those magical trees, in 1922. (Monet died in 1926.) We can follow his development from the time when Boudin suggested to him that he give up doing caricatures in Le Havre and look instead at the landscape and the sky. We watch him exploring light on water, or through mist or trees, until his final stage when he became more interested in the objects themselves, in the willow-trunks and the water-lilies. His pictures of these, dated 1920, are wild whirlpools, the lilies iridescent, painted in thick paint; full of energy, they are very different from his earlier quiet landscapes of the Seine valley. But they were sadly unsaleable; this at least has prevented the collection being dispersed.

I must confess to considerable bias about Monet, and I believe that I have seen every Monet that is on public view and some that are not. He has been much criticized for his lack of classical formalism, his lack of interest in perspective, his habit of leaving out the edge of the cathedral or the top of the palazzo. But then he also left out goddesses and plunging horses. A painter should be appreciated for what he gives us and not for what laws he upholds or breaks. Monet remains my favourite French painter and his greatness depends on his personal vision and his communication of it, rather than on having helped to start a new art movement.

There are other Impressionists in the Marmottan: works by Renoir, Sisley, Caillebotte and Pissarro. But these are not their most luminous or famous works, for which we should go to the Jeu de Paume.

The museum also houses the Wildenstein collection of European (mainly Flemish) thirteenth and fourteenth-century illuminated manuscripts and miniature paintings. For lovers of this period, these are fine treasures, with startling, brilliant colours. But they make a weird contrast with the Impressionists a few yards away and one may feel that they would be better housed in the Louvre.

Our second walk is a shorter and simpler affair; just the **Avenue du President Wilson**, a dull street with a number of buildings by Perret. But it contains six important and varied museums and we shall need

Père Lachaise Cemetery.

Beaubourg in the 1920s, by Charpentier,
founder of the Academie Charpentier.

Beaubourg today –
the Pompidou Centre.
Below Old Paris,
the Rue de
l'Hôtel-de-Ville.

The Bastille as it once was.
Below left En garde!
Below right Victor Hugo
in his youth.

The Marais – Hôtel de Sully.

The seventeenth-century
Place des Vosges.

The Rue Saint-Antoine, a
busy market street and the
oldest road in Paris.

Montmartre – the Place du Tertre with Saint-Pierre and the Sacré-Coeur in the background. *Below* The Moulin Rouge in Toulouse-Lautrec's day.

The Marais – Robert Le Lorrain's superb 'Horses of the Sun',
on the Hôtel de Rohan.

to be selective according to our interests. We start at Metro Trocadéro at the Place of the same name, on top of the Chaillot hill.

This hill, overlooking the Seine, has always been thought a desirable place and many famous names are associated with it. Catherine de Medici built a country house here, later occupied by a licentious friend of Henri IV, who went to the Bastille for offending Richelieu. Later Henrietta of Orléans, the daughter of Charles I of England, bought the house and turned it into a fashionable convent. Napoleon wanted to build a palace there for his son. Foch dominates the Place du Trocadéro. The forgotten name is Trocadéro itself, an obscure fortress in Spain, besieged by the French in 1823; its capture was celebrated on this hill by order of Chateaubriand, the Minister of Foreign Affairs, who had organized the expedition into Spain.

The present **Palais de Chaillot** was built for the 1937 Paris Exhibition and it consists of two curved low 'classical-style' buildings, wings to a central building which does not exist. The best that can be said for it is that it does not distract from the view, which is indeed remarkable. From the terrace we look across the Trocadéro Gardens with their fountains and ornamental pool, across the Seine to the Eiffel Tower, the Champ-de-Mars and the Ecole Militaire. In the distance are the domes of old Paris and the high-rise towers of the modern age. The Trocadéro fountains are much admired, especially at night when they are floodlit; and the biggest displays of fireworks are let off here on 14 July and special festive occasions.

Apart from this scenery, Chaillot contains three museums, a film library (*cinemathèque*), an aquarium, and two theatres, one of which, the Chaillot National Theatre, is underground, very large and modern, and is used for plays, concerts, operas, ballets and other less easily classified cultural events.

The Musée National des Monuments Français (north wing). Over the museum door we read a quotation from Paul Valéry: 'The wonder-working hand of the artist is the equal and rival of his thought. The one is nothing without the other.' It is a remark much debated among artists.

Inside we find irremovable objects, such as frescoed ceilings, façades, arches, columns and portals, collected in replica from all over France, and we can enjoy many of the great treasures of the provinces. The depressing entrance hall, with stained glass murdered by strong front lighting, must not deter us from going in.

The first sculptures of all (two great twelfth-century sculpted columns on either side as we enter the first room) are among the best. On the left 'Abraham sacrificing Isaac' defies any modern work in its vigour, terror and fantasy – yet the father and son cling to each other with real tenderness. (Trumeau, from Souillac, Lot). On the right, 'The Caryatids' (also Trumeau, from Beaulieu de Cor-rèze) achieves another paradox: the weight seems too great for the figures to bear, yet the grace of the columns' lines gives a sense of calm strength.

The ground-floor rooms are well lit by skylights which allow the daylight to play on the façades and figures. The works are shown in date order, but grouped by regions, so that we can get the distinct flavour of each time and place. We begin with the late eleventh century, '1066 and all that', but in fact the start of a great period of stone carving. Here we can see the huge portals of some of the twelfth-century cathedrals, still full of power and faith. Autun is here and the famous tympanum of the central narthex portal of Vézelay Abbey (c.1130). This great figure of Christ sending forth the Apostles seems to float as He stretches His (curiously big) hands towards us. We shall also admire the carved foliage from Bourges Cathedral (1159), and the huge Gothic figures from the west façade of Rheims Cathedral (thirteenth century).

The Black Death (1348) and the Hundred Years' War ended this period; builders now built castles and sculptors made tombs. We next see a whole hall of tombs; a scale model shows us the tombs of the kings at Saint-Denis, followed by replicas of some of them. Among them are two kings of England: Richard Cœur-de-Lion (d. 1199), a little unenthusiastically rendered, lies beside his mother, Eleanor of Aquitaine, and his father Henry II – an even more unflattering likeness. These come from Fontrevault Abbey on Queen Eleanor's estates and perhaps the monks were admirers of Thomas à Becket.

The famous soldier Du Guesclin (end of fourteenth century) has two splendid tombs, an unusual achievement. The monks of Saint-Denis buried his body, but the enterprising church of Saint-Laurent-du-Puy-en-Vélay secured his entrails. The liver-and-lights tomb has the more vitality and shows Du Guesclin lying with a dog at his feet.

When prosperity returned in the fifteenth-century, church building was resumed in a style which was beginning to be influenced by the Renaissance. The sixteenth-century sculpture is particularly delicate and beautiful, notably the carving from Limoges Cathedral (1533) and the perspective reliefs from the door of Beauvais south transept. Here are the well-known arch of the 'Grosse Horloge' in Rouen (1527) and a graceful fountain with dolphins and ribbons from Tours by François (1510). There are also works by the Renaissance sculptor Jean Goujon, Richier and Pilon; beautiful in themselves, they remind us how far art had moved from the fierce strength of the Middle Ages.

On the first floor (there are lifts) we can see seventeenth, eighteenth and nineteenth-century sculpture, including works by Pigalle and Houdon. They are mainly statues and busts in Græco-Roman poses and, if you wish to see a hundred togas, this is the place.

On the third and fourth floors, are the frescoes. Whole vaulted ceilings and walls have been copied, mainly from churches of the fourteenth, fifteenth and sixteenth centuries, but including the oldest fresco in France, from the crypt of Saint-Germain Abbey, Auxerre (twelfth century). We may feel that frescoes transplant to a museum much less successfully than monumental sculpture, perhaps because they depend much more on their setting. Since the colours of the originals have faded with time, we have to make an effort of imagination to see these as they must once have been. However, they are worth studying, if we have time; they give us much insight into mediæval points of view.

Once again we feel the terrible impact of the Black Death, in a fourteenth-century fresco 'Pestilence', transfixing the congregation with a hail of arrows (Church of Lavaudieu). There is also the 'Danse Macabre' from La-Chaise-Dieu Abbey Church. We may contrast these with the fifteenth-century 'Abundance', showing a great feast. The most famous works are from Berzé-la-Ville, Vic and Cahors Cathedral. A long series, using the 'narrative-strip' teaching-technique comes from Saint-Seine-l'Abbaye, near Dijon (1504). The most striking fresco is the huge 'St Christopher' (Lassay, 1496), and the most charming the flying 'Angel-musicians' from Kernascleden, Morbihan.

The Musée de l'Homme (south wing). This museum presents the early remains of mankind and the cultures, from all over the world, of prehistoric and primitive societies, including present-day cultures still similar to the Stone Age. Diagrams and displays explain how men lived in ancient times and show their tools and earliest industries.

On the first floor, galleries deal with anthropology and fossils, early stone implements and so on. Here, near the entrance, we may see the skeleton of Cro-Magnon Man, the first European *Homo sapiens sapiens*, found in 1872 in the stalagmite grotto of the Grimaldi caves at Menton in the south of France. He is just like a modern Frenchman, except that the race may have been taller; he is 5 foot 10, but was young and not fully grown; other skeletons found nearby were 6 foot 4. He is at least 30,000 years old and lived at the time when the last ice age was receding. His body was covered with red ochre and he wore a crown of shells, and bracelets and anklets made of shells. He was buried with his tools and animal bones, suggesting a belief in life after death.

Homo sapiens sapiens skeletons of a similar date from Africa and Australia can be compared with Cro-Magnon Man. The Museum points out that it was characteristic of them all to use artistic designs for their household objects and burial places, and to produce sculpture and mural paintings which indicate their religion.

Also on this floor are the 'Hottentot Venus' and the ivory 'Lespugue Venus'. There are fine collections of African art, of which the most exciting are probably the oldest, the copies of prehistoric wall-paintings and photographs of rock-paintings from caves in the mountainous Ahaggar region of the Sahara. These are full of the same vitality as the rather similar Lascaux cave-paintings, of which small drawings and photographs are also shown on this floor, near the entrance.

We shall enjoy the room of mediæval Christian Abyssinian murals. The figures of saints, which are somewhat Byzantine in style, have strong simple lines against a red background. Among the powerful Central African sculpture, we may note a huge drum carved with animals, from the Ivory Coast. It is in rich traditional local style, but must be recent, since one of the figures carries a gun. The disappointing European section is at the end. It shows the survival of primitive art and customs through folk costumes, festivals and masks.

The second floor is mainly devoted to the excellent collection of pre-Columbian, Maya and Aztec art, beginning on the staircase with a great carved stone relief from Mexico, the 'Disc of the Sun' or 'Aztec Calendar', a wonderful work. Among figures of the god Quetzlcoatl, a massive statue from the Maya civilization of Honduras dominates us; it seems curiously reminiscent of Asian styles, although so far away. Near it is the famous 'Crystal skull', finely carved out of a single giant rock-crystal. Although this fascinates many people, we may feel grateful that the finders of the Koh-i-noor and Hope Diamonds did not feel a similar urge.

The most awe-inspiring exhibit in the museum is the gigantic Easter Island head, gazing upwards, carved in volcanic rock. The statue surmounted a platform for the lying-in-state of the dead. Also on the second floor are further exhibits from the Pacific and from the Arctic, but the Far East is poorly represented. There are also costumes from many lands.

Unless we are already experts, the notices in the museum do not make it at all clear what date or place we are seeing. This is perhaps deliberate, since the emphasis is on the homogeneity of mankind rather than on its diversity. But there is a completely individual work outside the museum, a huge totem-pole carved from an entire British Columbian pine. This tells the legends of a North American chief's ancestors; one it seems, was hanged and another eaten by a crocodile. By any standards it is a splendid piece of sculpture.

The Musée de la Marine (south wing). This museum is devoted to sea power, shipping, underwater exploration and the ports of France. These are shown by models, lifesize and scale, pictures, dioramas, souvenirs and films. French achievements are particularly emphasized, though the model of Columbus's *Santa Maria* is an obvious exception. Of special interest is the reconstruction of the removal of the Luxor Obelisk from Egypt to the Place de la Concorde. We shall also note Alain Bombard's sailing-raft *Hérétique*, if only for its name.

Leaving Trocadéro, we walk down the Avenue du President Wilson to Metro Iéna, the statue of George Washington and the **Musée Guimet**, which is the home in Paris of the art of Eastern Asia. It has 300,000 objects and related documents and a library of 100,000 works, plus 120,000 photographs and prints. Concerts are held there and there is a music department with listening booths. It is much visited by Asians as well as Parisians, and it was here that a group of Tibetan lamas came, when they were expelled from Tibet, to copy their sacred art and texts and re-establish their lost tradition.

This is a very carefully watched-over museum but, even so, some of the best items are considered too fragile or precious to be put on general view. If we are experts in this field and can produce convincing credentials, we should write in advance (English is spoken) to the Conservator for permission to visit the reserve collection, especially the series of exquisite paintings of the life of Buddha, in the Tibetan Mandala.

On the ground floor, well lit by skylights, we see Khmer gateways with carved pediments from North Cambodia. These date from the eleventh century. If we have seen the French portals of almost the same date in the nearby Palais de Chaillot, the different spirit of these carvings must strike us. Unlike the majestic but static French sculpture, the Khmer figures dance and clap. There are also Khmer heads of Buddha and a Shiva from Vietnam.

In the Lamaist collection we can admire the very beautiful Tibetan and Nepalese banners, including the Mandala of Samvara. This is a mystic diagram, painted in gouache on textile, showing a square with four guarded doors within a double circle, presided over by the protecting but terrible God, Samvara. These banners cover a long span of time; one shows the Buddhist reforming monk Atisa (982–1055), another depicts the great Fifth Dalai Lama (1617–82) receiving Chinese and Mongolian ambassadors. Among other objects we may note the dancing Dakini bronze.

The first floor shows Indian sculpture of many centuries, from the third century BC onwards, including reliefs from North India and Hindu figures from the South. The museum attendants will point out to us the bronze sculpture of the Cosmic Dance (eleventh century) in the Dravidian style from South India. The God Shiva dances inside a circle of flames, symbolizing the Cosmos. With his foot he crushes a dwarf, symbol of the power chaining down souls.

The Chinese have an even longer history of art and their fine bronzes, also on this floor, date back as far as 2000 BC. The massive gravity of the Chinese style seems a constant feature of all periods, in contrast with the suppleness and rhythm of the Indian works. An interesting item is a great bronze ritual vase of the ninth century BC with intricate embossed patterns.

The Pakistan section is at present being reorganized.

The 'Bagram Treasure' from Afghanistan is a surprise here, because the small ivory or plaster figures and fragments are in the Hellenistic style of the first and second centuries BC, reflecting the Greek influence at that date. They are Indian, not Afghan, but were dug up in 1937 on the site of the old Afghan capital, near Kabul.

The second floor, now re-opened, shows fine collections of Chinese porcelain, mainly of the seventeenth and eighteenth centuries, and lacquer. The Buddhist banners are worth studying; the finest is a Korean fifteenth-century figure of Buddha, painted on silk.

In the Japanese section the twelfth-century wooden figures and the fourteenth-century paintings on silk have great dignity and severity. In a very different vein, a large painted and gilded 'Screen of the Barbarians of the South' (end of the sixteenth century), depicts the arrival in Japan of a Portuguese ship, carrying gifts. The dignitaries are seen being received by St Francis Xavier. The Elizabethan-style balloon-trousers and lace handkerchiefs evidently seemed very comical to the artist, who has caricatured the visitors.

We should choose a cool day for our visit to the Guimet, as ventilation seems to have been entirely forgotten.

The **Palais de Tokyo** is the next museum we come to as we walk down the Avenue du President Wilson. A large double building built for the 1937 Exhibition, it resembles in design its contemporary Palais de Chaillot. It originally housed the Museum of Modern Art, but has recently been renamed the Musée d'Art et d'Essai. It still has connections with modern art, although most of its greatest works have been transferred to the Pompidou Centre at Beaubourg.

We enter the right-hand building (south wing) from the Avenue and find, at the moment, the 'd'Orsay Collection'. The d'Orsay Museum is now being built inside the old station beside the Seine and the former Hôtel d'Orsay, which have been classified for preservation (see Chapter 4). It is intended to be opened in 1986 and will house art of all kinds of the period from 1848 to 1914, including photography. This is thought of as an important period of change – scientific, industrial and social – and one of the most fertile periods in French art. Paintings of this date now in the Louvre, the Jeu de

Paume and the Palais de Tokyo are to be transferred to the d'Orsay Museum.

Meanwhile we can see a large part of the Post-Impressionist collection destined for the d'Orsay Museum here, on the ground floor. The upper floors are closed for reconstruction.

'Post-Impressionist' is a vague phrase which embraces three distinct schools: *Symbolism and Art Nouveau*, with the school of *Pont-Aven* (Gauguin, Bernard, Sérusier, etc.); the *Nabis*, 1890 –1900, admirers of Gauguin (Bonnard, Vuillard, Denis, Maillol, Vallotton); and the *Neo-Impressionists* (Seurat, Signac, Cross and some works by Pissarro). These are usually known as *pointillistes*, because of their technique of using small adjoining dots or cubes of primary colour to convey light. The technique is based on the mosaic rather than on sweeps of the brush and it is certainly effective; the canvases seem to glow with light and heat. But it is also restricting; the human face, when they bothered to paint it at all, has to be much simplified. Both Seurat and Monet (whom he attacked) were trying to find a scientific way of rendering light, water and the Seine countryside. Which succeeded better is a matter of choice; we can enjoy them both.

But the most famous artists are not the only ones of interest here; there is a great variety, typical of our individualist century. For instance, in the first room, we may note a portrait of Leo Tolstoy in his old age (1901) by Leonid Pasternak, a recent donation. The Gauguins, including a curious relief-painting '*Soyez Mystérieuses*' (1890) are in the second room, where we may also like Maximilien Luce's pointilliste 'The Louvre and the Pont Neuf by Night' as a view of Paris. Bonnard's '*Le Peignoir*' (The Dressing-gown) is a good example of the 'Japanese' vogue of the time; the whole canvas is alight with golden colour. His arching cat is also one of his best.

If we are devotees of Art Nouveau, we should not miss a whole panelled room with clematis and wistaria carved in mahogany, by Alexandre Charpentier, 1900. It is puzzling to find a Burne-Jones and a Gustav Klimt together, but we must not lose our way among these very mixed rooms because the last room now has the Toulouse-Lautrecs, which were formerly in the Jeu de Paume.

It seems to be a good idea to separate Toulouse-Lautrec from the Impressionists, with whom he has often been grouped. Apart from a slight acquaintance with Van Gogh, he did not know them, and his aims were indeed different. Not for him the long hours of studying light on the Seine. His days were spent racing, his nights at the Moulin Rouge or the Mirliton, where he painted the dancers and singers, designed posters for La Goulue and the singer Aristide Bruant, and drank far too much, which brought about his early death. Here we have two panels which he painted for La Goulue's booth at the Moulin Rouge, and 'la clownesse Cha-U-Kao'. But personally I am drawn to a small portrait, '*La Femme aux Gants*' (The Woman with gloves). It is an extraordinary likeness of my grandmother Elinor, face, posture, clothes, gloves and all. And why not? She was in Paris at the time and would have pretended not to notice the little cripple on the next bench, sketching. One of her novels has a crippled artist who was a genius. But I do not think she ever heard of Lautrec.

The last remnants of the former National Museum of Modern Art on this site are now relegated to the basement and their future is uncertain. These are two over-large donation-collections by Dunoyer de Ségonzac and the sculptor Laurens and – amazingly in this deserted dungeon – a whole room of excellent works by Georges Rouault. We need a true cave-explorer's zeal to find them, but shall be rewarded by '*Le Christ aux Outrages*' (The Tormented Christ) and the '*Miserere – Le dur métier de vivre*'. We can see here that Rouault's talent was by no means limited to his well-known studies of clowns. Some of his works are quite unexpected; for instance '*Le Conférencier*' (The Speaker), a telling portrait of a man making a speech, looking over his glasses. The collection is buried here because the donors, Rouault's daughters, have refused to allow any of it to be moved to the Pompidou Centre.

The left wing of the Palais de Tokyo is still called the Museum of Modern Art of the City of Paris, but only a small part of its permanent collection of late nineteenth- and twentieth-century art is now on view, in two ground-floor rooms, on a rotating basis. The rest of the building is now used for temporary exhibitions, jazz concerts and so on, in an attempt to attract a larger attendance and interest Parisian youth.

We end our walk at the Place de l'Alma, where we find the Seine and a metro station (Alma-Marceau). Here in one of the many cafés we can rest our feet and eyes over a drink.

201

Our third and final walk in the Seizième is simply a stroll among the greenery of the **Bois de Boulogne**. Ideally it should be a ride, but if we cannot borrow a horse (or a bicycle – see Appendix A) we can always go by car or taxi and walk from our stopping-place. The Bois is very large, over two thousand acres, and except for certain areas and certain days, we shall be able to find solitude. For many centuries it was a private royal park. Although it was opened to the public by Louis XIV, who hardly needed it, it did not become fashionable till later. The present Bois is really the creation of Haussmann (of course!). He demolished the surrounding wall, landscaped the area with its lakes and riding tracks after the Hyde Park manner, and built some of the restaurants, the racecourses, and the main approach road, the Avenue Foch (then the Empress's Avenue).

Those who like a *but de promenade* may like to visit the **Jardin d'Acclimatation**, an area for children with many amusements including a children's zoo, a miniature railway, a theatre and much else. Others may prefer the **Bagatelle** area, with its shrubs, water-gardens, follies, rose-garden and glasshouses. The **Pré Catalan** area attracts many people, not only for its café and restaurant, but for the copper beech, said to be nearly two hundred years old; and for the **Shakespeare garden**, where all the trees and flowers are mentioned in his plays. Rather an academic method of gardening, one might think, but a remarkable example of Anglophilia.

Or we may go there simply to eat. The tradition of dining in the Bois has continued ever since the Second Empire, and the restaurants, Armenonville, the Pré Catalan, the Château de Madrid, try to continue the tradition of luxury. Because they now cater mainly for the tourist trade, we may find their food and service (but not their prices) less than imperial. However, if all goes well, we can have a pleasantly sumptuous evening under the great trees – though there usually seems to be some reason why we cannot dine out of doors that night. But at least the restaurants are open in August, a month when many other Paris restaurants are closed while their faithful customers are away. Of the Bois restaurants my favourite is also the most modest: the Chalet des Iles in the middle of the Lac Inférieur. We reach it by rowing across, a romantic way to start and finish an evening.

The Bois de Boulogne is much associated with sport. At the

southern end is the Roland Garros tennis stadium, where the French Open Championships are held in May. A hard court tournament, it attracts all the big names and almost rivals Wimbledon in prestige. But it is easier to get into.

And horses. The Bois is the headquarters of the Racing Club de France and the Société Hippique. But what bring the crowds are the two big racecourses. Auteuil has the jumps, including a wide water-jump. Longchamp is the flat course, a blend of Epsom and Ascot, and the course is said to be hard. The big week of the year is at the beginning of October, the climax on the first Sunday with the Prix de l'Arc de Triomphe. This is Europe's richest race and, unlike the Derby, it is not confined to three-year-old colts, so the choice is wider. To many British, Paris is the Arc and hotel beds are hard to find at this time. The Arc is also a big social event, culminating in the moment when an elegantly dressed lady, the wife of the owner, leads in the winner. She is very likely to be British.

CHAPTER 13

Le Shopping

Shopping in Paris is one of the main attractions of the city. There are many good reasons for coming to Paris, but shopping will certainly be one of them; everyone is expected to take home a few presents. For many, shopping is the main object of the expedition, with the Eiffel Tower and the 'Mona Lisa' thrown in as a sideline. For those on a tight budget, windowshopping in Paris can be a great pleasure – to see the latest fashions and enjoy the attractive window displays (see a suggested walk, on page 218). And we may well be tempted inside.

Prices, too, are tempting at the present time. With the franc continually weak and a favourable exchange rate, the sweater you long for may well be cheaper than you had feared. The major credit cards are accepted in all department stores (*grands magasins*), whether you are claiming your TVA refund or not. And presents will be gift-wrapped free and almost automatically.

Shopping hours are also convenient. The *grands magasins* and many of the larger boutiques stay open until 7.0 p.m. Small shops (*petits commerçants*) are open until 8.0 p.m., but many of them will be closed from 1.0 p.m. till 4 or 5.0 p.m. Some may be open on Sunday mornings and closed all day on Mondays – it depends on the habits of the shopkeeper and where he lives. Many boutiques and two *grands magasins* (Samaritaine and Bazar de l'Hôtel de Ville (BHV)) stay open once a week until 10.0 p.m. These late-night openings are called, rather romantically, *nocturnes*.

CLOTHES AND ACCESSORIES

People have been coming to Paris for clothes since the Middle Ages; they went to the stalls and booths round Saint-Merri church for their doublets and hose, silks and ribbons. But the present highly organized and commercialized *haute couture* industry began in the last century and is generally attributed to an Englishman called Worth, whose name is still found on scent bottles. My great-aunt, Lucile, and her protégé Molyneux also played their part in the Paris fashion world; designers may come from many lands, though they tend to congregate in a small area of the Right Bank. Opinions differ, names change like the fashions they design, but at the moment Saint-Laurent is generally thought to be the top designer, though the maison Dior keeps its prestige and its faithful clientèle. Chanel in the Rue Cambon is experiencing a great wave of popularity, especially with Americans; some of this may be due to the recent successful Broadway musical *Coco*. Coco Chanel dominated Paris *haute couture* for many years and it is good to know that her maison has survived both time and a terrorist bombing. But there are many others, some rising, some declining.

The *haute couture* maisons show their new fashions – called *collections* – twice a year, in February and September. These are fashionable affairs in every sense; you sit on gilt chairs, sip free champagne, and admire skinny models in extraordinary positions, often with their legs wide apart, their knees bent and leaning over backwards. The audience includes princesses, wholesale buyers, film-stars, fashion journalists and the wives of rich oil sheiks, an intriguing mixture. Admission is by invitation only; if you are the sort of person who gets these invitations, you need read no further in this chapter.

The main point is not the selling of clothes, though no maison will object to the entire collection being bought by Harrods or Neiman-Marcus or a Saudi-Arabian prince. The real object is to sell designs to the wholesalers and dealers, to be commissioned to dress a new theatrical spectacle and, generally, to introduce new ideas into the fashion world. It was thus that Christian Dior lowered the world's hemlines to calf-length (the 'New Look'), Saint-Laurent made every smart Frenchwoman wear Mondrian squares, and Paco Rabanne put them all into leather. Sometimes an outside influence intrudes, to the annoyance of the local designers. So it was that Albert Finney, in the film *Tom Jones*, made every girl wear knee-breeches and a black bow on the nape of her neck; more recently the Princess of Wales encouraged unwittingly the trend to black velvet

205

knickerbockers – both these fashions were at a time when the collections were featuring a soft, feminine look.

The *haute couture* maisons will, of course, design and make clothes for actual people; royal weddings, pop stars' galas, a big ball – these events bring out all the enthusiasm of a famous maison. But it is hardly the place for an ordinary shopper; many ladies, even those with plenty to spend, have emerged with nothing except a bruised ego. And, even if you should succeed, the prices will be fantastic. A rich French lady said to me recently. '*C'est impossible!* I prefer to spend my money on antique furniture' – a baffling remark, since you cannot easily wear an armchair at a party.

Gradually the big maisons realized how much money they were losing to the boutiques by freezing off the retail trade. Now they have all opened their own boutiques, either on their own ground floors or next door; or in the Rue du Faubourg Saint-Honoré or the Avenue Montaigne. Cardin and Saint-Laurent have even gone so far as to open boutiques on the Left Bank, and in other cities and other countries. In these boutiques you can either buy clothes off the peg or made to measure. Prices are high, but we have the satisfaction of dealing with a top house and a big name.

Many of these boutiques are in the Rue du Faubourg Saint-Honoré, which is in any case a must for fashion-conscious shoppers, window and otherwise (see also Chapter 6). Out of the many shops here are a few selected names:

Hermes, No.24. Still in the top bracket, but mainly for leather goods and horsey silk scarves. It is a place for the older woman, and you may emerge looking as if you were going to a county point-to-point.

Saint-Laurent-Rive-Gauche (though we are, of course, on the right bank). Arguably the top boutique in Paris, and more expensive than the branch on the real Rive Gauche.

Lanvin, No.18. Still fashionable, especially for scarves and scent and it has preserved a clientèle for clothes.

Emmanuel Ungaro, No.25 and also No.2 Avenue Montaigne. One of the smartest boutiques in Paris and the clothes here are all the rage. Who would have guessed that Hungarians were so fashion-conscious!

Charles Jourdan, No.10. For shoes. See later.

We shall also enjoy looking in at the windows of Laroche, Lapidus, Cardin, Courrèges and Louis Féraud.

In the Avenue Montaigne we shall find Ungaro, as already mentioned. Also **Nina Ricci** at No.37. At No.30 we find

Dior, one of the main attractions of this street and indeed of Paris. The boutique on the ground floor is closely linked with the couture maison and the *vendeuse* will gladly take your order for *couture* clothes or sell you something off the peg. Most boutiques sell accessories as well as clothes, but the accessories here are a great attraction, especially the scarves and costume jewellery, in particular the necklaces, which are reasonably priced. They will not, of course, be made of gold or precious stones at these prices, but they will be smart, modern and eye-catching. And, as you will let drop, Dior.

HAUTE COUTURE PRÊT-À-PORTER (READY TO WEAR)

This is a different area of the fashion world, but just as fashionable and 'in'. All clothes are sold off the peg, there is no ordering or making to measure, but the prices will be almost as high as in the Faubourg Saint-Honoré. Collections are held in March and October (entry once again only by invitation). The designers' names are different, but well known to the fashion-conscious Frenchwoman.

The centre here is the Place des Victoires, near the Palais-Royal Gardens. It is full of *recherché* expensive boutiques, as smart but not as touristy as the Faubourg Saint-Honoré. Some names:

Thierry Mugler, No.10. Very much an in-place, especially for evening dresses. No prices are marked, so be careful.

France Andrève, No.2. Women's clothes only, no accessories. The prices are reasonable and there is much to choose from. The clothes are ultra-smart, the sort of things which look dated after one season – or indeed one week.

Kenzo, also called **Jungle Jap**. This is rather an expensive boutique for both sexes, men on the ground floor, women on the first. Despite the outrageous window displays, there is an old-fashioned feel to the place, with its wooden staircase, its wooden counters with drawers and its flowery designs. There is, however, nothing old-fashioned about its clothes.

207

Tokio, round the corner, is a shoe shop, where you can buy shoes which look as if they had been painted by Jackson Pollock.

Cacharel, No.1 – next door to Kenzo, is a popular medium-priced boutique for men.

Incidentally, the **Place des Victoires**, dating back to the seventeenth century, is worth visiting for its own sake. A small-scale and damaged version of the Place Vendôme. The Banque de France was here for a while in a house designed by François Mansart, but since remodelled. The nineteenth-century equestrian statue of Louis XIV is by Bosio.

The Place du Marché Saint-Honoré leads off the Rue Saint-Honoré, near the Rue Daunou. This is another, rather smaller centre for the *prêt-à-porter* trade. The main attraction is **Castelbajac**'s boutique and, at No.31, **Bab's** (see below).

HAUTE COUTURE AT MARKED-DOWN PRICES

There are several reasons why smart clothes should be sold off cheaply: a change of mind by the designer; withdrawn from the collection because the secret design was leaked in advance; end of a series; slightly imperfect or shop-soiled. But the clothes themselves are in high fashion and the prices will be at least at a 40% discount. There will, however, be no designer's label inside.

Bab's, No.31 Place du Marché Saint-Honoré, is one of the main shops for this trade and the clothes here are very trendy. Another centre is the Rue Saint-Placide on the Left Bank, where there are many marked-down-price shops. Two leading designers, **Courrèges** (No.7 Rue Turbigo, first floor) and **Emmanuelle Khanh** (No.6 Rue Lescot, first floor) have both opened discount shops for their unwanted model dresses.

SHOES

Charles Jourdan, No.10 Rue du Faubourg Saint-Honoré and also in the Forum des Halles. Fashionable, but rather traditional in style.

Tokio, Place des Victoires. See earlier.

The real centre for smart shoes and boots is the Left Bank. Here we shall find **Bazile** and **François Villon**, both in the Rue Bonaparte (see end of this chapter), both smart names in the fashionable shoe world. In the parallel Rue de Rennes we have two more, **Sacha** and **Maud Frizon**. But the shoes or boots which we buy here will not be exactly for ordinary knockabout wear, a wet evening at a bus stop. For this sort of footwear we should go to a branch of Bally or Manfield, or any shoe shop in the Boulevard Saint-Michel. These shops are also the places to buy attractive cheap summer sandals.

LEATHER GOODS

Handbags can be bought at any boutique which sells accessories, but naturally we think first of **Hermès** (see earlier). The top floor of the Forum des Halles also has a number of boutiques which sell good leather, including coats. And then there is **Lancel** in the Place de l'Opéra, where you can buy luggage as well as bags and belts. The luggage is traditional in style, expensive and looks impressive, as it is meant to.

Those wanting something more swinging in bags, cases, luggage and sports bags should go to **La Bagagerie**, the smart shop for this sort of thing. The main shop is at No.12 Rue Tronchet, very near the Au Printemps store, but there are other branches in Paris including Saint-Germain-des Prés, and also in New York, Beverly Hills and Tokyo.

UMBRELLAS

La Farge at No.40 Rue Vignon, just off the Rue Tronchet and very near La Bagagerie and Au Printemps, concentrates entirely on fun umbrellas of all kinds. Those caught out in the rain and wanting a cheap one quickly should go to the nearest branch of Monoprix.

SCENT AND MAKE-UP

If you know the brand you want, the easiest place to buy it is the airport duty-free shop on the way home. But this is not the place to try out unfamiliar brands; nor are the *grands magasins*, where the system of stalls-by-firms restricts choice and the assistants are not inclined to let you dally. You should go to a *parfumerie*, a small shop like a chemist where beauty products are sold. These exist all over

Paris, but especially in the Rue de Rivoli. The assistants here will be very helpful, letting you try out many different brands, spraying the backs of your hands. If a Frenchman should kiss your hand later the same evening, he will reel in amazement.

Scent, in general, is made by the big *haute couture* houses and sold in their boutiques. If you would like to visit a *grande maison de parfum*, try **Guerlain** at No.68 Champs-Elysées or 2 Place Vendôme. You will appreciate the elegant, rather intimidating atmosphere and the scents made from a great variety of flowers, which even include non-allergic scent. It will be a unique but rather expensive experience.

Make-up should not be bought in Paris, except in an emergency, and then from a *parfumerie* or *pharmacie*. The same brands are available in Britain at a third of the price.

JEWELLERY

For the real stuff you should go to one of the big names in the Rue de la Paix or the Place Vendôme. The jewellers here usually have attractive window displays and often temporary exhibitions of old or interesting pieces. For cheaper and costume jewellery we should go to the Rue de Castiglione and the Rue de Rivoli.

RUE DE RIVOLI

The Rue de Rivoli is often thought by visitors to be Paris's smartest shopping street. The point is arguable. Certainly the section between the Louvre and the Place de la Concorde is a ponderous piece of Second Empire planning; a monotonous line of identical buildings with an arcade and globe lights. But the arcade shelters us from the rain or the August sun and the Tuileries Gardens on the south side provide pleasant greenery.

The shops are unashamedly for tourists and many are open on public holidays, though not on Sundays. Many sell souvenirs, trinkets and sketches of the Eiffel Tower. Otherwise it is a street to buy cheap jewellery, scent, scarves and stockings – also books and some prints. Here are some addresses:

Galerie Hautecœur, No.172. Founded in 1796, it has a big stock of old prints, watercolours etc, reasonably priced.

Verveine, No.186. For hand-painted silk clothes and accessories, beautifully finished.

La Dame Blanche, No.188. Pretty scarves, stockings, umbrellas.

Reine Fleurmay, No.204. Good cheap jewellery, *bijoux fantaisie*.

The English Bookshop, No.224. We can browse here and at **Angelina's** No.226, have tea. This famous tea-shop, founded in 1903, was originally called Rumpelmayer, but changed its name after the last war. The style is still luxurious, with its red carpet, marble, gilt decor and wrought-iron, and it is always crowded. The chestnut meringue cake is much recommended. It is a place for *le five o'clock* or morning coffee; no meals are served.

The **Hôtel Meurice**, No.228, is one of Paris's most prestigious hotels, now British-owned. During the last war it was the German military headquarters. Here, in August 1944, the Commandant, General von Cholitz, after much heart-searching, took the decision to disobey Hitler's order to burn down Paris. Lovers of Paris should remember his name with gratitude.

D'Aleçon, No.234. A wide range of stockings, underwear and tights. A nice shop for the girls.

Mademoiselle France, No.238. *Bijoux fantaisie*, necklaces, trinkets, etc. The *vendeuse* takes particular trouble.

Harold, No.240. Smart cheaper clothes.

d'Orly, No.242. For scarves.

Lanvin for men, on the corner of the Rue Cambon.

W. H. Smith's, on the opposite corner. Mainly paperbacks now. Upstairs is a popular restaurant and tea-shop.

Old books and prints

The obvious places to buy these are the bookstalls beside the Seine. These are on either bank in the Notre-Dame area and the pleasure of browsing and buying will be much increased by our surroundings. The bookstalls, however, are closed in the winter. The Galerie Hautecœur, for prints, was mentioned earlier. On the Left Bank are a number of second-hand bookshops, especially in the Rue du Vieux Colombier (see end of this chapter).

ANTIQUES

The Hôtel Drouot auctions are really only for professional dealers. But Paris is full of antique shops, where enthusiasts may potter and discover what they can. There are several on the Ile Saint-Louis and others on the Left Bank in the Rue de Beaune and the Rue Bonaparte. The 'Flea Market' (see next section) is another popular hunting-ground. But the real mecca of antique-hunters is the **Louvre des Antiquaires**, at No.2 Place du Palais-Royal, beside the Louvre. Here in one large building are 240 antique shops, arranged on three floors. It is open from 11.0 a.m. till 7.0 p.m. Tuesdays to Saturdays. Here you can browse for hours, occasionally chatting to likeminded and knowledgeable people. For lovers of the past, it is a way of life.

If, however, you should decide to buy something, you should bear in mind that the export of antiques and works of art from France is rigorously controlled. There is a list, familiar to every dealer and auctioneer, of works which may not leave the country. Exceptions to this can only be made on the highest level, for instance the Dufy painting given by President Mitterrand to the Prince of Wales as a wedding present. Otherwise all antiques and works of art need an export permit to leave the country; the object may have to go before a committee of the Beaux-Arts for this permission. Obtaining this permit is the responsibility of the seller or dealer and he is not allowed to accept any money from you until it is obtained. This is a complicated business and may take a month or more. An agent will almost certainly be necessary; he will look after the packing, crating, transport, documentation and Customs formalities, but he will be very expensive and his charges can only be justified for really valuable works.

Paintings done in the last twenty years by a living artist come into a special category and are easier to take out of France. But even here care is required and the work must be declared to the French Customs at the port or airport.

THE MARKETS

Marché des Puces – the 'Flea Market'. This famous market is on the outskirts of Paris at Saint-Ouen (Metro Porte de Saint-Ouen or

Porte de Clignancourt). It is open all day on Saturdays and Sundays, and on Monday mornings, but as it attracts a large and interesting crowd, both French and foreigners, we should go early in the day. On arriving in the big open square we may well wonder if the market sells anything except blue jeans. But we must persevere into the side streets and arcades, in particular the Rue Jules-Valles and the Rue des Rosiers, and we should visit Ali Baba's cave. The market sells everything except food, but it is best known for its antiques and *petits objets*. Prices are not as low as we might hope.

Marché Saint-Pierre, in Montmartre, beside the Sacré-Cœur. A workaday market for materials and fabrics. Open every day.

Marché de la Mouffe, in the Rue Mouffetard, leading off the Place de la Contrescarpe (Metro Monge). The market is open every morning, except Sundays and Mondays, and is a place to buy household goods, camelots, oddments, amusing objects, but not antiques.

Marché Place Maubert (Metro Maubert). Tuesday, Thursday and Saturday mornings. Food; but it is also possible to buy shirts.

Marché Buci, Rue de Buci, Saint-Germain-des-Prés (Metro Mabillon or Saint-Germain-des-Prés). Open every day except Mondays, mornings and evenings. Mainly food, but also flowers, eggcups, cheap pants, etc. On the whole visitors go to a food market for the atmosphere, and here it is very typical of the quarter. Unless you are housekeeping, you have not come to buy haddock. But a bag of shrimps or cherries will add to the enjoyment of a stroll beside the Seine.

FOOD AND WINE

Many visitors like to buy pâtés and terrines to take home. (In theory pâtés are made of a single ingredient, terrines of several; but the difference has now largely disappeared.) These can be bought at any *triperie* or *épicerie*, sometimes with a Maxim's label. But the best ones come from **Fauchon**, No.2 Place de la Madeleine, which is Paris's top food shop. The range of pâtés here is very wide, including many we had never even thought of. We can also consider tinned and bottled sauces, jams, spices and mustards. Dijon mustard makes a good and comparatively inexpensive present, especial-

213

ly if it is in a stone jar with a big red seal. Mustard can also, of course, be bought in any grocery chain store such as **Félix Potin**.

Cheese is available in any *crèmerie* or *fromagerie*, but all too often this will have been kept in a refrigerator and never allowed to ripen. The range too may be limited, as the French now seem to prefer *fromage blanc* or yoghourt. But connoisseurs of cheese can still find what they want at **Androuet**, No.41 Rue d'Amsterdam (Metro Saint-Lazare). Here we shall find every sort of cheese, familiar and unknown. As Androuet is also a restaurant, we can taste them at lunch first before making our choice (see Chapter 11). Less imposing is the **Fromagerie des Carmes** in the Place Maubert. Here we find a big range of good cheeses and the staff will take trouble to find what we want. I personally recommend the Brie de Melun, the Fourme d'Ambert from Auvergne and the Epoisse *affiné*, from Burgundy, especially in the autumn. As the shop also sells most dairy products, you may well be tempted by a box of quail's eggs, *œufs de cailles* (boil them for seven minutes and eat cold with red pepper), an inexpensive luxury. These are cultivated, not wild, so we are not going to make the species extinct.

Fauchon also sells good and selected wines, including vintage port, a rarity in France. But there are wineshops all over Paris and any branch of the **Nicolas** chain will provide everything from the cheapest *vin ordinaire* to the most expensive *haut crû*. If you should become bewildered by years and vintages, the manager will be both well-informed and helpful. He will know which wines are for immediate drinking and which for laying down, which are *léger* and which *corsé*. He will be accustomed to those on a limited budget and there will probably be special offers of good value. But we should remember that in France, unlike England, Burgundy is a much lighter wine than Bordeaux. The better brands of Beaujolais – Brouilly, Morgon, Moulin-à-vent – can be bought with confidence, but ordinary Beaujolais should be avoided, except for the Beaujolais Nouveau, which should be bought and drunk soon after 15 November. Its special quality depends on the year, but it always makes a good and fairly cheap talking-point. If you want to take home your Customs ration of spirits, you might consider Calvados, Vieux Marc or Armagnac, as a change from the traditional brandy. In general, however, the French themselves prefer to stick to whisky.

GRANDS MAGASINS – DEPARTMENT STORES

Many people do all their shopping in one of these. They are easy to find and it is simpler to have everything under the same roof. But it is hardly the most enjoyable way of shopping. Two tips should be given at the outset. You should wear very thin clothes, even if you shiver in the street outside your hotel. The shops are kept very hot and the assistants wear thin dresses. Anyone in an overcoat is liable to heatstroke. The second tip is to go in the morning, if possible. In the afternoons and evenings the stores become unbearably crowded (this does not apply to Aux Trois Quartiers or boutiques). This is even more so during sales, which are held in January and July.

BOULEVARD HAUSSMANN – the Oxford Street of Paris.
Splendidly lit up at Christmas

Galeries Lafayette, behind the Opéra, the best-known and busiest store (Metro Opéra or Chaussée d'Antin). The main building is centred round a courtyard with a fine glass roof and a nostalgic glimpse of the sky. The store sells almost everything, but it specializes in clothes for Madame and Mademoiselle; there is, however, a man's shop next door.

The ground floor is crowded, but somewhere in it we may find bags, jewellery, knitwear, toys and a small books and record section. Scent and make-up are also here but, as has already been indicated, these are better bought in a *parfumerie*. However, all the main brands are available here.

The first floor is largely occupied by mini-fashion boutiques and we may well look in at Cacharel, Rodier or Jousse. But the prices are the same as in the main boutiques, and the choice is smaller. The next floor is for expensive clothes, except for the 'Club 20 Ans', the teenage fashion section. There are also some cheaper clothes, with attractive designs and some good bargains. The blouses and shirts are recommended. The restaurant on the top floor has long queues because it is so popular. But we can also lunch at Au Printemps.

Au Printemps, Boulevard Haussmann (Metro Havre Caumartin). This is a more up-and-coming version than the Galeries Lafayette, and, in general, more enjoyable and with staff who are less brusque. But we pay a little more. There are two buildings, joined by a second-floor walkway. The Nouveau Magasin has clothes. Cheaper dresses are on the first floor and there is a large bathing-suit section and a good sports clothes area. The ground floor has stockings, tights and scarves – indeed this is the place for scarves, some designed by big names, others anonymous but also attractive.

The other building ('Havre') is mainly occupied by household objects. The amusing restaurant under the dome is a series of mini-self-service counters where you can choose salads, pizzas grills, German food, sandwiches, dessert and so on. The roof garden has a good view.

Marks & Spencer have a large and popular store in the Boulevard Haussmann. The main attractions here are English clothes and food. The former attracts the romantic French, who find it the next best thing to a real visit to Oxford Street. The latter brings in the homesick British, wanting sausage rolls, crumpets and wrapped, sliced bread.

BOULEVARD DE LA MADELEINE

Aux Trois Quartiers, almost opposite the Madeleine. This is Paris's luxury department store and the service is old-fashioned and de-lightful. If you are trying on gloves, they will bring you a velvet cushion for your elbow. But of course prices are much higher than elsewhere and it is rarely crowded, even in the evenings. The ground floor has the celebrated gloves and equally well-known handkerchiefs. The clothes, on the third floor, are rather expensive, but bargains can be found among the knitwear, which is always good. The 'Weekend' section is considerably cheaper. Aux Trois Quartiers can well be combined with a visit to Fauchon nearby – the same sort of person goes to both. It is closed on Mondays in August.

RUE DE RIVOLI

The part of the Rue de Rivoli east of the Palais-Royal has several department stores. Samaritaine also faces the Seine.

Samaritaine (Metro Pont Neuf) is one of the cheaper stores and prides itself on selling everything, from private zoos to portable bathrooms, from instant psychiatry to gimmicky telephones. It is not, however, the place for clothes. It delivers anywhere in Paris, COD, and there is a *nocturne* every Wednesday until 10.0 p.m. (The roof terrace bar with its wonderful view has already been recommended). If we live in Paris, this is where to come for bargain refrigerators, pressure-cookers and household goods, which are guaranteed and serviced.

C & A, Rue de Rivoli, very near Samaritaine. Clothes only, cheap, pretty ones as in other branches of this chain. The branch at the Tour Montparnasse has the same clothes but is less crowded.

BHV (Bazar de l'Hôtel de Ville), Rue de Rivoli, opposite the Hotel de Ville. This is a cheap store, selling mainly things for the home. There are five floors of do-it-yourself equipment, furniture, wallpaper, paint, fittings and so on. *Nocturne* on Wednesday till 10.0 p.m.

LEFT BANK

Au Bon Marché (Metro Sèvres-Babylone). Rather off the beaten track and so less crowded and less fashionable than the Boulevard Haussmann. Prices are also marginally lower. The store sells everything, including clothes, and for lunch we can regale ourselves in Le Bistroself, Le Fastfood or La Sandwicherie.

We end this chapter with a shopping walk on the Left Bank. We shall explore the Left Bank in later chapters, so this is simply a stroll for shoppers – window and serious. The smart quarter of the Left Bank is more compact than the Right Bank and so more suitable for walking. We shall also have the pleasure of seeing the girls of Saint-Germain-des-Prés, who look and dress very differently from their cousins in the Faubourg Saint-Honoré. The clothes in the shops are also different. However, there are other things on this walk besides dress shops – antique shops, bookshops, records. It is a walk for men as well as women. And both sexes will enjoy the narrow old streets, so full of the atmosphere of *vieux Paris*, before Haussmann changed it all.

We start at Metro Saint-Germain-des-Prés (see also Chapter 17) and head west along the Boulevard. Just beyond Lipp's we find

Aussi, a small boutique which specializes in modern, well-designed turquoise jewellery; bracelets, necklaces, brooches and so on. Reasonably priced, these make good presents.

At the Rue des Saints-Pères we turn left, away from the river. This street is full of boutiques of clothes and *bijoux fantaisie*. For instance, we can try **Nelly Valéry** (No.60, on right side), a shop for cheap, eye-catching jewellery, made of plate, enamel or even plastic; but colourful. At No.67, on the left, is **Catogan** for sweaters. These are very smart and, alas, very expensive. Opposite is **Laura Ashley**; very popular, but hardly for British visitors.

We cross the Rue de Grenelle and continue along the Rue des Saint-Pères. **Natalie Frangeul** is another shop for amusing cheap jewellery and then, for a change, we can look at the books and papers in the **Librairie Saints-Pères**. Just before the corner, **M.M.** (Marie Martine) is a boutique for funfurs, not overpriced for what they are.

Across the Rue de Sèvres, on the corner, is **Cellini**, an Italian *haute couture* boutique. Italian clothes have been fashionable for some time; here they are both smart and medium-priced. We turn left here into the Rue des Vieux Colombiers.

Both sides of this street are full of boutiques, and we can note only a few. **Fikipsy** (No.23) is for fashionable co-ordinates, but prices are low, especially for shirts. At No.19 is **Le Colombier**, the place for smart wedding-dresses, if you should happen to want one on your visit. Next door is **Marcel Lassance**, a good boutique for men's clothes. On the opposite side of the street is **Séraphina** (No.22), for French-style underwear, rather expensive.

Next door (No.20) is a bookshop, **L'Oeil Ecoute**, which is much recommended. Both the stall outside and the inside room are full of bargains, especially in second-hand art books and marked-down leatherbound volumes. The proprietor comes from Eastern Europe, a friendly man who will encourage you to browse as long as you like.

On the other, east, side of the Rue de Rennes, but still in the Rue du Vieux Colombier, we find that the boutiques have an older style. On the right side note the old shop-front of **Cyriaque** and, just into the Rue Madame, is **Chantal Thomas**. This well-known boutique from former times still has an old-fashioned charm. You sit on an antique chair while the *vendeuse* pulls drawers out of wooden

218

chests. The underwear she is selling, however, will be modern, not antique, and the prices are high.

A little further on we have **Au Plat d'Etain**, an antique shop specializing in old toys, for instance lead soldiers. Opposite are more second-hand bookshops.

We are now in the Place Saint-Sulpice (see also Chapter 17). On the corner of the Rue Bonaparte is **Saint-Laurent-Rive-Gauche for men**, which may well attract us. Continuing along the north side of the square, we consider buying a rosary, booking a pilgrimage or having a drink in the Café de la Mairie. But our goal is really **Saint-Laurent-Rive-Gauche** on the corner of the Rue des Canettes. This is the most glamorous boutique on the Left Bank, specializing in ready-to-wear dresses, accessories, scarves and evening clothes. It is not, however, for paupers.

We retrace our steps to the Rue Bonaparte and turn right along it towards Saint-Germain-des-Prés. This is the Rue du Faubourg Saint-Honoré of the Left Bank. The prices are about the same. The clientèle is equally well-heeled, the clothes equally fashionable, although more stylish and trendier. It is not compulsory for ladies to buy black velvet evening trousers here, but it is possible.

At the Saint-Sulpice end, facing the garage, is the centre of Italian fashion in Paris, with boutiques like **Giovanni Versace**, **Pisanti** (especially for sweaters), **Ventilo**, and **di Varni** (furs). All these are very expensive but they will give great pleasure to windowshoppers. By way of a change we pass an ivory shop and consider buying a statuette of the Pope.

Diagonally across the Rue du Four is **François Villon's** shoe shop and next to it, in the Rue du Four, **La Petite Gaminerie**. This is the place to buy children's clothes which are both smart and fun; the prices are not outrageous.

Continuing along the Rue Bonaparte we find some famous boutiques: **Bazile**'s for shoes, **Georges Rech**, and **Louis Féraud**, probably the most expensive boutique on the Left Bank, and the most fashionable. At the end on the left we have the metallic shop front of **Ted Lapidus**, for women as well as men.

We are now back at Saint-Germain-des-Prés, but we may like to continue our walk for a few minutes more, as there are some enticing shops we have not yet seen. So we retrace our steps to the Rue du Four and turn left at the *pharmacie*.

219

There are boutiques all round us here and the names change as fast as the fashions. But since the premises are licensed for commercial use, one boutique merely replaces another. The owners often buy from the big names in the Rue Bonaparte, so prices here are comparatively lower. Some names may be mentioned: **Georges Darmon** (for men, also in Saint-Tropez) and **Caroll** (Sweaters for women). Both these are on the left side; on the right we have **Tilbury**, excellent for leather goods of all kinds, including coats and shoes.

We reach the Boulevard Saint-Germain at Mabillon; opposite is the Marché de Buci, already referred to. We can turn right towards Odéon and here are more fashionable shops, but the prices are rather lower; for example, **Coroner** (No.127), for women (good sweaters), **Anthony** for men – I once bought a big synthetic fur coat there and looked like a great bear; **Emanuel Pariken** and **Daniel Hechter** – the last is more expensive because of the well-known name.

Or we can turn left, back to Saint-Germain-des-Prés. On the left is **La Gaminerie**. This boutique with its exciting decor and loud music is reminiscent of London in the 1960s. But there is nothing Sixtyish about the clothes or accessories which are right up to date. The assistants are friendly and the prices are about half of what you would have to pay in the Rue Bonaparte a few yards away. Much recommended.

We arrive back again at Saint-Germain-des-Prés, at Ted Lapidus and Vidal's record shop and the Drugstore. I suggest that we cross the Boulevard and sink into chairs at the Deux Magots. Here, over a cup of hot chocolate or a glass of something stronger, we can examine our booty with pride. We can also look back over our walk, which will, I hope, have been a rewarding one in more than one way.

In writing this chapter I have been much helped by my daughter Victoria, a keen shopper, some of whose friends design clothes in the fashion world. I should like to record my gratitude.

PART THREE

The Left Bank

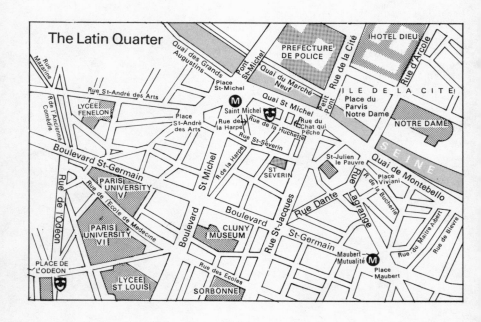

CHAPTER 14

The Latin Quarter

PREFECTURE DE POLICE

HOTEL DIEU

Quai des Grands Augustins

Pont St-Michel

Quai du Marché Neuf

Rue de la Cité

Rue d'Arcole

ILE DE LA CITE

Rue Mazarine

Rue St-André des Arts

Place St-Michel

Quai St Michel

Place du Parvis Notre Dame

NOTRE DAME

R. de l'Ancienne Comédie

LYCEE FENELON

Place St-André des Arts

Saint Michel

Rue de la Harpe

Rue de la Huchette

Rue du Chat qui Pêche

SEINE

Rue St-Séverin

St-Julien le Pauvre

Quai de Montebello

Boulevard St-Germain

St Michel

R. de la Harpe

ST SEVERIN

Place Viviani

R. de la Bûcherie

PARIS UNIVERSITY VI

Rue de l'Ecole de Medecine

Rue Lagrange

Rue du Maitre Albert

Boulevard

Rue St-Jacques

Rue Dante

Rue de Bièvre

Rue de l'Odéon

PARIS UNIVERSITY VII

CLUNY MUSEUM

Boulevard St-Germain

PLACE DE L'ODEON

Rue des Ecoles

Maubert Mutualité

Place Maubert

LYCEE ST LOUIS

SORBONNE

The Latin Quarter

The Left Bank – *la Rive Gauche* – has an atmosphere which is unique and we are aware of it the moment we cross the river. The architecture (particularly if it is nineteenth-century), the traffic and much of the to-and-fro may seem similar to other parts of Paris, yet we can tell the difference by looking at the shops and cafés and, especially, the people; they may not look happier than Parisians elsewhere, but they appear livelier and, in every sense, more colourful. The Left Bank is generally associated with youth, students, intellectuals, artists, books, poverty, freedom and a bohemian way of life – though in fact there are hundreds of thousands of people living on the Left Bank who have nothing to do with any of these things.

But the atmosphere remains, and with good reason. Anyone who has spent a term or a year at an art school or taken the short course in French Language and Civilization at the Sorbonne will always have nostalgic memories of that lost, unforgettable spring on the Left Bank. They will revisit their old haunts, look from the outside at their old window and wonder what has become of their one-time *copains*. For those of us who missed this experience, we can read and hear about it and, better still, try to rediscover its romance. As we stroll along the boulevards or the narrow streets, informally dressed and possibly munching pancakes, some of it will rub off on us. Henri Burger's novel *La Vie de Bohème*, and Puccini's opera which was based on it, not only publicized a lifestyle which had been going on for a very long time; both the author and the composer knew that they were on to a winner. (The word 'bohemian' in this connection comes from a double misunderstanding. The Left Bank 'bohemians' were vaguely identified with gypsies, who have a very different lifestyle; and all gipsies were thought to come from Bohemia.)

When the Roman city of Lutetia spread out from the Ile de la Cité, it expanded mainly on to the Left Bank, towards the sun, towards Rome. Only a few ruins remain of this civilization and the real history of the Left Bank began with the arrival of Christianity and the building of such abbeys as Cluny and Saint-Germain-des-Prés. It became the intellectual centre of Paris, of France and, arguably, of Europe. There were several causes: the removal of Abelard and his followers to the Cluny area; the foundation of the University of Paris (1215); the gift by St Louis of several houses to his confessor, Robert de Sorbon, for a theological college (1253); the first French printing works in the Sorbonne (1469); the founding of the Collège de France by François I in 1530. The whole area, the Latin Quarter, was ruled by the University (except the Collège de France, which has always retained a certain independence), and the University became a sort of autonomous state within Paris, strong enough to defy even the king, which it often did.

The University and the printing press naturally attracted scholars, writers and in due course publishers, even if they had nothing to do with the University itself. The artists arrived at the end of the nineteenth century (whatever Murger may have imagined), attracted from Montmartre by the studios, art schools and cafés of Montparnasse. The musicians, however, remained faithful to the Right Bank, where they were nearer to the Conservatoire, the Salle Pleyel and the Opéra.

A good starting-place for our walk is Metro Maubert-Mutualité, on the edge of the most picturesque part of the area, the huddle of tiny streets between the Seine and the Boulevard Saint-Germain and, east to west, between the Place Maubert and the Place Saint-Michel; the term Latin Quarter is sometimes applied exclusively to this part. Not that we are likely to hear any Latin here now. Apart from French, the most common languages spoken are from North Africa, the Eastern Mediterranean and South-East Asia. Every other house seems to be a small restaurant serving the meals of faraway places. In between are small grocers (*épiciers*) selling exotic food and spices. The little streets reek of *couscous*. We could be in Tunis or old Saigon or, come to that, Soho.

Many of the streets are now closed to traffic and are a pedestrian precinct. This will make our exploration on foot pleasanter, though not necessarily safer. French policemen do not pound a beat and

224

there has been a marked increase in pestering, drug-pushing and petty crime. But then there have always been perils in the Latin Quarter. The archetypal hero was not only the imaginary operatic Rodolfo, romantic, feckless and harmless; there are plenty like him still on the Left Bank and they are not always French; there was also the real François Villon, the fifteenth-century poet, violent criminal and Master of Arts at the Sorbonne. His poems and ballads were written in French slang, not Latin, and were barely comprehensible even in his own day. But his memory should not deter us from our walk and we are unlikely to come to any harm in daylight.

The **Place Maubert** was for centuries a place to be avoided, full of crime and such entertainments as public executions. Later it became the skid row of Paris, the haunt of drunken *clochards*. Now it is a respectable shopping area, architecturally uninteresting, but with a lively open-air market (mornings only on Tuesdays, Thursdays and Saturdays). Many people throng the place, attracted by the good value and the low prices. The name Maubert is possibly a corruption of Maître Albert, a Dominican teacher at the University, who held his classes in the open air.

A number of small streets lead down to the river. In the Rue de Bièvre we can see the private home of President Mitterrand. In the Rue du Maître Albert we find a small animal clinic, the Paris branch of the PDSA and the gift of the Duke of Windsor to his adopted city. But we shall probably walk along the Rue de la Bûcherie westwards to the Square Viviani. This is a delightful garden with benches, truncated columns, acacias and a wonderful view of Notre-Dame across the river.

Behind the Square is the small church of **Saint-Julien-le-Pauvre**. Many chapels have stood on this site; the present church is contemporary with Notre-Dame. It has no transepts, no stained glass or organ, but we can admire the Gothic vaulting in the aisles. The chancel, the east end, is rumoured to be very fine, but is shut off from our eyes by an iconostasis, a wall of icons and hanging lamps. For nearly a hundred years the church has been the centre of the Greek-Catholic Church in Paris, but it was originally intended as a church for the poor. It was named after the mediæval bishop of Le Mans, St Julien, who gave everything he had to the poor. Poorboxes abound in the church and it has for many centuries been the chapel of Hôtel-Dieu across the river; it is used especially for pauper funerals.

Outside the entrance, a few yards away, is another old building, **Les Oubliettes**. This is now a nightclub (no dancing), where we can drink and be entertained until the small hours by songs of the Middle Ages and later, sung by entertainers in fancy dress. Afterwards we can make a late night tour of the *oubliettes*, the deep dungeons from which few prisoners ever emerged.

Continuing along the Rue de la Bûcherie we find an English-language bookshop, Shakespeare and Company. This is named after the celebrated bookshop in the Rue de l'Odéon (which no longer exists), where Sylvia Beach provided a home-from-home, and often subsidies, for the hungry British and American writers of the Twenties and Thirties. The present bookshop has no connection with the old one.

We reach the Rue Saint-Jacques, a big straight street built on the old Roman road, cutting like a knife through the Latin Quarter. Unlike most roads, which lead to Rome, this one was supposed to lead to Spain, to Santiago, Saint James of Compostella, hence the name. In fact it leads to the Porte d'Orléans. Confusingly, the part nearest to the river, where we now stand, is called the Rue du Petit Pont. We cross the street and, walking away from the Seine, find the Rue de la Parcheminerie, a narrow street where parchment was made and sold. Leading off it is another pleasant garden, beside the cloisters of **Saint-Séverin**. The church, one of the finest in Paris, was for many centuries the parish church of the Left Bank and is now, officially, the University church. There is some dispute about which St Séverin it is named after; a hermit who lived on the site in the sixth century and who persuaded Clodoald (St Cloud), grandson of King Clovis, to become a priest; or a Swiss namesake; or the sixth-century philosopher Boethius, who was partly responsible for introducing Aristotle's works and thinking into Catholic theology. Some of his writings were translated into Anglo-Saxon by King Alfred. Boethius was eventually executed, declared a martyr and canonized as St Severinus.

The west façade is Romanesque, although the door comes from the thirteenth-century Saint-Pierre-aux-Bœufs on the Ile de la Cité, now demolished. The church, however, is mainly late Gothic, complete with gables and monstrous gargoyles which overhang the street. It is a curious building, as broad as it is long, without any transepts. Inside, only the first three columns have capitals and some of the arches at the east end were transformed into rounded late seventeenth-century arches on the orders of La Grande Mademoiselle (see Chapter 16); she had quarrelled with Saint-Sulpice and had transferred her devotions and her wealth to Saint-Séverin. Happily her influence did not last long.

The great glory of the church is the ambulatory behind the altar. A double row of slender columns, the centre one twisted, rise into the tracery of the vaulted ceiling and we seem to be wandering through a garden of fountains made of stone. There are no distant views; we are lost in a Gothic forest. A jarring note, however, is introduced by the modern windows by Jean Bazaine, who also did some mosaics for the UNESCO building (see Chapter 18). His original sketches were much admired for the way in which he followed and complemented the gothic columns. But the final effect is something else. The two blue windows, which can be seen from the nave, are dark and tolerable, but the four shocking-pink windows distract, I think, from the beauty of the church. The best time to see the ambulatory, in my view, is late on a dark November afternoon, when the columns are lit and the windows have disappeared. But on a fine summer morning lovers of stained glass can console themselves by looking up from the nave at the fine late-fifteenth-century glass in the clerestory. Bazaine, a leading figure in contemporary French glass, is more successful elsewhere.

The church has a good organ and is a centre for choral music. The concerts are often given by visiting choirs and we should take advantage of this, if our time schedule allows.

Returning to the Rue Saint-Jacques, we turn towards the river and then left into the famous **Rue de la Huchette** – Elliot Paul's Narrow Street – though in fact an even narrower street turns off it, the Rue du Chat qui Pêche, the narrowest street in Paris and a sad, almost windowless alley. Fortunately it is quite short and there is the quay at the end.

The Rue de la Huchette, by contrast, was known for centuries for its luxury, though luxurious is hardly a word we should use about it now. But it is pretty enough and full of excitement. On the left the **Caveau de la Huchette** is a jazz-cellar, where we can drink and dance into the small hours in another dungeon setting. A notice on the wall

227

COMPANION GUIDE TO PARIS

reminds us that sleep equals equilibrium; it was presumably not put there by the management. A little farther on the same side we find the small **Théâtre de la Huchette**, where a double bill of one-act plays by Ionesco has been running non-stop for twenty-five years (at the moment of writing), a record only beaten by a play in London. We should also note **No.10** where a young Brigadier-General Bonaparte, unemployed and unpaid, existed for several months in 1795, not yet on the road to glory. At the corner of the Rue de la Harpe we are in the heart of the *souk*; it is the moment, perhaps, for a cup of very black thick coffee.

We emerge on to the large Place Saint-Michel (metro), a nineteenth-century square complete with a large statue and fountain of St Michael which students climb and plaster with posters. The square teems with people and traffic; it is the junction of the quay and the Boulevard Saint-Michel, the main street of the Latin Quarter (see Chapter 15). We cross carefully at the lights and on the far side we find a smaller square, the Place Saint-André-des-Arts, an extension of the main square, though it is much older. It is a picturesque place, with its pavement cafés, and the restaurants provide French and Alsace food – we have left the Orient behind.

We follow the narrow Rue Saint-André-des-Arts, which is also a pedestrian precinct. At its end we are at a crossroads; ahead is the Marché de Buci (see Chapter 17). On the right is the **Rue Mazarine**, which has a nice view of the dome of the Institute; on the left is the Rue de l'Ancienne Comédie. At No.12 Rue Mazarine the young Molière made his first stage appearance. With the help of an inheritance, he reorganized the existing small company, built a theatre on the disused tennis-court and in effect founded the Comédie-Française.

After Molière's death (1673) the company continued under the direction of his widow, but in 1688 they were driven out by the teachers at the Institut college (see Chapter 4), who did not care for the proximity of actors, and rather irreverent ones at that, to their great college. Madame Molière found another tennis-court at No.14 Rue de l'Ancienne Comédie, which is really the same street, and in 1689 the theatre opened with Racine's *Phèdre* and Molière's *Médecin Malgré Lui*. The company remained there till 1770, when it moved to the Tuileries Palace Theatre. The theatre is now the office of a large publishing house, but it has been decorated with pictures and engravings to remind us of Molière and the early days of the Comédie-Française (occasional guided tours).

Facing us at No.13 is the old **Café Procope**, perhaps the oldest in Paris. It was for centuries the place where people went to hear the latest news and gossip and it was particularly busy during the years which preceded the Revolution. A plaque on the wall recalls some of the famous names, politicians and writers, who were clients of the café, and among them we may note Benjamin Franklin (the American envoy to France during the Peace of Versailles, 1783), Robespierre, Danton, Marat and Bonaparte. It was a centre of revolutionary thought. It was also a literary café, used by La Fontaine, Rousseau, Voltaire, Diderot and many others until the present day. A name missing from the plaque is Oscar Wilde, who drank there with the poet Verlaine. Poor old Verlaine, far over the hill, would sit there hoping that the prestigious Englishman would buy him another absinthe – something that Wilde unkindly sometimes failed to do. Later, after his own fall, Wilde would sit there hoping that someone would speak to him and buy him a drink.

The Procope is now a well-known restaurant and we should certainly eat there. Its décor has been preserved in eighteenth-century style, the service is excellent, and it is full of intelligent people, many of them literary. It appeals to those who enjoy good food at reasonable prices; in season we can eat *salmi de faisan*, washed down with a bottle of Beaujolais Nouveau or Crozes-Hermitage. The atmosphere is comfortable, almost luxurious, and we shall not be hustled.

Afterwards we can stroll along the street to the Carrefour de l'Odéon (metro), the square where many streets meet the Boulevard Saint-Germain. It is surrounded by cafés, cinemas, and bookshops selling medical textbooks; the Ecole de Médecine is at the east end. The *carrefour* is dominated by the bulky statue of Danton, calling in his best orator's style for more audacity and education and gazing enthusiastically towards the Procope.

Crossing the Boulevard we continue up the Rue de l'Odéon to the Place de l'Odéon, a half-moon-shaped square of simple 1780 houses and several restaurants. Facing us across the 'half-moon' is the colonnaded façade of the **Théâtre de l'Odéon**, one of the National Theatres of Paris. It was built in 1782, in the neo-Classical style then fashionable, to provide a more suitable home for the Comedians in

229

the Tuileries Palace. The new 'Théâtre Française' was possibly the last artistic achievement of the reign of Louis XVI. The company did well for ten years, but the Revolution split it. Some became Republicans and moved to a new theatre on the Right Bank, the present Comédie Française. The others went to the guillotine.

After the Revolution the theatre had a sad time. It was damaged by fire (and reconstructed), then used by failing companies for their productions. It was too far off the beaten track for the theatre-goers of the Belle Époque. Its revival started after World War Two, when it became the theatre of Jean-Louis Barrault, his wife Madeleine Renaud and their company. They produced modern plays, particularly by Claudel, Beckett, Ionesco, Genet, Albee, Sarraute and others, together with the rather incongruous Shakespeare. It was the most crowded theatre in Paris; the productions and acting were famous, particularly Claudel's *Partage de Midi* with Barrault and Edwige Feuillère.

All this came brutally to an end in the student riots of May 1968, when the theatre was occupied. The subsequent goings-on made good copy for the journalists, but they caused a good deal of damage to the theatre, the scenery and costumes, and to the company itself, which was once again divided politically. It is now an ordinary theatre, belonging to the State. Various projects are mooted, but what it really needs is a new Barrault – or Molière.

Beyond the theatre we are at the Luxembourg Gardens. We can either enter, or turn left along the Rue de Medicis to the Boulevard Saint-Michel (see Chapters 15 and 16). Or we can return, exploring various side streets on the way, to Danton's statue and the metro.

CHAPTER 15

The Montagne Sainte-Geneviève

The Montagne Sainte-Geneviève dominates the Left Bank. Not exactly a mountain, yet surprisingly steep in some streets, it was an obvious point both for worship and defence; in due course it became a centre of learning. On its north side, towards the Seine, we can number the Sorbonne, the medical and law schools, several schools devoted to technical subjects such as mining, the Collège de France, three large *lycées* (secondary schools) and the site of the Ecole Polytechnique, France's most prestigious centre of higher education. The summit of the mountain is the Panthéon, once the Church of Sainte-Geneviève, the patron saint of Paris. Soufflot's graceful dome, surrounded by a ring of columns, floats above the Left Bank and the city, a worthy crown.

Along the eastern flank of the Montagne runs the well-known **Boulevard Saint-Michel** – do not call it the Boul' Mich', unless you want to sound very old. Metro Saint-Michel makes a convenient starting-place for our walk. This is the street of students, careworn young people in jeans and sweaters and raincoats, carrying large folders and paperback books. The Boulevard is lined with bookshops, cafés and, surprisingly, shoe shops. The cafés, with their sandwiches and pinball machines are cheap (but expect higher prices in the Select-Latin) and full of rather solitary young people, sitting and spinning out a cup of coffee in the warm while they write their papers; if we glance over their shoulders, it usually seems to be algebra. For recreation they play at the pinball tables, which will cost them as much as another coffee or even a glass of beer. They look, even the blacks who form a large part of the local population, as if they are just recovering from flu, a combination possibly of too much black coffee, too many cigarettes and too little sleep.

Montagne Ste-Geneviève
& The Luxembourg

The liveliest period is October, the *rentrée des classes*, when the street and the bookshops are full of people buying books and pencil-sharpeners, getting ready for the new academic year. They will have spent their summer with their families or lying quite broke on a sunny beach or, more probably, working in a restaurant. It is also the time of year for changing girlfriends. The idea of the *rentrée* has spread now to the whole of Paris – the party season, the conversations about summer holidays in distant parts, the autumn fashions, the vintage, the cars, the new oysters. But it is not quite like that in the Boulevard Saint-Michel.

The Boulevard was the setting for the well-publicized student riots of May 1968, when the students burnt cars, broke shop windows, cut down trees as barricades and threw cobblestones at the police. Marxism and Anarchism still thrive in the area, judging from the leaflets lying on the ground, but several 'students' have since admitted publicly that they were never at any college, and even at the time it seemed that some of them were rather elderly for the part. Anyway, the trees have been replanted, the cobblestones covered with tarmac and the Boulevard returned to its normal studiousness.

Leaving Metro Saint-Michel, we follow the pavement southwards through the crowds, pausing perhaps to buy a newspaper from some other country, most of which are available in this area. Crossing the Boulevard Saint-Germain, we have a garden, some Roman ruins, a sixteenth-century *hôtel* and museum – Cluny, to which we shall return at the end of this chapter. (Metro Cluny is closed permanently.)

At the **Place de la Sorbonne** we can pause for a moment for breath. The square has recently been reconstructed for those on foot, lined with cafés, cleared of parked cars, and decorated with young lime trees. At the end is the façade and dome of the Sorbonne chapel, to which we shall also return. We can also consider the ornate statue of Auguste Comte (1798–1857), the Positivist (Humanist) philosopher admired by John Stuart Mill. His mottoes '*Famille, Patrie, Humanité*', and '*Ordre et Progrès*' make the ideas of the nineteenth century seem more comfortable than our own. Surprisingly, he was dismissed from his post as examiner in mathematics at the Ecole Polytechnique for his 'revolutionary' theories.

233

The Boulevard Saint-Michel meets the Luxembourg Gardens at a busy square (Place Edmond Rostand, Metro Luxembourg). On our left is a hamburger restaurant, once the celebrated student café, Capoulade's. We turn left here and climb the Rue Soufflot to the **Panthéon**.

There have been holy buildings on the summit of the Montagne since time immemorial; since the sixth century they have usually been dedicated to Ste Geneviève. But in the eighteenth century her abbey and church were in ruins and Louis XV, who was seriously ill, vowed that, if he should recover, he would build a noble church in her honour. He duly recovered and the task was entrusted to Germain Soufflot, who had royal connections through Madame de Pompadour. His ideas were grandiose indeed, in size and height: a gigantic classical temple with a dome under which the tomb of the saint would lie. But both time and money ran out and Soufflot never saw his dome. It was completed by his pupil Rondelet in 1789, the very eve of the Revolution.

It was soon declared a Temple of Fame, a great atheistic building fit to receive the bodies of the great men who had died in the time of French liberty. It became a church again under Napoleon I, a necropolis in 1830, a church again in the Second Empire, and finally once more a necropolis for the great atheists of France. Auguste Comte's idea of replacing the calendar of saints with another dedicated to scientists and scholars finds its temple here, but politics tend to come to the fore. We can visit the tombs of Rousseau, Voltaire, Victor Hugo, Emile Zola, Braille, Jean Jaurès (left-wing politician and orator, assassinated in 1914) and Jean Moulin, the Resistance leader in the Second World War, tortured to death in the Occupation. Elaborate though some of the monuments are, they seem rather lost in the vast expanse of the building. The Panthéon received a boost to its prestige when President Mitterrand in 1981 on his Inauguration Day visited it to pay homage to Jaurès and Moulin. He left Notre-Dame till the following day.

Below its dome the Panthéon is a grim building, better seen from a distance. The blank walls dominate the square like a prison and the super-colossal columns of the portico are of a grandeur which was never Rome. But standing under them, feeling dwarfed rather than uplifted, we can enjoy a fine view down the mountain, across the Luxembourg Gardens and Palace to the Eiffel Tower. Framing the view are two symmetrical façades, also by Soufflot, now occupied by the local *mairie* and law school.

One of the great men of the area (and, indeed, of France) is not honoured in the Panthéon, though a street leading off the Place is named after him. **King Clovis of the Franks** (466–511) was without doubt the founder of France and of much else in Europe. He defeated the Romans at Soissons and so ended the Roman Empire in Gaul, though the Romans, compromising, gave him the title of Proconsul. He fought off invasions from the East (from where the Franks had come originally) and incorporated dissident provinces into his new kingdom. Hard and ruthless, he gave France its own identity, based on Paris; a man of great ability, he organized the government and codified the laws. His conversion to Christianity by his wife, Clotilde of Burgundy, and Ste Geneviève, gave a new impetus to the young kingdom. His success in fusing the Teutonic and Gallic cultures started the French civilization and finally produced, it can fairly be said, the modern Frenchman.

He built a large church on the summit of the Montagne, where the Lycée Henri IV now stands, and where he, his wife and Ste Geneviève were buried. The saint soon became the personality of the Montagne and there were big processions in her honour through the streets, with elaborate decorations, bells and a vast crowd. These processions continued for centuries, until they were firmly suppressed by the Revolution.

The church attracted a monastery and then became an abbey, so rich and powerful that it was ripe for looting. Nothing remains now except the cellars and the belfry, known as Clovis's Tower, though it was of course built long after his time. The relics of Ste Geneviève were moved opposite to Saint-Etienne-du-Mont; the whereabouts of the remains of the King and Queen are unknown.

The church of **Saint-Etienne-du-Mont** is one of the finest Gothic churches in Paris. Originally the parish church of the abbey servants, it was rebuilt in the sixteenth century, starting with the belfry. A hundred years later in 1619 Queen Margot, the first wife of Henri IV, laid the foundation stone of the façade and the church was finally consecrated in 1626. The façade is indeed remarkable with its triple pediment. The east end, the chancel, is late Gothic in style; the windows of the nave were altered later to the rounded Renaissance manner.

Inside, it is a tall church, with elaborate late gothic vaulting and a hanging keystone. The eye is immediately taken by the rood screen, the only one surviving in Paris because, being basically an arch, it did not cut off the altar from the congregation. On either side two beautiful spiral staircases (late sixteenth-century) lead to the top of the rood screen and to the extensions towards the chancel. The organ is big and it makes a great sound at recitals, weddings and other big events. We should also notice the stained glass, particularly on the right side, where the gold and deep red glimmer in the dusk. The shrine of Ste Geneviève attracts much attention and many candles. Plaques also mark the burial places of the remains of Pascal and Racine. Marat, after a brief stay in the Panthéon, is buried in the charnel cloister, beyond the chancel. Before leaving the church we should also look at the wooden pulpit (1650), which is supported by a statue of Samson. Is he, we may wonder, about to pull down the whole church, or merely the pulpit and preacher? A slab marks the spot where an Archbishop of Paris was killed by an unfrocked priest.

Recrossing the Rue Clovis, we are back at the **Lycée Henri IV**. This is a pleasant building, dating from Napoleonic times, hardly integrated with its gothic belfry. It was here, when it was a monastery under the rule of the Abbot of Cluny, Peter the Venerable, that Abelard was given shelter after he fled from the Notre-Dame cloister and where he wrote his greatest works (see also Chapter 1). Dramatic though his private life may have been, it is his philosophical thinking which has given him his place in history. He was not the first philosopher to be accused of blasphemy (perhaps Socrates was), nor the last, but he was certainly the first of the modern school.

Abelard, although himself a religious believer, contended that Reason cannot lead to results at variance with Revelation and that dialectics must therefore be used in the service of theology. This amounted to saying 'I understand in order that I may believe,' in opposition to St Augustine's famous approach *'Credo ut intelligam'* – 'I believe in order that I may understand.' By putting intellect first, before Faith, Abelard became the founder of mediæval philosophy in France and was in line with later French thinkers, reaching to the present day, by way of the Goddess of Reason enthroned in Notre-Dame and the Panthéon. What Abelard would have thought of these developments cannot, fortunately, be guessed.

Farther down the Rue Clovis we meet the Rue Descartes. Whether **René Descartes** (1596–1650) ever lived there himself is doubtful; it was a street of brothels, la Rue des Bordels. But he was in Paris, on the Montagne, from 1613 to 1619 and again in 1625. His thinking, however, gained him no support either moral or in his livelihood, and he was forced to emigrate to Holland and finally to Sweden, where he had several admirers, among them Queen Christina. France, nevertheless, claims him as her greatest philosopher.

Descartes based philosophical reasoning on the principles and methods of mathematics, refusing to make any initial metaphysical assumptions. Instead, he took his own sense-experience as his *point de départ* in the well-known phrase: *'Cogito ergo sum'* – 'I think therefore I am.' He wrote three works in which he tried to prove by reasoning the existence of God (he was educated in a Jesuit college). This brought him under attack from both sides.

Descartes propounded and was largely responsible for the idea of Dualism, between mind and body, subject and object, idea and object, which later philosophers (Empiricists, Rationalists, Dogmatists and Hegelians) have struggled to resolve. Professor Gilbert Ryle has called it the myth of the mental ghost enclosed in the bodily machine.

Forgetting philosophy for the moment, we turn right into the Rue Descartes. On the left we can note the house where the poet Verlaine died in 1896; it is marked by a plaque and by a conspicuous sign, La Maison de Verlaine. Turning sharply left into the Rue Thouin and immediately right into the Rue du Cardinal Lemoine, we are at No.74, where Hemingway and his first wife lived for several years in the 1920s (a plaque is scheduled).

We are now in a picturesque little square, surrounded by cafés and shops. The **Place de la Contrescarpe** has been cleaned up a good deal since Hemingway's description of it in *A Movable Feast*. The bus stop, the public urinals and the *clochards* have gone, yet it and its frequenters still retain a certain atmosphere of seediness which some find attractive, others less so. Leading out of it is the **Rue Mouffetard**, a narrow pretty street full of shops, cafés and art galleries, much painted and photographed. Many of the houses are old and marked by carved signs and two quiet passages lead off the street, where we can for a moment escape the bustle. The Pot-de-Fer fountain at No.60, in Italianate style, was constructed for Marie de Medici as an overflow from the aqueduct which was to bring water to her new palace in the Luxembourg Gardens (see Chapter 16). At No.53 a hoard of 3500 gold coins was discovered in 1938, each bearing the head of Louis XV. They had been hidden there by the Royal Counsellor, Louis Nivelle, obviously an able and thrifty man in that extravagant age.

We return to the Place de la Contrescarpe for a pause and a drink, probably at La Chope, the two Hemingway cafés now joined together. Facing us is the site of the Pinecone cabaret, mentioned by Rabelais and existing until a few years ago. Its songs, I recall, had a strong Resistance and anti-German flavour, long after the Liberation of France. Perhaps it was time for it to close.

We walk back down the Rue du Cardinal Lemoine. At No.67, in an earlier house on the site, Pascal died in 1662. Next door is the **Foyer Sainte-Geneviève**, a girls' hostel. This is a fine building and was for many centuries the Scottish College, the centre of Scottish Catholicism in France (entrance by the goodwill of the concierge). The neo-Classical chapel on the first floor once held, as its principal relic, the brain of King James II of Great Britain, who died in exile in Saint-Germain-en-Laye in 1701.

Turning into the Rue Clovis, we find the pavement, narrow enough all the way, almost blocked by the ruins of King Philippe-Auguste's fortress wall. Over thirty feet high and thick in proportion, it reminds us that in the twelfth century Paris was indeed a fortified city and its walls were something invaders had to reckon with. On our right are the massive buildings of what was, until very recently, the Ecole Polytechnique. This is still France's prestige college; its members wear on occasions glittering uniforms and give an annual ball at the Opéra. Among its distinguished members we may note Auguste Comte, Foch, Jean Borotra the tennis champion and a great favourite at Wimbledon, André Citröen, the car designer, and President Giscard d'Estaing. It has been much attacked for its élitism, something which Giscard may have found an election disadvantage. It has recently moved to the suburbs and the buildings on the Montagne are renamed the Institut Auguste Comte, seeking, perhaps, a change of image.

We make our way back to the Panthéon. At the corner of the Rue Valette we can see the Bibliothèque Sainte-Geneviève, a nineteenth-century building. Originally the Montaigu College, it was famous through the centuries for its learning, its collection of manuscripts and its lice, fleas and bugs. Only those with readers' passes are admitted.

Turning right down the Rue Victor-Cousin or even the Boulevard Saint-Michel, we are back again at the Place de la Sorbonne, dominated by the **chapel of the Sorbonne**. It was built by Mercier for Richelieu, who had appointed himself Chancellor of the University, and it is a fine example of seventeenth-century architecture, the columns, pediments and the dome blending with the Gothic spirit which always lay underneath. More imposing is the north façade overlooking the courtyard of the Sorbonne and dominating it with its Corinthian columns, its pediment and, of course, the dome. Inside, the church is of neo-Classical design and no longer used for services (except for one mass a year for the soul of Richelieu, but no one seems to know exactly when it is said). It is used mainly for exhibitions of stained glass, tapestry and old manuscripts, which are usually well worth seeing. The Cardinal's red hat hangs from the ceiling and will remain there, the story goes, until his soul is released from Purgatory, when it will fall to the ground. He was condemned to long purgation, it is said, for his sin in supporting the Protestants in the Thirty Years' War. The story is popular even among the ecumenically minded and no doubt the hat has been firmly wired up, to continue the legend.

The Sorbonne was strongly anti-Protestant until the Revolution; nowadays religion plays only a small part in student talk. Many of the students are Marxists, Moslems or Buddhists, or a blend of these beliefs. 'Againstism' has always been part of the Sorbonne: anti-Protestant, anti the King, anti-authority, in particular the civil power in Paris, and even at times anti-France. During the Hundred Years' War it supported the English and the Burgundians against the French, even to the extent of sending one of its best orators, Bishop Cauchon, to Rouen to prosecute Joan of Arc.

It is sad that nothing remains of Richelieu's Sorbonne, apart from the church. But it was, of course, far too small for the horde of students who now study there. The building, now unromantically renamed **Paris University IV**, has as its centre the big courtyard, where the students talk and pass in the open or, if it is raining, under the arches. We are free to enter, walk about and talk to anyone we like. But, apart from the façade of the church, the nineteenth-century building is dreary indeed; as the main courtyard of a great university it can scarcely be compared with, say, the Great Court of Trinity College, Cambridge. But the building manages to house a large number of amphitheatres, smaller lecture rooms, offices for the teaching staff, laboratories, an astronomical observatory and so on. The amphitheatres (large lecture halls) are rather sad places, difficult acoustically for both the speaker and the listener (I have been both).

Nevertheless the main courtyard has had its dramatic moments, and will no doubt have many more. The most recent was during the riots of May 1968 when the University was occupied by the students and others, and was, so to speak, open to the public. It was a centre of revolution. When I had had enough of exploring, of reading leaflets on how to make Molotov cocktail-bombs, of the posters of Trotsky and Guevara and the scratched record of the 'Internationale', it was interesting to read the graffiti on the walls. Two of them stay in my mind: 'Father a kid to carry on the struggle,' and 'Invent new sexual positions'; which, between them, may explain the virtual disappearance of the girls from the riots after the first week or so.

We make our way through the imposing corridors to the front of the building, down the main steps into the Rue des Ecoles. In front of us is a statue of Montaigne, a pleasant garden where we can sit for a moment of quiet, and beyond it the old stones and the plane trees of the Hôtel de Cluny, which we shall soon visit. But, first, we should turn right, cross the Rue Saint-Jacques and look at the outside at least of the **Collège de France**.

This has a long past reaching back into the Roman era, part of the Cluny establishment, but it sank during the Middle Ages in scholarship and reputation. It was revived in the sixteenth century by François I, who wanted a rival to the Sorbonne. Twelve King's Scholars, paid by the King, were free to study and teach whatever they liked, including such forbidden and pagan writers as Virgil. Thereafter it prospered, especially in the seventeenth century when many new subjects were added, including French, as contrasted with classical, literature.

The Rue Mouffetard market.

A narrow street, the Rue Berton.
Below An original Art Nouveau metro station (Mouton-Duvernet).

Saint-Séverin in the Latin
Quarter.
Below Saint-Etienne-
du-Mont from
the Panthéon.

La Dame à la Licorne, the tapestry illustrating 'Sight', in the Cluny Museum.

The façade is mainly eighteenth-century, by Chalgrin, and is pleasant enough with its statue of Claude Bernard and its unpollarded trees. Behind the façade there has been much rebuilding in the following two centuries. It is not primarily a centre for undergraduates and we may compare similar colleges in England, perhaps All Souls', Oxford. The Collège has had many distinguished members: Claude Bernard, who did great research on the working of the human liver; Joliot-Curie, who split a uranium particle; Ampère, the physicist; Henri Bergson, the philosopher; Paul Valéry, the poet; and most recently Claude Lévi-Strauss, long-time professor of anthropology and one of the founders of Structuralism, the current French philosophy.

If you may think that there has been rather a lot of philosophy in this chapter (see also Chapter 17), it should be remembered that philosophy plays a much more important part in French life than it does in British, where it is considered something of a specialist interest. Every schoolchild in France studies 'philo' as a normal part of education, often in some depth. Many have written essays on Descartes or Bergson, and Structuralism started naturally on the Montagne, though it has since spread to many other countries, especially to Cambridge and Yale. This does not mean that the woman in front of you in the queue for cheese or fish and talking endlessly to madame is discussing Structuralism; she is probably giving the gory details of her sister's illness. But her children will be familiar with the philosophy and we have only to talk to the local bookseller or overhear the conversation in the nearby Brasserie Balzar (see later) to get the point.

Paris is not only a city of art and architecture, of politics and revolutions, of people and good food and sex. It is also a city of ideas, as Athens was in its time, which at heart are the basis for all else. To understand Paris and the French people, and to converse with them, it is a good idea to have a little knowledge of 'philo', even if it is rather sketchy. And so we should now take a quick look at Structuralism.

Structuralism, briefly defined as the search for 'structures' in human behaviour and institutions, applies recently developed mathematical structures to analyses of thought and behaviour. It has been claimed as a blueprint for the future of the social sciences, but in fact lays much stress on the past, studying the habits of primitive tribes still living in Stone Age cultures. Its trendy disciples enjoy interpreting contemporary mores in terms of anthropology, in particular the habits of Brazilian Indians.

A clue to the attitudes of Lévi-Strauss may be found in his early enthusiasms for geology and Marxism. His 'structures' seem to inherit a certain rigidity from both these disciplines, since developments of thought are claimed to be 'inevitable'. And so his followers see the French intellectual tradition, traced through the thinking of Descartes, Rousseau, Auguste Comte, Durkheim and Bergson, as a continuous stream and producing inevitably (and with considerable hindsight) such philosophers as Lévi-Strauss and his fellow Structuralists, Jean Piaget, the child-psychology theorist, who has had such an influence on modern education, and Roland Barthes, the literary critic.

Michel Foucault (died 1984), in his well known book *Les Mots et les Choses*, followed the Structure theme. He decided, arbitrarily, that the essential functions of language (any language) are Articulation, Designation, Derivation and Attribution. These he depicted in the form of a diamond-shaped quadrilateral and then claimed that his diagram marked out the possible structure of any science, notably Natural History, which is the main subject of *Les Mots et les Choses*.

Descartes and Comte would certainly have approved of Lévi-Strauss's and Foucault's zeal for mathematical method, but Structuralism was attacked during the upheavals of 1968, in the sessions at the Odéon, by the Trotskyists and Anarchists for attempting to find a pattern in life where none should exist. The debate continues.

Enough of 'philo' for the day! Many historical and visual pleasures lie in store for us in the Hôtel de Cluny a few yards away. But before then we should refresh ourselves and happily the Brasserie Balzar is close at hand, in the same street on the other side of the Sorbonne. The restaurant has much in common with Lipp (see Chapter 17) and indeed the two were for some time under the same management. There is the same atmosphere, with the waiters wearing long white aprons, the same attentive service and the food is similar, though rather cheaper. We sit on the *terrasse* or inside on *banquettes* under potted palms, with lace curtains shielding us from the stare of the passers-by. It is not a place for starving students, but a place for those who wish to talk and think while absorbing *bœuf gros sel avec ses légumes* and a bottle of Bordeaux (particularly good here) or a *sérieux* of Mutzig beer. It is a place for successful intellectuals, professors, editors, writers, artists, plus a sprinkling of the bourgeoisie who live in the quarter and have nothing to do with university life, but who happen to like oysters. Much of my work has been thought out, if not actually written, at the tables here. The Balzar is closed on Tuesdays; there is an arrangement with Lipp by which one or the other is always open, even in high summer.

And now it is time to look at the **Hôtel de Cluny**, the one-time residence of the abbots and, long before that, a centre of Roman civilization. The gardens facing the Boulevard Saint-Germain are open to the public and, under the shade of the great trees, beside the Roman ruins and the sixteenth-century house, they are a pleasant place to read or while away an hour, the Boulevard traffic notwithstanding. On the side facing the Boulevard Saint-Michel, we have the remains of the Roman baths, the caldarium (steam) and the tepidarium (cooling-off) beside the railings, the frigidarium (cold water) further inside. They are best seen on an autumn evening, floodlit, covered with fallen chestnut leaves and with the smell of roasting chestnuts coming from the stall on the corner.

The present house was completely rebuilt at the end of the fifteenth century by the Abbot of Jumièges in Normandy and it may seem to us more like a country manor house than a Paris *hôtel*. It is, however, far more elaborate than an English equivalent. It has, certainly, battlements and turrets, memories of the Middle Ages, but they are purely decorative. We shall also see arches, mullioned windows, decorated friezes and balustrades. Under the balustrade there are beautifully carved grapes and vine leaves. On the dormer windows are elaborate coats-of-arms and everywhere there are carved shells – Coquilles Saint-Jacques. Shells are traditionally the emblem of pilgrims and the Rue Saint-Jacques, the pilgrims' way, is only a few yards off. But when the decorators carved the shells, it is possible that they were thinking more of the taste of *coquilles*, that delicious seafood, than of the rigours of the long pilgrimage to Spain.

Comfort and luxury, these are the keynotes of the house. After the long centuries of mediæval austerity, France was enjoying the taste for riches, which had come from Italy. It was the mood of the Renaissance, of Lorenzo the Magnificent in Florence and finally, of the Field of the Cloth of Gold (1520). The well-proportioned rooms are neither too large for heating nor too small for parties. The many tapestries give a vivid picture of the life of the well-to-do; the ladies in rich, ornamented clothes with plenty of jewels and servants (or alternatively naked, having a bath), the gentlemen setting out for a day's hunting, the vintage. Wine (to be drunk out of gold goblets, also on view) is one of the themes of the building. Little of this luxury rubbed off on to the poverty-stricken peasantry, as Breughel made very clear in his pictures of life in the same century. But there are no Breughels in Cluny to disturb us.

In 1945 it was decided to make the house into a museum devoted exclusively to the Middle Ages in France, though the word seems to cover the whole period from Roman Paris to the sixteenth century. It attracts a great number of visitors.

We enter through the main courtyard in the Place Painlevé, facing the Sorbonne, and we should notice the big turret containing a spiral staircase (no longer in use) and the well with its beautiful iron well-curb (fifteenth-century). The ticket-office is on the right. We move into **Room I** and immediately we are among the tapestries, among them the Vintage ('*Les Vendanges*'). The tapestries are of the 'thousand flower' style and give a cavalcade of vigorous life. But we may find them restless and lacking in construction and artistic form; there is no attempt at perspective. However, we can enjoy them for what they are. In **Room IV** there are five large tapestries of *la vie seigneurale*. In the next room (**V**) is a tapestry, '*L'Embarquement*', in sharp contrast to the previous jollifications. One of the ships is sinking and there is much distress; it has also a primitive attempt at perspective, reminiscent, possibly of Uccello in Italy.

There is no space here to list all the treasures of the museum, but certain ones may catch our eye as we pass through. Among them will be the '**Descent from the Cross**', in **Room VIII** which dates from 1457 in Tarascon and is regarded as the most important painting in the museum. But it is not a picture gallery, and our attention will be taken more by the vessels, plaques and other objects which we shall see. Among these, in **Room XII**, is a Byzantine-style 'Christ in Glory' from the twelfth century, almost certainly made in Germany. An enamelled plaque, it shows a seated Christ within an oval enclosed space. Those who have seen the modern Sutherland tapestry in Coventry Cathedral may well find an artistic connection, eight centuries later.

244

The gold in **Rooms XIII and XIV** naturally attracts much interest, especially two double Crosses (Crosses of Lorraine) from the thirteenth century. But the prize exhibit, in **Room XIII**, is a golden rose. Late thirteenth-century, it was found in Basle and was probably a gift from the Pope to an important visitor. In **Room XXI** we shall see a fine bronze gryphon, German, fifteenth-century, one of the many heraldic beasts which abound in the museum.

Room XX is the **Chapel**, and here we should linger for a while. A small chapel, it is an architectural masterpiece. A slender central column branches out, like a palm-tree, into a roof of flamboyant vaulting, intricately decorated with, once again, suggestions of vines. Around us are niches with carved canopies, which once contained statues of the Amboise family.

The chapel was the scene of a curious romantic episode. In October 1514 the King, Louis XII, married again. His first wife, Anne of Brittany, had died without producing an heir. His new wife was Mary Tudor, the eldest sister of Henry VIII of England. He was in his fifties, she was a lively sixteen-year-old (and, as it happens, my ancestress). King Louis died three months later, exhausted by his young bride; the throne was seized by his twenty-year-old cousin, François I, and the Queen was sent to mourn in Cluny. But François was naturally worried in case the young widow might be pregnant, which would probably cost him his throne. However, his spies reported that she was having an affair with Charles Brandon, a man-at-arms or perhaps a *chevalier-servant*. The King arrived late one night with an armed guard and a priest and, finding the young couple in bed together, ordered them to this chapel, where they were married on the spot, by consent. He then sent them straight back to England. There was some anxiety in case Brandon might be sent to the Tower, or even the block, for treason. But Henry VIII was in an indulgent mood; perhaps he was fond of his sister, or knew of the affair and did not disapprove – it would have been interesting to have had an Englishman on the throne of France. Anyway Brandon was created Duke of Suffolk and nobody knows who was the real father of their eldest child. François I remained firmly on the French throne and the two kings must have made some bawdy jokes about it at the Field of the Cloth of Gold.

In a more austere mood, the chapel also contains fine tapestries, originally in Auxerre Cathedral, showing episodes from the life of

St Stephen, a popular saint in France. As we leave the chapel we see facing us, in **Room XIX**, a tapestry woven in 1490 of the saint's martyrdom. The dead body, with bloodstained stones, is being mourned by a lion and a unicorn. It is moving in its expression of grief, but without the artistic achievement which we shall find later. Lions, both winged and otherwise, abound in the museum; there is a historic connection between Christianity and lions, but these ones seem very friendly. We can find more in **Rooms IX and X**, carved on the romanesque capitals of the stone columns from Ste Geneviève's church (twelfth-century). A lion is also the main motif of a finely carved ivory hunting-horn ('Olifant') from southern Italy, eleventh-century, in **Room X**. And, of course, there is the great stone lion in the garden outside (originally at the Tour Saint-Jacques).

In Room X, the **Salle Archæologique**, we should note the column capitals from the nave of Saint-Germain-des-Prés; one of them is another oval 'Christ in Glory'. There is also a good thirteenth-century Adam, from Notre-Dame, and in two adjoining crypts we can see the tombs of five Grand Masters of the Order of St John of Malta (originally Rhodes, now generally known as St John of Jerusalem). Robed figures, they express both calm and strength.

We now descend into the **Salle Romaine**, originally the frigidarium. Built of stone with layers of brick, we may well find it a chilly place. Certain decorative designs suggest that it was built by the Boatmen's Guild of Paris; boatmen were an important part of Paris in Roman and mediæval times. Here we shall see the 'Boatmen's Pillar', Paris's oldest piece of sculpture, a column to Jupiter from the time of the Emperor Tiberius (AD 14–37) and originally in the temple where Notre-Dame now stands.

Against the back wall stand the heads of twenty-one kings, one of the great archæological finds of the century. They were discovered in 1977 during excavations in northern Paris and were originally on the façade of Notre-Dame. It was first thought that they were kings of France, including St Louis, as all were statues of kings, but it is now thought that they were the kings of Israel and Judah, claimed as the royal ancestors of the Virgin Mary. One of them is said to be Solomon, but it is hard to be sure. They are much battered by time, by venial canons who wanted the stone for their houses and, possibly, by revolutionaries. But even without their noses they exude a tremendous presence and they dominate the big room with their personality. We feel humbler in their presence; they were truly Kings.

But the best till the last; we have kept the great treat for the end. We ascend to the rotunda on the first floor (**Room XI**) and there we find the six beautiful and mysterious tapestries, '**The Lady and the Unicorn**' (*La Dame à la Licorne*). Designed in France and woven, it is said, in what is now Belgium, they date from the late fifteenth century. They are part of a series and similar in design. A blonde lady, richly dressed and wearing a jewelled collar, stands in the centre with an attendant. On either side are a lion and a unicorn, and beside them are the banners and poles of the de Viste family from Lyons, white crescents on a blue band against a red background. The tapestry background is also red, of the thousand flower type, and teeming with rabbits, dogs, monkeys, birds and other wild life. She stands on an oval of blue-green grass, full of flowers and more animals.

The tapestries portray the five senses – it was a sensuous time. For 'Touch' the Lady is shown holding the banner-pole and the unicorn's horn; for 'Taste', she takes a sweet from a bowl which she is possibly going to offer to a parakeet on her left hand. For 'Smell' she sniffs a rose taken from a bouquet, while a monkey smells another one behind her. For 'Sound' she plays a portable organ, pumped by her attendant; the design in this one is especially fine. And for 'Sight' the unicorn lies with its paws in her lap, gazing at itself in a mirror. (Can unicorns see themselves in mirrors? Dogs cannot.)

It is the sixth tapestry which baffles us. The lady stands at the door of a tent, which has its flaps open; on the tent is the motto *A Mon Seul Désir*. She is taking off the jewelled necklace which she has worn throughout and placing it in a box. This is supposed to be a gesture of renunciation or sacrifice and the unicorn raises its horn in salute. What does it mean? Is she giving her jewels to the beast? There is much conjecture about this, even to the point of supposing the sixth tapestry to have come from a different series. But this cannot be so; she is the same girl, they are the same animals throughout.

The motto suggests a gift and the tapestries, it has been suggested, were a wedding present from Jean de Chabannes (whose arms included a lion) to Claude de Viste, his bride. But this is unlikely. A unicorn is a wild noble beast, a symbol of power, sex and

247

purity, and it can only be tamed by a pure virgin. Claude de Viste was a widow, not a virgin, and moreover the lady never looks at the lion, although it is obviously begging for attention. Clearly she much prefers the unicorn. The museum supports the theory that the tapestries were made for Jean de Viste, '*President des Aides et Seigneur d'Arcy*', who died in 1500. But then, where does the motto come in?

Of course the lady does not have to be a Mademoiselle de Viste. She could be a saint, rather a luxury-loving one, or even the Virgin Mary, taming the noble savages round her. This idea is encouraged by a further six tapestries in the same style and possibly by the same artist, which now hang in the Cloisters, New York. These show the hunting of the unicorn, which, though wounded, savages the hounds with its horn, but finally lays its head meekly in the lady's lap.

In Chinese symbolism the unicorn is a rain-bringer and always fighting with the sun, the lion. This idea of the two beasts fighting each other also occurs in the English nursery rhyme, but not in these tapestries, or in the British coat-of-arms, where they tolerate each other.

I have a personal explanation of the sixth tapestry. It represents the sixth sense, which in this case is not extra-sensory perception, but quite simply Love. And in this I am supported by the motto *A Mon Seul Désir*.

But, intriguing though the subject is, and interpret them as we like, we cannot fail to enjoy their beauty. In design they are far superior to the tapestry mentioned earlier of the two beasts mourning the martyred St Stephen. The design is mainly triangular, the lady's head being at the apex of the triangle. On either side are upright features, banner-poles or trees, and below is the curved oval base. This use of the triangle is similar to the use of triangles in Italian Renaissance religious paintings. Contrasted with this geometry are the luxuriant landscape, abundant in flowers and animals, the swirling banners, the rich clothes of the lady. (Rabbits, which abound, are symbols of fertility, as are the crescents on the de Viste banners; so perhaps it was a wedding-present after all.)

Anyway these tapestries are to be enjoyed and we can spend a pleasant half-hour or more studying them. What we shall chiefly recall is the splendid unicorn, a noble beast indeed.

CHAPTER 16

The Luxembourg

The Luxembourg Palace and Gardens are the green heart of the Left Bank; the gardens are possibly the most enjoyable and certainly the most popular in Paris, thronged by children, prams, students, poets, sportsmen (of a sort) and strollers looking for fresh air, greenery and flowers in the bustling centre of the city. They are easily reached from the Latin Quarter, Saint-Germain-des-Prés and Montparnasse, but we should for preference enter them from the Boulevard Saint-Michel (Place Edmond-Rostand). We walk down an avenue, pausing perhaps to buy a balloon or hot chestnuts, until we reach the balustrade, from where we can see the gardens stretching in all directions, the formal pond below us, all dominated by the façade of the Palace, built between 1615 and 1625 by Salomon de Brosse on the orders of Queen Marie de Medici, second wife and widow of King Henri IV.

The first marriage of Henri IV (Henry of Navarre, as he then was) had been a disaster, after the murder of all his friends on the wedding day, in the Massacre of St Bartholomew, (see Chapter 9), arranged by his mother-in-law-to-be, Catherine de Medici. The marriage was childless and finally annulled, and it is curious that for his second bride he should have chosen to marry again into the same family. But Marie de Medici, the niece of the Grand Duke of Tuscany, had a dowry of 600,000 gold crowns and, after the civil wars of religion, France's treasury was very short of cash. Her appearance can only be judged by the series of pictures by Rubens in which she appears. These were in the Luxembourg Palace but now hang in the Louvre. They show her as a stately red-head of considerable presence, and Rubens would not have objected to her ample figure; the pictures were painted in 1621 and the following years.

249

Marie de Medici has been much criticized for her grossness, vulgarity, possessiveness of her son, her lovers and intrigues – though this was all part of the time. But the marriage produced children and she bore with her husband's infidelities. And we must be grateful to her for giving to Paris the Luxembourg.

When Henri IV was assassinated, her son (King Louis XIII) was only nine years old. Marie had brought with her to Paris her foster-sister and her husband, an uncouth bully called Concini, who rapidly became a duke and a marshal. The Queen Mother and Concini ruled the country, buying off the Guises and other important French families; the King was relegated to the nursery.

When he was fourteen the King became officially of age and one of his first acts was to authorize the murder of Concini, shot by the captain of the guard in the Cour Carrée of the Louvre. He then expelled his mother to Blois on the Loire. The new ruler of France was his chief falconer, Luynes, a man completely unfitted for the job. Fortunately for France his rule only lasted four years; he died, surprisingly for the times, of an illness. The Queen and her son became reconciled. This was brought about by a little-known provincial clergyman, who had managed to become Court Almoner: Armand de Richelieu. For his services he was made a Cardinal and President of the Council of State.

The Louvre was soon a nest of intrigue and counter-intrigue, as every reader of Dumas knows. Lovers, plots, ambitious hangers-on, whispering ladies-in-waiting; there were two queens, Marie de Medici herself, and her daughter-in-law, Anne of Austria, who after ten years of marriage to Louis XIII, was still childless and probably virgin. There was also the King himself: sad, sickly, pious, latently homosexual, easily influenced yet on occasions able to exercise his royal authority. His main recreation was hunting, and he built a hunting lodge at Versailles, later to become the great palace. He also took an interest in the arts and he and his mother encouraged the architects Le Vau and Marie (happily named) in the development of the Ile Saint-Louis. He also completed the Place des Vosges (see Chapter 10), begun in his father's reign, and he deserves his statue there. France, meanwhile, was ruled by Richelieu from the Palais-Cardinal, now the Palais-Royal.

It was time for the Queen Mother to move out and she bought the house and estate of Duke François of Luxembourg. She ordered her architect, de Brosse, to build her a palace which would remind her of her native Florence – though the result may look very French to us. It was enlarged in the nineteenth century; in particular, the façade facing the gardens was rebuilt and the two wing pavilions added, also the balustraded terrace with its statues. But the architect (Alphonse de Gisors) was faithful to de Brosse's original and the result with its simple design and harmonious proportions is very pleasing.

The main entrance is on the Rue de Vaugirard and here we can see more of the Italian influence, with its Tuscan columns and, perhaps, the cupola. The ground plan, with its enclosed courtyard, is however in the traditional French style.

Marie de Medici moved in in 1625 and herself supervised the final decorations and in particular the fountain, which still bears her name and about which more will be written later. She was also occupied by lovers and intriguers. On 10 November 1630, *la journée des dupes*, she made her son promise to dismiss Richelieu. Despite his nickname, Louis le Juste, the King revoked his promise the same day, and it was Marie de Medici who found herself in exile, in Cologne, where she died in 1642. The palace and gardens reverted to their original name, Luxembourg.

Abandoned for a while, it remained a royal palace and was the principal home of her grand-daughter, another French personality. Anne-Marie-Louise, Duchesse de Montpensier, known generally as **La Grande Mademoiselle**, was the daughter of the brother of Louis XIII, the Duc d'Anjou; the Princess Royal of France and, through her mother, probably the richest woman in the world. She was a trump card in the game of royal marriages, but neither Richelieu nor later Mazarin, neither inexpert in these matters, managed to find a suitable husband for her. They tried with Charles II of England, the King of Spain, the Holy Roman Emperor, the Archduke of the Netherlands, and even her cousin, Louis XIV. But there was no doing anything about her huge, ungainly size, her great feet, her Bourbon nose and her personality, sometimes capricious, sometimes obstinate.

She saw herself more as a man. During the Fronde rising, she was first up the scaling ladders at the walls of Orléans. She captured the Bastille and held it for a while. Twice she forced Mazarin into exile, but each time he, far cleverer than she, was back in power in a few

251

weeks. After the second return, he exiled her to her estates in the south and there she remained for many years, until she was no longer a desirable bride.

After Mazarin's death she returned to the Luxembourg. She was forty-two and largely forgotten and then she fell hopelessly in love with the future Count of Lauzun (see Chapter 3). He was younger and far smaller than she, a penniless adventurer, a braggart not averse to duelling, touchy and a womanizer. He was, however, a Captain of the Musketeers and not unknown to the king, Louis XIV. How his heart must have sunk when she first smiled lovingly at him, but he dared not antagonize such a formidable person. He dodged and evaded and the King did not approve of such a match. But somehow she obtained royal permission for a marriage, only a temporary permission, as it turned out. They were married secretly and Lauzun was immediately led away to prison, escorted by a company of his own musketeers, commanded by d'Artagnan, no less.

He remained there for ten years. Mademoiselle did her best to get him released. She begged, petitioned, intrigued and paid out much of her fortune in bribes. Typically inept, she always bribed the wrong royal mistress. But finally she got it right and the couple were reunited in March 1682 in Madame de Montespan's apartments at Saint-Germain-en-Laye. It seems to have been a silent reunion. Lauzun thanked her politely for her efforts, but he was appalled by the elderly lovesick Amazon he found to be his wife. Mademoiselle herself was too moved to say a word.

The couple moved into the Luxembourg and Lauzun consoled himself with the thought of the probable advantages in being the husband of La Grande Mademoiselle, as she was still called. But, to his surprise, he found that they were not to live as man and wife. He was to lodge elsewhere, with Rollinde the Intendant of her household, and to attend with many others her morning *levée*. He was also to pay her a longer visit in the evening, to play games. It does not seem that there was any question of a sex life.

Such an arrangement was unlikely to satisfy Lauzun for long and in August he bought the house on the Ile Saint-Louis which still bears his name. Where he found the money for this is not clear; perhaps some of her bribes had found their way to him. Anyway Mademoiselle was not pleased by the new arrangement and still less by the goings-on in the Hôtel de Lauzun, the affairs and seductions (his mistress was Madeleine Fouquet), the gambling parties at which the guests included such socially different persons as the Duke of Orléans and the butcher Tiber. It is said that she visited him secretly by boat, chasing him round the house while he escaped down secret staircases. But this seems unlikely. She was incapable of doing anything secretly. She did not visit, she commanded people to visit her, and his twice-daily visits now included a twice-daily scolding. The Hôtel de Lauzun was the talk of Paris and plenty of gossip reached the ears of Mademoiselle. At times the bantam-cock in Lauzun would assert itself: 'Grand-daughter of Henri IV, take off my boots!'. It is said that he beat her, and this is possible. When she fished for compliments, he would tell her that her clothes were too young for her. He was made to crawl the whole length of the long gallery at Eu in Normandy to beg her pardon.

Obviously it could not last. Lauzun hoped that the King would make him an aide-de-camp and send him to the wars, but this did not happen. Mademoiselle ordered him to leave Paris and hide; he would look ridiculous in Paris, a Captain of the Musketeers, when everyone else was at the wars. They would say it was her fault and this would make her very angry. The scene took place in the Luxembourg. Lauzun answered, 'I will go away as you wish, and I will say goodbye so as never to see you again in my life.' He bowed deeply and left the palace for ever. Mademoiselle lingered on for another nine years until she died. On hearing of her death Lauzun wore deep mourning, more out of panache, one must feel, than from grief.

Once the separation was public knowledge, Lauzun prospered. He was accepted back into royal circles; he sold his house on the Ile Saint-Louis and moved at last into Versailles. He was placed in charge of the musketeers who rescued King James II of England and his wife Mary of Modena from Whitehall and installed them in safety in Saint-Germain-en-Laye, a mission which he accomplished efficiently. The road from the Luxembourg to Versailles, as Madame de Sévigné put it, led through Whitehall. Two years later, in 1690, he commanded the French troops, with much less success, at the Battle of the Boyne in Ireland. However, he survived this and was made a duke. Aged sixty-three he was given a rich young bride of fourteen. When he died he was ninety, a respected old man who figures in eighteenth-century memoirs and later romances. But his only visible memorial is the *hôtel* on the Ile Saint-Louis, which he occupied so briefly and boisterously.

The Luxembourg, still a royal palace, was neglected for nearly a hundred years, though it was used for a time as a monastery. At the Revolution and afterwards it was an annexe of the Conciergerie and several notable people were imprisoned there, including the aristocratic de Noailles family and Danton. Among the famous trials held there were those of Camille Desmoulins (guillotined), Marshal Ney (shot by a firing squad), and Louis-Napoleon Bonaparte, the future Emperor Napoleon III, who finally died in exile and is buried at Farnham, Surrey. In 1870 the Commune used it for the trials of those supporters who had become dissatisfied with the authoritarian regime and turned against it. During the German occupation it was a military headquarters. It is now the home of the Senate and it is closed to the public, unless we have official political business there, and even then we may have to suffer long delays for bureaucratic and security reasons. But there are guided tours on Sundays. However, as the interior was completely transformed in the nineteenth century by Chalgrin (the architect of the Arc de Triomphe, among other things) little of Marie de Medici's time remains.

Some of the panelling and paintings from her private apartments survive in the Golden Book Room, while in the library are paintings by Delacroix of such personalities as Virgil, Dante, Alexander holding the epics of Homer and so on. There is also a Zodiac ceiling by Jordaens. But we may well prefer to spend our Sunday in the gardens themselves, like so many other Parisians.

The **Senate** is France's Second Chamber, like the House of Lords, and has equally little power, because it can be overruled by the Assemblée Nationale (Parliament). However, it is a respected advisory body and the French are evidently attached to it as they have voted against its abolition in a series of referenda between 1946 and 1969. Senators have prestige and their number has grown to 315 in 1983; a good deal of rebuilding has been necessary in the Luxembourg to give each of them his own office.

The President of the Senate takes over the powers of the President of the Republic when the position becomes vacant. Monsieur Alain Poher has twice done so, after General de Gaulle's retirement and President Pompidou's death. However, he has to call a Presidential election within 35 days; as he cannot call a referendum or alter the Constitution, and as the existing Prime Minister is still in office, he cannot make much impact on the nation. He can, of course, run as a Presidential candidate himself, but so far Monsieur Poher has had no success here.

Senators, who must be aged at least thirty-five, are chosen by a system of indirect election through municipal and district councils. This has a built-in rural bias, because the voting basis is weighted against the large towns. The Senators include 160 mayors and others are local worthies such as the heads of provincial building societies and development boards. Their term is for nine years and the Senate is only renewed by one-third at a time. All this is thought to be a stabilizing factor in French politics.

The Senate also represents French settlements outside France – for example, the island of Mayotte has its own Senator – and 'Frenchmen established outside France'.

The gardens are a delight at all times of year, even in midwinter when mists and grey light shroud the bare trees. In the spring we go to see the crocuses, the daffodils, the azaleas in flower and the first green leaves on the chestnuts. All these are near the Saint-Michel entrance, and in summer there is an open-air café, where we can sit under the trees and watch the world at play. We could be part of a picture by Manet, except that nowadays nobody is likely to be wearing a top hat.

But our first port of call must be the **Medici Fountain** which has inspired so much fiction and poetry. It is not exactly as Marie de Medici intended. Dominating it is a large grotto (built in 1863 by Ottin), inside which is a naked loving couple, said to be Acis and Galatea. Above them, peering over the rocks, is a great bearded giant, perhaps Polyphemus, watching them and awaiting his chance to destroy them or, more likely, to abduct the girl from her rather wan lover. The water flows out under their feet over three semi-circular steps into a long pool full of golden carp. This is the pool as Marie de Medici saw it, lined with big stone vases and very Italianate in design. From the far end there is a curious *trompe l'œil* effect that the water is flowing uphill to the fountain. The plane trees, for once unpollarded, meet overhead and there are plenty of benches and chairs where we can sit. It is a very romantic place, especially in the autumn when the leaves have turned, popular with

255

loving couples and others, more solitary, reading or writing poetry.

I may perhaps recall my small personal contribution to the fountain. One day, sitting there, I noticed that the pool was covered with leaves, the fish were gasping for oxygen, and no water was flowing from the grotto. The fountain was dead and the fish would soon be dead too. Typically British, I went in search of a gardener, whom I found sweeping up leaves. After some discussion, not due to language problems, he got my point: I wanted the water turned on. He unlocked a wooden door in the side of the grotto; inside, along with the rakes and spades, was a vertical, rather wonky pipe with a tap in the middle. He turned on the tap. *Voilà, monsieur!* I thanked him suitably and returned to my chair and poem. Gradually the water began to overflow the first step, the second, the third into the pool. The leaves started to drift down to the grating, the fish stopped gasping, the fountain was alive again, though I do not think that the loving couples noticed. It is, at the moment of writing, still flowing.

Moving on reluctantly, we reach the terrace with its balustrade and view of the palace and the pond. This is the more formal part of the garden, where the trees are clipped and the flowers planted in regular municipal patterns. Behind us is a semi-circle of statues, erected in the nineteenth century, of eminent French women. They are not in themselves of great artistic interest, but we may note with some amusement two almost adjoining ladies of very different temperament: Ste Geneviève and Marie Stuart, Reine de France (Mary Queen of Scots).

Below us is the *Bassin*, the central pond with its fountain, filled with toy sailing-boats. These can be hired from a kiosk at hand and give great pleasure, not only to children. On the far side we re-enter the trees and watch games of *pétanque*, a complicated form of bowls imported from the south and played on rough sand. Beyond, in fine weather, are tables for card-players. I cannot understand the game, which is played with tarot packs, but we can admire the ferocity with which the players throw down their cards. There are also tennis courts, a marionette theatre (times of performances are announced on posters), and an exotic garden. There is a large children's playground with a tree-house. This part of the gardens, beside the Rue Guynemer, is more in the English style. The trees are unclipped and some of them are very old.

We stroll back towards the palace where we find the **Orangerie** (not the one at the Tuileries) where delicate plants are housed in the winter. In summer it is often used for exhibitions of modern art. The choice of these is at the discretion of the Senate or, in French style, of an influential senator. Back in the Rue de Vaugirard, we find the Petit Luxembourg, the official residence of the Senate President. Across the street are some pleasant buildings of eighteenth-century origin, which are now part of the Senate. The doorway of No.36 was built by Boffrand and has since been incorporated in a later building.

Beside the Petit Luxembourg is the **Musée du Luxembourg**, recently renovated and much used for exhibitions of modern art, including the well-known Salon de Femmes Peintres. The choice of these salons is once again at the discretion of the Senate and as usual much depends on their relations with the Salon president. Whether Marie de Medici would have approved of the emphasis of some of these exhibitions on politics, womens' lib and sex cannot be known, but with our knowledge of her personality and career, she might well have been pleased.

257

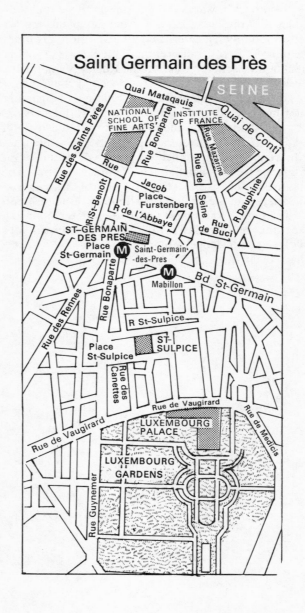

Saint Germain des Près

SEINE

Quai Mataqauis

NATIONAL SCHOOL OF FINE ARTS

INSTITUTE OF FRANCE

Quai de Conti

Rue des Saints Pères

Rue Bonaparte

Rue Mazarine

Rue

R/St-Benoît

Jacob

Place Furstenberg

R de l'Abbaye

Rue de Seine

R Dauphine

ST-GERMAIN DES PRES

Place St-Germain

Saint-Germain-des-Pres

Rue de Buci

Rue des Rennes

Rue Bonaparte

Mabillon

Bd St-Germain

R St-Sulpice

Place St-Sulpice

ST-SULPICE

Rue des Canettes

Rue de Vaugirard

Rue de Vaugirard

LUXEMBOURG PALACE

Rue de Medicis

Rue Guynemer

LUXEMBOURG GARDENS

CHAPTER 17

Saint-Germain-des-Prés

Saint-Germain-des-Prés – Saint Germanus in the Fields – is the intellectual and literary centre of Paris. This statement may cause dissent at the Sorbonne or in Montparnasse, neither very far away on foot. Yet it remains true. In the Place Saint-Germain, under the steeple of the great church (Metro Saint-Germain-des-Prés), in the narrow streets around and behind, much of French thought has grown and been disseminated for several hundred years.

To the modern tourist, and to journalists writing about intellectual Paris, Saint-Germain-des-Prés means the decade or more following the Second World War, the Fifties, the era of the rediscovery of Paris after the Occupation and, especially, the philosophy called **Existentialism**. It started in Saint-Germain, partly because the whole area has always been a think-tank, and partly because Sartre lived above the Café Bonaparte. Its main areas of concentration were the two cafés, the Deux Magots on the Place (and in particular the wall banquette nearest to the window) and the Flore on the next corner. Also involved were the Montana Bar (immediately behind the Flore), where a rather obscure philosopher, Merleau-Ponty, tried to teach the essentials of Existentialism to the singer Juliette Greco; the Bar Rouge in the Rue Jacob and the jazz-cellar, Le Tabou, in the Rue Dauphine, all of which still continue. The philosophy attracted many followers, who became well-publicized for their appearance, blue-jeans, sandals, beards and a fierce, gloomy expression. The leaders of the movement, the mandarins, held themselves a little aloof. Sartre always dressed like a bank manager; Simone de Beauvoir was concerned about her hairstyle. Many of the Existentialists could scarcely understand the subtle difference between Being and Existing, but jazz was a great common thread. In Existentialist books many of the characters spend time listening to jazz singers and clarinettists. When, near the end of Simone de Beauvoir's very long novel *Les Mandarins*, we find Nadia listening to César Franck rather than jazz, we are to understand that she has abandoned Existentialism in favour of family life.

Politics was also a common thread, in particular protest against atom-bomb tests. The slogan, 'I think day and night of the animals at Bikini,' was plastered everywhere, even in the staid Deux Magots.

Existentialism is a difficult philosophy to explain in a few words. It has links with Germany (Heidegger's *Da-Sein* 'being there') but basically it grew out of the Resistance, the revolt against the German occupation. To put it briefly, everyone is in their own and separate hell; hell is also other people, who can impinge and torture us but with whom we can never communicate. The Existentialists produced a group of fine writers and playwrights, two of them Nobel prizewinners (though Sartre refused the award). They understood, like Plato many centuries before, that philosophy can often be better explained in fiction than in a thesis. And so, rather than slog our way through Sartre's monumental book *L'Etre et le Néant* (Being and Nothing), we would do better to read his short novel *La Nausée* (Nausea), his one-act play *Huis Clos* (Vicious Circle) or Camus's short novel *L'Etranger* (The Outsider) – the titles themselves give clues to this sad and lonely philosophy.

It was a passing phase, though some aging Existentialists can still be seen around Saint-Germain-des-Prés. Anti-bomb protests still continue, but bikini now means a minimal bathing-suit, jazz gave way to rock, blue-jeans became a symbol of American influence and Sartre himself moved to Montparnasse. The philosophy became a form of dissident Communism and has now been superseded by Structuralism (see Chapter 15).

Saint-Germain, however, still continues, as it has done for centuries, and perhaps improved by the disappearance of the philosophic gloom. Never has it been fuller or livelier, its streets and cafés more crowded. To sit on one of the café terraces for an hour or two and watch the world go by is to have a fashion display by people of all ages. The Boulevard Saint-Germain in this area is the centre of swinging Paris; the clothes and the atmosphere are far from the Faubourg Saint-Honoré on the Right Bank. This is the world of girls in breeches or urchin-style trousers and elegant boots, not of suits and skirts just below the knee; of intelligent faces, of quick dialogue and of people who would never answer a thoughtful remark with the words *'Ah, bon?'*. There are certainly many bourgeois families living in expensive flats in the quarter, but somehow they seem to be lost in the crowd.

The centre of the quarter is the **Place Saint-Germain**, where the Rue Bonaparte crosses the Boulevard Saint-Germain, between the famous church and the Deux Magots. It has recently been made more agreeable for strollers by the widening of the pavements, the planting of many lime trees and the channelling of the Rue Bonaparte traffic into a single one-way street. As we sit in spring or summer on the terrace of the **Deux Magots**, sipping an expensive apéritif, we shall be entertained by a series, often rather competitive, of accordionists, jugglers, flame-swallowers, guitarists, American folk-singers and poets reciting their unpublished works, passing round the hat at faster and faster speed. It is often disconcerting to those who have come to the café to talk business.

The business is mainly literary and the Deux Magots calls itself the *Rendezvous de l'Elite intellectuelle*. Most French publishers have their offices in the neighbourhood and the café is thronged by writers, publishers, agents, journalists and swinging people who have little connection with literature or the arts – plus, of course, those who live locally and who like a cup of coffee (*un express*) in congenial surroundings – and a crowd of tourists. Inside, in colder weather, the café is brightly lit and crowded, especially at night. The two *magots* (mandarins) gaze down benevolently on those discussing contracts or politics or philosophy, or simply reading *Le Monde*.

The next café, at the corner of the Rue Saint-Benoît, is the **Flore**, which has something of the same reputation and the best coffee in Paris, but it became some years ago the rendezvous of the 'gay' people, of both sexes, and this has rather changed its atmosphere. Heterosexual apéritif-sippers can, however, enjoy the presence of pretty photographers' models, waiting to change their clothes yet again in the small lavatories upstairs. The service is excellent.

Facing the Flore, across the Boulevard Saint-Germain, is the well-known **Brasserie Lipp**, one of the landmarks of the quarter, and of Paris too. Founded at the end of the last century by a refugee from Alsace (then under German rule), it quickly gained a reputation for its beer and *choucroute garnie*. This has grown enormously but it has retained its décor and atmosphere, the ceilings covered by gigantic black, very full-bosomed, nude ladies, the waiters in old-fashioned black waistcoats and long white aprons.

It is always crowded (closed Mondays and occasional periods of staff holidays) and reservations are scarcely possible. An intimidating notice beside the revolving door warns of a ninety-minute wait. But it is amazing that, if we are known and welcome to the owner or his nephew, who seem to be permanently on duty, we shall be shown to a table within a few minutes. Monsieur Cazes likes to think that he organizes his restaurant as a good hostess organizes a dinner-party. The restaurant is a rendezvous for the world of literature, politics and art – the type of artist who can afford the prices and whose posters do not conflict with the décor. But we do not have to be famous to gain admittance; unknowns are welcome, if they seem to have the right personality and trendy appearance – neckties are not important if we are the sort of people he wants.

The food is simple brasserie food, excellently served by an attentive staff, and there is nothing wrong with *gigot rôti avec flageolets*, washed down with a bottle of Bourgogne Lipp. Prices are on the high side, as they usually are in places where we go to see the world, but we shall not grudge it. Or we can sit on the small terrace, now permanently glassed in, or at one of the tables just inside the door, and enjoy an apéritif or perhaps *la petite carte* – oysters, smoked salmon, foie gras or even just potato salad and beer, as described by Hemingway in *A Movable Feast*.

Lipp's has its own life and it is not a place for those who wish to sit and watch the passing scene on the boulevard. We can do this more cheaply and less fashionably at one of the cafés further along the Boulevard such as the Apollinaire, the Sainte-Claude, the Mabillon or Old Navy.

In a smart area it is not surprising that there should be plenty of boutiques (see Chapter 13). These come and go, but if we want to buy or try on ladies clothes, we shall certainly visit Kashiyama and La Gaminerie, both on the Boulevard. Men's clothes are catered for at Ted Lapidus (women's too) in the Place Saint-Germain or at Saint Laurent Rive Gauche in the Place Saint-Sulpice. The accent here is on casual dress, suitable for a cabin cruiser; but it is not every businessman who wishes to arrive in his office in short check trousers, a tight navy blue blazer with brass buttons and a silk scarf, so there are formal clothes too. For those wanting to browse among modern books (not only French) there is La Hune, next to the Flore (open until late at night), and for music lovers, pop and classical, there is Vidal on the Place, next to Lapidus.

But Saint-Germain-des-Prés is not only the Place, the Boulevard and the celebrated cafés. We shall certainly explore the little streets which lead to the river and, on the other side of the Boulevard, to the Place Saint-Sulpice, and beyond to the Luxembourg Gardens. These narrow streets are full of art galleries, publishing houses, both small and great, cheap restaurants, antique shops and cafés. The Marché de Buci, at the corner of the Rue de Seine and the Rue de Buci, is a lively area (closed Sundays and, naturally, lunchtime). The Rue de Seine, which continues down to the river, is lined with art galleries. We are free to wander into any of them and see what is going on in the world of modern art in Paris. This does not necessarily mean French art; painters, sculptors and tapestry designers of many nations and continents show in these galleries. The Rue Jacob and the Rue Jacques Callot (which turn off the Rue de Seine), the Rue des Beaux-Arts which (behind a high wall and a courtyard) houses the famous art school, the Rue Dauphine and other streets adjoining are full of galleries too.

If there is a formal opening (*un vernissage* – a 'varnishing', not that any modern art is ever varnished), we are free to join in, look at the work, talk to anyone we like, perhaps drink a glass of red wine. If we put our names and addresses in the visitors' book, we shall be invited to the next *vernissage* the following month. It is a good way of seeing modern art and of making friends.

Between the Rue de l'Abbaye and the Rue Jacob is a charming old square, the **Place Furstemberg**. It has elaborate white-globed lamp-posts and old paulownia trees, and it is often used by film-makers shooting backgrounds of old Paris. Delacroix had his studio at No.6 (open to the public, a museum), but his greatest works are in the Louvre and elsewhere. We should, however, recall the date 1830, the high point of French Romanticism. It is sometimes said that this was a hangover from Napoleonic Glory, but the year produced three remarkable works – Victor Hugo's *Hernani*, Delacroix's *Trois Glorieuses* and Berlioz's *Symphonie Fantastique*. They were received with little enthusiasm and *Hernani* provoked a riot (organized) in the theatre, which drove Hugo permanently out of playwriting. The other works survive and the symphony is now a popular work everywhere.

Returning, of course, to the Place Saint-Germain, we should walk along the **Rue de l'Abbaye**. Little remains of the original abbey, built by Pierre of Montereau in 1239, which was burnt during the Revolution, but it has been well rebuilt. The **Abbot's palace** (No.5) had a pavilion and later a Renaissance façade. These have been restored to something approaching their original appearance and the interior is now used for small concerts and lectures. In summer, perched among the trees which surround the church, we can listen to Bach or Mozart in delightful surroundings.

The church of **Saint-Germain-des-Prés** is the reason for the special existence of the quarter. It is the oldest church in Paris and all that remains of the powerful Benedictine abbey. It dates from Merovingian times (AD 542) and its builder, King Childebert, the son of Clovis, King of the Franks, is buried there with St Germanus, Bishop of Paris (496–576). Constantly destroyed by the Normans, it was rebuilt in 1163; the Pope himself attended the consecration but the Bishop of Paris was not invited – Saint-Germain has always prided itself on its independence. But its rule eventually decayed and in the seventeenth century it turned to the austere Congregation of St Maur. It soon became a centre, not only of worship, but of scholarship and literature. Two of its greatest scholars, Montfaucon and Mabillon, were distinguished Greek scholars, historians and men of letters and they left behind them a vast quantity of folios which happily were saved at the Revolution and are now in the Bibliothèque Nationale. Both men were attacked by the Trappists, who held that such work was not the business of monks; both men defended their views splendidly and at great length. A bust of Mabillon (1632–1707) stands in a niche on the west wall overlooking the Place. The Maurists were also attacked for being secret Jansenists (near-Protestant) and there may be some truth in this. The church still has strong links with the Anglican Church. And the literary and independent tradition continues.

The building itself has altered greatly. Only a few stones remain of the Merovingian church and the eleventh-century romanesque monastery chapel has been much rebuilt. The north wall is still

The Medici Fountain, the Paris of Romance.

Saint-Germain-de-Prés cafés, the Flore and the Deux Magots.

The Invalides Dome, Hardouin-Mansart's masterpiece.

The Montparnasse
Tower (Vari), the
tallest building
in Europe.

mostly of this date. The chancel at the east end was rebuilt in the twelfth century and there we can find the tombstones of Mabillon, Montfaucon and, surprisingly, Descartes. The outside was given its beautiful flying buttresses in the same century, more or less contemporary with Notre-Dame.

It was a three-towered building, but the two towers above the chancel were removed in the last century, the main tower with its rounded arches remains. The steeple which crowns it, and has become the symbol of Saint-Germain-des-Prés, is a replacement done in the nineteenth-century. The building on the south side of the entrance is the presbytery, a pleasant eighteenth-century façade which enhances the attractions of the Place. On the north side is a little garden, where we can sit surrounded by flowering trees and some Merovingian stones. There is also Picasso's sculpture, a tribute to Apollinaire, and a reminder of the tolerance which Saint-Germain always shows to all kinds of thought.

The inside of the church, however, is a disappointment. Crudely restored with garish colours and glass and indifferent frescoes (by Flandrin, a pupil of Ingres), it has little feeling either of antiquity or sanctity. But parts of the chancel and ambulatory at the east end are still from King Childebert's church; we should note the columns with their Romanesque capitals. Apart from services, Anglican occasionally as well as Catholic, the church is used for concerts, discussions and lectures on contemporary subjects such as Faith and Anthropology.

Moving to the other great church of the quarter, we cross the Boulevard and walk along the Rue Bonaparte till we reach the **Place Saint-Sulpice**, a huge square with pink-flowering chestnuts and a big fountain with lions. All were destroyed a few years ago to make an underground car park, but they have since been replaced, though it is doubted if the trees will ever have a sufficient depth of earth to grow properly. The fountain, dedicated to the Four Cardinal Points, is a joke not only about geography but about the four eminent clergymen (statues) who never became cardinals – *point* in French means not at all.

Standing there, we can consider the monumental façade of **Saint-Sulpice**, which catches the evening sunlight, as it is no doubt meant to do. Originally founded by the Abbey of Saint-Germain-des-Prés as a parish church, the two soon went their separate ways,

Saint-Germain with its independent and ecumenical outlook, Saint-Sulpice valuing its links with Rome. It was supported by a lay society formed to encourage more zealous and ascetic training of priests. The church has always been associated with the priesthood, training, ordination and subsequent councils. Until very recently the square was surrounded by little shops selling rosaries, crucifixes and little ivory images of the Virgin or the Pope (which were often given to the newly-ordained priest by his family), bookshops selling missals and other devotional books, travel agencies organizing pilgrimages to Lourdes and Rome. Many of these have disappeared with recent changes in thought, but a number still remain.

The church has been rebuilt several times, most of it in the seventeenth century, but surprisingly ponderous for that time. By the eighteenth century, reconstruction had reached the portals and, especially, the façade. It was felt that 'classical architecture' since the Renaissance and particularly in the eighteenth century had not been faithful to Roman tradition; it was the time of the excavation of Pompeii and Herculaneum. A competition was held, won by the Italian architect Servandoni, and his plan for a vast Roman temple was accepted.

The design was much altered in building. The huge pediment was abandoned in favour of an equally huge balustrade. The towers, asymmetrical (the south one was never finished), were crowned by balustrades instead of Renaissance pinnacles. The effect of the façade is overwhelming for its size, if not for its beauty, and we may well prefer the south portal in the Rue Palatine for its simpler, lighter design. Built by the eighteenth-century architect Delamaire (who also built the Hôtel de Rohan, the stables at Chantilly, and the Hôtel Matignon, where the Prime Minister now lives), it is an example of the eighteenth-century classical architecture which Servandoni was trying to avoid.

We enter, however, from the west, up the massive stairs. The interior is equally imposing for its size and heaviness. There are three points of interest, the first immediately on our right, the Delacroix chapel. The two frescoes (of Jacob wrestling and the expulsion of Heliodorus) and the ceiling (St Michael and the Dragon) are full of Delacroix's usual energy and sense of line. He took a long time to paint them, as he only worked there during services; he said that the music inspired him, though the connection between Heliodorus and Monteverdi seems obscure.

In the chancel a metal band, embedded in the floor, runs due north and south, and it shows us the exact time at midday on the solstices and equinoxes – another indication that the church was, in its far origins, a sun temple. At the east end, in the Lady Chapel, we find a nineteenth-century picture of the Immaculate Conception and note, with some irony, that the artist was called Pigalle.

Outside in the square we can pause for an apéritif in the Café de la Mairie (closed Sundays) while we consider where to eat. Apart from Lipp, Saint-Germain-des-Prés does not have any great restaurants, but the quarter has a multitude of small restaurants where we can eat well or badly, expensively or cheaply, as we choose; and we should bear in mind that 'expensive' does not necessarily mean 'good'. But we have a vast choice. On our left as we sit in the café, the narrow Rue des Canettes is full of bistros, some for people with special tastes. We might do better to return to the Boulevard and the Place Saint-Germain.

This area has just been renamed the Place du Québec and, as a gift to Paris, Québec has presented it with a new fountain, immediately in front of the Lapidus and Vidal shops. The fountain, by Charles Daudelin, is called 'Embâcle' or Blockage. It keeps a low profile and shows what local people call a burst water-main throwing up some of the paving-stones.

Straight lines, simplicity and destruction – three key themes of fashionable art. Revolution might be added. The sculptor has described it as a conflict between lateral and vertical pressures, another way of saying the same thing. *France-Soir* merely commented 'Ah bon?', but sculptors like it.

The Drugstore attracts a large clientèle, but is planned for quick turnover, not for the more leisurely and discerning diner. Across the Boulevard, next to the Flore, is the Rue Saint-Benoît, another pretty street lined with restaurants; in warm weather we can eat on the pavements, probably being entertained by poets and singers. My personal favourite is the Petit Saint-Benoît at the end of the street, almost at the Rue Jacob. An old-style bistro, which looks, wrongly, as if it had never been redecorated, it offers a surprisingly large range of *plats du jour* and cheese (try the *hachis parmentier*), a very friendly atmosphere, and very low prices. We should also notice the charming and celebrated blue-and-white-check wash-bowl in the lavabo; it should have a red towel hanging above it. A few yards away (No.40 Rue Jacob) is Aux Assassins which provides *coq au vin* and a merry, rather bawdy evening for those whose French is up to it.

On the other, south, side of the Boulevard, the Restaurant des Saints-Pères, at the corner of the Rue des Saints-Pères, specializes in game. We could well try marinaded wild boar (*sanglier*); it is also fairly inexpensive. Saint-Germain also has two excellent fish restaurants. The Port Saint-Germain on the Boulevard, next door to Lipp, offers us a regatta-style decor and such dishes as *brandade de morue* and *escalope de saumon soufflée*. Meat dishes are also available, but the prices are higher than in the bistros previously mentioned. The other fish restaurant, Saint-Germain-de-la-Mer, is just behind in the tiny Rue du Sabot, which can be reached from the Rue du Dragon or the big Rue de Rennes. Here the décor is fisherman-style; a big wall screen shows us changing scenes of the sea and harbours, and sometimes there is the (taped) mewing of seagulls. The cold table of twenty different sorts of hors d'œuvre from which we help ourselves is recommended. The prices are reasonable.

After dinner we can stroll the two yards across the street to the Club Rive Gauche for a last drink. Or perhaps to the London Tavern next door, where we can sing 'It's a long way to Piccadilly' to a very familiar tune.

CHAPTER 18
The Septième Arrondissement

The Seventh Arrondissement is another *beau quartier*, an area of good addresses, where smart people live and pay high rents. But there are some subtle differences between it and the Sixteenth. The architecture is largely older and more pleasing; it has several historic monuments, which attract visitors; and it is on the Left Bank, although it has nothing in common with the Latin Quarter despite a street named, for historic reasons, the Rue de l'Université.

It is a large arrondissement, shaped like a segment of a circle, with the Seine flowing along the northern, curved side. A number of long avenues or boulevards run across it north and south, among them la Motte-Picquet, Suffren, La Bourdonnais, Bosquet, Latour-Maubourg, Invalides and Saint-Germain. Running across them from side to side are four long streets: the Rue de l'Université, the Rue Saint-Dominique, the Rue de Grenelle and the Rue de Babylone. These are rather narrow streets with big doorways suitable for coaches (*portes-cochères*). Behind them are courtyards and large *hôtels*, which are now usually embassies or ministries. There are many of both in the Septième, including the Soviet Embassy and the Hôtel Matignon, the official residence of the Prime Minister.

The avenues and the streets are long and for this reason the area is not really suitable for a sightseeing walk; the sights are too far apart and it would be a pity to spend a morning tramping the length of the Avenue de la Motte-Picquet when we ought to be queuing for the lifts on the Eiffel Tower. For this reason we shall confine ourselves to the major monuments, which can be reached separately by metro.

The area, however, is not only long avenues and embassies. For those who like a stroll and to explore pretty corners of old Paris, the Septième has something to offer. The Rue Monsieur (Metro Saint-

269

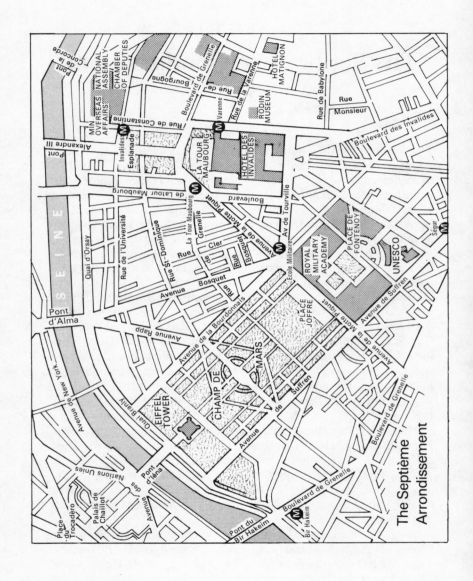

The Septième
Arrondissement

François-Xavier) is an attractive short street; Nancy Mitford lived here for many years. Or, near Metro Ecole-Militaire, there is the Rue Cler, a pedestrian area and open shopping market. The adjoining streets are agreeable – note the Rue Bosquet. Another picturesque corner is the Fontaine de Mars, in the Rue Saint-Dominique near the Avenue Bosquet. In warm weather we can eat out under the colonnades surrounding the fountain. The nearby streets are, except for the Rumanian Embassy, pleasant to look at.

However, most people do not come to the Septième to explore quiet corners. They come for the main tourist attractions, and we may as well start with Number One.

THE EIFFEL TOWER

In less than a hundred years *La Tour Eiffel* has become the symbol of Paris, the welcoming finger, the most easily recognized building in the world, even by those who have never seen it. Eiffel himself called it a flagpole three hundred metres high and in its *joie de vivre* and lack of function it is a festival in itself. Nor is it, as it turns out, useless; it is France's tallest radio mast and her big tourist attraction. Half a million people visit the top in August, and lesser numbers through the rest of the year.

Gustave Eiffel (1832–1923) was an engineer specializing in viaducts and pylons and the idea of a tall tower was a natural consequence of this. The occasion was the Paris Exhibition of 1889 – the centenary of the Fall of the Bastille. Although it was intended only as a temporary folly, it was at once a subject of controversy. A petition to have it immediately removed was signed by three hundred distinguished men, including Garnier (the architect of the Opéra and the Monte Carlo casino), Gounod, Maupassant and the younger Dumas. Verlaine went out of his way to avoid having to see it.

On the other hand Cocteau called it the Queen of Paris, *Notre-Dame de la Rive Gauche*. (The tower is feminine, despite Freud.) It, or she, was also praised by Apollinaire, Pissarro, Dufy, Utrillo and others. A British architect has called it, on television, the world's most beautiful building, marred only by the second floor which added a tiresome horizontal line. He was admiring its graceful lines and proportion, and also the fact that it was uninhabited. We are a

271

long way from Le Corbusier's idea of the *machine à habiter*; but he himself wrote; '*La Tour Eiffel est signe de Paris aimé et signe aimé de Paris.*' A very different but equally remarkable view of the tower is from underneath looking upwards – an amazing perspective of lacework done in pig-iron.

After twenty years the concession expired and the tower was due to be pulled down. It was saved by the sheer difficulty and expense of dismantling a rusty pylon and by the fact that it was now of value as a radio transmitter. Later there was competition between it and the Empire State Building in New York to be the tallest building in the world, each adding on further TV masts. Now both have been overtaken by buildings elsewhere; the tallest at the moment is the Sears Building in Chicago.

For those who want the statistics, the Eiffel Tower is now 1051 feet high; the first floor is 187 and the second 377 feet high. The top only sways 4½ inches in the strongest winds, but the height can vary by six inches in extremes of temperature. The tower is said to weigh seven thousand tonnes, but a thousand tonnes of cement have just been removed from the first floor in the course of repairs, so perhaps the tower needs re-weighing. If we imagine a three-dimensional oblong which could contain the tower, the air inside the oblong would weigh more than the tower. This seems inconceivable to me, but then, not being Pascal, I do not know the weight of air. The dead weight of the tower per square inch is roughly the same as that of a man sitting on a chair. And so on.

The view from the top extends almost fifty miles, but haze or cloud may reduce this. Paris too seems to get lost beneath us and, though we must of course go to the top at least once, we may prefer the view from the lower floors, from which we can recognize the familiar landmarks. The second floor is a good restaurant, the **Jules Verne**, reached by special lift. The first floor has recently been completely replanned and its inauguration was a memorable occasion for those invited to participate. It has a brasserie in (need one say it?) Style Rétro; a steak-and-chippery, a snack bar, a souvenir shop, a post office where our cards can be franked with a special stamp, a tourist-office for hotel-booking, a car showroom (how do they get the cars up there?) a conference room called the Salle Gustave Eiffel, a video museum attractive to children, and a small cinema. This at present shows a short, rather arty film of the tower witnessing the changing scene of the last hundred years; we meet again Harold Lloyd, Charles Chaplin, Josephine Baker, Adolf Hitler and others who have been photographed at the tower.

A few tips may be given to those visiting the tower. We must expect queues. The ride to the top and back will take two hours, more in the high holiday season. In cold or windy weather we should wrap up warmly: we queue in the open air. If we decide to eat on the tower and want a window table in the Brasserie, a reservation is essential.

The restaurants and the lifts close at 11.0 p.m. The energetic, impatient or thrifty who wish to climb to the first or even the second floor on foot should be moderately free of vertigo and fit. Girls should wear trousers.

The Champ-de-Mars (Metro; as for the Eiffel Tower)

This large rectangular park is one of the pleasant features of the Septième arrondissement. Originally the parade ground of the Ecole Militaire (hence the name), it is now a playground for all. The façade of the Ecole Militaire stands at one end, the Eiffel Tower at the other, near the Seine. This part of the park is the most attractive; not only is there the soaring tower, of which we have a wonderful view, but the park has been landscaped with small cascades, shrubs, flowering trees and a pool. It is a delightful place in the spring when the blossom is out. Beside the tower is an organ-grinder and we shall certainly ask him to play one of Paris's traditional tunes. We shall also, of course, buy a red balloon, to keep or release into the air. Ballooning has always been associated with the Champ-de-Mars. In 1780 a physicist called Charles launched the first hydrogen balloon here; it landed near Le Bourget. The following year the balloonist Blanchard floated away himself in the basket of a balloon, landing safely at Billancourt, near the Bois de Boulogne.

The Champ-de-Mars now has other attractions besides balloons. There is a marionette theatre and a children's playground. The peripheral track is much used by joggers and those exercising dogs, while the transverse road, closed to traffic, has become a roller-skating and skateboard rink. There are also football grounds.

Unexpectedly, the Champ-de-Mars has religious associations. On the first anniversary of the Fall of the Bastille, Talleyrand, in his capacity as Bishop of Autun, celebrated mass here in the presence of the King, Lafayette and a vast crowd who all took oaths of loyalty to the nation. Four years later, religion having been abolished in the meanwhile by the Revolution, Robespierre proclaimed his doctrine of the Supreme Being here. And, very recently, Pope John Paul II celebrated mass here before a huge crowd. Few noticed the irony, the Pope who preaches peace on the Champ-de-Mars.

THE INVALIDES

The Invalides is one of the most visited places in France. Most people go simply to see Napoleon's tomb and the beautiful dome above it which is visible from many parts of Paris. But the whole place is so full of historic and architectural interest that we should not rush our visit. Those who merely wish to glance at the Tomb can do so while the taxi waits. But the whole architectural ensemble comprising the Hôtel des Invalides, two churches, the Cour d'Honneur, the Army Museum, the front garden and the Esplanade, deserves a little more of our time. It is one of the marvels of Europe.

It started, however, in a humdrum way. Louis XIV, concerned about the state of his old soldiers, many of whom had become beggars, ordered the architect Liberal Bruand to build a barracks for them, the Hôtel des Invalides (we may compare the Chelsea Hospital in London of approximately the same date). The barracks were finished in 1676 and paid for out of the pay of serving soldiers together with a levy on the local markets. The thoughts of the serving soldiers and the stallholders are not known, but it is the pensioners who are known as *grognards* or grumblers. Their barracks were lavish enough to look at, though probably not very comfortable inside. There are now only a hundred pensioners left and they do not wear scarlet uniforms. Many are in wheelchairs and the others act as guardians or oddjob men.

The ideas of Louis XIV grew more glorious, and in the following year he commissioned Jules Hardouin-Mansart to build a second **church** with a dome and a semi-circular colonnade, like St Peter's in Rome. The colonnade was abandoned in favour of an avenue (the Avenue de Bréteuil), but the rest of the church is as Hardouin-Mansart planned it, one of the masterpieces of the seventeenth

274

century, the *grand siècle*. With his innate sense of form and line, which we have noticed elsewhere, allied to his technical expertise, he produced a baroque church of great beauty and simplicity. The façade has Doric columns and a single pediment. Above it rises the drum with forty columns and windows; and above this the dome, crowned with a lantern and spire. The dome is decorated with trophies and garlands and the spire rises to a height of 351 feet, a little lower than its contemporary St Paul's in London, but equally imposing.

The dome was first covered in gold leaf in 1715, an eye-catching and sun-catching effect. The gold leaf has been replaced several times since and it needs it again badly now. But did Hardouin-Mansart see it as a golden dome? He died in 1708, and the church with its gilding was finished by his brother-in-law, Robert de Cotte. There is a statue of Hardouin-Mansart near the main door; but if you seek his monument, look up!

The inside of the dome is elaborately painted by distinguished artists of the period and shows the Evangelists, the Kings of France and the Apostles, in that order. At the top is St Louis presenting Christ with a sword, thus striking from the very start a military note. It is very possible that both the King and the architect had martial glory in mind all the time; after all, the *grognards* can hardly have wanted a second church.

> *Louis Quatorze*
> *Was addicted to wars.*
> *He sent Turenne to the Palatinate*
> *With orders to flatten it.*

Louis XIV would have been very happy to know that Turenne was the first soldier to be buried in the Dome church. He was re-interred here in 1800 on the orders of Napoleon, and from that moment the Invalides became the French Valhalla. It was separated from the other church, Saint-Louis-des-Invalides, and no longer used for services, but a notice reminds us to remove our hats and speak in low voices. We are in a shrine. Those entombed here include Turenne, Vauban, Bertrand, Duroc, Foch and two Bonaparte brothers (rather out of their element, we might think). In the centre, dominating everything, lies the Emperor himself.

Napoleon died in St Helena in 1821. In 1840, after years of

political negotiations, the British agreed to his body being brought home to France. He himself had said, 'Paris will still cry *"Vive l'Empereur!"* ' A party went to St Helena including Louis-Philippe's son, General Bertrand, the writer Las Cases who had helped Napoleon to write his memoirs, and his valet Marchand. In their presence the coffin was exhumed and opened. To general astonishment it was found that, after nineteen years in the warm damp earth, the body was still perfectly preserved – a tribute either to Napoleon's personality or to the skill of the local coffin-makers.

The body was brought home to Le Havre, the Arc de Triomphe and finally the Invalides. The present **tomb**, however, was not ready until 1861. It was designed by Visconti and is one of his finest achievements, both majestic and simple. Napoleon lies inside seven coffins: the first is of iron, the second of mahogany, the third of lead, the fourth of lead, the fifth of ebony, the sixth of oak and the seventh, the visible sarcophagus, of red porphyry. It reads like a verse from *Revelation* and indeed there is something apocalyptic about it all. As we gaze down on the tomb, the charisma reaches us through the years, through the coffins. Whether we think of Napoleon as a man who spread revolutionary enlightenment, law and order through Europe, or as an ambitious soldier who brought war and death to unfortunate millions, one thing cannot be denied: few men in history have aroused such fervent hero-worship.

Napoleon spent his six years on St Helena re-creating his image, with the help of the sycophantic Las Cases. But now it was the image of the benevolent ruler, the wise law-giver. Julius Cæsar had been replaced by Justinian. Round the tomb, on the lower, crypt level are wall-plaques illustrating this; one shows Napoleon with his arms outstretched, one hand touching the Laws of Justinian, the other the Code Napoléon. There is a quotation from his memoirs which may be translated, 'In every country where I ruled, the permanent trace remains of my good deeds.' Other quotations emphasize the Code Napoléon, his work for education, the restoration of law and order and the suppression of dishonesty in the public services. There is not much about liberty or fraternity, nothing about the Grande Armée. But on the marble floor of the tomb are the names of his chief battles. Against the pillars are twelve huge classical figures, by Pradier, representing the campaigns from Rivoli to Waterloo; dignified and sorrowful, their laurel wreaths are lowered in mourning. Whatever Las Cases may have thought, we are in the presence of a commander-in-chief.

In a niche beside the tomb is the grave of his young son, the King of Rome – not that he ever saw Rome. He died aged twenty-one in Vienna and was buried in the Habsburg crypt, but his body was returned to France in 1940, an unexpected present from Hitler to Paris. He lies beneath a dominating statue of his father and there are often fresh flowers on his grave. Who puts them there, and why, is a mystery. Perhaps they are really intended for his father.

The other church, **Saint-Louis-des-Invalides**, once shared a sanctuary with the Dome church. Now completely separated, we enter it (free) from the far end in the Cour d'Honneur. The work of the original Invalides architect, Liberal Bruand, it has been criticized for its severity. But in fact it is a pleasantly proportioned classical church with an interesting ceiling; the more intricate organ-loft is by Hardouin-Mansart and a plate-glass window over the altar allows a glimpse into the Dome church. The most conspicuous features are the captured banners which hang from the upper gallery; many of them were burnt by the governor of the Invalides in 1814 to prevent them falling into the hands of the Allies, but plenty still remain. It is called the Soldiers' Church and services are held here on Sundays; but it is best known for its military funerals and memorial masses – Berlioz's **Requiem** was first performed here. In the crypt (not open) are the tombs of more soldiers, including Joffre, Leclerc and Juin.

We emerge into the great **Cour d'Honneur**, Bruand's best achievement and a fine example of *grand siècle* architecture. Completely formal and symmetrical, it has arcades below and pitched roofs above. But Bruand has broken up the horizontal lines with four pavilions and pediments, prancing horses on the corners of the roof, oval dormer windows and sundials. Under the arcades are a number of captured cannon of great size and weight, most of them with names and histories. The south wall is also the church façade and in the middle of it is a large statue of Napoleon by Seurre, which at one time stood on top of the Vendôme column.

The cobbled courtyard is the scene of many parades and military occasions. It was here that Captain Dreyfus was publicly disgraced. On a pleasanter note we may like to recall the select number of men, some of them foreign, who have been publicly honoured here with the traditional kiss on the cheek bestowed by a Frenchman of equal rank. It was here that Churchill was kissed by de Gaulle, Montgomery by Juin. I do not know who kissed Eisenhower.

On either side of the courtyard, occupying three floors, is the **Army Museum**, which we should certainly visit. (An entry ticket for the Tomb of Napoleon is also valid for the museum, and lasts two days.) If we are short of time or energy, we should concentrate on the east side of the courtyard. This part of the museum is devoted to the French Army from Louis XIV to the Crimean War and of course includes Napoleon's own campaigns, which will be much in our mind.

We shall see many uniforms, much armour, a great deal of it mounted on realistic models; there are also many swords, daggers, harnesses, pistols and rifles. The uniforms are tight, elaborate and much covered with lace; the weapons are richly chased or engraved and signed. As we look at them, it is hard to realize that we are seeing the material from a bloody battle, and indeed there is nothing in the museum to suggest that war is an unpleasant business – except perhaps the bullet which killed Turenne, and this is hard to find. There is also an absence of models or sand-tables which would help us to understand the tactics of the various battles. We seem to be in a gunsmiths' shop or a military outfitters, wondering how on earth it was possible to move, let alone fight, in such tight clothes.

Several things remain in the memory, chiefly relics of Napoleon. His death-mask, taken by a British doctor in St Helena, has only recently been presented to the museum. Also eye-catching are his solid portable desk; his big white dog, which was his companion on Elba, (stuffed), and the well-known portrait by Delaroche of him at Fontainebleau in 1814 after his first abdication, a brooding figure.

We leave the Cour d'Honneur on the north side, emerging into the garden, full of clipped yews and cannons and surrounded by a dry moat. This is a good point from which to see the façade; long, sternly classical, emphasizing the flat horizontal lines. Impressive rather than attractive, it looks like a barracks – and indeed that was what Bruand was ordered to build. However, he provided some variation with the two end pavilions and the fine central portal. Above this is a statue of (by way of a change) Louis XIV on horseback, assisted by Justice and Prudence, not qualities with which he is generally associated. The statue dates from 1815, the original by Coustou having been destroyed in the Revolution. The dormer windows are decorated with helmets, which gives them a grotesque, semi-human appearance.

Beyond the garden stretches the **Esplanade** which reaches to the Seine. It was planned by Robert de Cotte, who completed the Invalides dome, and provides another of those magnificent perspectives which the French admire so much. The trees are kept low and indeed with underground car parks and transport terminals they have little depth of earth. The only building actually on the Esplanade is the Air France Terminal (Metro Invalides, also RER) and this keeps a deliberately low profile. Nothing must be allowed to spoil the view from the Seine and the Pont Alexandre III. Five hundred yards away the dome seems to float over the Hôtel des Invalides.

Centre Culturel Britannique

The Centre Culturel Britannique, which is also the elegant and imposing offices of the British Council, is 9 Rue de Constantine, overlooking the Esplanade des Invalides. Here a private organization, the Association France-Grande Bretagne, organizes occasional lectures in French on some aspect of British life. The British Council also arranges lectures and *tables rondes*, in English, with distinguished guest-speakers. Otherwise, the main attraction is the English-language library. Here we can borrow up to five books and two records at a time, for a period of three weeks. We have, of course, to pay a subscription and also give a Paris address which is not a hotel.

The British Institute. At the same address as the British Council, but next door. A link between Paris and London Universities; organizes courses in English literature and current affairs.

Ecole Militaire

The Royal Military Academy was possibly the brainchild of Madame de Pompadour, the mistress of Louis XV. At any rate it was she who obtained a grudging permission from the bored King and some finance. Gabriel, the architect of the Place de la Concorde, produced elaborate plans, which had for financial reasons to be much modified by Paris-Duverney, who was responsible for Army finances. Nevertheless, the buildings are an elegant example of eighteenth-century architecture and lavish for an army school; they were finished in 1772.

From the Champ-de-Mars we can see the central pavilion with its Corinthian columns, pediment, statues and dome. The statue (1939) is of Joffre. From the opposite side in the Place Fonténoy, we catch a glimpse of the main courtyard with its porticoes and columns in pairs, flanking the central pavilion. The rest of the building is nineteenth-century.

Among the cadets who successfully completed the three-year course was the young Napoleon Bonaparte, whose report said that he was likely to go far in favourable circumstances. The Ecole Militaire now houses the Staff College and the War Studies School. It is not open to the public except for Sunday morning services in the chapel.

UNESCO

The UNESCO Building, the work of three architects, Nervi, Breuer and Zehrfuss, was completed in 1958 and is a typical example of twentieth-century architecture, except that it is not high-rise. Indeed, much of it seems to be underground. As the headquarters of the educational, scientific and cultural side of the United Nations, it is both busy and influential, particularly in the Third World, many of whose members we shall see hurrying along the corridors, looking for their conference rooms. There are up to sixty conferences here every day and (I write from experience) they tend to go on for a very long time. Folk music is apparently an unending topic of interest. For the visitor there are film shows of folk-dancing three times a day and sometimes opportunities for hearing lectures or debates. Information about the organization's current activities can be obtained from the souvenir desk in the main entrance hall.

The UNESCO Building is also a miniature museum of modern art, most of it First World. We may visit it on weekdays, but must telephone or write for permission. As we wander about we may see tapestries by Le Corbusier and Lurçat, frescoes by Picasso, a relief by Arp, a wall by Miró, a mosaic by Bazaine, sculpture by Giacometti and Kelly. The two biggest works are outside the main building; a huge reclining figure by Henry Moore and a swinging mobile by Alexander Calder.

THE RODIN MUSEUM

The Musée Rodin, a must for lovers of sculpture, is in the house and the garden of the Hôtel Biron at No.77 Rue de Varenne, on the corner of the Boulevard des Invalides. It would be hard to imagine a more perfect setting for the works of a sculptor. Rodin's works would seem impressive anywhere, but it is pleasant to have them in a classical setting which is neither overwhelming nor cramped.

The **Hôtel Biron** would be worth a visit for itself alone; it is possibly the only *hôtel*, in an area noted for its fine houses, which is open to the public. Eighteenth-century, with columns and pediments, it was designed by Gabriel for a rich wig-maker, and was later the home of the Duke of Maine, the illegitimate son of Louis XIV and Madame de Montespan, who married the grand-daughter of Le Grand Condé. Biron, a general in the Revolution, occupied it briefly before being guillotined. Later it became a convent and unfortunately the Mother Superior had the white and gold eighteenth-century panelling ripped out for being both materialistic and baroque. However, the panelling in the two end rotundas survives, a beautiful example of eighteenth-century decor, even though it is now plain wood-coloured; this provides a better background for marble statues.

Later the house became an official home for those connected with the arts, an earlier Cité des Arts. Among those who lived there were the German poet Rilke, the British dancer Isadora Duncan, and Auguste Rodin from 1908 until his death in 1917. They paid for their lodging by presenting their works to the state, though it is not clear what Madame Duncan presented. But we must be permanently grateful for the Rodin collection, which also includes works by other artists, which he possessed.

Coming to his own sculpture, we may well be amazed at its strength and vitality, by the mastery with which he handled the change from the classical to the modern idiom, and by the variety of themes which he studied. One of the principal themes is emergence

– hands and heads emerging from rough rock or water, the creation of humanity. In 'The Hand of God', a hand emerging from limbo holds Adam and Eve in a gentle grasp. In one of his most celebrated works, 'The Cathedral' (1908), two large hands emerge from rock, the tips touching in a prayerful attitude, forming a sort of chancel arch. The close observer will note that it is not a pair of hands, but two right hands. Indeed, with one exception, all his studies of hands are right hands, sometimes sensitive, sometimes stubby-fingered, as in 'The Secret' (1910), usually holding something or someone; the left-handed exception is *La Main du Diable*, the devil's hand crushing humanity.

Feet were another of his themes. His walking men, his barefoot figures, when they have legs at all, have large muscular feet with strong toes. But his main theme was the torso, the human body, usually nude. Even in marble or bronze, the women are soft, the men have well-muscled backs. This is especially noticeable in his famous marble, 'The Kiss', which is remarkable both for its delicate eroticism and for its harmonious design. The bodies are beautifully shaped, but the faces hardly exist. The same applies to many of his imaginative works and also, of course, to his headless torsos; one might be forgiven for thinking that Rodin was not much interested in the human face. And then we look at his heads of Balzac, Hugo and Clemenceau, so full of life and character, Balzac's with almost a Dionysiac twinkle, and we see that Rodin was a fine portraitist. But it was a different facet of his art.

The Hugo busts and the Balzac statues are on the first floor. Rodin made several statues of Balzac, including a nude. But Balzac's portly figure hardly looks at its best nude, despite a resemblance to a middle-aged Bacchus, a resemblance perhaps justified by Balzac's own lifestyle. But a great novelist should not appear thus to the passing crowds and we must feel that it was right to choose a clothed, cloaked version for the Boulevard Montparnasse.

In the garden are some of Rodin's largest and best-known works. We shall look carefully at the bronze *'Le Penseur'* – 'The Thinker'. This was at one time in a park in Lübeck, Germany, where it was painted by the Norwegian Expressionist Edvard Munch, a picture which is now in the museum. The sculpture was bought back, with money raised by public subscription, and is now on the right of the entrance. The Thinker sits, his chin on his hand, his elbow on his knee, his legs crossed, his body present, his mind far away. The dominating features are, once again, the great hands and feet; the head, by contrast, seems rather small. Perhaps the artist's model was not a great thinker – this is a problem which confronts many sculptors.

On the other side is the well-known group 'The Burghers of Calais'. Rodin made several versions of this in plaster and we may well prefer the more homogeneous one, which is on the first floor of the museum. Against the east wall is a vast, extraordinary work, 'The Gates of Hell'. This shows writhing bodies, Michelangelo-style, being sucked down, while over them sits a smaller version of our old friend '*Le Penseur*'. Above him, over the doors, are three shades, the same figure in three different positions. In this work, the symbolism eludes me, nor can I imagine Rodin's purpose, except that sculptors like writhing bodies. It can hardly have been intended as the portal of a church, and it looks out of place in the beautiful garden.

Before leaving we may well dawdle for some pleasant minutes in the garden, where there are sometimes temporary exhibitions. But even if not, we shall enjoy the garden for itself. In many ways it is the quintessence of much that is best and most typical in Paris. There are no long perspectives or picturesque old corners, but it is the sort of place which the French themselves enjoy; the pool, the statues, the trees, the overshadowing dome, the classical façade of the house, the quietness. We might be in the eighteenth century. Being British, we may wish that they would not pollard the trees quite so savagely, but no Frenchman would agree with us.

The Septième arrondissement is not an area full of famous res-taurants. Those who live here tend to eat at home or in the canteens of their embassies or ministries. All the same, good food on every level can be found.

If we are tempted by steamed oysters in a white leek sauce, we should head for Le Bourdonnais, No.113 Avenue de la Bourdon-nais. It is fairly expensive and closed on Sundays and Mondays. Chez Marius, No.9 Rue de Bourgogne, is rather cheaper and is used by politicians from the nearby Chambre des Députés; the *gratin de langouste* is popular (closed Saturdays and in August). La Fontaine de Mars, No.129 Rue Saint-Dominique, is a cheap little bistro beside the fountain of the same name. In warm weather we can eat out under the colonnade and we shall certainly order the *cassoulet de canard* and a bottle of Cahors wine.

Unexpectedly, one of the best restaurants hereabouts is in the Invalides Air Terminal. Called Chez Françoise after a cashier who left a quarter of a century ago, the restaurant is not for hurried air travellers. Indeed, few of our fellow-lunchers are likely to be catching a plane anywhere. It is, however, a place where we can enjoy at our leisure *escalope de saumon aux poireaux* (leeks seem to be popular in these parts) or *rable de lièvre, sauce poivrade*. Or even, in season, roast partridge. Underground, we eat in an enclosed green bower. Those who like to chew with a view may prefer the Hilton roof restaurant (No.18 Avenue de Suffren) – or the Eiffel Tower.

CHAPTER 19

Montparnasse

Montparnasse may fairly be called the cradle of modern art. All contemporary art is, of course, 'modern', but Montparnasse was the forcing-house of all those ideas which had been germinating in our civilization and which came to harvest in the first forty years of this century. In the plastic, visual arts, its influence was worldwide; generally referred to as 'modern art', it was also called the Ecole de Paris, though its influence soon spread. Many of its leading figures were not French in origin; sometimes they were refugees from foreign tyrannies, sometimes simply enjoying the freedom of expression, the general café *ambiance* and the meetings of sympathetic minds, all of which they found in Montparnasse. Nor was it confined to the plastic arts. Some were writers, political thinkers, composers, dancers, theatre designers or those connected with the new art-form, films. Many of their successors are still there and can be seen in the evenings in the Coupole or the Select. There were also many hangers-on, with less talent, and a good picture of Montparnasse in the Twenties can be read in the first half of Hemingway's early novel, *Fiesta*, (*The Sun Also Rises*) and in his memoir, *A Movable Feast*.

We can start our walk with Hemingway, at the eastern end of the Boulevard du Montparnasse (see page 287), but first we can pause for a cup of coffee while we consider the life of Montparnasse and its fascinating history.

It was not concerned specifically with painting, originally. In the seventeenth century many poets and students (often much the same thing), finding the Pont Neuf too noisy and the near presence of Queen Margot discouraging, took to the nearby countryside to declaim their works. The 'mountain' was hardly worthy of the name; it was merely a heap of stones from disused quarries, covered

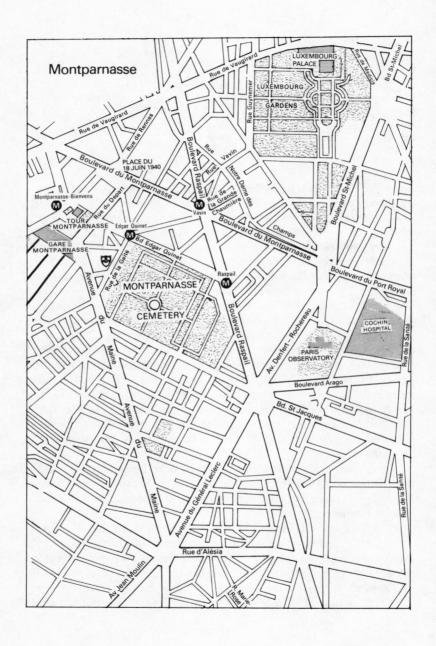

Montparnasse

Rue de Vaugirard

LUXEMBOURG PALACE

LUXEMBOURG GARDENS

Bd St-Michel

Rue de Médicis

Rue de Vaugirard

Rue de Vaugirard

Rue de Rennes

Boulevard Raspail

Rue Guynemer

PLACE DU 18 JUIN 1940

Rue Vavin

Rue

Notre Dame des Champs

Boulevard du Montparnasse

Montparnasse-Bienvenu

M

Rue du Depart

Vavin

M

Rue de la Grande Chaumière

Boulevard St-Michel

TOUR MONTPARNASSE

Edgar Quinet

Boulevard du Montparnasse

GARE MONTPARNASSE

Bd Edgar Quinet

M

Rue de la Gaité

Raspail

M

Boulevard du Port Royal

MONTPARNASSE CEMETERY

Boulevard Raspail

Avenue du Maine

Av. Denfert - Rochereau

PARIS OBSERVATORY

COCHIN HOSPITAL

Rue de la Santé

Boulevard Arago

Avenue du Maine

Bd. St Jacques

Avenue du Général Leclerc

Rue de la Santé

Rue d'Alésia

Av. Jean Moulin

R. Marie-Rose

with grass, but it was given the nickname of Mount Parnassus. It has long since disappeared and the area was built over, becoming a lively centre of Paris, with cafés, cabarets and dance-halls. The cancan was danced here, before it ever appeared at the Moulin Rouge. Much of the quarter was rebuilt by Haussmann in the nineteenth century, in particular the two wide boulevards, the Boulevard du Montparnasse (which preserved the colloquial name) and the Boulevard d'Enfer, now the Boulevard Raspail, a very long street which Hemingway's 'Jake' 'could not stand to ride along', though he did not mind walking along it. An interesting building is No.26 Rue Vavin, a block of flats built in 1911 and covered almost entirely in white tiles. The flats are stepped back from each other to give each one an open-air terrace, very unfashionable in these glass-tower days. But as a piece of Art Nouveau it is remarkable. Otherwise, the quarter is of little interest architecturally; atmospherically it is fascinating.

The first writer to move in was the satirist, Alfred Jarry; the first painter, Rousseau le Douanier. After the 1900 Exhibition, the wine pavilion was reconstructed to provide modest lodgings and studios, known informally as the Beehive (*La Ruche*), and among its first tenants were Modigliani, Chagall, Léger, Soutine and Zadkine. Apollinaire, the poet who coined the word Cubism, arrived early on the scene, followed soon after by Picasso, Braque, Juan Gris and Van Dongen, who had previously been centred in Montmartre, but were attracted by the liveliness of the new quarter.

We may drop some further famous names: Kandinsky, Klee, Matisse, Rouault; Pascin; Scott Fitzgerald, Gertrude Stein, James Joyce, Hilaire Belloc, Ford Madox Ford, Max Jacob, Henry Miller, Samuel Beckett; Stravinsky, Satie, de Falla, Milhaud; Cocteau, Eisenstein. There were some 25,000 Russians living in Paris during this time, many, but not all, refugees from the Tsarist régime, and they would argue with each other all evening in the Montparnasse cafés. Among them were Lenin and Trotsky. It is possible to visit Lenin's flat (see page 293).

Unless we have other transport, our walk is reached from Metro Vavin, along the Boulevard du Montparnasse, eastwards towards the Boulevard de l'Observatoire. When Hemingway came to Montparnasse from the Place de la Contrescarpe, he and his family lived at No.113 Rue Notre-Dame-des-Champs, just round the corner from the **Closerie des Lilas**. This was the literary café of the area and, as he liked writing in public, he would sit at a table on the pavement, writing in his notebooks, greeting his friends, sometimes snubbing them, sometimes, absorbed in his work, not even seeing them. In the evening, according to some who still remember him, he would stroll along the boulevard to the Dôme café, where he would join a table and from then on dominate the conversation, although he was hardly the world figure he later became.

The Closerie des Lilas is no longer a café, but an elegant and rather expensive restaurant. It still has literary associations, one of the places where established writers and aspiring winners of the Prix Goncourt should be seen. In spring and summer we can eat in the garden, among the lilacs, enjoying fresh asparagus, and *rognons de veau* in a cream sauce *aux herbes d'Alpilles*. In the evening we dine inside, to the accompaniment of some rather sad piano music. The atmosphere is not quite the same as at the beginning of the century, when the writer Paul Fort held his rowdy Tuesday evenings there; or when Lady Duff-Twiston (Hemingway's 'Brett') danced the Charleston there.

Outside the garden of the Closerie we find the celebrated **statue of Marshal Ney**, the French tactical commander at Waterloo, brandishing his sword among the trees, only a few yards from the place where he was executed. The responsibility for his trial and death (7 December 1815) lay with the Duke de Richelieu, who ruled France in the name of the Bourbon king, Louis XVIII. The King, rather out of his depth in a country divided between Royalists and Bonapartists, was accused by both sides of weakness and only too glad to leave politics to Richelieu, a close friend of the Tsar.

We are now at the meeting of four boulevards and there are fine views through the trees of the Observatoire, the dome of the church of Val-de-Grâce and, down the Observatoire avenue, the distant façade of the Luxembourg Palace.

However, we shall stroll (*flâner*) with many others along the Boulevard du Montparnasse. The first part is not very interesting and soon we shall see the blank façade of New Jimmy's, Montparnasse's most prestigious nightclub and part of Régine's empire. (She is a lady who says she hates the sight of daylight. See Chapter 20.)

Opposite is a small street, the Rue de la Grande Chaumière,

which we shall certainly look at. The **Grande Chaumière** was a cabaret and 'dancing', a rather noisy one, which started during the Revolution. It is now Paris's best-known private art school and, as there is no entrance examination, anyone from anywhere can enrol on payment. The students sit in crowded rooms, doing charcoal drawings of plaster saints or female figures, clothed and nude. If they are lucky, their work may be corrected and scribbled over by Yves Brayer, an admired traditionalist painter, who does not seem even to have heard of Picasso. Watching the young people emerging for their lunchtime break and coffee in the Select, we can try to guess which are serious artists and which are merely passing a year or two in pleasant, artistic surroundings.

Almost opposite is an excellent artists' colourman, Gattégno, a shop which will sell canvases, paints, brushes and so on in almost unlimited sizes and shapes to everyone, professionals and students alike. Next door to the Grande Chaumière is a very cheap bistro, the Wadja, which has been there for a long time. Small and humble, it is favoured by professional artists who like to eat well and very cheaply. But no fresh asparagus for them.

Returning to the Boulevard, we are at the Carrefour, the cross-roads with the Boulevard Raspail. There we find Rodin's famous **statue of Balzac**, which certainly deserves our attention. Rodin's basic idea was that a statue was both a figure and a rock, one emerging from the other, and the Balzac statue combines both. Rodin worked long on it, making many sketches, and the result has been hailed as a masterpiece, though some have found it over-praised. It is certainly a dominating tribute to two great men, near contemporaries.

At the Carrefour, back at Metro Vavin, we are in the heart of the quarter, crowded with people and life, not much connected with art. Two well-known cafés, the Dôme and the Rotonde, face each other. Neither are what they were in the days when the tables stretched down the street to the next café. Here Modigliani would hawk his pictures from table to table, with moderate financial success; there must be many people alive now who wish that their grandparents had disbursed a few francs on those occasions. Both cafés are now mainly restaurants, full of nostalgic reminders of the Twenties, but with small, glassed-in terraces, and filled by the better-off bourgeoisie slurping down oysters. Montparnasse seems to specialize in seafood and the boulevard could almost be called a street of oysters.

Beyond the Rue Vavin is the **Select**, which appears in many novels. This is a true café (though sandwiches and excellent omelettes are available); there is not an oyster in sight. Instead we have a crowd of artists or pseudo-artists drinking and talking, and the walls are covered with posters of current shows. A glance at these will give us a good idea of what is going on in the art world that season. Artists are convivial people and we shall have no trouble in making friends. We may well be asked to see their studios and their work in the hope, of course, of selling us a picture. If we are lucky and choose right, our grandchildren may find themselves millionaires. But it is a long-odds gamble.

Opposite it is the **Coupole**, a large café-restaurant and the artistic and literary heart of the quarter. It is a place where we go to see who is there, especially in the late evening. Here too there are posters on the walls; every artist having a show has to have his poster in the Coupole. More and more it is being turned over to food, the drinkers and talkers being eased on to the glassed-in terrace or the bar. But it is crowded every evening and we should try to get a table in the centre, near the big vase of flowers. There is also an underground 'dancing', with partners available, but many visitors never discover this. We have not come to the Coupole to dance.

Moving on down the Boulevard, past the cafés, cinemas and small shops (and even a church, Notre-Dame-des-Champs, neo-Byzantine, on the site of an old country church), we reach the crossroads with the Rue de Rennes, the Place du 18 Juin 1940 – the name recalls the date of de Gaulle's historic broadcast from London. Facing us is the Maine-Montparnasse Building Complex, dominated by the Tower.

The **Montparnasse Tower** indeed dominates, not only the quarter but the whole of central Paris. It was completed in the last decade and was part of the plan to renovate a rather decaying area with new business facilities. From the point of view of transport and the metro, it was ideally situated and the tower has many qualities. Nearly seven hundred feet high (two hundred metres) it is the tallest office block in Europe – we can hardly call it 'inhabited'. It has 39,000 square metres of glass. Built by SEFRI Construction (Georges Vari), it is a beautiful skyscraper, the work of a team of

French architects, Cassan, Beaudouin, de Marien and Saubot. Unlike some new North American towers, it has a curved shape, not over-severe, and reminiscent possibly of the Pirelli Building in Milan. One could almost call it a piece of giant sculpture. But whether it is placed in the right city is a matter of continuing debate.

Seven thousand people work there. But we shall ignore them and ascend to the 56th floor by a fast lift, well signposted. Here we have a panorama, not only of Paris but of twenty-five miles of the Ile-de-France. This is on fine days; on wet days the clouds swirl round the windows, romantically. At night we have a million twinkling lights below us. There is a restaurant and bar (piano music in the evening), but the food and service are disappointing, for such high prices. This does not matter much, we have not come up here for the meal.

It is a view which should be seen, though personally I think Paris looks better from lower down. What we see from the top of the Tower are the other high-rise buildings, La Défense, and the new apartment blocks which now encircle Paris. The famous avenues, domes, palaces and churches which we have come to see are lost far below us and we shall have some trouble in identifying them, even with the help of the painted encircling map.

Two flights higher (on foot) we find ourselves on the open-air terrace able to see, if we wish, the distant airports and Mont Valérian. On a windy day we may have the feelings of a main-topman furling the sails in a westerly gale or a mountaineer who has continued the ascent against the advice of his guide. There are careful precautions against suicide, one of the problems of high-rise architects and one to which Eiffel did not, perhaps, give enough attention.

Returning to the ground, we find ourselves in the big building complex, the commercial centre. This is on eight levels, six of them underground and served by lifts or escalators. There are two department stores (Galeries Lafayette and C & A); about sixty boutiques; cafés; snack-bars; a sports centre; swimming pool; the main offices of Air France and the International Textile Centre, the export offices of over two hundred companies. It was originally intended that the complex should be an art centre, revitalizing the artistic life of the quarter, and for a time this seemed to be coming about. A huge tent was erected in the piazza behind the Tower,

291

where several exhibitions and salons were held. But then the plan was dropped in favour of concentrating the arts at Beaubourg and the Montparnasse Centre was given over wholly to business and businessmen, who rarely live in the quarter. In a bustling area traditionally devoted to art and entertainment, the biggest architectural feature is largely empty at night.

The Tower and the commercial centre are built on the site of the nineteenth-century Gare Montparnasse and our walk ends here. In August 1944 General Leclerc and his armoured division arrived from the Porte d'Orléans and made their headquarters in the station; no trains were of course running. On 25 August, he accepted the surrender of the German military governor there, as is recorded by a plaque on the left side of the commercial centre. The new **Gare Montparnasse** is now a few hundred yards farther down the line. It is the most modern railway station in Europe, following Rome and Euston. The trains run into a tall canyon of glass, steel and concrete, and every possible amenity is provided for the traveller, including a chapel and a statue of St Bernard, carved from an old railway sleeper. But the station only serves Brittany, lower Normandy and the Atlantic coast. It has no long-distance or international traffic, which bring so much glamour to the aging stations elsewhere, and it is mainly used by commuters, who are always in a hurry.

Nevertheless, Montparnasse remains a centre of attraction. Many of the artists may have been forced by rising rents to live farther out, but they return frequently for the *ambiance* and one anothers' company. Many people come for the night-life, which goes on till all hours and is centred, suitably, on the Rue de la Gaîté. This was originally an old country road lined with cafés and cabarets, and it continues the tradition with many nightclubs, cinemas and restaurants where we shall find a very mixed crowd of visitors and local inhabitants. The street also has two 'straight' theatres and the Bobino music-hall (see Chapter 20), the Left Bank equivalent of the Olympia on the Right Bank. Many of the prominent pop singers appear here, and it was the favourite theatre of the modern troubadour, Georges Brassens, whose records are known internationally. There are more nightclubs in the Rues Vavin and Bréa, near the intersection with the Boulevard Raspail. One of these caters for transvestites.

Lest it may be thought that Montparnasse is, and has always

been, just a place for fun and revelry, we can pause for a moment to consider the more serious side. The places of interest are scattered and can be reached by Metro from Montparnasse-Bienvenue.

Lenin lived from 1909 to 1912 at No.4 **Rue Marie-Rose** (Metro Alésia). His apartment, and the adjoining one, are now a museum. We can visit this, but we should telephone the conservator first at his private number (665–9922) to arrange a rendezvous. It helps, also, to consult the Soviet Embassy.

The three-room flat is modest, fifty-nine square metres, but an ample lodging by modern Paris or Russian standards, and it had central heating, its own lavatory and a kitchen with an old-fashioned range. Lenin worked in the front room which overlooked the small street, the trees and the wall opposite (the hideous red-brick church which now dominates the street was not there in his time). The flat, which he shared with Kroupskaya and her mother, has been redecorated to look much as it did in 1909, comfortable but not luxurious. His and Kroupskaya's bedroom has no outside ventilation and he was short of furniture, writing at a kitchen table and keeping his books stacked on the floor.

He had other problems too, apart from politics. His printer went bankrupt, leaving him short of money, like any other bourgeois. His correspondence was hindered by a postal strike, about which he expressed himself forcefully. His letters were also watched and he was forced to clandestine and rather romantic methods; Kroupskaya's mother would copy out old and harmless texts and, between the lines, her daughter would write Lenin's manifestoes in invisible ink, schoolgirl-style. However, he also managed some more public events: political meetings in the Puits Rouge café, since demolished, at the corner of the Avenue Jean-Moulin (then the Avenue de Châtillon), facing the church at Metro Alésia. The area was then part of the Montrouge district, and the word and colour *rouge* must have been much in his mind. The fifth Communist Party congress was held in a dance-hall at 99 Rue d'Alésia in 1909.

On the centenary of his birth, 1970, moves were made to rename the street Rue Lénine, but there was fierce opposition and the flat was sacked by right-wingers. Behind the smashed mirror over his writing-chair a piece of the original wallpaper was found. This relic was sent to Russia where it was copied and printed and now the whole flat is papered with it, a design of laurel sprigs in pinkish-buff.

This and the oil lamps give an idea of the time and, in a sense, of the man. The apartment next door contains books, manifestoes and photographs, among them the British Museum Reading Room, more identified in our minds with Marx than with Lenin. The plaque outside was erected in April 1945, before the end of the war, and obviously prepared well in advance by the Resistance.

In 1912 Lenin decided to leave Paris, no longer a suitable headquarters for his work. In June of that year, he said goodbye to his colleagues at the Pavillon du Lac in the nearby Parc Montsouris, and started on the long, fateful journey through Switzerland and Germany to the Finland Station in St Petersburg, which he reached in 1917.

Revolutionaries, however, continued to exist in Montparnasse, though Lenin might not have approved of their dissenting ideas. In recent times Sartre lived his last years near the main Montparnasse-Raspail cross-roads, and often lunched late in the Coupole, speaking to nobody except his adopted Algerian daughter, to whom he talked incessantly. She never replied. It has often been thus in Montparnasse.

At the east end of the boulevard was the Port Royal convent, a centre of the Jansenist (near-Protestant) movement so cruelly persecuted in the reign of Louis XIV; it is now part of the Cochin hospital (Metro Saint-Jacques) next door. We see the big hospital itself, where de Gaulle was operated on for prostate. Or we may pass the Santé prison (Metro Glacière) where the guillotine blade fell fairly recently, and probably for the last time. Although we are unlikely to enter, we can stop at the café, A Votre Santé, and sip a glass of rum, the traditional 'last drink'. And then on to the **Montparnasse cemetery** (Metro Raspail), which at least we can enter from the Boulevard Edgar-Quinet. Here we shall find the graves of several artists previously mentioned, plus those of Baudelaire, Maupassant, Citroën, César Franck and Saint-Saëns; also two recent and much-publicized suicides, who were married for a time: the film-star Jean Seberg and the novelist Romain Gary. Then, to cheer ourselves up, we shall cross the Rue Emile-Richard (the longest street in Paris without houses) to the eastern part of the cemetery. There, beside the Boulevard Raspail, we shall find Brancusi's statue 'The Kiss', which will remind us that Montparnasse has always been a place of romance. A simple monolithic gravestone, it conveys in the modern idiom a touching devotion, and it invites comparison with Rodin's famous work on the same subject.

Recovering our appetites, we shall head back to the Boulevard Montparnasse, probably to the Coupole (Metro Vavin), where we can enjoy a *plateau de fruits de mer* as a prelude to what will be a long and multilingual evening, there and in the Select opposite.

CHAPTER 20

Paris by Night

The night-life of Paris has long been famous. Indeed the whole idea of 'Gay Paree' is based on the city's night-life rather than on the other attractions which have been discussed in the previous chapters. Paris is a city which never seems to sleep. If we happen to be out in the middle of the night, we shall find people going about, on pleasure or unimaginable business. Unlike French provincial towns, which firmly turn out all the lights at ten o'clock, Paris goes on all night, *la ville lumière*. For those who do not wish to go to bed, Paris offers a wide choice. Whether we are wanting a girl-show or a poetry-reading, a glamorous gala or a tramp along the boulevards in Henry Miller style, we can find it. All I can do here is to indicate some of the ways in which people enjoy Paris by night and leave you to make your choice. *Chacun à son goût.*

To many the thought of a night out in Paris is associated with the stomach and the palate. Many cafés and restaurants have been mentioned in this book, but I can bring some of them together as suggestions for a pleasant evening: a cocktail or apéritif in pleasant surroundings, followed by a memorable dinner and ending with coffee and a last drink at a boulevard café, watching the never-ceasing world go by.

If we are in the **Champs-Elysées**, we could start with a champagne cocktail at Fouqet, followed by dinner in the same place or at Lasserre and ending with an Armagnac at a pavement table on the Avenue, looking at the floodlighting and the fountains. In the **Concorde area**, wanting fashionable life, we could start at the Crillon Bar, dine at Maxim's and remain there afterwards. In the **Opéra area**, we might start with a very dry martini at Harry's Bar, followed by dinner at Drouant or the Grand Véfour, and end on the terrace of the Café de la Paix. On the **Ile Saint-Louis** I would suggest a vermouth at the Brasserie, followed by dinner at the Orangerie, or even at the Tour d'Argent just across the river, ending on the pavement of Le Lutétia, overlooking the Seine and the floodlit buildings.

If we should prefer something more Bohemian and a little cheaper, we could spend the evening on the **Butte de Montmartre**. We could start with a *kir* (if you find that drinkable) at the Clairon des Chasseurs, followed by dinner at La Mère Catherine, and end in one of the many places along the Rue Norvins. In **Saint-Germain-des-Prés** we shall of course start with an apéritif, a Pernod or a Ricard, on the terrace of the Deux Magots, followed by dinner at Lipp and ending in the Club Saint-Germain or the London Tavern. In **Montparnasse** we might like to start with a cocktail on the top of the Tower, followed by dinner at the Coupole or the Closerie des Lilas and ending on the terrace of the Select.

Any of these evenings can be varied at will, but they will all give us a pleasant and memorable evening. Except for Lipp, which works on a different principle, reservations are essential at the restaurants.

However we may want a more organized entertainment, perhaps a **theatre**. A useful magazine, *Pariscope*, which appears weekly will give us much information about what is on in Paris on any particular evening and can be bought at any newsagent or bookstall. We can also find out the details of theatres and films from the entertainments pages of *France-Soir*. Paris has many theatres of all types, and somewhere we shall find what we want: famous classic or with-it farce, lavish spectacle or intimate revue.

Paris theatres usually have a matinée on Sunday afternoons and are closed on Sunday evenings and Mondays. They are also usually closed in August, a month which may extend from mid-July to mid-September. Tickets should be bought in advance, either from the theatre itself, from your hotel concierge or from an agency, of which there are many. The theatre agency of American Express, 5 Rue Scribe, is very helpful, particularly when tickets are hard to get. (The Comédie-Française, incidentally, being a small theatre, is often hard to get into, except when Corneille is being played.) Remember to tip the usherette who shows you to your seats (a couple of francs per person) or you may find her torch flashing in your eyes all the evening. This tipping also applies to circuses, cabarets and, increasingly, to cinemas.

Chansonniers have always been part of the Paris theatrical scene, but now only two are left, one in Clichy, the other at République. This type of intimate revue needs a good command of fast French slang and the topical scene. Imitations are not very amusing if you have not heard of the person being imitated.

Café-concerts and '*café-théatres*' were in vogue about fifteen years ago, combining entertainment with a drink, but many of them have now closed, including one in the Ile Saint-Louis. However, pavement entertainers come and go outside popular cafés, especially in summer, and are busier than ever. Saint-Germain-des-Prés, Montparnasse and Beaubourg are main centres.

The French are great film-goers and Paris is full of **cinemas**, many of them small. Some of the big old houses have been divided into three or four small cinemas, each showing a different film, so the choice is vast. English-language films are usually shown in the original version (v.o.) but may be dubbed into French (v.f.). The English version is usually screened on the Right Bank, the French version on the Left, despite the proximity of the Sorbonne and Berlitz. Modern French youth prides itself increasingly on seeing the original version, even if it is in Japanese.

Music-lovers will find three theatres giving opera or ballet and there are several concert halls. The programmes are shown on posters on tall cylinders with green hats which stand in many streets and are often mistaken for public urinals. The concerts, however, are of international standard and indeed are given by the same famous performers as in London and elsewhere. Jazz and jazz cellars have long been part of the Paris scene and several have survived the pop takeover. Among these are the Caveau de la Huchette in the Latin Quarter and that old existentialist haunt, the Tabou in the Rue Dauphine, Saint-Germain-des-Prés, which preserve their own atmosphere.

French pop has a sound of its own, which never seems to change, decade after decade, and indeed the names of the singers do not seem to change. The songs are usually written by the musician himself and the rather sentimental words are as important as the tune itself. It has a long tradition and can be said to go back to Villon or even further, although you would not guess this when listening to Sylvie Vartan or Gilbert Bécaud. The sound and the personalities, however, continue to draw the crowds to Olympia or the Bobino.

Or should there be a big gala we may even venture to the Palais des Sports on the outskirts, where, with a vast screaming crowd, we can hear Johnny Hallyday or a visiting group such as the Rolling Stones.

Gambling is one of the few evening activities for which Paris does not cater. There are a few private clubs, whose addresses are confidential, but if we wish to see the roulette wheels spinning, we shall have to go to Enghien-les-Bains, near the port of Gennevilliers. Here we shall find a pleasant casino beside a lake. Although it is technically outside Paris, it is only half an hour to an hour's drive from the Gare du Nord. We should bring our passports as well as our money.

If we should want to **dance**, there are hundreds of nightclubs and discothèques in Paris, all the way from Montmartre to Montparnasse. The oldest and most prestigious disco is Castel's in Saint-Germain-des-Prés, which operates on five floors, including restaurants and a cinema; but it is strictly for members and their guests, as are such celebrated night-spots as New Jimmy's and Régine's.

La Scala, the newest and brashest disco in Paris, offers three floors of noise, drinks but as yet no food. At No. 188 *bis* Rue de Rivoli, near the Palais-Royal (on the site of the old Magasins du Louvre), it is open to all comers all and every night. But the management reserves the right to exclude anyone without reason. In these times of single dancing they do not want too much 'living sculpture'. Ladies are admitted free except at weekends.

Other discos which have been recommended are the Club 79 (No.79 Champs-Elysées), the Wagram (No.39 Avenue Wagram), the Whisky-à-Gogo (No.57 Rue de Seine), the Club Saint-Germain (No.13 Rue Saint-Benoît) and that old Existentialist jazz-cellar Le Tabou (No.33 Rue Dauphine), now a disco. More names can be found in the current edition of *Pariscope*.

And so to sex. Paris night-life is generally associated with **girl-shows** which can be anything from a single stripper to a lavish spectacle. It is this last category which has made Paris night-life world-famous. There are three types of show: those which are simply theatrical spectacles like ballets (Folies Bergère, Casino de Paris); those which give three shows each evening – you dine during the first performance and drink during the others (Moulin Rouge (see Chapter 11), Lido, Eléphant Bleu, Eléphant Blanc); and those

299

where you simply drink and watch (Don Camilo, Crazy Horse Saloon).

At the **Folies Bergère**, we sit in stalls and watch the show; we do not dine or drink while it is going on, although in the interval we may visit the celebrated bar. The show is a long one, lasting over three hours, too long, some people think. But the spectacle is breathtaking; how do they manage to change the elaborate sets so quickly? The stage is relatively shallow, so much use has to be made of staircases, down which come girls in glittering outfits. Or they may be completely nude and we shall notice that the nude girls are much plumper than the dressed ones. Many of them, incidentally, are British or German. Between the spectacular scenes are simple, rather crude sketches, which can be easily understood by those who speak no French. We emerge, finally, dazed, hungry but having had a good eyeful and a good money's worth.

The **Crazy Horse Saloon**, at No.12 Avenue George V, is for many people the best and most famous thing in Paris and the main reason for their visit. Founded in 1951 by Alain Bernardin, it has been open every night ever since and has recently welcomed its five millionth guest. Starting as a burlesque Western bar, it has changed into a sophisticated and beautifully produced show, although the stage is very small. In place of the cowboy note, there is sometimes a military or other theme, but the emphasis is on the female nude body, in particular the bottom.

Other cabaret managers hold to their belief in the beauty of the long-legged Anglo-Saxon girl, from either side of the Atlantic. But Monsieur Bernardin prefers girls of mixed race. So far he has shown us, among others, girls of mixed Polish and Italian origins, or English-Japanese, or Spanish-African. They all have gorgeous pseudonyms like Bianca Polaris, Vanilla Banana and Brenda Rainbow. The current star is called Diva Terminus; she is half Breton, half Chinese.

Reservations should be made in advance. We can either sip our champagne at the bar or, for a closer view, sit in the *salle*. Prices here are half as high again, but we have not come to Le Crazy to economize.

Despite the fact that Monsieur Bernardin, in his art student days, was censured by his professor for pornography, the Crazy Horse advertises itself as a place where a woman can bring her husband

without blushing. And indeed that applies to all the shows previously mentioned here; they may be daring, but they are as clean
as a Rubens, as innocent as an Ingres. If we want something
else, *une soirée hard*, we shall have to go elsewhere, probably to
Pigalle.

I have already written about Pigalle in Chapter 13. But I can give
a few further addresses for those with 'special' tastes. At La Cirque
de Minou (No.47 Rue La Rochefoucauld) the waitresses are top-
less. The Lolita Club (No.73 Rue Pigalle) has a lesbian show. Love
in Paris (No.7 Rue Fontaine) also has lesbian shows, slave-girls in
cages and 'Special hard striptease'. Elle et Lui (No.29 Rue Vavin,
Montparnasse) has a transvestite idea. Les Deux Boules (No.28
Rue des Ecoles) has a 'diapositive which revolutionizes voyeurism'.
And at No.16 Rue des Bernardins, near the Place Maubert, we find
'Le Quartz' (formerly 'Gay Club'), which is open every night until
eight o'clock in the morning. But by then we shall be far away.

The traditional way of ending a night out in Paris is at Les Halles,
and it is still the right way, even though the great market may have
gone. At one of the restaurants there, probably Au Pied de Cochon,
we can eat onion soup with melted cheese, drink café crème or even
a last bottle of champagne.

It has been a long night. We have dined and wined, we have
listened to fast, brilliant dialogue, we have danced the smurf, we have
seen many beautiful girls, we have walked miles along the boulevards. And now it is dawn, the Paris sky is growing pink, the pigeons
are beginning to coo on the rooftops. It is time to part; you have a
journey ahead of you, I am thinking of my bed.

But you will certainly come back. Hemingway wrote that Paris is
a movable feast; wherever you go for the rest of your life it stays with
you. Yes, but it is better to see it on its own site, beside the Seine.
We shall certainly meet again, next year or even sooner – in front of
your favourite building or masterpiece, strolling down a wide
boulevard or narrow street, sitting on the terrace of your favourite
café. Together we shall look again at the flying-buttresses of Notre-
Dame and at Monet's water-lilies. We shall windowshop in Saint-
Germain-des-Prés and picnic beside the Seine. We shall drink
Pernod and eat roast quails in a gin and cream sauce. And we may
even stand on the star of Kilomètre Zero.

301

Yes, we shall certainly meet again. But in the meantime it is Goodbye. Or, as a modern French novelist has put it, '*Au, dit-il, revoir.*'

Appendices

APPENDIX A

Public Holidays in France

1 January
Easter Monday
1 May
8 May (Victory)
Ascension Day (a Thursday)
Whit Monday
14 July (Bastille)
15 August (Assumption)
1 November (All Saints)
11 November (Armistice)
25 December (Christmas Day)

NOTE If we arrive in Paris, as we often do, for the weekend of Easter or Whitsun, we shall find the Arc de Triomphe closed on Sunday and Monday. The Louvre and the Jeu de Paume Museum are closed, both at Easter and Whitsun, on Sunday, Monday AND Tuesday. However, the Eiffel Tower and Tour Montparnasse are open every day of the year, and we can also visit the Pompidou Centre, Notre-Dame Cathedral and the Sainte-Chapelle.

Telephone Numbers

Telephone numbers are frequently changed in Paris, but the numbers given in this book were correct at the time of going to press. France is changing to an 8-figure telephone system during 1985, and as from 25th October 1985 all Paris numbers will be prefixed by the extra figure 4.

APPENDIX B

Opening Hours

1. Ile de la Cité

(See Chapter 2 for details of Notre-Dame Cathedral)

Archæological Crypt, Parvis Notre-Dame, 4ᵉ. Metro Cité. TEL: 329:8351. Open every day (except 1 Jan., 1 May, 14 July, 1 Nov., 11 Nov., 25 Dec.) from 10.0 a.m. to 6.0 p.m. in summer (1 April to 30 Sept.); 10.0 a.m. to 5.0 p.m. in winter. Half-price on Sundays.

Deportation Memorial (beside Passerelle Bridge). Open every day of the year from 10.0 a.m. to 12 noon and 2.0 p.m. to 5.0 p.m.

Sainte-Chapelle, Boulevard du Palais, 4ᵉ. Metro Cité. TEL: 354:3009. Open every day (except 1 Jan., 1 May, 14 July, 1 Nov., 11 Nov., 25 Dec.) from 10.0 a.m. to 5.45 p.m. in summer; 10.0 a.m. to 4.45 p.m. in winter. Guided Tours: apply Hôtel de Sully, 62 Rue Saint-Antoine, 4ᵉ. TEL: 274:2222.

Conciergerie, 1 Quai de l'Horloge, 4ᵉ. Metro Cité. TEL: 354:3006. Open every day, except when Sainte-Chapelle closed (combined ticket), from 10.0 a.m. to 5.25 p.m. in summer; 10.0 a.m. to 4.25 p.m. in winter.

2. Notre-Dame Cathedral

Place du Parvis Notre-Dame, 4ᵉ. Metro Cité. TEL: 354:2263. Open daily. Services announced at entrance.

Visit to Towers: daily 10.0 a.m. to 5.30 p.m.; access outside, at corner adjoining Rue du Cloître Notre-Dame.

Treasure: Visits daily 10.0 a.m. to 5.0 p.m., except Sundays and public holidays. Apply on right of choir.

Guided Tours: Saturdays 2.30 p.m.; Sundays 2.0 p.m.

Organ Recitals: every Sunday at 5.45 p.m.

Crown of Thorns and other relics, displayed on Good Fridays.

Museum of Notre-Dame de Paris: 10 Rue du Cloître Notre-Dame, open Saturdays and Sundays from 2.30 p.m. to 6.0 p.m. TEL: 325:4292.

WARNING: Bag-snatchers are rife in Notre-Dame. Hold your bag in front of you.

3. Ile Saint-Louis

Metros: Cité (for west end); Pont Marie (centre); Sully-Morland (for eastern end).

Hôtel de Lauzun: Guided tours on certain days only. Apply Hôtel de Sully (Bureau of Historic Monuments), 62 Rue Saint-Antoine 4ᵉ. TEL: 887:2414.

4. The Seine

River Cruise-Boats (including *bateaux-mouches*)

Bateaux Parisiens – Tour Eiffel:– Metro Bir Hakeim or Trocadéro. TEL: 551:3308. From foot of Eiffel Tower. Daily 9.30 a.m. to 10.30 p.m. every 30 minutes.

Vedettes de Paris:– Metro Bir Hakeim. TEL: 705:7129. From Port de Suffren (etc.) daily 10.0 a.m. to 5.30 p.m. every 30 minutes. Also Floodlit Cruise.

Vedettes du Pont Neuf:– Metro Pont Neuf. TEL: 633:9338. From Pont Neuf. Daily; first boat 10.30 a.m., last 6.30 p.m. also Lunch and Floodlit Cruises.

Bateaux-Mouches:– Metro Alma-Marceau. TEL: 225:9610. From Pont de l'Alma (right bank). Daily every 30 minutes from 10.0 a.m. to 12 noon and 2.0 p.m. to 10.30 p.m. Also Floodlit Cruise.

Patache Eautobus (Quiztour). Metro Solferino. TEL: 874:7530. From Quai Anatole France. Half-day cruises on Seine and Canal Saint-Martin. April to November daily, except Mondays and public holidays. Reservations needed.

The Zoo ('La Menagerie du Jardin des Plantes'), 3 Quai Saint-Bernard, 5ᵉ. Metro Gare d'Austerlitz. TEL: 336:1441. Open daily 9.0 a.m. to 6.0 p.m.

La Monnaie de Paris (The Mint), 11 Quai Conti, 6ᵉ. Metro Pont Neuf. TEL: 329:1248. Open 11.0 a.m. to 5.0 p.m. on weekdays. Closed Sats., Suns. and public holidays. Entrance free.

Académie Française, Institut de France, Quai de Conti, 6ᵉ. Lecture tours on Saturdays and Sundays at 3.0 p.m.

d'Orsay Museum, 1 Place Henri Montherlant, 7ᵉ. Opening projected in 1986. Collection mainly housed, meanwhile, in Palais de Tokyo. See Chapter 12.

5. *The Champs-Elysées*
Etoile – Champs-Elysées – Concorde – Arc de Triomphe – Tuileries (Jeu de Paume) – Rond Point – Grand Palais.

Metros: Charles de Gaulle-Etoile; George V; Franklin D Roosevelt; Champs-Elysées-Clemenceau; Concorde.

Arc de Triomphe. Metro and RER: Charles de Gaulle – Etoile. TEL: 380:3131. Open for ascent daily from 10.0 a.m. to 4.30 p.m. except on public holidays; also closed on Easter Sunday and Whit Sunday.

St George's Anglican Church, 7 Rue August Vacquerie, 16ᵉ. Metros: George V or Etoile. TEL: 720:2251.

The American Cathedral, 23 Avenue George V, 8ᵉ. Metro George V. TEL: 720:1792.

Palais de la Découverte, Avenue Franklin Roosevelt, 8ᵉ. Metro Champs-Elysées-Clemenceau or Franklin D. Roosevelt. TEL: 359:1665. Open daily 10.0 a.m. to 6.0 p.m. Closed on Mondays and public holidays.

Grand Palais, Avenue du General Eisenhower, 8ᵉ. Metro Champs-Elysées. TEL: 261:5410. Open daily, except Tuesdays, from 10.0 a.m. to 8.0 p.m. (10.0 p.m. Weds.).

Petit Palais, Avenue Winston Churchill, 8ᵉ. Metro Champs-Elysées. TEL: 265:1273. Open daily except Mondays and public holidays from 10.0 a.m. to 5.40 p.m. Free on Sundays.

Jeu de Paume Museum, Place de la Concorde, 1ᵉʳ. Metro Concorde. TEL: 260:1207. Open daily from 9.45 a.m. to 5.15 p.m. (Sats. & Suns. 11.30 a.m. to 5.15 p.m.). Closed on Tuesdays and all public holidays, plus Easter Sunday and Whit Sunday. Free on Wednesdays; half-price Sundays.

6. Opéra
Madeleine – Opéra – Grands Boulevards – Palais-Royal.

Metros: Concorde; Madeleine; Opéra; Bourse; Palais-Royal.

British Embassy, 35 Rue du Faubourg Saint-Honoré, 8ᵉ. Metro Madeleine or Concorde. TEL: 266:9142.

British Consulate, 109 Rue du Faubourg Saint-Honoré, 8ᵉ. Metro Philippe du Roule. TEL: 266:9142.

Embassy Church: St Michael's (Anglican), 5 Rue d'Aguesseau, 8ᵉ (opposite Embassy). TEL: 742:7088.

The Madeleine, Place de la Madeleine, 8ᵉ. Metro Madeleine. TEL: 265:5217. Open daily 7.30 a.m. to 7.0 p.m.

Cognac-Jay Museum 25 Boulevard des Capucines, 2ᵉ. Metro Opéra. TEL: 742:9471. Open daily except Mondays, from 10.0 a.m. to 5.40 p.m.

The Opera, Place de l'Opéra, 9ᵉ. Metro Opéra, RER Auber. TEL: 266:5022. Open daily from 11.0 a.m. to 4.30 p.m. for visitors (guided tours).

Opéra Comique (Salle Favart), 5 Rue Favart, 9ᵉ. Metro Richelieu-Drouot. TEL: 296:0611.

Grévin Museum, 10 Boulevard Montmartre, 9ᵉ. Metro Montmartre. TEL: 770:8505. Open daily 1.0 p.m. to 7.0 p.m. Sundays 1.0 p.m. to 6.0 p.m.

Bibliothèque Nationale, 58 Rue de Richelieu, 2ᵉ. Metros Palais-Royal or Bourse or 4 Septembre. TEL: 261:8283. Closed on Sundays. (Includes *Musée des Medailles et Antiques*. Open daily except public holidays, 1.0 p.m. to 5.0 p.m.)

Bourse de Paris (Stock Exchange), Palais de la Bourse, 2ᵉ. Metro Bourse. TEL: 233:9983. Visits daily, 11.0 a.m. to 1.0 p.m.

Louvre des Antiquaires, 2 Place du Palais-Royal, 1ᵉʳ. Metro Palais-Royal. TEL: 297:2700. See Chapter 13.

7. The Louvre

Rue de Rivoli, 1ᵉʳ. Metro Palais-Royal. (Metro Louvre is not as near.) TEL: 260:3926.

The whole Museum is closed on Tuesdays and public holidays. Also closed on Easter Sunday and Whit Sunday. The entrance-building (European Painting; Greek and Roman Sculpture; Egyptian Crypt) is open on all other days from 9.45 a.m. to 5.0 p.m., with an extension until 6.30 p.m. for French Paintings and some Italians, including the Mona Lisa.
The whole Museum is open on Mondays and Wednesdays. But only the entrance-building is open at lunchtime. Other sections close from 12.30 to 2 p.m. Entrance is free on Sundays and Wednesdays.

8. Beaubourg
Pompidou Centre – Defender of Time Clock – Forum des Halles – Saint-Eustache.

Metros: Rambuteau; Châtelet or Les Halles. Also RER Châtelet-Les Halles, with underground connection to Metro Châtelet.

Centre Georges Pompidou, 120 Rue Saint-Martin, 4ᵉ. Metros Hôtel de Ville; Rambuteau or Châtelet. TEL: 277:1233. Closed on Tuesdays. Open on every other day of the year, except 1 May, from 12 noon to 10.0 p.m. Saturdays and Sundays, 10.0 a.m. to 10.0 p.m. Free on Wednesdays, Sundays and public holidays.

Defender of Time Clock, Quartier de l'Horloge, 4e. Movement of figures hourly; 9.0 a.m. to 10.0 p.m.

Forum des Halles shopping centre, 1–7 Rue Pierre Lescot, 1er (entrance Rue Rambuteau). Metro and RER Châtelet. TEL: 296:6874.

9. Eastern Paris
Saint-Germain L'Auxerrois – Saint-Gervais – Bastille-Père Lachaise Cemetery.

Metros: Louvre; Pont Neuf; Châtelet; Bastille; République; Père Lachaise.

Hôtel de Ville (Town Hall), 29 Rue de Rivoli, 4e. Metro Hôtel de Ville. TEL: 276:4242. (Office of Tourism.) Guided Tour Mondays at 10.30 a.m.

Père Lachaise Cemetery, Boulevard de Ménilmontant, 20e. Metro Père Lachaise. TEL: 370:7033.

10. The Marais
The Hôtels – *Victor Hugo Museum – Place des Vosges – Carnavalet Museum.*

Metros: Pont Marie; Saint-Paul-le-Marais; Chemin Vert.

Hôtel de Sully, 62 Rue Saint-Antoine, 4e. Metro Saint-Paul. TEL: 274:2222. Open daily 10.0 a.m. to 12.30 p.m. and 2.0 p.m. to 6.0 p.m. Guided tours Wed., Sat. and Sun. afternoons.

Bureau of Historic Monuments. At Hôtel Sully. (Gives details about other Hôtels and guided tours, including Sainte-Chapelle.)

Hôtel Salé, 5 Rue Thorigny, 3e. Metro Saint-Sébastien. Future Picasso Museum (1985).

Hôtel d'Aumont, 7 Rue de Jouy, 3ᵉ. Metro Saint-Paul. TEL: 278:4024.

Hôtel de Sens and Bibliothèque Forney, 1 Rue du Figuier, 4ᵉ. Metros Pont Marie; Saint-Paul. TEL: 278:1460. Open daily, except Sundays and Mondays, from 1.30 p.m. to 8.0 p.m.

Victor Hugo Museum, 6 Place des Vosges, 4ᵉ. Metros Chemin Vert; Saint-Paul. TEL: 272:1665. Open daily except Mondays from 10.0 a.m. to 5.40 p.m. Free on Sundays.

Carnavalet Museum, 23 Rue de Sévigné, 3ᵉ. Metros Saint-Paul; Chemin Vert. TEL: 272:2113. Open daily except Mondays, from 10.0 a.m. to 5.40 p.m. Free on Sundays.

Hôtel de Soubise, 60 Rue des Francs-Bourgeois, 3ᵉ. Metros Rambuteau or Hôtel de Ville. TEL: 277:1130. Includes *Museum of French History* and *National Archives*. Open daily except Tuesdays, from 2.0 p.m. to 5.0 p.m. Free on Wednesdays; Half-price on Sundays.

Hôtel de Rohan, 87 Rue Vieille du Temple, 4ᵉ. Twinned with Hôtel de Soubise (same entrance-ticket).

Hôtel de Beauvais, 68 Rue François Miron, 4ᵉ. Metro Saint-Paul. TEL: 887:7431. Open daily except Sundays from 2.0 p.m. to 6.0 p.m.

The Arsénal, 1 Rue de Sully, 4ᵉ. Metro Sully-Morland. Library open on weekdays from 10.0 a.m. to 5.0 p.m.

Centre Culturel du Marais (Contemporary Culture), 26–28 Rue des Francs-Bourgeois, 3ᵉ. Metro Saint-Paul. TEL: 272:7352.

Village Saint Paul, 4ᵉ, (Antiques). Metro Sully-Morland. Open daily, except Tuesdays and Wednesdays, from 11.0 a.m. to 6.0 p.m.

11. Montmartre

Place du Tertre – Sacré-Cœur – Restaurants and Nightclubs – Pigalle.

Metros: Abbesses; Pigalle; Blanche; Clichy.
Funicular: from Marché Saint-Pierre: 6.45 a.m. to 12.45 a.m. daily.

Sacré-Cœur Basilica, Place du Parvis du Sacré-Cœur, 18ᵉ. Metro Anvers. TEL: 251:1702. Open daily from 6.0 a.m. to 11.0 p.m.

Museum of Montmartre, 12 Rue Cortot, 18ᵉ. Metro Lamarck. TEL: 606:6111. Open daily from 2.30 p.m. to 5.30 p.m. Sundays 11.0 a.m. to 5.30 p.m.

Montmartre Cemetery, 20 Avenue Rachel, 18ᵉ. Metro Blanche or Place Clichy. TEL: 387:6424.

12. *The Seizième Arrondissement*
The 'Beau Quartier' – Passy – Balzac's House – Marmottan Museum – Palais de Chaillot – Guimet Museum – Palais de Tokyo – Bois de Boulogne – Tennis – Racecourses.

Maison de Radio France, 116 Avenue du President Kennedy, 16ᵉ. Metro Charles Michels. TEL: re visits: weekdays 230:2180, weekends 230:3384.

Wine Museum, 5 Square Charles Dickens, 16ᵉ. Metro Passy. TEL: 525:6326. Open daily from 2.0 p.m. to 6.0 p.m.

Balzac's House, 47 Rue Raynouard, 16ᵉ. Metros Passy; La Muette. TEL: 224:5638. Open daily, except Mondays, from 10.0 a.m. to 5.40 p.m. Free on Sundays.

Marmottan Museum, 2 Rue Louis Boilly, 16ᵉ. Metro La Muette. TEL: 224:0702. Open daily, except Mondays, from 10.0 a.m. to 6.0 p.m.

Palais de Chaillot, Place du Trocadéro, 16ᵉ. Metro Trocadéro. Houses several Museums:–
Musée National des Monuments Français (Left entrance). TEL: 727:3574. Open daily except Tuesdays, from 9.45 a.m. to 12.30 p.m. and from 2.0 p.m. to 5.15 p.m. Half-price on Sundays.
Musée de l'Homme (Right entrance). TEL: 553:7060. Open daily, except Tuesdays, from 9.45 a.m. to 5.15 p.m.
Musée de la Marine (also Right entrance). TEL: 553:3170. Open daily, except Tuesdays and public holidays, from 10.0 a.m. to 6.0 p.m.

Musée Guimet, 6 Place d'Iéna, 16ᵉ. Metro Iéna. TEL: 723:6165. Open daily, except Tuesdays, from 9.45 to 12 noon and 1.30 p.m. to 5.15 p.m. Free on Wednesdays. Half-price Sundays.

Palais de Tokyo, 13 Avenue du President Wilson, 16ᵉ. Metros Iéna; Alma-Marceau. Houses several collections under new name:
Musée d'Art et d'Essai. TEL: 723:3653. Post-Impressionism. Includes some remains of the former Musée National d'Art Moderne; also d'Orsay Collection, until 1986. Open daily except Tuesdays, from 9.45 a.m. to 5.15 p.m.

Musée d'Art Moderne de la Ville de Paris, 11 Avenue du President Wilson, 16ᵉ. Metros Iéna or Alma-Marceau. TEL: 723: 6127. Open daily, except Mondays, from 10.0 a.m. to 5.30 p.m. Extension on Wednesdays until 8.30 p.m. Free on Sundays.

Bois de Boulogne, 16ᵉ. Metros: Porte Maillot; Porte Dauphine; Les Sablons; Porte d'Auteuil; Porte de Passy. Attractions:
Jardin d'Acclimatation (Children's Zoo, etc.) Metro Sablons. TEL: 624:1080. Open daily from 9.0 a.m. until dusk.
Bagatelle Rose-Garden (and other flowers) all the year. In northwest of Bois. Metro Pont de Neuilly. TEL: 624:6700.
Pré-Catalan Area: near the great waterfall.
Roland Garros Tennis Stadium, 2 Avenue Gordon Bennet, 16ᵉ. Metro Porte d'Auteuil. TEL: 743:9681.
Auteuil Racecourse. Metro Porte d'Auteuil. TEL: 527:1225. Seasons: mid Feb. to end April; end May to mid-July; mid-Oct. to mid-Dec.
Longchamp Racecourse. Metros Porte Maillot or Porte d'Auteuil, then on by bus. TEL: 772:5733. Seasons: May, Sept. and Oct.

13. 'Le Shopping'

Duty-Free and Hors-Taxe

'Duty-Free', in the original sense 'free of *Customs and Excise Duty*' applies only to purchases in airports, ports, ships and aircraft, outside the national Customs barriers. In Paris we may often see the sign 'Duty Free' or 'Hors-Taxe', but it only means that the shop is licensed to give *VAT (in French TVA) Rebate-Forms* to visiting (non-resident) foreigners. Department stores ('Grands Magasins') and major boutiques operate this VAT Rebate system. We must produce a foreign passport and round-trip travel ticket and ask for an export 'détaxe' form. The VAT is then refundable at the Bureaux Détaxe of the port or airport as we leave France. Such purchases, we are officially reminded, should be declared on going home, and VAT is then due on them in our home country.

'Détaxe' can only be claimed on single items costing 1400 francs or more, if we are Common Market nationals (800 francs for others). It is substantial on goods such as furs or scent, which carry a 'Luxury' 33% rate of VAT in France. Rates vary, but the standard French VAT is currently 18.6%.

If in doubt, telephone Centre Renseignements Douanier, 260:3590, Mondays to Fridays.

14. The Latin Quarter
Left Bank – Narrow Streets – Saint-Séverin – Odéon.

Saint-Julien-le-Pauvre, Quai-Saint-Michel, 5ᵉ. Metros Saint-Michel, Maubert-Mutualité, Cité. Open 8.0 a.m. to 7.0 p.m. except 12.0 to 2.0 p.m.

Saint-Séverin, 1 Rue des Prêtres-Saint-Séverin, 6ᵉ. Metro Saint-Michel. Open 8.0 a.m. to 7.0 p.m. except 12.0 to 2.0 p.m.

Théâtre de l'Odéon, 1 Place Paul-Claudel, 6ᵉ. Metro Odéon. TEL: 325:7032.

15. The Montagne Sainte-Geneviève
Sorbonne – Cluny – Boulevard Saint-Michel – Panthéon.

Metros: Saint-Michel; Odéon; Cardinal Lemoine, RER Luxembourg.

The Panthéon, Place du Panthéon, 5ᵉ. RER (B) Luxembourg. Metro (not very close) Maubert-Mutualité. TEL: 354:3451. Open daily from 10.0 a.m. to 5.0 p.m.

Cluny Museum, 6 Place Paul Painlevé, 5ᵉ. Metros Odéon; Saint-

Michel. TEL: 325:6200. Open daily, except Tuesdays, from 9.45 to
12.30 p.m. and 2.0 p.m. to 5.15 p.m. Free on Wednesdays; half-
price Sundays.

16. The Luxembourg
Luxembourg Gardens – Fountain – Palace – The Senate.

RER: Luxembourg. Metros: Saint-Michel; Odéon; Saint-Sulpice;
Saint-Germain-des-Prés; Vavin.

Luxembourg Palace (The Senate). Apply at 15 Rue de Vaugirard,
6ᵉ, for tours on Sundays: 9.30 to 11.0 a.m. and 2.0 p.m. to 4.0 p.m.

Luxembourg Museum. Temporary exhibitions only. 19 Rue de
Vaugirard, 6ᵉ. (Original collection transferred to Museum of
Modern Art.)

17. Saint-Germain-des-Prés
*The Quarter and Cafés – Saint-Germain-des-Prés Church –
Saint-Sulpice.*

Metros: Saint-German-des-Prés; Mabillon.

Eugène Delacroix Museum and Studio, 6 Place de Furstemberg, 6ᵉ.
Metro Saint-Germain-des-Prés. TEL: 354:0487. Open daily except
Tuesdays, from 9.45 a.m. to 5.15 p.m. Free on Weds. Half-price
Sundays.

18. The Septième Arrondissement
Eiffel Tower – Invalides – UNESCO – Rodin Museum.

Eiffel Tower, Champ-de-Mars, 7ᵉ. Metros: Bir Hakeim; Champ-de-
Mars. RER (C). TEL: 550:3456. Open every day of the year. Lifts
run from 10.0 a.m. to 11.0 p.m. Stairs (to 2nd floor only) closed
from 6.0 p.m. Restaurant reservations: 555:2004. Salle Gustave
Eiffel Conference Room reservation 550:3456. Express-Lift to
Jules Verne Restaurant.

Les Invalides (Napoleon's Tomb), 2 Avenue de Tourville, 7ᵉ, or Esplanade des Invalides, 7ᵉ. Metros: Ecole Militaire or La Tour Maubourg (NOT Invalides). TEL: 555:9230 *Includes*: *l'Hôtel des Invalides* and *Army Museum*. Open daily from 10.0 a.m. to 5.0 p.m. in winter (1 Oct. to 31 Mar.). 10.0 a.m. to 6.0 p.m. in summer.

Centre Culturel Britannique (British Council), 9 Rue de Constantine, Paris 7ᵉ. Metro Invalides. TEL: 555.9595. *Library* open 11.0 a.m. to 6.0 p.m. on weekdays. Weds. 11.0 a.m. to 7.0 p.m. Closed Sats. and Suns.

British Institute, 9 Rue de Constantine, 7ᵉ. TEL: 555:7199. Open on weekdays 10.15 a.m. to 1.0 p.m. and 2.0 p.m. to 5.45 p.m.

Ecole Militaire Metro Ecole Militaire.

UNESCO Building, 9 Place de Fontenoy, 7ᵉ. Metro Ségur or Ecole Militaire. TEL: 568:1000. Visits possible on weekdays, but telephone in advance for permission.

Rodin Museum, Hôtel Biron, 77 Rue de Varenne, 7ᵉ. Metro Varenne. TEL: 705:0134. Open daily, except Tuesdays, from 10.0 a.m. to 5.0 p.m. (6 p.m. in summer).

19. *Montparnasse*

Modern Art – Hemingway – Montparnasse Tower – Lenin Museum – Montparnasse Cemetery.

Metros: Vavin; Montparnasse-Bienvenu; Raspail; Edgar Quinet.

Montparnasse Tower, 33 Avenue du Maine, 15ᵉ. Metro Montparnasse-Bienvenu. TEL: 538:5256. Open every day of the year from 9.30 a.m. to 11.30 p.m. in summer; 10.0 a.m. to 10.0 p.m. in winter (1 Oct. to 31 Mar.)

Montparnasse Cemetery, 3 Boulevard Edgar Quinet, 14ᵉ. Metro Edgar Quinet. TEL: 320:6852.

20. Paris by Night
Some of the Paris Revues and 'Dîners-Spectacles'.

REVUES:

Crazy Horse Saloon, 12 Avenue George V, 8ᵉ. Metro George V. TEL: 723:3232.

Folies Bergère, 32 Rue Richer, 9ᵉ. Metro Cadet. TEL: 246:7711.

'DÎNERS-SPECTACLES' (Dinner-Shows)

Alcazar de Paris, 62 Rue Mazarine, 6ᵉ. Metro Odéon. TEL: 329:0220.

Lido, 116 *bis* Avenue des Champs-Elysées, 8ᵉ. Metro Georve V or Etoile. TEL: 563:1161.

Moulin Rouge, Place Blanche, 9ᵉ. Metro Blanche. TEL: 606:0019.

Paradis Latin, 28 Rue du Cardinal Lemoine, 5ᵉ. Metro Cardinal Lemoine. TEL: 325:2828.

MUSIC HALLS:

Olympia, 28 Boulevard des Capucines, 9ᵉ. Metro Opéra. TEL: 742:2106.

Bobino, 20 Rue de la Gaité, 14ᵉ. Metro Cité or Edgar Quinet. TEL: 322:7484.

APPENDIX C

How to get about

Paris, now the biggest city in Europe with over nine million inhabitants, is divided into the Ville de Paris and the suburbs. The Ville de Paris, which is what this book is concerned with, is divided into twenty arrondissements or districts. Each of these has its own mayor, town hall and a limited amount of self-administration. Each, too, has its own atmosphere and lifestyle; to know the number of someone's arrondissement is to get a rough idea of his social position and interests. Arrondissement No. 1 is right in the centre of Paris, including part of the Ile de la Cité, the Hôtel de Ville and the Palais de Justice. After this the arrondissements spiral out clockwise to No. 20 which is on the eastern city limits.

A very useful little book, *Plan de Paris*, can be bought at any newsagent or *tabac*. This gives maps of Paris, the suburbs, the metro, detailed maps of each arrondissement, the location of every street in Paris with arrondissement number and nearest metro station, and also diagrams of all the bus routes. Even lifelong Parisians find it invaluable.

Streets are numbered from the end of the street nearest to the river, odd numbers on the left. If the river is at both ends, as on the islands, then the numbering starts from the southern end, the end nearest to Rome. If the street runs parallel to the Seine, then the numbering goes downstream, with the flow of the river. It must, however, be admitted that this information is useless to many people, particularly if they happen to be far from the Seine. Some streets too, after redevelopment, do not obey the rule – for instance, the long Rue de Vaugirard. But the principle holds.

On foot. Walking still remains the pleasantest way of getting about and exploring the areas which appeal to us. Most of the chapters in this book have been based on a walk, which can be shortened or altered according to wish; everyone likes to make his private discoveries and this is best done on foot. However, there are some hazards. The pavements may be cluttered with parked cars or motorcycles; cars may drive forwards or backwards along them, or shoot suddenly out of or into underground car parks; dog-dirt is a hazard, since French dog-owners usually walk their dogs off the lead, and the dogs are understandably reluctant to go out into the road; we may be run into by boys on roller-skates or skate-boards, their ears deafened by radio headphones. We should use traffic-lights or pedestrian crossings to cross main roads, but even here we should be careful; strict obedience to regulations is not something the French pride themselves on. Nevertheless, despite all this, a summer's day stroll along one of the great boulevards can still be one of the most enjoyable experiences to be found anywhere.

Driving. Many people bring their cars to Paris on their way to the south and have the interesting experience of driving in this city. The obvious resemblance is to a chariot-race. We should resign ourselves to bumps and dents; Paris cars carry their scars proudly. French drivers change lanes abruptly and without signalling – this adds to the excitement. They also have an interesting theory that you can go the wrong way down a one-way street provided that you go backwards. We should treat this theory with caution.

But we should obey carefully the 'Rule of the Right', which is in force in all European countries except Britain. Unless lights or signs say otherwise, the car coming in from the right has right of way over the car going straight ahead. Many British drivers go across Paris, and indeed Europe, without knowing this, and many collisions arise.

Traffic lights should be obeyed, whatever other cars may choose to do. However, should there be a policeman on point-duty as well (for instance, in rush-hours) then we should obey the policeman rather than the lights. Should there be two policemen on duty, the position becomes more complicated and we should follow the cars round us.

Parking is a problem in Paris, as in other cities. If possible, we should use one of the underground car parks which have recently been dug. These, however, are not guarded and so cars should be locked. Kerb parking, being free, is universal, though free places are increasingly hard to find. Many drivers find manœuvring into a too-small gap a good sporting event and, having succeeded, leave again; it is estimated that a third of Paris cars are not going anywhere in particular, and they disappear in bad weather. Should we find a gap, we should of course reverse into it; if, while we are doing this, another car nips in forwards in our place, a lively scene will certainly ensue – one of the features of Paris street life ('Have you bought the street, Monsieur?'). We should never park in front of a courtyard gateway (*porte-cochère*), on a pedestrian crossing or on a corner. Infringements bring a fine (*contravention*), the piece of paper we find under the windscreen-wiper after dinner. Cars with foreign numbers, which cannot easily be traced, may get away with it for a time, but they can be towed away or immobilized with a metal clamp on the wheel. Getting this removed is a slow and expensive business. There is a night-and-day car breakdown service *Dépannage Auto*, telephone 236:1000.

The Metro. The Paris metro, one of the oldest in the world, is still one of the best and the normal way of getting about. Trains run frequently – almost nose to tail in rush hours – and there are many stations. Nowhere in Paris is very far from the nearest metro station. Recently the rolling-stock has been renewed, the stations have been modernized with escalators and travelators, and extra police drafted in to check the crime. More than this, the authorities have attempted to make the metro a way of life by providing festival weeks, concerts, art exhibitions, cafés, restaurants, shops, and information and reservation centres. It is possible to spend all day and much of the night (until 1.0 a.m.) below ground, all for the price of one metro ticket.

However, I assume that we are using the metro mainly for purposes of transport, and the first thing to know is how to find our way about. Every metro station has maps, both outside and inside and some even have electric push-button maps to tell us which way to go. The secret is to ignore the ostensible number of the line, which nobody knows, and concentrate on the final station on the line, which gives its name to the line. This will be marked 'Direction Mairie d'Ivry' or similar. Should we have to change lines (*correspondance*), we follow another Direction towards a different and distant destination, which we shall certainly never reach (like characters in an Anouilh play). For example, if we want to go by metro from the Gare du Nord to the Arc de Triomphe, like many

321

people, we first study the map. Then we take Direction Porte d'Orléans as far as Châtelet, where we change, taking the tunnel marked 'Correspondance'. Then we follow the signs marked 'Direction Neuilly' as far as the station Etoile-Charles de Gaulle, where we emerge. All very simple, quick and cheap.

We can buy metro tickets at every station, and in some *tabacs* too. We should buy them in blocks of ten (*carnets*), which are half-price. For short visits, tourists can buy 'Sesame' tickets covering unlimited Paris bus or metro travel for two, four or seven days, sold at most metro or railway stations. If we plan to be in Paris more than three months and to use public transport regularly, we might consider buying a Carte Orange, which offers further reductions. Both it and ordinary metro tickets are also used on buses. To stamp the ticket, we put it through an electric gate, which will then let us through. (Never try to jump the gate, like many young men.) Arriving on the platform, we make our way quickly to a second-class carriage, unless, by mistake, we happen to have bought first-class tickets. Before 9.0 a.m. or after 5.0 p.m., second-class tickets are valid for first-class carriages. To open the doors we press a button or raise a lever; the rest is automatic. The doors close automatically when the guard decides that there are no more travellers getting off or on. In crowded rush-hours it is usually easier to push yourself on backwards; the other passengers will smile sympathetically. If, on leaving the station, we should find our way blocked by glass doors, we should remember to push the glass panel and not the metal rim.

The RER. This is the suburban network, providing fast travel to the suburbs, including Versailles, Saint-Germain-en-Laye and both airports. It interconnects at several *correspondances* with the ordinary metro, but stations are much less frequent and ordinary tickets are only valid inside the city limits. We need our tickets to get *out*, as well as in.

Buses. These are one of the pleasantest ways of getting about Paris in daylight, but they take time and do not usually run after nine o'clock in the evening, except for a special night service. On Sundays they run only occasionally. There are diagrams of bus routes, not only in *Plan de Paris*, but also at every bus stop, which are often sheltered; some have telephones. The system, which takes some mastering, produces enjoyable travel. We clip our ticket ourselves (the same ticket as for the metro) beside the driver and gradually make our way down to the exit door, pressing a button on our way to ask for the door to be opened. There are no conductors. A single ticket (unlike the metro) will not take you all the way. For a journey covering more than two 'sections' you will have to clip two tickets. The driver will advise you, monosyllabically. Bus stops are hard to find, especially in one-way streets, and you are advised to concentrate on one route until you are familiar with it, before tackling another. Personally I use Paris buses a good deal, but only on one route. Unlike other cities, the drivers do not leave you standing at the stop because the bus is nominally 'full'.

Taxis. These are increasingly hard to find, especially in rush-hours or on wet days. However, we may be lucky. Cruising taxis rarely stop; we find taxis at railway stations or at taxi-ranks (*Têtes de station*) which occur throughout the city. The driver will ask us where we are going – he is not obliged to carry anyone anywhere, and he hopes we are going a long way, preferably to an airport. If he refuses to take us, we should try the other taxis behind him – this is the normal practice. On leaving, we should tip normally, about 15% of the fare. Radio Taxis may be useful, after a certain wait, listening to music. We may get one, in *'cinq minutes'* or hear simply *'Pas de voitures'*. Once again rush-hours or wet days can be difficult, but restaurant proprietors often seem to have a secret knack of getting them. The telephone numbers are: 203:9999 or 200:6789 or 205:7777 or 793:3333 or 270:4422.

Guided Tours (or with an official guide in our own car): details from Office de Tourisme de Paris, telephone 723:6172.

Helicopters. Reservations needed. Heli-France, telephone 557:5367 or Helicap, telephone 557:7551. From Heliport de Paris, 4 and 14 Avenue de la Porte de Sèvres, 15ᵉ. Metro: Balard.

Bicycles. Can be hired. Telephone 337:5922 or 766:5592.

APPENDIX D

Some Paris Hotels

A personal selection

Reservations may be made at the Office de Tourisme de Paris, 127 Champs-Elysées, 8ᵉ. (Telephone 723:6172.) Open every day in the year. Also at its branches at four railway stations (Nord, Est, Austerlitz, Lyon), both airports, the Hôtel de Ville and the Eiffel Tower (summer only).

LUXURY
Inter-Continental, 3 Rue Castiglione, 1ᵉʳ. Telephone 260:3780
Meurice, 228 Rue de Rivoli, 1ᵉʳ. Telephone 260:3860
Ritz, 15 Place Vendôme, 1ᵉʳ. Telephone 260:3830
l'Hôtel, 13 Rue des Beaux-Arts, 6ᵉ. Telephone 325:2722
   (where Oscar Wilde died: 'I am dying above my means.')
Bristol, 112 Faubourg Saint-Honoré, 8ᵉ. Telephone 266:9145
Crillon, 10 Place de la Concorde, 8ᵉ. Telephone 296:1081
Lancaster, 7 Rue de Berri, 8ᵉ. Telephone 359:9043
Nova-Park, 51 Rue François Ier, 8ᵉ. Telephone 562:6364
   (reputed to be the most expensive in Paris)
PLM, 17 Boulevard Saint-Jacques, 14ᵉ. Telephone 589:8980

THREE STARS
Sainte-Anne, 10 Rue Sainte-Anne, 1ᵉʳ. Telephone 296:1018
Arènes, 51 Rue Monge, 5ᵉ. Telephone 325:0926
Claude Bernard, 43 Rue des Ecoles, 5ᵉ. Telephone 326:3252
Lutèce, 65 Rue Saint-Louis-en-l'Ile, 4ᵉ. Telephone 326:2352
Pas de Calais, 59 Rue des Saints-Pères, 6ᵉ. Telephone 548:7874

TWO STARS
Crystal, 24 Rue Saint-Benôit, 6ᵉ. Telephone 548:8514

YOUTH HOSTEL
Auberge de Jeunesse de Paris, 8 Boulevard Jules Ferry, 11ᵉ.
(Metro République). Telephone 357:5560

APPENDIX E

Paris Restaurants

A Paris restaurant can be anything from a luxurious establishment with white tablecloths and fresh roses to a simple room where we find paper tablecloths on which we can write poems or telephone numbers. These are often called *bistros*; they usually have an informal bar and Madame sometimes does the cooking herself. Many names and addresses of restaurants of all types have been given in this book and some of these names are recapitulated in a later appendix. These recommendations are personal and are based on the quality of food and service, or on the atmosphere which may be amusing and intriguing, or sometimes on fashionability, if we go to see smart people.

A *brasserie* (literally, beerhouse) is a type of eating place which is becoming increasingly popular. It stays open for late lunches and dinners. Once again, it may be smart and expensive, or very simple, scarcely more than a café annexe. The food is normally plainer than in a restaurant: roasts, grills, Alsace food and, usually, oysters. Beer obviously is important, probably Mutzig or Kronenbourg, served in *demis* (half-litre glasses) or German-style *pots, sérieux* or *formidables* (holding one litre), but there will also be a good choice of wines. The waiters probably wear the traditional *brasserie* uniform of black waistcoat and long white apron.

A third type of restaurant is the *self-service* or *self*, which is French for cafeteria. We push a tray along a counter, helping ourselves and paying at the cash desk at the end. Cheap and crowded, *selfs* are much used by office staff in rushed lunch-hours. A *lunch*, incidentally, is a small buffet, usually a private one.

All restaurants, brasseries and selfs (except for a few very grand restaurants which seem to be above the law) are required to display their bill of fare (*la carte*), so that we may study it before we venture in. This will give us an idea of the place and prices before committing ourselves. It will also give us a chance to consider the *plat du jour*, the special dish of today. Specially recommended by the restaurant or brasserie, freshly prepared, rapidly served, it is usually a good choice and provides an element of variety in an otherwise fixed *carte*. Otherwise we can choose from the whole range of the *carte*, though we must not be surprised if many of the printed dishes are not in fact available that day.

As well as a *carte*, every restaurant and brasserie is obliged to offer a *menu*. This is a fixed-price meal of usually three courses, chosen from the cheapest parts of the *carte* and not always including the *plat du jour*. The *menu* is often cheap and satisfying, but the French usually prefer to eat *à la carte*, leaving the *menu* to foreigners who may be bewildered by a long *carte* in French. Service charges are normally included; a ration of drink may or may not be – this will be stated on the *menu*. We should, however, beware of restaurants which offer unlimited wine on their *menu*; neither the wine nor the company are likely to be agreeable.

There is also a type of restaurant, often rather expensive, which offers nothing but a *menu*, but with four or even five courses, which we have to pay for, whether or not we wish to eat so much. This type of restaurant caters mainly for hungry tourists, especially those who wish above all to be freed from the burden of choice.

Whether we are eating the *menu* or *à la carte*, the service charge will be included in the final bill (*l'addition*), but it is polite to leave the small change and an odd franc or two, especially if the service has been good. In expensive restaurants we must remember to tip the head waiter, the wine waiter and the cloakroom attendant as well. A waiter should be addressed as 'Monsieur', never as 'Garçon'. If we know him well, we can call him 'Monsieur Jean-Claude', etc. In certain restaurants and cafés we may call the waiters by their first names straight, but otherwise we should be wary about this. Waitresses, a rare species, are always 'Madame' or 'Mademoiselle', depending on age. The *patron* is 'Monsieur Jean-Paul', his wife 'Madame Jean-Paul' and not 'Madame Françoise'. We have to be matey indeed to be on first-name terms, but, equally, surnames are rarely heard. The present compromise pleasantly combines informality with politeness.

And so *Bon Appetit*! – a phrase which we shall hear many times.

Glossary of Paris restaurant 'codewords'

Paris restaurants often use 'codewords' to describe a number of standard dishes, which we shall often eat. The descriptions may not always be exact or adequate. The dishes may well be elaborately prepared and with variations; every cook likes to improvise on occasions. But a short glossary may be helpful.

à l'ancienne	anyhow, using up stock and leftovers
anglaise	plain boiled or fried
Sauce anglaise	Worcestershire sauce, unpronounceable in French
armoricaine, now usually spelt *américaine* (the Armoricae lived in west Normandy, before the Norsemen arrived in the eighth century)	a sauce of shellfish, white fish, tomatoes, white wine and brandy. Often tinned
basquaise, also *catalane, espagnole*	with tomatoes and sliced red and green peppers
bercy	a white wine sauce with shallots (onions)
bordelaise	a red wine sauce with beef stock and marrow. For steak
bourguignonne	stewed in red wine until it is thick and dark. For beef and kidneys
Caen, à la mode de	cooked with calvados (apple brandy), usually for tripe
catalane	see *basquaise*
chasseur	a thin brown sauce, with mushrooms and herbs. Usually for rabbit
dieppoise	with shrimps and sometimes mussels
dijonnaise	with a mustard sauce
espagnole	see *basquaise*

328

financière	with a thick white sauce, for sweetbreads
florentine	with tinned spinach
grand mère	a thick brown sauce, with bacon and mushrooms
grenobloise	with capers
herbes de Provence	with thyme, rosemary, etc. Not garlic.
jardinière	with diced, mixed vegetables, probably tinned
lyonnaise	with tomatoes and onions
maison	how we always do it here
maître d'hôtel	a parsley-butter sauce
meunière	dusted with flour and fried
milanaise	with spaghetti
à la mode	with tinned carrots
mornay	with a cheese sauce
niçoise	with olives and anchovies, usually a salad
normande	with a sauce of butter, cream, egg-yolks, and calvados (apple brandy)
printanière	with grated raw carrots, usually an egg salad
provençale	with garlic
Provence, herbes de	see above
rouennaise	game cooked in its own blood and giblets
suprème	an almost tasteless white sauce, for chicken
toulouse	with sausages, whole or sliced
viennoise	coated with breadcrumbs and fried
vin, marchand de	a red wine sauce with chopped shallots and lemon juice. For steak.

Paris Restaurants: A Personal Choice

For details see the descriptions in the text.

LUXURY
Grand Véfour, 17 Rue de Beaujolais, 1er. Telephone: 296:5627
Maxim's, 3 Rue Royale, 8e. Telephone: 265:2794
Tour d'Argent, 15 Quai de la Tournelle, 5e. Telephone: 354:2331
Drouant, Place Gaillon, 2e. Telephone: 742:5661
Fouquet's, 99 Champs-Elysées, 8e. Telephone: 723:7060
Taillevent, 15 Rue Lammenais, 11e. Telephone: 561:1290
Lasserre, 17 Avenue Franklin D. Roosevelt, 8e. Telephone:
    359:5343
Jules Verne, Eiffel Tower (2nd Floor). Telephone: 555:2004

MEDIUM-PRICED
Closerie des Lilas, 171 Boulevard du Montparnasse, 6e.
L'Ilot Vache, 35 Rue Saint-Louis-en-l'Ile, 4e.
Androuet, 41 Rue d'Amsterdam, 8e.
Chartier, 7 Rue Faubourg Montmartre, 9e.
Port Saint-Germain, 155 Boulevard Saint-Germain, 6e.
La Mère Catherine, 6 Place du Tertre, 18e.
Le Grand Café, 4 Boulevard des Capucines, 9e.
Le Procope, 13 Rue de l'Ancienne Comédie, 6e.

BRASSERIES
Lipp, 151 Boulevard Saint-Germain, 6e.
Bofinger, 5 Rue de la Bastille, 4e.
Balzar, 49 Rue des Ecoles, 5e.
Coupole, 102 Boulevard du Montparnasse, 14e.
Strasbourgeoise, 5 Rue du 8 Mai, 10e.
Ile Saint-Louis, 55 Quai de Bourbon, 4e.
Au Pied de Cochon, 6 Rue Coquillère, 1er.

BISTROS

Vieux Bistro, 14 Rue Cloître Notre-Dame, 4e.

Petit Saint-Benôit, 4 Rue Saint-Benôit, 6e.

Saints-Pères, Boulevard Saint-Germain (corner of Rue des Saints-Pêres).

Aux Assassins, Rue Jacob, 6e.

Lutétia, 33 Quai de Bourbon, 4e.

Fleur de Lys, 5 Rue Rameau, 2e.

Wadja, Rue de la Grande Chaumière, 6e.

Orestias, 4 Rue Grégoire de Tours, 6e.

Les Arcades, 18 Rue du Louvre, 1er.

La Fontaine de Mars, 129 Rue Saint-Dominique, 7e.

APPENDIX F

La Défense

New suburb between Pont de Neuilly and Nanterre. Motorway A 14. Metro, RER and railway station. Publications available from the co-ordinating body, EPAD, Tour Fiat, Cedex 1, 92080 Paris La Défense. Telephone 796: 2424.

La Défense is Paris's biggest business suburb. It is a rival to London's Barbican, and the name has a similar meaning: a monument commemorates the defence of Paris in the 1870 war. Many of the major public utilities and commercial enterprises of France have their offices here, particularly the American firms. It is too far out to be a good headquarters for visitors to Paris, but, if we have come to do business, we shall find that the district is self-contained, with its own hotels, motels and amenities. Some businessmen arrive straight from the airport, do their business and fly home, without realizing that they have not been to Paris. Sightseers should start by calling at the EPAD information centre (Fiat Building) to study the large model of the quarter.

La Défense was planned nearly thirty years ago with the chief object of keeping skyscrapers out of Paris; this was not the only object in which it failed. Building has gone on ever since and the ups and downs of this still unfinished project have made town-planning history. It was at first conceived as an avenue of high-rise blocks, a sort of triumphal way continuing the Champs-Elysées beyond the Pont de Neuilly.

This image soon gave way to the 'group of towers in a park' idea, made fashionable by Le Corbusier in the 1950s. It was to be a mixed residential and commercial centre where 'a new vision of the town' would 'enforce on the world a conception of life in total rupture with humanity's past'. A huge open space described as an 'architectural

332

silence' was to cut pedestrians off entirely from traffic, so that the inhabitant would never even hear a car. But Parisians, who are attached to their way of life and to their cars, decided not to live there. They took a great dislike to the whole project, especially when the first towers began to dominate the Paris skyline and the famous view up the Champs-Elysées. Even the popular Salon de Mai was boycotted when it was held at La Défense, although the CNIT Exhibition Hall is a remarkable place, shaped like an up-turned shell.

Office building went ahead, but on such purely profit-oriented lines that in the 1970s a major public outcry broke out. The towers, it was claimed, were outmoded before they were built and paid scant respect to French æsthetic and town-planning standards. Staff refused to work in them until something was done about ventilation, lighting and sound-proofing. Office blocks stood empty, sites were left vacant and finances plunged into a huge deficit. Resources were diverted to Créteil, the newer new-town, where high-rise development was rejected.

This crisis was a turning-point for La Défense. The planners at EPAD must be congratulated on having reacted with a new initiative which took La Défense into its third and more varied stage, taking public opinion into account at last. It has now taken shape in a real sense and become, finally, a success. Visually the new towers are more elegant, and their edging with more imaginative lower buildings along the motorway gives the quarter a new cohesion. Modern sculpture is a feature (note Calder's last work, a huge red stabile 'The Spider') and fountains and gardens have been laid out. The change proved to be financially rewarding and the area has started to pay its way. There has been a return of big-business tenants, led by IBM, which has its European registered offices in its own IBM Tower. The Manhattan Tower has been bought by Kuwait. The CNIT Exhibition Centre has huge commercial shows and attracts vast numbers of visitors. Even Parisians have softened towards La Défense: 'We have got our Brasilia without realizing it.'

Those like myself who enjoy a good skyscraper will think these towers rather small by US standards, but we can find a number of buildings to admire as well as some to regret. The succession of styles, already spanning a generation, begins with the Nobel Tower, with its all-metal frame. The shining 45-storey FIAT Tower belongs to the much-criticized middle period, but it has its qualities; the green GAN Tower came next. The Aurore Tower, with bronze-tinted glass layers, and 'Porte Sud' are more recent, and the latest twin-towers 'Les Miroirs' (only 16 floors) show the trend of the 1980s. If it is dusk, we can see La Défense at its best, with its skyline framing the lights rising over us in the towers. This un-Parisian city has its own magic, after all.

The current 'Tête-Défense' prestige project, funded by the government, is intended to be the last stage of building, completing the whole plan and giving La Défense a less purely commercial image. This is announced as an 'International Communications Exchange' which will be 'resolutely oriented towards the twenty-first century' and is to keep France to the fore in video, telecommunications and cinema. Few people understand exactly what these phrases mean, but the project is thought of as 'President Mitterand's Beaubourg'. It is rumoured that it will be modelled on the Arc de Triomphe.

APPENDIX G

Paris Insolite *(Off-beat Paris)*

The Sewers

Metro Alma-Marceau. The Sewers are open to the public from 2.0 p.m. to 5.0 p.m. on Mondays, Wednesdays and the last Saturday in each month. They are closed on public holidays and the days before and after; also during heavy rain or flooding.

The Sewers are one of Paris's big attractions and it is worth being ten minutes early to avoid queuing (in the open). Across the Seine from Alma-Marceau, we find, opposite 93 Quai d'Orsay, the entrance sign. The visit lasts an hour, including a good film, a photograph exhibition and a visit down the tunnel to the sewers themselves, with the chance of seeing the *égouteurs* at work. Full-length cruises, however, are no longer allowed, since a famous bank vault robbery via the drains.

The sewers have been described as Haussmann's finest achievement, and are still considered unique; they enlarged and modernized the earlier system, built in 1740, which replaced the mediæval open drains. They now reach to 65 feet down and the big tunnels are 18 feet high, 14 feet wide, with a raised path on either side. Every street in Paris has one under it, and a map of the sewers would also be a street map of Paris. Knowing Paris, Jean Valjean, the persecuted hero of *Les Misérables*, was well able to find his way among the sewers, although, if laid end to end, they would reach from Paris to Istanbul.

They all have to be cleaned all the time, by *égouteurs* who wear waders and helmets; they walk behind special machines and drive special boats, and take a great pride in their work. They remove enough rubbish – sand, obstructions and such unlikely objects as bedsteads – to fill six hundred barges a year. The stink is appalling

335

but nobody, *égouteur* or visitor, is so poor-spirited as to mention it.

The sewage moves entirely by gravity. After 13 hours it reaches one of the four sewage-farms outside Paris – the largest is in the Forêt Saint-Germain. Here it is allowed to settle and then bio-degraded and pumped back into the Seine, theoretically clean. The sewers also carry, hooked to the tunnel roofs, the clean water pipes of Paris, the telephone wires, the traffic-light cables and the pneumatic postal network. We used to be able to send a billet-doux to a girl-friend by *pneu*, which travelled through the sewers on its way. But the system was closed in 1984.

The catacombs
Metro Denfert-Rochereau. Entrance at 2 bis Place Denfert-Rochereau. Telephone 321:5800 to find out when guided groups are being shown round.

The Catacombs were once quarries, and extend for many miles under Paris. Often attributed to the Romans, they are certainly much older, going back to prehistoric times and Cernunnus. Single visitors are not allowed because, once lost, you would never be found again. A torch and a warm coat are essential, at all times of year.

Museum of Public Assistance
Metro Maubert-Mutualité. 47 Quai de la Tournelle, 5e. Open daily, except Mondays and Tuesdays, from 10.0 a.m. to 5.0 p.m.

Museum-maniacs may like to know of this, the least visited of Paris museums. Set in a pleasant seventeenth-century house with some good period chests-of-drawers, it is devoted to hospital life in Paris during the last three centuries. Most of the exhibits are documents, engravings, portraits of doctors or benefactors. However, it is always interesting to see a picture of a surgeon performing a mastectomy, wearing a top-hat.

APPENDIX H

How to live in Paris

Many people come to Paris for several months or a year on a sabbatical, research project, or because they (or husband) have a job here. They often feel lost and lonely, and may like some advice.

How to find a flat Choose the quarter where you wish to live and go to the local agencies (*Immobilières*). Also read the small ads in *Le Figaro* and *France-Soir*. These can be divided into *appartements de grand standing, deux pièces* (more than one room), *studios* (large one-room flats with mod. cons.), *studettes* (bed-sitters) and *chambres-de-bonne* (garret rooms, with shared WC, formerly occupied by living-in maids). Rents vary according to area, number of stairs and quarter. Except for *chambres-de-bonne*, flats are usually unfurnished. Furniture can be bought economically at Samaritaine, BHV, or Habitat in the Montparnasse shopping centre.

You have to pay two months' rent in advance as a deposit, plus the normal one month in advance, plus agency fees (about a month's rent). This can add up to a lot of money, but you cannot sign the lease (*bail*) until it is paid. The deposit is refundable, but there are somehow always deductions.

If you are hard up, *chambres-de-bonne* are cheap and, with their views of the roofs of Paris, romantic for the young and strong-legged. Make sure that there is a communal WC on the same floor, with light; that the room has running water and an electric socket where you can plug in a drink-heater, a small cooking-ring or even a small bowl-fire, should no heating be provided.

How not to starve in a garret (for students on insufficient grants, artists, etc.) Use the electric socket in your *chambre-de-bonne*. There's no need to live on cold cooked chicken (expensive) and keep warm all day in a cinema, as many visitors do.

337

Fresh sardines, mackerel, or chicken livers (bought from the greengrocer), are very cheap and flavour a large quantity of ready-cooked rice (also easy to get). Guests can be impressed by apparent luxuries: oysters, artichokes, slices of seafood *pâté*, which are much cheaper in Paris than elsewhere. The latter also make good sand-wiches. Shop in side streets, always much cheaper than the main thoroughfares. A hot *plat du jour*, sold 'to go' in *triperies* and many small restaurants, is delicious and would cost double in a café. Overcome your prejudices and try tripe or hamburgers from the local horse-butcher – cheaper and tastier than in other shops.

Doctors. The best way of finding one is a recommendation from a friend or, failing this, your chemist (*pharmacien*) will advise you. There are health centres in many places (one is at Opéra), which are excellent and do lab tests and X-rays on the spot. A free booklet giving details of Paris hospital services is available at any hospital, clinic or health service. The maternity services of the Saint-Vincent-de-Paul and Hôtel-Dieu hospitals are thought to be particularly good. But, in any event, your own doctor will advise you. For urgencies, telephone 'SOS Médecin' 707:7777, or at night 337:7777. The emergency ambulance is SAMU, 567:5050. SOS Dentist 337:5100.

If you are entitled to Social Security (compulsory for all workers in France after the first year), you will pay very little, and nothing at all if you are in hospital for an operation, or illness for more than a month. Otherwise you should have some private insurance of your own, valid in France.

If you must have an English-speaking hospital, both the British and American Hospitals are available, but expensive. French pri-vate clinics come under the Social Security scheme. If you are of executive grade (*'cadre'*), you will get a private room without extra charge.

Carte de Séjour (Residence Permit). This is compulsory for all foreigners, even members of the EEC, after three months. This is issued by the Prefecture of Police on the Ile de la Cité, even if they pass you on to a local sub-office, but it is as well to get a statement of address from your local police station. You will need your passport, two photographs, proof of means such as a bank letter or a form from your employer and stamped addressed envelope. You should allow some six afternoons for appointments and interviews, after which you will receive a temporary card. When this expires, you do it all again, for a longer-term card.

Schools for your children. Much depends on how long you mean to stay and whether your children are heading for the British or French system, the *baccaleauréat* or A-levels. For infants, the Montessori Bilingue at 65 Quai d'Orsay provides happy playway, if not ambitious education. The American school is tougher physically. There is an English school in the suburbs (bus from the Palais de Chaillot), which is a prep school, preparing for a British boarding-school. The Ecole Bilingue is near the Parc Monceau at 7 Rue Alfred de Vigny, but there are several other branches in Paris. These are mainly French-speaking and preparing for the *bac* and French universities. There are also a large number of private French-speaking Catholic schools in all parts, which are cheap and where your child will learn, among others things, perfect French. Teenagers, with a year to spare, usually find the Sorbonne course in French culture and civilization enjoyable and rewarding. The American Library in Paris, 10 rue du Général Camou, 7e, (telephone 551:4682) has books in English.

Meeting the British community. The Cercle Interallié in the Faubourg Saint-Honoré is expensive and you have to be proposed by two members. Squash and swimming are available. The Country Club at Meudon provides tennis and swimming and is a haunt of British businessmen and their families. Children especially enjoy it. The Franco-British Junior Chamber of Commerce organizes lots of social functions, to which wives may be brought. All applicants are accepted (even secretaries) and the parties are usually fun and youthful. After the age of forty you move to the Senior Chamber. The two Anglican churches (see Chapters 5 and 6) also organize many meetings and events; St George's also has the Cardew Club for lost au pair girls in Paris.

Lost Property Office is at 36 Rue des Morillons, 15e. Metro Convention. Telephone 531:1480. Open weekdays 8.30 a.m. to 5.0 p.m.

339

Indexes

The Index is in two sections: *a* persons; *b* places, streets, buildings and subjects; page numbers in bold show the place where the entry is most fully dealt with.

Churches, cafés, restaurants and theatres are grouped together (in their own alphabetical order) under those respective general headings in section *b*.

The names of hotels, nightclubs, restaurants, shops or stores appearing in the Appendix or the special shopping and night-life chapters are not included in the Index, as they will be easily and immediately traced by reference to the sections dealing with them; they are, however, indexed when they are also mentioned in the body of the book.

INDEX OF PERSONS

345

INDEX OF PLACES

INDEX